T0325490

Mines

The Gauntlet of Golden Tech
Or
The Engineering Academy

By
Dave & Ralph Dougherty

Mines: The Gauntlet of Golden Tech Or The Engineering Academy
Cover design by Vincent Rospond
This edition published in 2019

Wrong Way Books, is an imprint of

Pike and Powder Publishing Group LLC
1525 Hulse Rd, Unit 1
Point Pleasant, NJ 08742

Copyright © Dave and Ralph Dougherty
ISBN 978-1-945430-65-7
LCN 2019931664

Bibliographical References and Index
1. History. 2. Education. 3. Colorado

Pike and Powder Publishing Group LLC All rights reserved
For more information on Pike and Powder Publishing Group, LLC,
visit us at www.PikeandPowder.com & www.wingedhussarpublishing.com

twitter: @pike_powder
facebook: @PikeandPowder

This work is dedicated to Regis Chauvenet, the visionary who nearly single-handedly created the Colorado School of Mines as the world's foremost mineral engineering school. The authors had the great fortune to benefit from his creation.

Table of Contents

Preface

The saga of the first hundred years of the Colorado School of Mines (CSM) would make an unbelievable novel in the proper form. Founded to fulfill a technological need in Colorado Territory, CSM rose to greatness through the establishment of a harsh, unforgiving environment with arguably the strictest academic standards ever seen on the North American continent. Its graduates dominated earth science industries having passed mental and physical tests of knowledge and endurance unthinkable in today's academic institutions. Even with selective admissions, CSM ultimately graduated about one-third of its students, and many of those long after the normal four years of study.

The men of Mines were the type who had built the nation in its first hundred years, the dominant Scotch-Irish frontiersman, and they accepted the challenge to further the United States in its second hundred after proving their abilities under the most adverse conditions. Patriotic and hardened men, Miners responded unhesitatingly to calls for service, and were decimated by World War Two, perhaps more than any American university other than West Point or Annapolis. Although records on students withdrawing before graduation are incomplete, Mines lost at least ninety-nine of its brethren during the war and suffered uncounted wounded and other casualties. Theirs was a sacrifice well beyond that expected from college men.

The first century of Mines was dominated by one man's vision for the school, Dr. Regis Chauvenet, President from 1883 to 1902. Chauvenet's father was instrumental in designing the standards, requirements, and academic programs for the United States Naval Academy, and the son went his father one better. Chauvenet designed an incredibly tough engineering academy, complete with brutal freshman hazing, designed to build student élan, personal initiative, and a spirit of cooperation to solve any problem and do any job. Mines became a school like no other in the United States, essentially a third service academy: after the US Military Academy at West Point and the US Naval Academy at Annapolis, there now was the Engineering Academy at Golden.

Since World War II it has come under fire from all quarters: state politicians who felt that Colorado could not afford a world-class school representing the nation rather than the state, social reformers who held no truck with elitism and were more interested on the school graduating students in proportional representation to the Colorado population instead of capability, educators who endeavored to make college a fun experience, accreditation institutions that showed a pronounced trend to level education standards on the lowest common denominator, the American Association for University Professors, essentially a faculty union, looking to safeguard their members, and faculty looking for a life-long sinecure that allowed them to devote more time to leisure and personal activities.

Producing giants in engineering, Mines was a glorious phoenix arising from the turmoil of Jefferson Territory's early days and reaching an apex during the nineteen-fifties when Mines graduates could do anything - it was not fated to last long. In an orgy of change during the late 1960s, engineering was de-emphasized, and a year and a half of engineering and technology courses yanked from the curriculum. Mines life was radically altered.

Although this work criticizes the subordination of engineering education in the United States to progressive education standards developed from the time of John Dewey, the authors nonetheless believe that all curricula should fit into a continuum of liberal education from fine arts to the professions of medicine, science, and engineering. Unfortunately, the American education establishment has decreed in very large measure that undergraduate coursework should prepare a student for life, and to be able to enjoy life. Some college presidents even believe engineering and other technological programs do not belong in a university, but rather should be relegated to vocational and trade school institutions. Facing these "levelling" pressures, it is perhaps remarkable that American engineering schools have continued to produce capable graduates at all. The trend is toward ever-decreasing rigor in higher education while at the same time raising grade point averages to maintain an appearance of excellence.

This short history recounts the story of Mines, particularly from 1947 to the early 1960s, its student life, and the traditions and excellence lost in the avalanche of political correctness at the end of its first century of existence. Nothing lasts forever in one form, particularly institutions subject to tinkering by social scientists and politicians unable to recognize the value of engineering. Teachers were replaced by corporate managers and research scientists, and students were recruited to represent the image Mines presidents wished to present to the state and the surrounding community. In addition to this book there is also an alternate history of Mines put out by the Colorado School of Mines History Project under an eleven-person planning and editorial committee. This work by Wilton E. Eckley, titled *Rocky Mountain to the World A History of the Colorado School Of Mines* was extensively funded by individual donors and sponsored by the CSM Alumni Association. Dr. Eckley was a CSM faculty member in the Department of Humanities and Social Studies. The volume was published in 2004, and is an extremely well-produced, superb coffee-table book, with some 265 illustrations and photos over its 223 pages, and 55 sidebars and vignettes in the modern popular style to reach indifferent readers. Eckley presented Mines history from the progressive education side, writing a congratulatory paean to the wisdom and prescience of the Mines administration in difficult and changing times. To him, the Mines administration has apparently done everything right. Obviously, this work takes a very different view.

Whether or not the School of Mines survives in the coming years without a definite niche in the mass of institutions of higher education as questioned in this work remains to be seen. Mines transformed itself into a research-based institution for funding by the federal government and expanded from six degree-granting programs to over seventy. The creation of so many majors was designed to attract students with a wide range of interests, of which engineering was only one. Science came into the forefront, and in advanced degrees, the school's technological and humanistic course offerings expanded considerably. *De jure* tenure came into being under pressure by the AAUP (American Association of University Professors), new faculty hires became almost universally PhDs, and "publish or perish" became the slogan for gaining tenure. Graduate programs were expanded to provide worker bees for faculty to use on their research projects and in writing scholarly papers. In short, Mines has become almost indistinguishable from the many institutes of technology throughout the United States. There will be increasing pressure from the Colorado Legislature, dominated by graduates from Colorado University, to make Mines part of the Colorado University system, as already there is significant redundancy between programs at Mines and CU. Other states have incorporated schools labeled "Institute of Technology" into their main state university, and Colorado may well follow suit.

At the same time, the cost of a college education has sky-rocketed, not the least due to burgeoning administrative costs, higher faculty salaries, and pensions, without correspondingly higher teaching loads. The yearly cost of an education at Mines, not counting room and board, had gone up by a factor of 24 from 1961 to 2015, a rise even higher than that of new cars. In fact, the rising costs of a college education far exceed the vast majority of price increases in goods and services, and are fast reaching the breaking point. The driving force is that a college education is no longer seen as the precursor to obtaining a good job, and for many students, a graduate degree has become a necessity.

Estimations are currently being made that other than community colleges with untenured faculty and few terminal degrees, few colleges and universities with less than 10,000 students will survive into the 2030s. The costs will be too great, the students will not be able to pay the tuitions, and research funding will only go to large and prominent institutions. On this basis, Mines is definitely at risk. Smart money appears to be betting that Mines will become "Colorado University at Golden."

One can be hopeful for the future of Mines, but it will have to find a way to regain its fame and singularity in engineering excellence. Engineering expertise seems today to be the province of certain ethnic groups, primarily Asian and Middle Eastern, with American schools producing significantly less qualified and trained individuals. This does not have to be, and hopefully the tradition of American excellence in all things will once again rise to lead the world.

Chapter 1 - The Mining Engineer

One of the most iconic symbols of the Colorado School of Mines is its official/unofficial song, "The Mining Engineer." Where other universities sing some politically correct Alma Mater, Mines confronts the world with an anachronistic challenge in its school song, making no bones about its prowess, and establishing the school as one bad-ass institution. It is appropriate that this work starts off with the song:

I wish I had a barrel of rum and sugar three hundred pounds.
A college bell to mix it in and clapper to stir it round.
Like every honest fellow, I take my whiskey clear,
I'm a rambling wreck from Golden Tech, a helluva engineer.

Chorus: A helluva, helluva, helluva, helluva, helluva engineer,
A helluva, helluva, helluva, helluva, helluva engineer,
Like every honest fellow, I take my whisky clear,
I'm a rambling wreck from Golden Tech, a helluva engineer.

And if I had a daughter, I'd dress her up in green.
I'd send her up to Boulder to coach the football team.
But if I had a son, sir, I'd tell you what he'd do,
He'd yell, "To Hell with Boulder!" like his daddy used to do.

Chorus: He'd yell, "To Hell with Boulder!" Like his daddy used to do.
He'd yell, "To Hell with Boulder!" Like his daddy used to do.
But if I had a son, sir, I'd tell you what he'd do,
He would yell, "To Hell with Boulder!" like his daddy used to do.

Now here we have a mining man, in either hand a gun.
He's not afraid of anything, he's never know to run.
He dearly loves his whiskey, he dearly loves his beer.
He's a shootin', fightin', dynamitin', mining engineer.

Chorus: A shootin', fightin', dynamitin', mining engineer.
A shootin', fightin', dynamitin', mining engineer.
He dearly loves his whiskey, he dearly loves his beer.
He's a shootin', fightin', dynamitin', mining engineer.

If you want to gear the planets that revolve around the sun,
we'll do the job right nicely, and we'll only call it fun.
And if you want a bridge to Mars, or a ten foot shaft to Hell,
we're the engineers of a thousand years, and we'll do the job right well.

Chorus: The engineers of a thousand years, and we'll do the job right
well.
The engineers of a thousand years, and we'll do the job right well.
And if you want a bridge to Mars, or a ten foot shaft to Hell,
we're the engineers of a thousand years, and we'll do the job right well.

My father was a miner on the Upper Malemute.
My mother was a madam in a house of ill repute.
They sent me off to Golden, where all they make is beer,
and they said, "Grow up, you sonofabitch, and become an engineer."

Singing, hail, hail, the gang's all here,
What the Hell do we care,
Just so we get our share.
Hail, hail, the gang's all here -- (hit it!)
M! I! N! E! S!
What the hell do we care now.

The Mining Engineer was adapted from the old English drinking song, "The Son Of A Gambolier." The last verse is sung to the tune of "Hail, Hail, The Gang's All Here," followed by spelling Mines in yells. Other, even bawdier verses have appeared from time to time, as well as slight variations in wording.

Earliest documentary mention of the song's use dates from 1892, but at that time it was already a popular glee club number. All evidence points to its originating in the Mines glee club under Dr. Milton Moss's tutelage, 1878 to 1883, although verses could have been sung earlier. The second verse was apparently added after Mines obliterated Colorado University in a football game by the score of 103 to 0 in 1890. Coors beer was first brewed in Golden in 1873, and "The Upper Malemute" replaced "Clear Creek's northern chute" following the Alaskan gold rush.

The North Fork of Clear Creek was the site of Gregory's fabulous strike in 1859, and the towns of Central City and Blackhawk. Allowing for uncertainty, the best guess for the debut of "The Mining Engineer" in public is 1876 to 1880.

Occasionally individuals associated with Georgia Tech have attempted to attribute the song's origin to their institution. Nothing could be further from the truth. Georgia Tech first started holding classes in 1888, some ten years after "The Mining Engineer's" emergence at Mines. Even the most ardent proponent of Georgia Tech's authorship cannot show its appearance on the Atlanta campus before 1898. In the early 1950s arguments raged back and forth between Mines and Georgia Tech until Tech's claims were clearly refuted. A Georgia Tech spokesman summed up his position at the end, "Maybe we didn't originate the song, but we were the ones who made it famous. Who ever heard of Colorado School of Mines, anyway?"

Who indeed? At the same time that Mines was a world famous engineering school, Georgia Tech was being referred to in professional circles as Atlanta Junior College. Nonetheless, there is a lesson in the Tech's supporter's statement for Colorado.

In the little town of Golden, once the capital of Colorado Territory, a school existed that produced men who knew no boundaries to what they could do, for after all, they had survived the toughest engineering school in the world. It was designed to be as tough or tougher than the US Naval Academy and be an Engineering Academy. It even featured freshman hazing like the Naval Academy. Three times Mines was forced to relinquish some of its rigor and lower the real or apparent workload on its students in an attempt to mollify outside pressure - 1947, 1953, and 1957.

Finally, under the stewardship President Orlo Childs in the 1960s, Mines gave up all pretensions of being an Engineering Academy, and by the 1970s, only advanced degrees received silver diplomas. A Bachelor of Science in Metallurgy required only 138.5 hours of credit, a far cry from the 175 to 205 semester hours required in the 1950s for the degree of Professional Engineer in Metallurgy. By the 21st century, degrees were being granted in liberal arts, business and economics, and the specialty engineering school, the Old Mines so loved by the authors, was a thing of the past.

This is the story of Mines primarily in its first 100 years. Mines went through four distinct stages: the early days (1874 to 1900), the Chauvenet-designed Academy from 1900 to 1962, an engineering college seeking to find itself in a sea of change from 1965 to 1996, and the research-oriented institute of engineering from 1996 to the present. The primary emphasis is on the decade of the 1950s that saw the introduction of the Horizon Plan, and in many ways became the last hurrah for the old Mines, the Engineering Academy. The Horizon Plan envisioned the near-total rebuilding of the physical college, ultimately to accommodate an enrollment of up to 10,000 students, undergraduate, and graduate.

In the 1960s, Mines succumbed to progressive education pressures from the North Central Accreditation Association and was ultimately remade into a mostly technical school along the lines of eastern engineering and technical schools. In 1961 the school granted six undergraduate Professional Engineer degrees, in Mining Engineering, Metallurgical Engineering, Geological Engineering, Geophysical Engineering, Petroleum Production Engineering, and Petroleum Refining Engineering. In 2015, the school granted sixteen Bachelor of Science degrees. In addition, Mines offered twenty-four Master of Science degrees, some requiring a thesis and some not, four non-thesis Master of Engineering degrees, three non-theses Professional Masters degrees, and twenty-four PhD degrees.

It must be emphasized that the school a reader encounters in this work is not the Mines of today. It did not promote diversity, sustainability, wealth distribution, equality, human rights, Agenda 21, or worry about the future of the Earth in the 21st or 22nd centuries. It produced engineers of incredible ability, forged in the harshest of educational institutions, and who knew no limitations. That was its mission, and it was wildly successful.

Chapter 2 - The Silver Diploma

Imagine a sheet of sterling silver, 5-3.5" by 4/78" (nominally 6" by 5"), and 40 mil thick. Imagine further that it is engraved by the Colorado School of Mines conferring on its subject the degree of Metallurgical, Mining, Geophysical, Geological, Petroleum Production, or Petroleum Refining Engineer. This is what Mines graduates received from 1934 to 1968.

The president of the school was forced to use a vibrating stylus to scratch his signature laboriously by hand onto each diploma, the only signature not pre-engraved on the silver sheet. It must have taken him a while to sign a hundred to two hundred diplomas. One president, Dr. John W (middle name only the letter "W") Vanderwilt, said it took several minutes to sign each diploma, but because of the stress on his arm and hand, he could only sign about a dozen on a good day. He was forced to begin the signing process in March of each year to be ready for the June graduation. For those familiar with the Harvard-educated Dr. Vanderwilt, his inability to handle the stress was understandable.

Yet this was only the most well-known symbol of the greatness of Colorado Mines. All other universities in the world issued paper or parchment diplomas, but the requirements for gaining degrees in those institutions were much less than at Mines.

Not only was Mines a specialty school, imparting knowledge in great depth on specific subjects, but it also certified that its graduates possessed basic mineral engineering knowledge across what in other schools would be considered minor disciplines. For example, all students took ten hours of geology, geomorphology, historical geology, crystallography, and minerology, and were required to memorize the geological timetable and even the stratigraphy of Colorado's Front Range. As one professor said, "It was unthinkable that Mines would graduate someone who wouldn't be able to identify the rock layers exposed on the hogback of the Front Range."

All engineers had to be able to draw, sketch, and possess the ability to make maps and engineering drawings of all types. Graduates found engineers from other schools amazed that Miners could produce better work than corporate drafting departments, having just joined industrial corporations as an entry-level engineer.

Typically, a geophysicist earned more credits in geology than geology majors at most universities, and metallurgists clearly accumulated more credits in chemistry than chemical engineers from other schools. And everyone could work in summers as a surveyor after the single intensive surveying course taught between the freshman and sophomore years.

But perhaps the single most important feature of Mines' teaching was that it required students to work their way through homework problems before they were covered in a professor's lecture. That might not sound so bad by itself, but the homework was graded, and those grades amounted to as much as twenty-five percent of the course grade. The technique required the student to solve problems before he was taught how — something beyond the capabilities of many, if not most, college students today. In fact, the inability to think creatively and logically was a major reason students flunked out of Mines, probably second only to not having sufficient dedication to do what was necessary to obtain a Mines degree. The ability to memorize was of only some help, and certainly not decisive. Yet the payoff in industry was stunning. If a student survived Mines' regimen, the pedagogical technique used in course after course often put Mines graduates far above their contemporaries.

One metallurgist had worked only in the steel industry with high strength steels before being hired away by General Electric and put to work rolling and fabricating items from refractory metals such as tungsten, molybdenum, tantalum, and alloys of titanium. None of those metals had been covered at Mines. Nonetheless, the Miner applied the sound metallurgical principles he had learned at Mines, and within three weeks he had created a successful process for metalizing tungsten slabs from pressed and sintered ingots and reliably produced rolled tungsten products.

He had observed that the high level of cracking occurred only on the top edge of the ingots as sintered, thus concluding that hot-pressing was occurring during the process sufficiently to forestall cracking on the bottom. Without even checking the grain structures, he rotated the ingots midway through the sintering process to produce more uniform grain structures, and the cracking disappeared. The cost saving was enormous. His ferrous metallurgy experience had helped, but Mines had taught him to go beyond what he knew.

His second test came in the rolling of three-inch thick molybdenum slabs. In the breakdown rolling mill where the highly pressed and sintered powder metallurgy ingot was first worked, the loss through cracking was unsustainable. A quick look at the grain structure revealed that passes below a twenty percent reduction in cross-sectional area failed to penetrate to the center of the ingot and were causing the cracks. But the mill was rated at only three million pounds of separating force, and the strain gauges were showing the mill approaching that on its current settings.

Knowing that engineers always build in a safety factor in operating levels, the Mines graduate had the bolts holding the mill chocks machined to half their cross-sectional area as his own safety factor, and then went for the gold. The area around the rolling mill was evacuated, the hydrogen-atmosphere electric furnaces protected from flying objects, and the mill's rolls were screwed down until the gap between them was only two inches, and the tests began.

The mill screamed horribly, and everyone in the production area departed for safer areas except for the roller, a mechanical engineer responsible for the mill, and our Mines graduate. At a little over eight million pounds the bolts gave way, but no one was hurt, and the equipment was undamaged (except for the bolts). Most importantly, a fifty percent reduction in a single pass had been achieved. Full bolts replaced the necked-down bolt failures, and the mill was thereafter operated regularly at five million pounds of separating force, twenty percent reduction was achieved, and the cracking was history.

As a result of these coups and other innovations, the Mines grad was put in charge of all production metallurgy for refractory metals, and his boss wanted to take him to Cincinnati and work in the GE jet engine division, another job far removed from his Mines instruction.

In spite of the enormous work load at Mines, the main thing taught was an attitude — that the Miner could solve the problem by applying himself and thinking beyond what he had been taught and what others knew. Geologists went to work for Procter and Gamble making soap, and became managers of production processes totally different from anything they had studied at Mines. Petroleum production engineers morphed into civil engineers in California, and others started their own companies or were successful in industries not even remotely associated with their degrees. What was learned at Mines was self-discipline and the ability to think through situations to solve whatever problems might arise. The graduates were engineers who applied engineering methodologies across the board, regardless of their narrow specialty. One graduate became one of the two top agent handlers in Europe running spies against East Germany, Poland, and the Soviet Union at the height of the Cold War. Many became lawyers, some in patent and intellectually property law where their engineering background helped immensely, but others in general corporate law. One became the Director of the Office of Management and Budget under President Reagan. Another started a company in 1970 that utilized ARPANET and by 1974 was using CRTs for data input, concentrators at various sites, and processing on large remote computers in a forerunner of the Cloud. His company became a recognized pioneer in client-server technology, and this by the middle 1970s. Still another started working in 1978 with the Pick Operating System and its post-relational data base management system, and by 2000 had arguably become the most prolific programmer in the world, writing over two dozen major application systems in widely different industries and producing over three million lines of computer code. One of the authors of this work who had never taken a history course in his life, started producing a series of highly acclaimed history books in his seventies.

Yes, Mines graduates could do anything, inside engineering or out.

This then was the meaning of the silver diploma: that its holder could get the job done, whatever that job was.

Perhaps the best example was Miner Wendell W. Fertig, a man who attended Mines in the late 1920s and early 1930s but failed to graduate. He was hired as a mining engineer in the Philippines, was also a member of the Army Reserve, rising to the rank of lieutenant colonel by the time the Japanese attacked Pearl Harbor. He performed well in the Philippines as both a mining and civil engineer, and was ordered out of Corregidor to Mindanao to take command of all engineering projects in the southern Philippines. When General Sharp, in command on Mindanao, chose to follow General Wainwright's order to surrender, Colonel Fertig exercised his freedom of choice to remain free and fight.

Colonel Fertig was arguably the most successful guerrilla leader in history, eventually commanding over 30,000 troops and guerrillas, and seizing control of most of Mindanao before MacArthur returned to the Philippines. Normally, he should have been promoted to lieutenant general for commanding a corps size unit, but the rabidly jealous MacArthur purposefully failed to promote Fertig to a reasonable rank. After the war, Fertig was returned to Mines to command the ROTC detachment, a job befitting his rank, but not his accomplishments. After five years commanding ROTC, Colonel Fertig retired and became the Executive Secretary of the Alumni Association.

According to Larry Schmidt in his 1982 master's thesis "The American Involvement in the Filipino Resistance on Mindanao During the Japanese Occupation," Fertig was effective because "His experience as an engineer...and methods of attacking problems would serve him in the challenges he would face as the leader of the Mindanao guerrillas... It was due primarily to his personal leadership qualities that the Mindanao resistance movement was unified under one leader and became the most successful of all the guerrilla units in the Philippines." In short, it was his Mines training that enabled him to be extraordinarily successful as an unconventional military leader.

When all is said and done, every silver diploma was earned under adverse and harsh conditions identifying its holder as a special breed of man or woman. Mines taught far more than engineering, and if the student was able to survive the regimen developed over the first seventy years of the school's existence, he joined a race of giants who knew no bounds on innovation, ingenuity, and the ability to produce. Mines would have been nothing without its graduates, dispersed to the world, carrying the banner of excellence. One such graduate was Bob Waterman, Geophysical Engineer of 1958, who would write with his co-author Tom Peters In Search of Excellence in 1982. Mines graduates knew what excellence was, and how to achieve it.

Even those students who fell by the wayside were influenced by Mines. In the early days students often dropped out to work in their chosen industry or start their own companies. Any training from the Colorado School of Mines was looked upon as an asset, often making the difference between obtaining a job or not. Yale might be the elite school for the east coast, government and politics, but Mines was the elite school for engineering in the real world.

Like West Point and the Naval Academy, Miners could and did excel in many occupations, in engineering and non-engineering. Private industry and even government recognized Miners as leaders driven by the need to perform at the highest level. Only the journeyman administrators of Mines after World War II failed to recognize what Mines was producing. Many of its graduates were polymaths, able to excel in many endeavors and technologies, far beyond the abilities of Mines presidents and many trustees to recognize and treasure. Unable to understand the greatness in front of them, they destroyed it and installed something more like what they had experienced on other campuses. Chauvenet's vision (described in Chapter 7) had become an unqualified success, making Mines fully the equal of the service academies. American citizens readily accorded service academy graduates the respect and expectation that they could excel in non-military positions, but Mines administrators could not understand that Mines graduates could excel in non-engineering positions. The reasons why reflect the administrators' nearsightedness, not any deficiency on the part of Mines graduates.

For many years, only two other schools gave professional degrees like Mines, the California Institute of Technology, and Massachusetts Institute of Technology. But Cal Tech was primarily a research school, generating graduates who would go on to acquire post-graduate degrees, then work in academia or research facilities. MIT was similar to Cal Tech, but somewhat less research oriented. Both cultivated the "engineering nerd" type of individual, one for whom science was an end to itself. Mines produced graduates who worked in private industry, to produce products for the benefit of all mankind. Research was not fundamental or theoretical, but applied, to be put to good use as rapidly as possible. There was little of the ivory tower approach in a Miner's life, all of his engineering was practical and useful to the average citizen.

While a guest lecturer at MIT in 1954, Mines professor Paul Keating was introduced by the MIT Dean, who ended his introduction by twitting Prof Keating (who did not have a PhD). He said: "Professor, I want you to know that here at MIT we turn out the finest engineers in the world." Keating took the lectern and said, "Thank you Dean H__. Please keep up the good work in producing fine engineers; our Mines boys are always looking for people to hire."

In World War II and the Korean War, Mines supplied the most reserve officers to the Corps of Engineers of any institution in the US, clearly showing the practical engineering side of the Mines curriculum as discussed in Chapter 15. Mines graduates performed distinguish service, and endured the casualties to prove CSM's importance to the military effort. After both World War II and the Korean War, veterans enrolled at Mines in great numbers and substantially impacted student life. The rough and tumble aspect of Mines life increased dramatically, especially as epitomized by Senior Day which gave new meaning to faculty evaluations. Good faculty members were rewarded, but bad instructors were in for a very rough time. Students felt that was only right: if excellence was to be demanded of them, then why not of the faculty?

The silver diploma stood for all of this, and simply to have earned the coveted symbol of excellence made a person proud. It may not have been Skull and Bones at Yale, but that was given to well-connected individuals rather than for achievement. Mines was egalitarian. Achievement was open to all, and indeed, often the students from wealthy families disappeared from the campus before their first semester had ended. Less than thirty percent graduated in four years, and this was from individuals scoring high on their SATs and the Pre-Engineering Inventory Exam in the first place. It took more than intelligence to graduate from Mines. It took grit, tenacity, endurance, and dedication.

The freshman Gauntlet that was a required prerequisite to joining any social or honorary fraternity, epitomized the years of study at Mines. Shortly before Thanksgiving, every freshman ran a gauntlet of all the upper-classmen swinging belts. One ran a different type of gauntlet daily, and it was the faculty that stood alongside and attempted to beat the runners until they dropped out. Most students did, and the silver diploma only went to the few left running.

It all started with the class of 1934, but the exact story of the silver diploma's origination is disputed. One story is that Charles A. Hull (or Hill) created an engraved silver diploma for his son when the boy graduated from Mines in 1933. President Coolbaugh was impressed, and decided to hand out similar silver diplomas in the May, 1934, commencement to all graduates. Another version says it was the idea of Gayland Warren of the 1934 graduating class. Students did the design under the direction of George W. Salzer (class of 1921), Professor of Engineering Drawing and Descriptive Geometry, and Charles Hull (or Hill) did the etching. In any case, the sterling silver diplomas rapidly made the school famous.

Nothing lasts forever, however, and following the elimination of the Professional Engineer degree at Mines in 1968 as the standard undergraduate degree and its replacement with run-of-the-mill Bachelor of Science degrees, the school administration decided to give silver diplomas only for graduate degrees. This began in 1969, but by 1980, the administration decided the diplomas would be discontinued for all. The situation was saved when ASARCO's President, Ralph L. Hennebach, EM '41, offered to provide the silver free of charge for professional and graduate degrees. The administration was more or less forced by the alumni to continue issuing silver diplomas, but undergraduate degrees remained on paper.

Then came the great cheapening. In 2001, silver-nickel (as opposed to sterling silver) diplomas were issued for all undergraduate degrees, even though they represented a year and a half less work than the professional degrees of old. The bachelor degrees were a far cry from the professional degree, and making them of an ersatz metal alloy, essentially a cheap imitation of silver, automatically lessened the silver diplomas still being issued. It was like a debasement of currency that has occurred so often in human history and always led to the demise of the empire or country lowering the precious metal content of its coinage. It remains to be seen if this rule will hold true for Mines.

The "M" seen from campus

Chapter 3 - The "M" & Nostalgia

To Colorado's citizens, the most commonly recognized aspect of the school is probably the giant "M" on a mountain overlooking Golden. Like everything else about Mines, it has a long and distinguished history. Joseph Francis O'Byrne, one of the founders of the Kappa Sigma fraternity at Mines, originated the idea for an "M" on Mount Zion while still an undergraduate in 1905. He proudly laid out the first "M" on the mountain, but discovered his work was subject to distortion when viewed from various vantage points below. An ardent designer and artist who later became a full Professor of Descriptive Geometry and head of the department at Mines, Joe O'Byrne went back to the drawing board and reworked his letter into a perfect block "M" for all locations in Golden, the road between the Table Mountains, and the Old Golden Road from Denver.

Other students were enlisted in the "M" Project, and W. S. Brown turned O'Byrne's design into reality by fencing in a square just below the mountain's peak to contain the "M." The workers then staked out the mammoth letter, correcting O'Byrne's earlier effort. A fever possessed the school, and with only a handful missing, the entire faculty and student body of Mines ascended the mountain on May 16, 1908, to construct the "M". Requiring most of a day to build, the "M" proved the correctness and excellence of O'Byrne's vision and Brown's layout (why are we not surprised?) The "M" conformed to Mount Zion's contours, naturally and esthetically, and was ultimately the subject of a graduate thesis in Descriptive Geometry.

The construction of the letter was no mean feat when one remembers the present road, Lariat Loop, was not in existence at the time. Students and faculty trudged upwards carrying all materials on burros, a mode of transportation befitting Mines' mascot, Blaster. In early days when roads were mere trails where they existed at all, burros were the pack animals of choice for miners and prospectors. The sure-footed little beasts were perfect for negotiating steep hillsides and were relatively insensitive to hostile environments. In this case, everything had to be carried in pack trains; food, water, cement, whitewash, and tools. Rocks were endemic, but even they were often carried long distances as the square's surface to contain the "M" was smoothed to produce an emblem of which every Mines graduate and friend of the school could be proud.

The lights came much later although flares were used to illuminate the "M" on homecoming nights during the first twenty years of its existence. In 1931, Professor S. Power (Pi) Warren of the Metallurgy Department took up the banner and persuaded honorary society Blue Key to arrange electric lights for homecoming. Professor Warren had helped build the "M" as a freshman, and spent a number of years with Professor O'Byrne on the Mines faculty and in Square and Compass, CSM's Masonic fraternity. Pi manifested more school spirit than most students, and using the professor's extensive industrial contacts, Blue Key collected materials and equipment necessary for temporary lighting. They obtained 350 light bulbs on loan from Mines' staunch supporter, the Colorado Central Power Company, wiring and a generator were liberated from the Mines physics laboratory, and the State Industrial School contributed the use of a Fordson tractor. As could be expected, the lighting was a raging success and a marvel to all on campus.

A campaign to install permanent lights immediately ensued, and by the following summer almost twelve hundred dollars had been collected through contributions and the sale of "Light the 'M'" tags by students. In the depths of the Great Depression, this was a major feat for what most Denverites, and particularly the ever-hostile Denver press, felt was a needless extravagance.

More than 400 forty-watt light bulbs were installed to illuminate the "M", using almost 2,000 feet of wire within the fenced square. A power line was constructed from the vicinity of Brooks Field to the "M", a distance of 4,600 feet, to supply power at 2,300 volts. By the 1932 homecoming everything was in place, and the "M" has shown brightly with minor interruptions ever since.

From the beginning maintenance was performed each fall by the freshman class as a standard part of their introduction to Mines traditions. Blue Key took attendance at this as well as all other freshman orientation functions, and participation in these activities was required for a student to be eligible for any Mines social or honorary organization. In 1952 Senior Day activities were coming increasingly under fire by the Denver media, and in an effort to divert energies to more constructive activities, the senior class renovated and whitewashed the "M" prior to graduation in the spring. Following the total abolition of the raucous and traditional Senior Day activities in 1953, the spring cleaning by seniors became an annual event.

Over the years the "M" has proven an irresistible attraction for students of other schools to vandalize. During the fifties fraternities routinely guarded the "M" at critical times such as homecoming or before grudge football games, foiling several attacks and apprehend the culprits. An efficient system was organized to seal off the road from Lookout Mountain before it intersected Route 40 and block the lower exit of Lariat Loop. Pledges from each fraternity took turns guarding the "M" high on Mount Zion and were connected with a command center on campus by an Army field telephone.

The most famous incident occurred in 1958 when three CU students were caught just before they lit a thirty second fuse on over a hundred sticks of dynamite. Alerted by guards, a convoy of students ascended the mountain and narrowly averted a major tragedy. The CU students would have perished in the resulting explosion and landslide had they carried their plan to fruition.

As it was, they were taken to the Sigma Phi Epsilon house on 15th Street. There they were subjected to an initiation rite that members of the Theta Tau honorary fraternity sometimes visited on their rival Sigma Gamma Epsilon counterparts — plastering. Following Mines tradition, the CU miscreants were stripped, then completely covered with Plaster of Paris from their chests to their knees, which of course were widely spread to accommodate an inordinate amount of hardening plaster to protect certain private parts. The plaster was well mixed into their body hair, and a small hole was left through which the individual could relieve himself. After the plaster set, the now fully remorseful three would-be dynamiters were bundled into their car and released for their return to Boulder.

Much to everyone's surprise the story did not end there. One of the CU students went to a Boulder hospital to have the plaster removed instead of chipping it away himself. Supposedly it was a very painful process, and anesthesia was administered to help the poor little boy through his terrible ordeal. *The Rocky Mountain News* pounced on the incident like a starving piranha, and lambasted Mines with relish on its front page. The student's father flew out from California and threatened to sue Mines and everyone involved. His son and the other students claimed they were innocent of any wrong doing, and merely accosted by miners in Golden because they were from Colorado University. The press had a field day.

Forced to defend themselves, Mines students grudgingly produced the confiscated dynamite, and gave statements to the Jefferson County Sheriff as to how the dynamite had been dangerously and incompetently rigged. A small article appeared in the News concerning Mines' disclosures in the controversy as a correction buried deep in the newspaper, but the plastering was still held to be a barbaric punishment. Nonetheless, the counter-offensive by Mines did the trick. Threatened with lawsuits and possible criminal arrest, the CU students recanted their stories, and the troublesome father disappeared back to California. Unfortunately, the large quantity of dynamite remained in official hands rather than being put to good use by Mines students.

The Denver papers had earlier enjoyed a field day with Mines in 1953 when the ATOs caught four Denver University (DU) students breaking lights on the "M". Their heads were shaved, and the letters M, I, N, and E were painted on their heads. *The Rocky Mountain News* front page photo showed the culprits' bald, bowed heads, and reporters blamed the incident on hooliganism at Mines. It was a flashback to the 30s when three CU students had been caught and one had an "M" burned into his head with silver nitrate. The letter was a permanent brand, so other forms of punishment had been adopted. The individual involved became a dentist practicing in Denver, and periodically his punishment was revived as proof by certain legislators that Mines should be eliminated as a separate institution.

Not all vandalism attempts were so successfully foiled. In 1949 the emblem fell mightily to unknown assailants. On the night before CSM's 75th anniversary celebration the "M" was essentially destroyed. Most of its rocks were scattered down Mount Zion, all lightbulbs were smashed, and the wiring cut into hundreds of tiny pieces. Obviously many individuals were involved, and they were able to make good their escape before the "M"'s absence was noted. Mines' unquenchable spirit rose to face this crisis, and CSM's beloved "M" was restored for the following evening's festivities. Almost half of the school's enrollment responded to the "M"'s hour of need, and by noon its rocks were replaced and whitewashed. Somehow wiring and bulbs were obtained and installed during the afternoon, and the fraternity guard system was inaugurated to prevent future occurrences of such heinous attacks on Mines pride.

In 1960, the fraternity guard system had fallen into disuse, and in the second week of December about half of the lights were smashed by persons unknown. The lights were not replaced until after New Year's, and many students took this as a sign of declining school spirit. The administration had begun bullying the fraternities to move into a fraternity row or else, and the IFC had been made a subordinate organization to the Student Council, effectively stripping the fraternity system of its independence. A formal pledging system had been inaugurated, and as it appeared to the students, the administration was instituting onerous rules with increasing frequency. Obviously, an era was coming to an end.

Until the sixties Mines was able to boast that its "M", the world's largest electrically lighted letter at 104 by 107 feet, had never remained unlighted, defaced, or damaged for more than one day. It had been rudely painted, dynamited, lost its wiring, suffered thousands of broken bulbs, but was always restored to pristine condition by loving Mines students and faculty. It was a symbol of pride to Golden, Mines, and Colorado, well worth defending against all depredations. Blue Key changed the bulbs to red in honor of Christmas each holiday season, and Golden glowed with the cooperative Yuletide spirit thus generated. That Mines was an indelible part of the local community even when most students were absent was understood by all. The lights that had been broken in 1960 had been the red lights, and that was a sad Christmas for the Golden and the Mines community.

As an unintended consequence of declining school spirit during the sixties, the "M" fell upon hard times, and partial losses of lighting went unrepaired for days and even weeks. CSM's administration had taken an adversarial position vis a vis the fraternities and wanted to bring the frats under administrative control. Every problem was addressed by first threatening the offending fraternity with being put on social probation or outright expulsion from campus activities. Finally flexing its eminent domain muscles, in the 1960s the administration forced the fraternities to give up their cherished houses scattered throughout the campus and move to a remote and segregated fraternity row.

The system of guards and early warning operated by the fraternities went dormant, but the Mines administration was caught short, and did nothing to protect the "M." It was not until Mines established a campus police force that someone again took responsibility for maintaining the "M"'s security. Unfortunately, the campus police proved a poor substitute for student guards protecting the "M" at critical times. The Mines spirit among students was vastly reduced, and the administration proved itself ineffective at maintaining the traditions of Mines. In fact, it seemed intent on eradicating the traditions that had stood the school in such good stead for so long. But what followed was the deluge.

As Mines' most visible symbol, the "M" showed the school was taking hits, possibly even mortal body blows, from which recovery was only problematical. It seemed as though the school administration, as well as the rapidly changing student body, no longer cared. The baby boomer generation had arrived, and it was intent on establishing a new United States with institutes of higher education following the principles of progressive education. The old Mines was probably the most recalcitrant and tradition-bound educational institution in America, with standards that turned non-elite middle-class Americans into captains of industry, and it had to go. Surprisingly, it went with only a whimper.

Colorado School of Mines Peak:

As the "M" seemed to be the only symbol of Mines seen by the transient vacationers in Colorado, various individuals felt that something additional was needed. Well, Colorado had plenty of mountains, and some were still unnamed.

Languishing somewhat behind Ivy League schools which had captured the Collegiate Range with Harvard, Yale, and Princeton peaks (as if those schools had anything to do with Colorado), CSM therefore began a project in 1952 to locate and name an appropriate mountain in Colorado after itself. Theta Tau, one of Mines' professional engineering fraternities, undertook the study at the suggestion of Dr. LeRoy, then head of the Geology Department and a long-time Mines booster.

Amazingly, none of the mountains in Colorado carried the name of any Colorado institution, and the team headed by Neal Harr, President of Theta Tau, determined that Mines should take initial honors. Why Colorado had not yet honored any of its own educational institutions with a peak almost defied imagination. All the peaks over 14,000 feet elevation already were named, as were the vast majority of those easily visible from major highways. It was imperative that an unnamed peak be found visible from a trans-continental highway, significant in elevation, and preferably one associated some way with Mines or mining history.

After wading through over eighty pounds of Colorado quadrangle maps Harr discovered a prime candidate located immediately east of Berthoud Pass with an elevation of 12,486 feet. Captain Edward L. Berthoud, one of Colorado's early pioneers and a professor, trustee, and major backer of Mines, had discovered the pass in 1860, and the mountain peak overlooking the pass was appropriate in every respect.

Harr presented CSM's case before the board on geological names in Washington D.C., and no objection to naming the peak was found. An exhaustive search was made to determine if the peak had borne other names in the past, but it seemed that somehow the mountain had been overlooked. With no clear competition from a past designation or any interested group, the mountain's new name was adopted by all interested governmental agencies. The Colorado Highway Department placed a marker along US 40 giving the peak's name and a short description of its features. Until the Eisenhower Tunnel opened under Loveland pass (named for William A. H. Loveland, the first president of Mines' Board of Trustees), US Highway 40 was the main route heading west from Denver across the Continental Divide.

On April 16, 1954, a team of Miners ascended the mountain and staged "official" dedication ceremonies. The team included three students; Neal Harr (1954), Student Council President Kent Miller (1954), and William Harvey (1955); one administrator, Charles Morris, the director of public relations; and one faculty member, Dr. Leslie W. LeRoy of the Geology Department. An "M" flag was unfurled on top of the peak, and CSM took its place alongside Berthoud's Pass.

The student newspaper, *The Oredigger*, announced the event in its edition of April 27, 1954:

"It seems fitting that the peak should be named in honor of the Colorado School of Mines. Each year students make extensive study of the peak...to observe the outstanding examples of the effect of glaciation on its topography. Secondly, the peak commemorates the contributions made to the mineral industries...for over 80 years by graduates and faculty members. And last, the peak is near Berthold Pass, named in honor of Captain E. L. Berthold, who devoted much of his energy to the School of Mines in its early days."

Although it might seem that the school would seize upon the peak to build a mountain-climbing tradition in Theta Tau or other organization, that did not occur. School traditions started disappearing in the fifties under Harvard-educated President Vanderwilt, and the naming of Colorado School of Mines Peak became a kind of last hurrah. Instead of opening new visions and vistas, the dedication of the peak heralded the end of an era.

The Stranded Football Fan:

And then there was the "Stranded Football Fan", a poem written by Richard Broad, Jr., around 1911. Broad was not a Mines graduate, and may not even have been a student for the four years as related in the poem, but became one of its strongest boosters in the early part of the 20th century.

A football fan from Golden was stranded in Salt Lake,
With nary a cent to bless him, nor drink his thirst to slake,
But the "M" upon his sweater soon caught a passing eye,
And a stranger stood beside him and bade him cease to cry.

And the fan's eyes quickly brightened as he heard the stranger say —
"Hailest thou from dear old Golden, if so with me you'll stay,
For I once lived at Golden and I studied at the Mines,
And to me there is no fairer place on which the warn sun shines.

The "M" upon Mt. Zion, with its freshly painted stones,
The church bells all a ringing with their soothing, dulcet tones,
The pool balls clicking, and the sounds of chips at night,
And oft unto my vision comes each entrancing sight.

The "Lab.," the "Gym," the library at Guggenheim and all
Those old familiar buildings to me in fancy call.
The moonlight nights beneath the trees, when she and I were there,
Ah me, but those were happy times and life seemed far from care.

Alas, she chose a butcher's boy and he and she were wed,
Any many a night I got soused and wished that I were dead.
But all came out all right at last, I found another lass
Who beat the first by forty rods – was in another class,

And she agreed to share my lot, she shares it yet today,
And there's a kid – we call him "Mines," who round our home doth play,

I'm happy and I'm prosperous, yet oft in fancy roam
Back to the dear old School of Mines, which always seems like home.

And oft I long to be once more within those classic walls,
Where Patton, Fleck, Haldane and Trapp, each one for study calls.
And oft I realize again that those were happy times
When I stayed four years in Golden at the dear old School of Mines.

So he took the stranded football fan and held him to his breast,
And liquids bought, and things to eat, so you can guess the rest,
And when the football fan woke up, he vowed he'd cease to roam;
Upon the train he had been placed and carried free back home.

Moral:
Of all the schools upon the earth, the Mines is sure the best,
Its graduates throughout the world are scattered east and west.
No matter where you chance to be, if you for succor call,
You'll find some Mines men somewhere round, and they're the best of
all.

Richard (Dick) Broad, Jr., was born in 1863 at Superior Mine, Michigan, and came to Colorado as a child in 1870. His family first settled in Central City, but after a year, moved to a farm on Ralston Creek. In 1885 he relocated to Golden where he became a City Commissioner. He made Golden his permanent home, residing at 1422 Washington Street (later a rooming house for seven Mines students), was on the Golden City Council in 1890-91, became mayor of Golden in 1903, then a Jefferson County commissioner, and later a state senator in the Colorado Legislature. He was also chairman of the State Silver Republican Central Committee, and a Trustee of the State Normal School at Greeley, now Northern Colorado University, for ten years. Mr. Broad was a prominent member of the Golden community until his death in 1936. This was truly a Mines supporter.

Chapter 4 - The Early Colorado Environment

The story of Mines is a reflection of Colorado history from the days of its founding to the present. In a very large sense, Mines mirrored Colorado society, or at least the industrial side of it. When Mines was founded, Colorado was only marginally civilized, and the mining and engineering professions required highly competent and hardened individuals. For eighty years Mines produced those individuals, and in so doing, built an international reputation. It is well to review the history of Colorado to understand CSM's heritage, starting with the Indian inhabitants, of whom few remain.

Of the tribes found in Colorado by explorers in the early nineteenth century, only the Utes had lived in the state for any appreciable length of time. The Sioux were forced out of the Wisconsin forests onto the plains by the Chippawas, and in turn pushed the Cheyenne and Arapaho out of South Dakota and the Black Hills in the 18th century.

At the same time, Utes were working eastwards, laying claim to all mountainous territory in Colorado. Decades of savage conflict saw the extermination of a number of lesser tribes. During the first forty years of the nineteenth century warfare was more or less constant between the three groups; Utes, Cheyenne and Arapaho, and Kiowa and Comanche.

The Denver-Golden area was first opened up by Louis Vasquez and Andrew Sublette who built a trading post named Fort Vasquez in 1836 (some sources say 1832) on the South Platte immediately north of the site of Denver. Representing the Rocky Mountain Fur Company, they were the Bent brothers' chief rivals in Colorado. Clear Creek was first named Vasquez Creek in honor of Louis, but the name was changed after Fort Vasquez was sold to Locke and Randolph in 1840. The fur trade declined after 1840 and in 1842 the post was captured and razed by an Arapaho war party. The Front Range area remained a wilderness for over a dozen years, although settlements further south slowly took hold in the face of great adversity.

In 1858 a party of Georgians and Cherokees headed by William Green Russell panned a small amount of gold from Cherry Creek within the present city limits of Denver. Another party from Lawrence, Kansas, drifted up from Pikes Peak following news of Russell's discoveries, and constructed a series of log huts on the eastern bank of the South Platte along what is now West Evans

Avenue. They named their settlement Montana City. Two traders, John Smith and William McGaa founded another settlement on the north bank of Cherry Creek near its confluence with the South Platte and named their town St. Charles. A number of the Montana City men joined forces with Smith and McGaa believing the traders possessed influence with nearby Arapahos, and Montana City fell by the wayside.

Officers were elected at St. Charles in September, 1858, and knowing the gold finds in Cherry Creek were insignificant, a group of St. Charles entrepreneurs headed by Charles Nichols set out for eastern Kansas and Missouri to recruit new residents for their town. In their absence some of Russell's party returned from prospecting in the mountains and founded another town on the south side of Cherry Creek and enlisted Smith's and McGaa's assistance. The town of Auraria rose rapidly from the mud.

The alarmed St. Charles promoters hurriedly returned to find their town site being taken over by a new town company of recent Kansas arrivals headed by William Larimer. He had arrived at Cherry Creek on November 16, 1858, expecting to sell building lots in a boomtown he hoped to found. Larimer simply jumped the claims of St. Charles, and when Nichols protested such high-handed affairs, Larimer cowed the St. Charles men into silence with threats of violence. Larimer organized the Denver City Town Company on the former sites of Montana City and St. Charles, naming the town for James W. Denver, the Territorial Governor of Kansas. Denver had sent three officials west with Larimer's party to incorporate the area as Arapahoe County, Kansas Territory, and they had supported Larimer. Choosing Denver's name was a shrewd move, even though the Governor no longer held office by the time Larimer's town company was formed. Using Denver's name, Larimer's party appeared to have a political seal of approval that tended to eliminate opposition.

Meanwhile, the exaggerated tales of great strikes caused major excitement in the East, and before winter began in earnest, hundreds of enthusiastic gold-seekers had found their way to the Denver Basin. The cold and snow suspended migrations during the winter, but with the earliest breaks in harsh weather thousands trekked westward from Missouri and Eastern Kansas to seek their fortune. Alas, the Cherry Creek strike was ephemeral, and many returned back across the plains decrying the "Pikes Peak Hoax".

The twin towns of Denver and Auraria glared at each other across Cherry Creek and formed an intense rivalry. *The Rocky Mountain News* built its offices on stilts over Cherry Creek on the boundary between the two towns attempting to maintain a semblance of neutrality. With forty houses, Auraria possessed twice the number of Denver, and boasted of Colorado's first saloon, established by Uncle Dick Wootton with his Taos Lightning from New Mexico.

The "Pikes Peak or Bust" rush in the following spring was even larger in numbers than the California gold rush of 1849, and easily its equal in hardships. Provisions were scarce, the miners were ill-prepared for adversity, and the Indians were hostile. In the midst of a great general despondency in the Denver Basin came news that gold was discovered by George Jackson and John Gregory in 1859 on tributaries of Clear Creek within a few miles of each other and less than twenty-five miles from Golden. Almost immediately, another strike was made as well in Boulder Canyon at Gold Hill. Shortly thereafter, Green Russell led a prospecting party north of Jackson's strike and panned some $20,000 worth of gold out of what became known as Russell Gulch. Within a week over four thousand miners were crammed into the Idaho Springs, Russell Gulch, and Gregory Gulch areas, and with economic success barely snatched from certain misery, the region's politicians began to agitate for becoming the State of Jefferson.

In the summer of 1859, Golden took shape, absorbing the placer mining camp of Arapahoe Bar between the Table Mountains. Most historians agree that it was named for Tom Golden, a prospector who panned Clear Creek near the present Washington Street Bridge. Nonetheless, the town's founding occurred to a very large degree as the result of work and promotion accomplished by William A. H. Loveland, helped by George West. West founded the *Western Mountaineer* with the press formerly owned by John Merrick, an early rival to William Byers, the cantankerous editor of the *Rocky Mountain News*. When Merrick's first issue hit the streets of Denver and Auraria twenty minutes after the News' initial edition, Merrick sold out to Byers and his partner Thomas Gibson for a thirty-dollar grubstake and headed for the gold fields. Gibson split with Byers and took Merrick's press to Central City and produced the *Gold Reporter* for less than a month during August, 1859. West brought the much-traveled press to Golden, but sold it again when he departed to fight in the Civil War in 1861.

Golden City, incorporated in 1859, became a major outfitting and supply center for prospectors going into the mountains to make their fortune. The secure source of good water from Clear Creek enabled the founding of businesses engaged in milling and smelting. Other early industries included a candy factory, brickmaking, quarrying, glass making, and the brewing of beer. In 1870, Golden featured three flour mills, 2 breweries, one paper mill, three brick kilns, and five smelters. By 1880, Adolf Coors was the sole owner of the Golden Brewery, and the town boasted of having over 110 businesses, including fifty mercantile shops and 14 saloons.

These early days were characterized by the rude but generally fair form of justice which normally traveled with the westward migrating Scotch-Irish pioneers. Probably the most efficient human predators in history, the Scotch-Irish settled the West, nearly exterminating Indian tribes with whom they came into contact, and forming their own government entities as warranted. Colorado and its home-grown self-organized Jefferson Territory was a perfect example of their attitudes and society. Mostly Protestant and with most influential individuals active in freemasonry, Colorado went from two hundred white settlers in 1858 to statehood in eighteen years. During that time the new Coloradans fought a Civil War, neutralized five tribes of bitterly hostile Indians, and created all the necessary major governmental and social institutions.

Prior to 1876 the Jefferson Territory Miners' and People's courts dispensed justice firmly and with no nonsense. Statutes were clear and direct, designed to maintain law and order with minimum inconvenience to the honest inhabitants. Lawyers were looked upon as rogues whose presence was an anathema to an effective criminal justice system. Many courts forbade the use of lawyers; allowing their presence only if a litigant or accused individual happened to be an attorney himself. Justice was not a subject for tampering, and legal niceties were not allowed to interfere. The vast majority of courts were astoundingly fair and just, but the Denver People's Court system broke down in the fall of 1860, in large part due to the rising tensions between the North and South.

All claims became illegal since there was no mechanism to convert the federal government's ownership on lands and mineral rights to private individuals. Congress couldn't do anything about the situation, so the miners handled it themselves. Vigilante committees were formed, and after a few miscreants were found dangling from trees, many major transgressors fled the Territory, and

Denver and the area returned to a more orderly system.

Miners' Courts were notable for limiting greed and spreading the wealth of diggings equitably among working miners. Severe limits were placed on what an individual could claim, and a miner had to work his claim to retain his interest. Territorial law later was substantially stricter than the first Federal mining law, and as stated in Creede's code of 1892, "Prospecting shall be done with a pick and shovel, not with a penknife and lead pencil."

Placer mining was fine as a jump-start to Colorado's economy, but most influential citizens recognized that a true, long-term industry was needed, coupled with effective transportation facilities. In that respect, Colorado communities girded themselves to battle for the railroads which seemed to be the key to prosperity. With an imposing wall of mountains in its backyard, Denver was at a decided disadvantage. Captain Edward L. Berthoud was sent west from Denver with mountain man Jim Bridger to find a reasonable pass for a railroad in 1861, but in spite of his best efforts to tout Berthoud Pass, both the Overland Stage and Union Pacific elected to use routes through Wyoming. Berthoud's credentials were impeccable, having been a construction engineer and surveyor on the Panama Isthmus Railway during the 1850s, but the grades were too steep, and Berthoud Pass too high. A tunnel through the divide was proposed almost immediately, and in 1936 was finally completed as the Moffat Tunnel connecting Denver with Winter Park. A special Moffat Tunnel Tax was still being paid by Denver residents in the 1950s.

Undaunted by his failure to attract a railroad, Captain Berthoud began building a wagon road over his pass in 1862 after attracting several partners and investors. For a while he enlisted the assistance of *Rocky Mountain News* Editor Byers, but Berthoud eventually sold the uncompleted road to a Georgetown banker, William Cushman. The road bankrupted Cushman, and it wasn't until W. A. Hamill completed the work in 1875 that the first stage crossed the divide. Until completion of the Eisenhower Tunnel under Loveland Pass in 1979, Berthoud Pass was the primary route between Denver and Salt Lake City.

William Austin Hamilton Loveland also enmeshed himself in railroad affairs and built the Colorado Central from Denver to Central City through Clear Creek Canyon in 1872. Loveland possessed hopes of pushing his railway over Berthoud Pass, and thwarted by Berthoud's steep grades, envisioned a cable tram carrying passengers over the divide to meet the railroad in Winter Park.

Loveland was the primary early promoter of the town of Golden and built the town's first mercantile store. When the Colorado Territory was established from about sixty percent of Jefferson Territory in 1861, Loveland lobbied successfully to make Golden the territorial capital. One of the few influential citizens to remain aloof from serving in the Civil War, Loveland was able to establish a premier position as the leading citizen of Golden during the 1870's and the Colorado Territorial Legislature met in his building during 1866. After the capital was moved to Denver, Loveland threw his energy into supporting the establishment of the Colorado School of Mines.

In many ways Denver, Golden, and Colorado School of Mines embodied an eighteenth-century frontier culture which lasted until after World War II in Colorado and a few other western states. Formed by the dominant Scotch-Irish segment in the American Colonies before the Revolutionary War, this culture would set the tone for life in Golden and at Mines until the 1960s.

What cannot be denied by their detractors, is that the Scotch-Irish believed all political power belonged to the people, and that education was the key to personal success. A thousand miles away from any other population center, Colorado legislators promoted public schooling as one of their highest priorities.

CSM was not the only success for the people of Colorado and their legilators. Colorado was able to reduce its illiteracy rate from 4.2% in 1900 to 2.8% in 1930, far below the 2016 illiteracy rate in the adult U.S. population of 14%. As Colorado's population became increasingly diverse, however, its schools adopted progressive education principles. Functional illiteracy grew in estimates to over 10% by 2003. Twenty percent of Colorado high school graduates now cannot read beyond a fifth-grade level — a development that would be unbelievable to the Mines educators in the 1930s.

Chapter 5 - Early Mines History

In many ways, the Colorado School of Mines owes its parentage to a brief moment in history when settlers in the Rocky Mountains Front Range governed themselves independently as Jefferson Territory. With the gold strikes in 1859, a mining fever began that would culminate in the establishment of the Colorado School of Mines to serve an increasing need for engineering expertise on the frontier. The independent spirit moved more than mountains of ore, it established a milieu of tough-mindedness which became a hallmark of Mines life and its graduates.

Within six months of the Clear Creek strikes, Golden City was founded, and a town company called the Boston Company was formed. Headed by William A.H. Loveland, it included such notables as George W. West, and Edward L. Berthoud. All three became extremely influential citizens in Colorado and passionately involved with CSM.

Loveland lived to give his name to Loveland Pass and the city of Loveland, founded the city of Lakewood in 1878, was President of CSM's Board of Trustees from 1874 to 1878, and Professor in Charge from 1875 to 1876. George West became a Brigadier-General in the Civil War and returned to establish the *Colorado Transcript* where he remained as its editor for many years. Colorado National Guard Camp George West was named in his honor, and it was General West who battled the *Rocky Mountain News* at the time Mines was created. Not only did the contentious *News* editor believe the State should not involve itself in supporting educational and scientific institutions, but stated a wagon road would be more useful to Colorado than a School of Mines. E. L. Berthoud was honored with Berthoud Pass, the town of Berthoud, and Berthoud Hall. He became a territorial legislator and Speaker of the House, Professor of Civil Engineering and Geology in 1872, and Member of the CSM Board of Trustees from1874 to1904.

After having been the capital of Jefferson Territory, bustling Golden became the second capital of Colorado Territory in 1862. Congress established the territory with the present State's boundaries in 1861, and after the Legislature's initial choice, Colorado City (the west side of Colorado Springs) proved ill-advised, the capital was moved to Golden. Competition from Denver, that newly (1861) amalgamated city of Auraria and Denver City in the flood-stricken basin where Cherry Creek and the South Platt joined, wrested capital honors away in 1867. But Golden's pre-eminence in history remained with Golden City Lodge Number 1, A. F. & A. M., the first masonic lodge in Nebraska and Colorado Territories, and Denver never acquired a world class institution of higher education to challenge Mines.

But what about the founding of the Colorado School of Mines? According to Trustee Captain James T. Smith in 1905,

> *"The Colorado School of Mines was founded in 1864 by the voluntary action of the miners of Gilpin and Clear Creek Counties. When those pioneers of Colorado's present wonderful mineral industry were confronted with 'cap rock' below the level of the free-gold material they appealed to science for a solution of their difficulty, setting aside a portion of the value of each mining claim patented or sold for the purpose of aiding a school in which metallurgy and mining would be nurtured and taught."*

Nothing is known about where the school initially operated, who was in charge, or the numbers of students, and Smith's testimony is the only evidence of an 1864 founding. This date 1864, if true, would be important, as it would mean that the founding of the two greatest schools of mines in the US, the Columbia University School of Mines in New York City and the other in Golden, took place in the same year. Thomas Eggleston, a well-known mineralogist and graduate of Yale University and the Ecole of Mines in Paris, France, originated plans for the school of mines at Columbia, and definitely became its first professor of mineralogy and metallurgy in 1864. Most historians have therefore credited Columbia's school being in operation before Mines, and use 1874 as CSM's founding. Nevertheless, the territorial government soon became involved, indicating something was going on in Colorado. While still meeting in Golden, the Council and House of Representatives of Colorado Territory approved the incorporation of a Colorado Mining College on January 11, 1867, the conceptual forerunner to a state-owned Colorado School of Mines.

This approval of a mining school may or may not have involved Episcopal Bishop George M. Randall, who had begun agitating for a multi-college university after arriving in the Denver basin in 1866. If a mining school was operating somewhere in Golden at the time, Randall might well have combined forces with it to lobby the Legislature. Although offered sites in Denver for his institution, Bishop Randall chose Golden as his preference and obtained a gift of twelve acres from Charles C. Welch upon which he would found his school. Located on the present site of the State Industrial School for Boys on the south edge of Golden, this acreage became CSM's first home.

Armed with state encouragement, Bishop Randall received private funding from George A. Jarvis and other friends in Boston, and began construction on Jarvis Hall in 1868. Originally the Right Reverend Randall conceived three college units; Jarvis Hall for a general college, Matthews Hall for a divinity school, and another building for the School of Mines.

With government still in an embryonic stage, early schools in the territory were all church-supported; Colorado Seminary (1864 - later Denver University) was Methodist, Loretto Heights (1864) was Catholic, and Colorado College (1874) was Congregational. State schools (other than Mines) came later; Colorado University at Boulder in 1877, Colorado Agricultural & Mechanical College at Ft. Collins (now Colorado State University) 1879, and the State Normal School at Greeley (Colorado State College of Education, now University of Northern Colorado) 1890.

While Jarvis Hall was under construction, a severe windstorm wrecked the half-completed building, and necessitated building a second structure. Bishop Randall actively sought help to deal with this calamity, and during its session of 1870, the Territorial Legislature voted $3,872.00 to assist the Bishop in his reconstruction for the specific purpose of erecting a building to house a School of Mines. Without this timely State involvement, Mines might have remained a private church-supported school and failed for lack of funds.

Jarvis Hall was opened for classes in 1871, followed by Matthews Hall in 1872, and the School of Mines building in 1873, in spite of the brick work on the building and tower being essentially completed by November 23, 1870. Students took courses leading to the School of Mines in Jarvis Hall during the 1871 and 1872 sessions, and Professor E. J. Mallett was listed as Jarvis Hall faculty to teach assaying and chemistry, and Professor in Charge of the School of Mines.

On September 3, 1873, three years after Jarvis Hall had opened its doors, all three buildings were operational for the first time. Aged 63, Randall had seen his vision realized, but he had almost no time to enjoy it, dying three weeks later on September 28. Athletics came to Mines shortly thereafter, with the establishment of a baseball and cricket club on November 12.

No photographs of Jarvis Hall or its two associated buildings are believed to exist, certainly not one that can be authenticated, and drawings of the facility are inconsistent. The commonly accepted likeness printed in Dean Jesse R. Morgan's book, *A World School The Colorado School of Mines*, and various *Prospectors* (the student yearbook), shows a large, ornate Victorian structure with a mansard roof. Another published by Baskin in 1880 depicts a smaller structure with a steeply pitched roof and more modest appearance. Interestingly, the Baskin drawing shows twenty-six students playing a form of rugby or soccer on the grounds. Jarvis Hall is depicted as wooden with clapboard siding, but the other two school buildings, as well as a fourth storeroom or stable, are brick.

Operating independently, the three schools shared the campus with assaying and chemical testing being taught at the School of Mines until 1874. That year fires burned Jarvis and Matthews halls to the ground, the first by accident, the second by arson. The schools then took refuge in the building later occupied by Golden's Old Capitol Grill on Washington Avenue.

Meanwhile, a political ruckus had broken out, with opinion pieces in the *Rocky Mountain News* and *Colorado Transcript* decrying the fact that public funds were being used to support the School of Mines, then owned by the Episcopal Church.

For the first time, but not the last, Denver and the Colorado Legislature injected themselves into the operation of the School of Mines. In 1874, a hot debate ensued in legislative chambers. Opponents of the School of Mines decreed the school must be moved to Denver and controlled by the State or closed completely. Colorado University would not open its doors for another three years, and the State desired to reach out and establish its dominance in higher education.

CU had first been projected as a mining school in 1861, but Golden had moved faster. The legislature authorized both the University of Colorado at Boulder and the School of Mines at Golden in November of 1861, but CU was still in the planning stage in 1873, while Mines was an actuality.

General George West led the fight to retain the school in Golden, championing as a major advantage its unique location near mining activities. It would be the second school of its kind in the United States, as only New York City's Columbia University, which specialized in Geology, possessed a prior claim. After much rancor and speechifying, legislation to establish a territorial School of Mines in or around Golden was passed on February 9, 1874.

The Territorial School of Mines, Colorado's first public institution of higher education, was now official, if not highly prized by the Legislature. The territorial government voted an appropriation of $5,000.00 on a bill introduced by Dr. Levi Harsh, the representative from Jefferson County. The ownership of the School of Mines building and five acres of land on which it resided adjacent to Jarvis Hall was deeded by donation to the State to be used for the Colorado School of Mines. At that point, the Legislature earmarked $4,500.00 of the appropriation for equipment and the salary of Professor Mallett, and $500.00 was paid to the Episcopal Church for its interest in the school's building and grounds and a spring on Table Mountain.

Denver was not done with its machinations, however, and Professor Mallett was hired away in 1875 to found another "Colorado School of Mines and Metallurgy" in Denver, also called the "School of Mines - Denver City," at Curtis and Fifteenth. This competing college failed to obtain significant support and recognition, and soon disappeared from Colorado history along with Professor Mallett. In the crisis over Mallett's resignation, Loveland assumed the duties of Professor in Charge at Mines until a replacement could be located.

The school recruited an eminent individual in the person of Gregory Board, a graduate of the Royal School of Mines (Great Britain), and holder of a diploma from the British Museum where he headed the Department of Minerals. His avowed purpose was to make the Colorado School of Mines the foremost school of mining and metallurgy in the United States. It was a lofty goal, but he believed it reachable with state and private support. In those early days of Carbonate Kings in Leadville and other local fortunes in the state, the School of Mines held its own as the darling of Colorado industry. Silver kings like Winfield Stratton donated to CSM, and in spite of its physical plant value expanding two hundred-fold in thirty years, Mines became free of debt before World War One. A key individual in managing this growth was Captain James T. Smith, an associate of West's at the *Colorado Transcript* and a member of the Board of Trustees from 1876 to 1922. Captain Smith was an ardent proponent of Mines, and his journalistic endeavors with various Colorado newspapers did much to ameliorate the effects of opposing views on the school's activities.

Meanwhile, CU had come into being in 1877 with forty-four students, none of whom could meet the stated entrance requirements. Preparatory courses were established, and the first freshman class enrolled in 1878 with twelve members. The university was organized by President Joseph A, Sewell, and its first seven graduates were produced in 1883, the same year in which CSM graduated its first two.

In 1879, when F. W. Pitkin was Governor of Colorado, the school was removed from the former Jarvis Hall campus to a more prominent and central location in Golden. The Board of Trustees purchased land in the southwest section of Golden in 1879, and an additional four blocks were acquired by donation and purchase by 1905, embracing the best locations in Golden. Money was appropriated for building facilities, and the Legislature voted a one-fifth millage tax on property for permanent support of CSM. Private citizens in Golden donated land between Fourteenth and Fifteenth streets west of Washington Street during 1879 and 1880, and construction began on a hall which would become known as the 1880 Building and ultimately a wing of the first Chemistry Building. By 1940 the campus was located mostly between Arapaho and Maple Streets on the east and west, and 13th and 16th Streets on the north and south. The Jarvis Hall complex became the State Industrial School for Boys which had opened in 1881 as a vocational training school for delinquents aged six through sixteen.

From the very beginning Golden and the School of Mines worked in harmony as partners. Donations of land and money poured in from local citizens, and, without facilities on campus except for fraternities (from the early twentieth century) to house and feed students, private homes provided lodging, and local establishments food and other daily needs for the majority of students during the first seventy-five years.

A drawing of Golden published by Fossett in 1876 shows the town concentrated in the low-lying area of downtown and along Clear Creek. The Golden School built in 1873 which would eventually end its days as the Mines Physics Building is almost alone atop the north edge of the large, relatively flat-topped hill comprising the southwest section of town. The hill is treeless, as is most of Golden except near Clear Creek.

Early sketches of Golden emphasize its industry, and a drawing published by the Denver and Rio Grande Railroad in 1878 show three large brick kilns, a paper mill, and two flour mills. Others published by Baskin in 1889 depict four smelters along Clear Creek between the Table Mountains; Golden Smelting, Malachite, French Smelting, and Moore Smelting and Refining. Baskin also shows other factories of unknown types, and the Golden Brewery with a pond to the West apparently on the site where the older portion of the Coors Brewery is today.

One of the early donations was made by Winfield Scott Stratton. An excellent carpenter in Colorado Springs, Stratton went prospecting on Pisgah Mountain in the spring of 1891. His wife decided his lack of attention was too much for her to bear, and divorced him for non-support while he was gone in the mountains. But Stratton knew something about mining from his coursework at Colorado College, and staked out claims on the Independence and Washington lodes near Cripple Creek in July, 1891. Lady luck smiled twice, and by the turn of the century Stratton was worth more than fifteen million dollars. In 1902 he donated $25,000 to the school which was used to help build Stratton Hall on the Mines campus.

Although there is some evidence Stratton was something of a misogynist, his disastrous marriage soured him permanently on the institution. His wife was pregnant at the time they traded vows, and Stratton doubted the son born soon afterwards was really his. At any rate, his subsequent liaisons with females all avoided matrimony. He lived modestly and incurred the wrath of everyone around him who expected him to live in the grand style then in vogue for mining kings. Even the *Denver Post* declared him to be a fool because he didn't spend his money on yachts and mansions. Instead, Stratton was generous to a fault; giving almost five million to Colorado Springs for civic projects, and hundreds of thousands to other worthwhile causes like Mines, the Salvation Army, and founding a home for destitute children and old people. During one winter he purchased coal to heat all the shacks in Victor, and was reputed to never refuse a request by someone in need. His eccentricities became legend, particularly when he gave every laundry maid in Colorado Springs a bicycle. The homeless and incapacitated were his major concern, and his Myron Stratton Home was built specifically to take care of those who couldn't provide for themselves.

A tall, slender man with light blue-grey eyes and silver hair, Stratton hated lawyers for their machinations in the gold fields, and like many a good miner, he took the side of individuals against corporations and their legal beagles. During his lifetime he held lawyers in utter contempt, but they had the last laugh. What sealed his doom shortly before he died was his statement that he wished he had ten million dollars and would use every cent to put every lawyer in Colorado in jail.

When he left seven million in his estate, almost all of which was to maintain the Myron Stratton Home for the destitute, the lawyers came out in droves. They tried to prove him incompetent, and even the Attorney General vowed to get all Stratton's money for the State of Colorado. His wastrel son from his failed marriage showed up under the influence of shifty attorneys looking for their own pot of gold. Aided by questionable judgements from the bench, the son won a large settlement of which his lawyers took half and he lost the rest in speculation within a few months. There were some thirty-five million dollars in suits filed in fraudulent claims, and it took over fifteen years to settle. The lawyers destroyed Stratton's estate and reputation, actively aided by the judges. Over a dozen women came forth claiming Stratton had married them and were therefore entitled to his estate.

The claims were legion and pressed by many attorneys, and yet when all was said and done, the will was upheld. It was probably the Colorado legal community's most shameful and avaricious hour. The Stratton story was a terrible account of legal greed which will never be told on American television. At least Mines benefited from Stratton's largess. It was also well-known that Stratton intended to make further donations, but unfortunately his premature death intervened.

From a struggling institution in 1879, when the tax support was provided by the State Legislature ($70,000 per annum by 1905), the Colorado School of Mines progressed to the head of its class in technical and higher education, not in America alone, but in the civilized world. It was favored with the most varied environment in mining and metallurgy, its students having access to mines, smelters, refineries, and mills worth millions and later billions of dollars, presenting a wider scope in ore treatment than is offered anywhere else in the US. Captain Smith asserted in 1905 that Mines carried upon its rolls a larger number of students in mining than any of its college contemporaries and drew to its classes in metallurgy a greater number of graduates from other universities, colleges and foreign lands than any other American school. Thus, it had become not only a state school in scope and influence, but a national and international institution, as wide as the industry of mining, metallurgy, oil, and other extraction and processing industries.

The course of study at Mines, which later proved its value in results exceeding all expectations, was established in 1883 by its president, Dr. Regis Chauvenet, whose father, the well-known author of works in higher mathematics, had created a rigorous curriculum at the U.S. Naval Academy. His son decided to out-do his father, and produce a civilian school that could compete successfully with the graduates of the Naval Academy in engineering. In effect, it was to be the Engineering Academy.

Dr. Chauvenet adopted hazing practices for first year students to help weld the student body into a cohesive unit, and increased the work load so that there was no time during the week for students to pursue non-scholastic or non-athletic activities. The emphasis would be 100% on undergraduate education, and as the ensigns being graduated from Annapolis could immediately perform as naval officers, graduates from Mines could be immediately productive as engineers. Both Annapolis and West Point at the time were turning out engineers for their military specialties, and Mines would turn out equally proficient engineers for the extractive and production industries.

He emphasized the formation of traditions, all to underscore the uniqueness of Mines and the excellence of its graduates. The role of the engineer in society was elevated to the highest level: indeed, it was the engineer who made all things possible. Science was fine, but it was engineering that turned science into practical reality and bettered people's lives. Within a few short years, Mines graduates began making their presence felt world-wide, and the school attained national and international recognition.

A number of women had enrolled at Mines from 1880 to 1887, the yearly high being thirty-three. Like many of the male students, they were enrolled in special courses that did not lead to a degree. These were called "scrap courses" and had been instituted to raise enrollments. Dr. Chauvenet changed the emphasis from numbers to excellence and eliminated all such courses in 1887 as being outside the mission of his engineering academy. For all practical purposes, Mines became a men's school. Until 1962, the official but unstated policy was to "not encourage female enrollment," and Mines graduated only eleven women before 1969. They were individuals who withstood the conditions and conquered the level of coursework required; one each in 1898, 1903, 1920, 1949, 1961, 1962,

1964, and two each in 1966 and 1967.

Dr. Chauvenet resigned as president in 1902, at which time and for some years previously, enrollment at Mines exceeded the capacity of the institution. The principle of attaining excellence through academic demands far exceeding any others in existence, had been established, and it only remained for future presidents to hold the line.

The first class to graduate was in 1883, consisting of two members, William B. Middleton of New York, and Walter H. Wiley of Idaho Springs, Colo. The former became one of the extraction experts for the Venture Corporation of London, while the latter became well-known in the mining districts of Colorado and other Western States. From two graduates in 1883, the total increased to 324 by 1905 when the average number of graduates was running from 35 to 40 each year. The capacity of the institution was only 300 students, so enrollments were at a maximum, despite the exacting conditions and difficult course of study. Captain Smith maintained that recent (by 1905) developments in mining and metallurgy in the United States, Mexico, South Africa, Central America, South America, Australia, and Korea owed much to the Colorado School of Mines. In all of those countries her graduates ranked equal or higher than the products of more ancient and publically better known institutions.

In the school year of 1904-05 enrollments were as follows: seniors 50; juniors 58; sophomores, 86; freshman, 96, for a total of 290. Colorado furnished the majority of students with 211, seventy-three came from other states, and six from foreign countries. The surviving alumni were spread across the country and the world: Colorado, 125, other states, 95, and other countries, 48. A high death rate among the alumni was evident, as 56 had died in the 23 years of producing graduates (18.5% versus a normal rate of 4-7%). This could be expected in following years, as Mines graduates were risk-takers, pushing the boundaries of human endeavors forward at every opportunity. There would be casualties.

After Colorado University opened following ten years of existence on paper, various legislators espoused a combination of the two schools into a single university. Over the years this idea would be repeatedly put forward in legislative chambers, to be defeated each time with increasingly hard feelings and difficulty. Other mining schools like those in Texas and New Mexico were absorbed into state university systems, and even Missouri Mines, perhaps the best known mining school next to CSM, ultimately lost its identity and became the University of Missouri at Rolla. The idea of teaching mining and the production of metals, petroleum, and materials from earthly deposits had become politically anathema among progressive politicians in both major political parties. Many universities moved to regulatory technology such as environmental engineering and newly emerging disciplines such as alternative energies, computer engineering, and cybernetics. At the bottom was fossil fuel energy, and metals and materials production which made the application of the new sciences possible. During all this, somehow Colorado Mines hung on. But as everyone knew, there was ONLY ONE "Mines."

In the face of serious opposition from Colorado University supporters in the Legislature, Mines prospered due to its powerful industrial allies and local support. In spite of the majority of its graduates leaving Colorado after accepting their sterling silver diplomas, the importance of earth science engineering to the State kept CSM's position secure until the advent of the computer age.

Mines was Colorado's single claim to excellence in higher education, and its proponents argued the brain drain was a small price to pay for world recognition. Colorado College developed into a liberal arts institution with an elite reputation and wealthy and genteel student body while Colorado University became known primarily as a party school, both in summer and winter, competing with other universities equally famous for their social, athletic, and leisure time activities such as Maryland and Wisconsin. It was not until 1955 when the Air Force Academy came to Lowry Field in Denver that competition to Mines for academic honors arose in the State.

One of the features of Mines that defined it from World War I to the Vietnam War was the Reserve Officer Training Corps, or ROTC. It was a natural successor to the military science taught at Mines by General George West, who introduced the teaching of military engineering in the earliest days of the college, possibly as early as 1873. West's program to produce part-time officers for the Colorado National Guard at Mines flourished, and in 1911, President Victor C. Alderson granted credit for courses in military science that applied toward graduation.

When the armory building in Golden was completed in 1913, it became the headquarters for the National Guard students and later the ROTC detachment until after World War II. This cobblestone building, built to look like a castle, reflected the insignia of the U.S. Army Corps of Engineers. It was furnished with a rifle range and a drill hall, as well as limited facilities to house and feed students who were enrolled in military science courses.

World War I brought about the federalization of the Colorado National Guard, and the students, local alumni, and other Golden recruits formed Company A, 115th Engineers, 40th Division, in April 1917. The 115th Engineers was shipped to France where it earned a unit citation.

In 1919, CSM was selected by the War Department to be in the first batch of colleges and universities in the United States for a ROTC detachment. Mines was assigned to the control of the Corps of Engineers, and graduates of its two-year elective advanced program were assigned to the Engineering Branch unless unable to qualify for a combat branch due to physical limitations. Completion of the two-year basic ROTC program became required of all able-bodied male citizens, although the amount of college credit was minimal. Not surprisingly, given the strict regimen at Mines and its normally patriotic student body, ROTC thrived. Until after World War II, enrollments in the advanced program were very high, sometimes up to ninety percent of the upper division students. In the years leading up to World War II, it was common for fifty to seventy students per year to earn their commissions. During World War II, Mines, with over 2,000 former students and alumni serving in the army, became known as "The West Point of the Rockies."

Not only did Mines produce a plethora of very high-quality engineering reserve officers, it also fielded an award-winning rifle team. This became a tradition at Mines that continued throughout the 1950s. When World War II came to the United States, Mines graduates responded like no other engineering or technological school. They served in every theater, and as the largest supplier of ROTC engineering officers of all colleges and universities in the US, Mines was termed by Major General Eugene Reybold, Chief of Engineers, as "The Backbone of the Corps of Engineers."

The ROTC program at Mines was suspended during World War II, and the boondoggle known as the Army Specialized Training Program (ASTP) made its appearance. In 1943, 500 army personnel arrived for the eighteen month ASTP program. The idea was to take Army personnel with high IQs and leadership potential out of the ranks, put them in college to earn bachelor's degrees, and then bring them back into regular army formations as officers. In practice, sons of influential individuals were assigned to the program to escape combat duty for eighteen months, hoping the war would be over before they returned to duty. The ASTP men wore uniforms and marched in groups to and from classes. In late 1944, the program came under congressional fire as a haven for the rich, and ASTP was summarily abolished. ASTP soldiers were sent to replacement depots in Europe where they were assigned to combat units to maintain the desired strength levels. With little appropriate training, the former ASTP personnel experienced the worst of all worlds and suffered abnormally high casualties.

When the war was over, the ROTC program was reactivated at Mines. Its strength was rebuilt from 1946 to 1950, as returning veterans availed themselves of the GI Bill and came to Mines to resume their schooling. Mines enrollments burgeoned, and in 1947, over 76 percent of the enrolled students were vets. Many were married and highly motivated to complete their educations. Senior Day took on added dimensions of terror for the less proficient faculty, and, in a sense, this time became a golden age for excellence in teaching and learning. This was the springboard that catapulted the fifties into the apex period of CSM's undergraduate excellence.

On the other hand, the heavy increases in married student enrollments caused demands for housing that Mines simply could not meet. Temporary facilities were obtained from various military installations, and makeshift barracks and dilapidated trailers were erected in Prospector Park, the field west of Brooks Field, and even in Steinhauer Fieldhouse.

The influences of the veterans receded following the Korean War, and after a period of stability, the mid-1960s ushered in the baby boomers. ROTC was no longer looked upon as appropriate at a college, and when the Vietnam War heated up, many students began questioning their obligation to serve in the military. Nonetheless, ROTC offered scholarships that paid for tuition, books, fees, and a monthly per diem, and enrollments in the advanced program continued to be more popular at Mines than in the vast majority of colleges and universities across America. Only two Mines students failed to honor their commitment to serve, but outside agitators and some students, usually freshmen, made ROTC's continued presence on campus controversial.

Late in the 1960s an anti-war movement developed and pushed for making ROTC optional rather than mandatory, and some even demanded that the ROTC detachment be removed altogether. Women, foreign students, veterans, conscientious objectors and upper division transfers were already exempt from the mandatory basic ROTC, but political and public support for the military ebbed dramatically. It would never recover, at least not on American college campuses. As President Obama opined in 2008, military service was the last resort for young people who did not go to college. The service academies would supply the elite leadership, and Officers Candidate School would fill the lower ranking positions. Military service was evidently no longer seen as a college graduate's moral duty.

In 1969, 600 students signed a petition to make the basic two years of ROTC voluntary. Mines was the only school in Colorado that required the two-year basic ROTC program, and that could not be allowed to continue much longer. Twenty-three students submitted a thirty-six-page brief on why basic ROTC should be voluntary. Another movement emerged that was opposed to anything that violated the civil rights of students, attacking both ROTC and school traditions. Notably, the movement's leader graduated from Mines with a BS, but did not become involved with the alumni, and his current whereabouts are unknown. Long hair was defined as a civil right, and Mines suffered many of the indignities that were rocking other institutions of higher learning. In 1970, the Board of Trustees gave the students half of what they wanted — only the freshman year of ROTC would still be required. At the same time, all harassment of freshmen was abolished. Class cohesion, pride in accomplishment, and the idea of brotherhood in the student body disappeared.

With the advent of Dr. Guy T. McBride's presidency, ROTC came under increased pressure. The Colorado legislature considered a bill to make all military training at state universities optional — a law that would only affect Mines — but the bill was never passed. As usual, students, including freshmen who would never graduate, gave their opinions on the quality of military courses, and recommended all such courses be voluntary. The faculty supported the rebelling students, but ROTC soldiered on.

In 1991 the Mines ROTC unit was deactivated, and the Mines program became part of the one at Colorado University. Mines was able to keep a Military Science Department, but the days of military engineering being a functional part of the Mines curriculum passed into history.

It is questionable that the U.S. will be able to maintain the civil liberties demanded so stridently by the Mines students from 1968 to 1973 without institutions likes Mines providing patriotic young men to keep those liberties safe. In the 21st century the military was something to be avoided by left-leaning faculty and students in universities, and politicians and public figures across the nation. By 2016, about 21 million veterans were still living in the United States (6.5% of the population), and the political power of such a small group had become negligible. The citizen army had gone the way of the dinosaur, just like Dr. Chauvenet's Mines. Whether or not American youths still possessed the necessary patriotism to rise and do their duty again if necessary is a question for the future.

Instead of becoming a "laboratory for liberalism" like most American universities with many liberal faculty members, broad curricula, and extensive social amenities, Mines had taken the opposite tack until the 1970s. Life in mining and petroleum exploration camps was hard, and to be successful, graduates of Mines had to be tougher and more capable of conquering adversity than their peers. Student life at Mines reflected that philosophy. Long hours, institutionalized hazing, unforgiving academic policies, and an almost hostile campus environment became lifestyle characteristics which students accepted as normal fare. Once again, Dr. Chauvenet's idea of imitating the Naval Academy was proven correct in practice. Much like West Point with its harsh physical, social, and academic challenges, Mines prepared its students for careers in the industries it served and eschewed "fun" courses and those with little content. Mines hewed true to the saying so prominently displayed; "May there be reared within these walls that sterling character and intellectual power which are basic to the development of the mineral industry of our nation."

Until requirements were lessened in the sixties as part of the remolding of Mines, the graduation rate was less than one-third, and the number of students able to achieve a diploma on schedule in four years was only about twenty-five percent. Some students opted for establishing a 5-year plan upon matriculating, while other students lengthened their stays to an unplanned five years, and some as long as nine or ten. Others avoided Mines' freshman year "flunk out" courses by transferring from other accredited state schools as sophomores or juniors. Of an entering freshman class, a fifth to a quarter would be gone by Christmas, and fifty percent would disappear within three semesters.

Transferring in from other schools was not always a sure-fire way to avoid flunking out early. In 1952, two transfers from Cal Tech ignominiously failed the three placement tests in Math, Chemistry, and English, and were assigned to the remedial class in each subject. They had passed those courses in their first year at Cal Tech, but ended up in "dumbbell" Math 05, Chemistry 01, and English 01 at Mines.

Mines' success in turning out astoundingly capable engineers meeting every adversity almost proved its undoing on a number of occasions. Legislators perennially attacked Mines as being a world class institution, something that Colorado could not afford. During the late 1940s and 1950s, fewer than fifty percent of the students were from Colorado and far fewer remained in the State after graduation. Somewhat less than twenty percent employed their skills to Colorado's benefit, about seventy percent lived in other American states, and over ten percent went abroad.

In all respects these statistics overstated Colorado's portion; some students (and their families) moved to Colorado to avoid out-of-state tuition, and many married in the State to achieve Colorado residency even though they were originally from other states. Graduates often retained Colorado resident status while on overseas assignments and mailing addresses while in military service reflected their home state of entry on active duty. Eventually Mines enjoyed the unenviable position of having the highest out-of-state tuition of any state-supported college in the United States, but out-of-state students still flocked to Mines to attain the quality education offered openly and cheaply to Colorado residents. In 1957, one enterprising family moved to Golden and purchased the service station on the northwest corner of 19th and Illinois. The father and mother ran the station, paying in-state tuition while their son attended Mines. Unfortunately, the boy flunked out the first year, and the family disappeared from Golden.

In the late 1940s and early 1950s, Denver was in the throes of introducing non-judgmental progressive education. Only two grades were given: PN-progressing normally in relation to a student's ability; and N-needs improvement as the student has not produced a quality of work consistent with his ability. This program was prematurely heralded as a great success and influenced educators throughout the state who wanted to be politically correct. The areas of basic knowledge and understandings being covered at the high school level were Algebra, English, Fine Arts, Foreign Languages (Latin and Spanish), General Science, Home Economics, Applied Arts, Mathematics, Music, Newswriting, Physical Education, Social Studies, Speech, and Typewriting. Denver public schools stressed work habits, personal development, and social development rather than learning the three "Rs" and science, and became little more than laboratories testing progressive educational theory.

The program had little effect on Mines since teachers in college preparatory courses continued to stress learning rather than social and personal development. Nonetheless, the K-12 schools had begun the "dumbing down" process that would prove so detrimental to American education.

During the 1950s out-of-state enrollments briefly topped a whopping seventy percent, in part as a result of the experimental failures in the Denver public schools.

Year	Non-Resident %	Year	Non-Resident %
1947	55.9	1951	69.9
1948	63.8	1952	69.4
1949	69.2	1953	66.9
1950	72.5	1954	66.0

A hue and cry erupted again in the Legislature over the luxury of maintaining a school for the education of non-Coloradans. A major assault on the school began in 1951 with the repeal of the 1925 act which assigned one-third of Colorado's oil royalties to Mines for its Petroleum Engineering Department. The Legislature declared Mines to be an expensive technological anachronism. The administration was unable or unwilling to face funding adversity, and instituted changes almost every year during the 1950s to soften the school and placate its critics.

Many school traditions ended abruptly when incidents occurred that brought extremely negative publicity promulgated by CSM's old adversary, Denver's *Rocky Mountain News*. In the sixties the school's administration took action to counter such publicity, and change the school into a more liberal institution. It undertook extensive efforts to recruit females and minorities, eliminate hazing, and provide a full range of student services. Alumni input was disregarded in the stampede for higher enrollments, and the graduation rate more than doubled to over seventy percent in the latter part of the 20th century. Graduate students were extensively recruited, and research-oriented professors were added in droves to replace the old undergraduate teaching faculty. Action by alumni eventually forestalled a name change to the Colorado Institute of Technology in 1964, but Mines' rough and tumble past was consigned to history. So was its unparalleled excellence in its undergraduate school. When the changes were completed, Mines could no longer compete with West Point, the Naval Academy, or the Air Force Academy, in the training and excellence of its graduates.

Stratton Hall

Chapter 6 - Golden & Mines

Until the late 1960s, Golden was a small town, and there was a strong sense of community between the town and the school. There was no housing on campus for unmarried students until 1954, and students lived in fraternities or throughout Golden in rooms in private homes. By 1930, Golden had only 2,420 inhabitants. Colorado at that time was five percent Hispanic, with 12,000 black or African Americans, and about 800 Indians. Golden grew slowly and featured a population of less than seven thousand in the fifties, not counting some seven to nine hundred students housed with the citizens. The fraternities could provide beds for no more than 190 students, and more fraternity members lived in private housing than in frat houses. Married student housing in Prospector Park on 19th Street and US 6 was limited, and at any rate, many wives of students worked in Golden. Relations between townies and students were close. In addition, there were three hundred employees, administration and faculty, at Mines, and most of them lived in Golden because Mines Park faculty housing, on Lookout Mountain Road west of US 6, was limited in space.

Students were often looked upon as adopted sons by local residents, and bonds were formed between the townspeople and students which were among the strongest of any school and community in the United States. Private homes were present all around and even inside the campus. The west side of Maple, behind Guggenheim Hall was all private, as were the north side of 15th and the north and south sides of 16th, east of Illinois.

There was no school bookstore, and textbook purchases were made in downtown Golden, either at Strawn's School and Office Supplies or Jeffco Engineering Supply. Strawn's book store had been selling books and supplies to Mines students since 1874, beginning as Robinson's Cash Book Store, then after Strawn's was Lloyd's, but that came to an end when the Student Union was built and furnished with an in-house book store. All that money which formerly went to Golden residents was switched to the State. Colorado had decided to compete with its tax-paying citizens.

The fraternities served food only through Saturday noon, and most students flooded the town on Sundays and ate either at the Golden Café, Dud's, the Spudnut Shop, Holland House, Golden Bowl at Ford and 24th, Foss's Drug Store (opened in 1916 and the place students could cash personal checks), A&W Root Beer, or Sena's Pizza. The school cafeteria in its wooden barracks building was well-known for poor food, and was regularly referred to as the "Ptomaine Palace." It had a captive market in that all dormitory residents were required to purchase meal plans in the cafeteria.

Golden laundries such as Wooley's ½ Hour Laundry, Paramount Cleaners and Shirt Laundry, One Hour Golden Cleaners, E-Z Way Laundry, Clean Clothes Corral, Selfserv Laundry, and the Golden Laundrymat did a land-office business, as did the three barbershops on Washington Streets, Del's Tonsorial Parlor, Slick's, and the Metropolitan Barber Shop. Wendell Plummer took care of Miners' jewelry needs, Jimmie's Shoe Shop repaired their footwear and sold engineer boots, and Gus City Tailor, (August Berninghausen since 1920) handled tailoring. Cars were repaired at Sparks Motor Company or Peterson's Gulf, and tires were re-treaded at Merritt Tire Shop for $4.00 per tire. Clothing was bought at Ellis Department Store, Eakers Department Store, and McKeehen's (the place that Mines seniors bought their "Open Road" Stetson hats.) Gas could be purchased for a quarter a gallon at the self-serve on Ford Avenue, but probably only 35% of Mines students had cars.

The bars also did good business, particularly on Friday nights. The Golden Nugget, Ace High, Dud's, Lookout, and the Big M Lounge, were all on Washington Avenue in downtown. 3.2 beer could be sold to 18-year olds, but the hard stuff required the purchaser to be twenty-one. IDs were rarely checked, however, and one of the authors had his first drink in a Golden (or Lakewood) Bar called the Rock Rest on the Old Golden Road when he was sixteen, paying twenty-five cents for a scotch on the rocks. For the adventuresome, there was always the Matinee, the Rock Rest, Duke's on West 44th Street, Jake's Tavern on 10th Street, Barney's Tavern, or Sam's Cowhide Corners on the top of Lookout Mountain. A glass of beer was a dime, and usually baskets of French fries were a quarter. One couldn't afford not to drink at those prices. The Holland House, originally the Hotel Berrimoor, then the La Ray Hotel, then the Holland House, also had a bar, but it featured Denver prices. Last, but not least, there was the Golden Theater at the corner of Washington and 13th Street. Students got in for a quarter, and the balcony was a great place to relax. There was always a double feature, and the movies changed at least twice a week. Students were often employed as ushers, ticket takers, and marquee changers.

The tragedy of Mines was that when the school was a member of the Golden community, the campus mixed with private dwellings and fraternity houses providing a true sense of community integration. That was lost when the school sealed itself off from Golden in the tradition of Yale University and other eastern institutions, providing facilities for the students at state expense and holding them on campus.

Students were such an integral part of the local businesses on Washington Street that when the student union opened in the mid-sixties, a number of local businesses folded. The Sputnut Shop, where many students ate breakfast, reduced its size by two-thirds. Golden's downtown died a painful death, mostly due to the administration's decision to provide facilities to isolate students from the community. Beginning in the 1950s, the school administration broadened its power base to build a nearly self-contained city.

Until the sixties an average student lived on less than a hundred dollars per month and spent probably forty dollars of it in downtown Golden. It was a different day and age. Many families in Golden rented rooms to Mines students in a family atmosphere. Houses were never locked, nor were any of the rooms. On Sundays students usually read the paper and spent time with their host families. All for fifteen to twenty dollars per month. In the sixties, however, everything began to be locked, double-locked, and chained.. The sign over Washington Street, "Where The West Remains," no longer spoke the truth for Golden residents, but remained as wishful thinking. Even that was deleted in 2008 when the sign was changed to "Where The West Lives." Maybe, but only in the minds of a few. Mostly the town has been taken over by environmentalists and sandal-wearers, riding bikes and attending trumped-up "traditions" like an Oktoberfest.

Starting more or less at the same time as the Horizon Plan, the long-range plan worked out by the Mines Administration in the early 1950s to improve the physical plant at Mines and change it to an on-campus residence school, Mines changed its academic policies, first reducing the formal hours of credit for individual required courses, and then the requirements themselves. In 1959, the administration hired a director of student affairs, and made strenuous efforts to provide a more comely social atmosphere for students. After copying Eastern schools with dormitory construction, it built a *Student Union* in 1964. None of this was requested by students. The Integral Club (what passed for a student union in the 40s and

50s) and miscellaneous offices made available to student organizations were more than adequate earlier, and only backwards when compared to Eastern finery. Students had no time to enjoy student union activities and facilities — those students who did flunked out. One is forced to conclude that the union was constructed for the administration's ego, not for student benefit. One must remember that during the time the *Student Union* was planned, John W Vanderwilt was president, and he came from Yale University.

The town-school relationship began to change with the new construction in the early 1950s. Alderson Hall was built in the old city park across from the Kappa Sigma and ATO fraternity houses on Illinois, and the Jefferson County Courthouse and Sheriff's Office went up behind Alderson and in front of the Beta Theta Pi house. Government and law enforcement had moved into the campus and created a block to further campus expansion towards the southeast. Although the massive population growth in Jefferson County from 1950 to 2016 (56,000 to 560,000) would cause the county to later build an enormous county government complex to the south of Golden, this construction in the early 1950s forced the school to plan its expansion to the west and south, into the clay pits and areas away from downtown Golden. Worst of all, US Highway 6 was completed in 1952 up Clear Creek Canyon, firmly anchoring Golden to Denver as a suburb and gateway to Central City. Only the discontinued railroad had gone up the canyon formerly, and the change destroyed Golden's isolation behind the Table Mountains.

Perhaps no better example existed for the partnering of students and townies than the story of the Sheriff of Central City. In a rooming house near Washington and Fourteenth, lived an old man who claimed to have been the sheriff for 25 years in the cowboy boom times. He was 96 years old in 1957, and still alert. He regaled students with stories about running the town, exciting gunfights, and where gold and silver could still be found. Various students took the old man to Russell Gulch and other sites where they were astounded by his knowledge of the area. The outings were sometimes "rock hunting", but often they were trips back in time.

The old man claimed to have had no fear of "fanners" who would fan the hammer of their six shooters with their left hands to fire more rapidly. When he would hear of a gunfighter in town, his first question would be to find out if the man was a fanner. If he were, the sheriff would go out and kill him by aiming carefully and firing slowly. If he wasn't, the sheriff would get the drop on him with a shotgun.

According to the sheriff, the Teller mine still had a great deal of gold and silver ore, some of it already in mine cars ready for recovery. The mine had flooded below the fourth level which was below Gilpin Creek's water table. On the seventh level were the remains of trapped miners and the ore they had already broken up for lifting at the time the water rushed into the mine. Pumping had not worked, divers had found the shafts too murky for visibility, and no one had figured out how to divert the water to drain the mine. The mine, ore, and miners were still there. Some students took to finding a solution, but soon found out they were not welcome in Central City which had no interest in re-opening any mines.

The old man died in the summer, but Paul Keating, a seventy year old Geology Professor, confirmed that the ex-sheriff was telling the truth. Crystal Paul, as Keating was known, was an old salt who knew the Front Range like the back of his hand. Crystal Paul himself was someone who had stepped out of the 19th century. Nonetheless, he seemed to enjoy an inexhaustible supply of young ladies who hung on his every word at the Holland House.

Golden was represented on the Mines Board of Trustees from the earliest days to the 1960s, and it took more than passing interest in the school's welfare. The city had donated land to the college, and many citizens made contributions to the school and supported its athletic events. Local complaints concerning the rowdiness of Mines students were almost unknown. The faculty normally became good Golden citizens, sometimes city councilmen and even the mayor, and the local chapter of Freemasons was studded with representatives from the Mines administration, its faculty and students. Many Mines students became involved in local churches and church activities. All, especially the students, patronized local business establishments, and the Golden economy owed much of its prosperity to the school's presence.

During the veteran enrollment boom from 1946 to 1950, temporary housing was provided for veterans and married students. During that period, enrollments averaged over 1,100 students in the fall, and a hundred to two hundred less in the spring. From 1951 to 1954 enrollments were in the 900s. The construction of Bradford Hall in 1954 provided beds for 84 students, and money previously paid to Golden residents now went to the State. Randall Hall provided another 84 beds in 1957, but enrollments had gone back to 1,100 during 1956-1957, and demand for rooms in local residences remained strong. Nonetheless, the principle had been put into effect: henceforth the State would compete with Golden homeowners for the student's housing dollars: a situation bad for Golden, and probably bad for the students.

With respect to boarding expenses, students ate in local boarding houses, cafés, fraternity houses, their own homes or rooms, and the school cafeteria. The fraternities hired local cooks feeding up to 450 students per day for lunch, approximately 60-80 married students ate at home or brown-bagged their lunches, and local options probably handled another 350 to 400. The remainder ate in the school cafeteria (poor souls.)

As the school grew during the 1960s and forced the fraternities to incur substantial expenses in relocating and building new houses, two fraternities folded and later three sororities were added. By the 21st century, only six fraternities were at Mines to serve over 75% of the student population, while three sororities were present for about 25%. For many years after fraternities had been organized on campus, 40-55% of the students were fraternity members, but in 2001 they were less than 10% and declining. Meanwhile, the fraternity-sorority system had fallen far behind in providing meals to students. Mines added a number of other eating and snack facilities, in the Student Union and other new construction, as the administration strove to keep its students on campus.

As a footnote to Golden's history, one might consider the saga of Golden's rail connection to Denver. In 1893, Golden founder and Mines booster William A. H. Loveland built the Denver, Lakewood and Golden Railroad, later to be variously called the Denver-Golden Interurban, the Denver and Golden Intermountain Railroad, and the Denver Tramway Interurban Railroad. The line ran from Denver through Lakewood around the south and west sides of South Table Mountain to its depot in downtown Golden on Washington Street. Another route connected downtown Golden with Denver following State Highway 58 past the Coors Brewery between the Table Mountains to Arvada, Lakeside Amusement Park (after 1908), and to Denver. The line was purchased by the Denver Tramway Company in 1909 and electrified, continuing in service until 1950. At that time Denver adopted a policy to eliminate electric trolleys and busses in favor of diesel powered busses, ostensibly so that public transportation would be available to move large numbers of people out of metropolitan Denver in case of nuclear attack. Clean Denver rapidly became smelly Denver, and polluting smog, or what was called "smaze" (smoky haze), soared to where a person could no longer see the Front Range from Denver's Mountain View Park.

All this changed forty years later with the introduction of Agenda 21 and the de-emphasis on fossil fuels in the 1990s. Government planning reversed itself 180 degrees. Denver proposed its FasTracks System of light rail transportation, a system substantially inferior to its former system of streetcars and Marmon-Herrington electric trolley buses, and one that would only service selected areas such as the Denver Federal Center. Included was the West Corridor (West Rail Line) route, built largely on Loveland's old right-of-way through Lakewood to Golden, but stopping short of downtown Golden at the Jefferson County Government Complex. The new line followed Loveland's route through Denver and Lakewood, turned south on the former Remaco (Remington Arms Co) spur into the Denver Federal Center, then headed out to Golden along the Sixth Avenue Freeway rather than the old Golden Interurban trolley path.

Constructed by government, the disinterment of the Interurban Railroad cost only $700 million—cheap because for years the Regional Transportation District had maintained ownership of Loveland's old right-of-way. Nonetheless, Loveland's railroad had been a private enterprise, and had cost the citizens of Denver, Lakewood, and Golden nothing to build. Now the Regional Transit Authority in Denver was spending billions. Sic transit cives!

Washington Street and downtown Golden looking north (c 1961)

Chapter 7 - CSM Board of Trustees & Staff

As usual for state-supported institutions of higher education, the Board of Trustees is appointed by the governor, in CSM's case, the Governor of Colorado. Somewhat unusual for a world famous institution, the Board of Trustees remained studded with local personalities throughout the life of Mines. As an example, Lester Thomas was President of the Board from 1949 until 1957, and although a Mines graduate, he was only an automobile dealer in Denver. Jesse Rubey, on the Board from 1915 through 1926, was a two-time mayor of Golden and a local banker, William Loveland was Golden's most prominent citizen early in Mines' history and a Board member from 1874 through 1878, and James T. Smith, a Board member and usually its secretary from 1876 through 1921, was the editor of the *Colorado Transcript*. William Smiley was the superintendent of the Denver Public Schools and a Board member from 1925 through 1933, serving as president from 1926.

Many trustees were local lawyers in Denver and Jefferson County. The kings in longevity were the Frederick C. Steinhauers, with the father serving in two periods: from 1879 to 1898 as president, and from 1911 through 1914, during which time he served from 1913 to 1914 again as president. His son with the same name, a graduate in 1899, served from 1931 through 1946, as vice president from 1933 to 1942 and president from 1943 to 1946.

Mines had always been a "citizen's school" with a local Board, capable of producing graduates from middle-class backgrounds who were able to challenge elites from expensive eastern schools. The middle class backgrounds changed somewhat in the 1940s and 1950s. Wealth and influence made their appearance when Texas and Oklahoma oilmen chose Mines for their sons with increasing frequency, but the Board itself remained local in orientation.

It is almost difficult to understand how such excellence could arise without influential and nationally prominent individuals being on the Board, but such was the case. Apparently, famous names were not necessarily a precursor to excellence when an environment and curriculum such as Dr. Chauvenet's was in place. To prove the point, no one knows or cares who populates the "Boards of Visitors" (the boards of trustees) of the service academies.

Most critically in Colorado, Mines generated only a minimum of respect. Possibly it was the old saying, "familiarity breeds contempt," but more likely Colorado residents simply could not believe that a world class school could be right next door. Another applicable saying was that "the expertise of a consultant increases by the square of the distance he has to travel." But there was also another very good reason for CSM's problems in the state: the Legislature and political class in Colorado was dominated by graduates of the University of Colorado and the standard eastern Ivy League schools. In those schools a student took 120 hours to graduate in political science, liberal arts, general studies, education, and yes, engineering. The Professional Engineer degree was deemed to be worth considerably less than bachelor degrees in pre-law and others by the graduates of elite schools, mainly because those holding that opinion had no basis for comparison. The trustees by 1950 who had not graduated from Mines were looking to build Mines into a western MIT, whereas Mines had already exceeded what MIT demanded from its students by a wide margin.

To a large degree, the alumni were unhelpful to the Board during the 1950s and 60s, and although the Board was consistently dominated by Mines graduates (by statute), they went willy-nilly along with initiatives to change the school. Clearly, their behavior begs the question, why? The answer was probably that most Mines graduates came away with a love-hate relationship with Mines, and were seriously conflicted over supporting what they had experienced as a brutal, arbitrary, and needlessly demanding existence while in Golden as a student. Only after working for a few years did most of the graduates come around to comprehending that they had come away from Mines far better prepared than even the graduates of elite Ivy League schools. Sure it was tough, but so was becoming a Navy Seal. The difference was that almost everyone understood that completing the requirements to become a Seal made a person one of the few, one of the very best. Mines did the same thing, but most people outside of the specialties taught at Mines could not comprehend that the school turned out far superior graduates, how Mines did it, or even why.

One of the most common feelings after receiving one's sheet of silver in the 1950s was to put Mines in the rear view mirror as rapidly as possible. It was like escaping Alcatraz, few could do the time, and there was no desire to ever return. Rude hand and arm gestures while driving away were normal, but within a year or two, nostalgia set in for one's brothers that had helped each other graduate. All graduates were noble, and difficulties in the past were forgotten. Then came the drive to see the old concentration camp, talk to professors who were now earning a fraction of what the graduate was earning, and re-live those not always good old times.

When one of the authors contacted a Mines graduate from 1956 regarding his recollections, he declined to offer any, stating: "That was not a good time for me." Yet he had been a campus leader, and later became an outstanding patent attorney and an executive officer in a major steel company. His Mines education and experience had served him very well, but time had never softened his attitude toward the school.

For some graduates, even though they had benefitted greatly from CSM's policies and curricula, there was the desire to make sure no one else would ever have to suffer as they did. Perhaps that was what inclined the Mines graduates on the Board to embrace the watering down of Mines, and to make Mines fun to attend and graduation obtainable for most entering freshmen. Whatever the reason, the Board, with a majority comprised of alumni that should have protected the school, went along with the efforts to make Mines a kinder, gentler institution in the 50s and 60s.

It was at this time that the Board's lack of prominence in politics and academia became apparent. When the North Central Association (NCA) gave the school fits over accreditation, the Board's lack of political muscle became a severe problem, whether or not the Board wanted to resist the pressures to change. The selection of John W Vanderwilt as President of Mines in 1950 was meant to mollify out-of-state education leaders and their criticisms, as Vanderwilt was a progressive from Yale and sure to move Mines more into the mainstream. In the event, he did precisely that.

With the blessing of the Board, the team of Trustee Ben H. Parker and President Vanderwilt went to work to change the school, starting first with the most easily changed aspect, the physical plant. The Horizon Plan was the brainchild of Parker and Vanderwilt in 1951, and although not formally presented to the public until 1954, all construction, beginning in 1952 with the new chemistry building, Coolbaugh Hall, was accomplished under the general outlines of the Horizon Plan. Vanderwilt razed the decrepit and unstable Old Chem Building (which was never even considered for renovation) and the buildings that replaced it were critical to the continuing functioning of Mines. Alderson Hall followed shortly afterwards. It housed Petroleum Refining, which had been temporary buildings in World War II, and other departments such as Descriptive Geometry that was displaced by the demolition of Old Chem. Construction continued on campus with the metallurgy building on the site of Old Chem, and a new gym where the publications building had been,

Parker and Vanderwilt also ventured in a new area: the construction of state-owned facilities to house and board students and provide living and social amenities. It was charged that they were attempting to create an entirely new academic community along the lines of Ivy League universities.

The Board rubber-stamped the Horizon Plan, and the change in Mines was dramatic. The Mines man was replaced by the Mines student, a ward whose every need would be met by the State. The administration grew in leaps and bounds, and from an administrative staff of ten individuals dealing with student services in 1952 (a ratio of one staff individual for every hundred students), and a budget of less than $40,000, the administration of student affairs burgeoned to a current (2015) ratio of nearly five staff positions for every hundred students, and a budget of over $8,000,000.

The largest building on campus in 2016 was the *Student Recreation Center* - a building that would have been unused in the 1950s. There simply was not time for the students in the 1950s to recreate, and social events were essentially limited to Saturdays. Even the new gym, built in 1959, saw little use other than for varsity and intermural sports, and facilities like the handball courts did not bother to take reservations. Swimming in the Olympic-sized pool was open to all students except when being used by the varsity swimming team, as were most other facilities when not used for varsity sports. The State's largess was impressive, but went unused. *The Integral Club*, the de facto student union before the *Parker Student Union* was built, seldom had more than three or four students using it as a lounge or to play pool at any one time.

Nonetheless, the Board plowed forward, creating world-class facilities with public money. They lowered academic requirements to increase enrollments and give the students time to make use of the State's cornucopia of goodies. There was much back-slapping and congratulating as Mines expanded, as if that was the goal. "Coordinators" sprang up like weeds, and every new office received its full staff of personnel and student work-study personnel. In the 1950s, there was no such thing as "work-study." New job titles came into being such as "research professor" (meaning the individual performed research but did not teach) and "research associate" as research activities expanded and personnel were hired to open the federal government's financial spigots.

The one good thing the Board accomplished to help the school occurred in 1975. Until then, any private or corporate philanthropic gifts to the school were offset by a reduction in state funding - an almost unbelievably punitive law that left Mines at the mercy of the state legislature and severely hampered CSM's ability to attract the funds necessary for its survival. The Board was able to get this changed, with a new law, §24-70-104, amended C.R.S., 1973. Mines would henceforth no longer be fully dependent on friendly legislators for handouts.

The 1960s and 1970s were decades of change that tore at the fabric of America, and the Board could not withstand the political pressure for change. But once a change was implemented, there was no going back. The Board began to reflect the political realities of an institution attempting to survive by growth and research grants, and soon there was no longer a place for undergraduate excellence.

Until the 1970s the Board consisted of five voting members, but under the push for growth and the transformation into a research institution, the administration felt the board needed to be expanded to enable better political outreach. Meanwhile, political correctness made its appearance at Mines, and the Board was expanded to include representatives of the faculty and students and various advisory members. Henceforth, the Board would be "diverse", and could be looked upon with favor by Colorado's politicians, particularly the Democrat Party that normally was dominant.

The offices of secretary and treasurer were not necessarily filled by Board members, and if not, the individuals holding those offices could not vote. Later bylaws governing the expanded Board specified that at least four, but no more than five, members were to have graduated from Mines at least ten years before being appointed to the Board. The current nine-members members are chosen according to the Colorado Revised Statutes (§23-41-101, C.R.S., et seq.) Seven voting members of the Board are appointed by the Governor of Colorado, with the advice and consent of the Colorado Senate, to serve staggered four-year terms. The elected representative of the student body, a full-time junior or senior, is a non-voting member as is the faculty trustee elected by a majority of at least 67 percent of his peers. The student trustee serves a one-year term, beginning July 1st. The faculty trustee serves a two-year term commencing on January 1st of each odd-numbered year.

The faculty board member came about through pressure from the American Association of University Professors. Although at first blush it might seem that including a faculty representative would improve a Board, that is not necessarily the case. The AAUP promoted (and promotes today) two ideas that had given so much power to academicians in Germany: the concept of lifetime-guaranteed employment through a legal right to a position called tenure; and academic freedom, the right to teach, perform research, and literally do anything a faculty member wants to do without being restrained or controlled by his employer — the university and the taxpayers. Under AAUP contracts, institutions, even public, citizen-funded universities, cannot terminate (except for criminal behavior or in overall reductions of faculty) a faculty member or restrict his activities in any fashion.

Creating a student representative position on the Board was a politically-correct move, creating the impression that the students would have a voice (but not a vote) to counter the increasing control of their lives by the administration. It sounded good, especially in light of increasing student disturbances at many universities, but in reality, the student representatives have had little power or influence.

Beginning in 2001, the position of non-voting advisory members of the Board was created by the Colorado legislature. There are to be no fewer than nine and no more than fifteen advisory members of the board to be appointed by the Governor at times of his choosing. They serve staggered, four-year terms, and do not have to be residents of Colorado. The intent was to add heavyweights to the Board, although these positions could also be mere gratuities granted for donations or political support. As is stated in the Board's by-laws, "the advisory members...shall be representative of national and international industries as well as research and academic institutions...whose role shall be to provide advice to the Board in their areas of expertise and contribute to the development and enrichment of Mines, including, but not limited to its academic and research programs, [and] shall meet with the Board at least once per year."

An interesting aspect of Board membership is that following one's service on the Board, ex-Board members automatically become Emeritus Trustees for life, regardless of how long the individual served as a trustee. The Emeritus Trustees have the right to support CSM's "mission and programs through participation in Mines events and public representation of Mines." In short, they become certified ambassadors of Mines. The student trustees were included in this boon, but the faculty ones were not. It is difficult to avoid the conclusion that this omission was on purpose for various unstated reasons.

But somehow all this misses the point that the wide-ranging alumni are the best ambassadors on earth for Mines — or at least, those disposed to extoll and continue the Mines that had produced such excellence in individuals such as themselves. Yet for many years, alumni were only hounded for contributions while the Board and the administration treated them as red-headed stepchildren. Scorning its alumni, Mines increasingly looked to the federal government for funding and research support, and never glanced back.

Administration and Staff in the 50's

During the 1950s, some of the Administrative personnel and members of the faculty were truly inspiring and worthy of every student's respect. William V. Burger, the Dean of Students and Registrar, was a colorful character who was always accessible to students, and seemed to take an interest in every individual. He lived in the old President's House on 15th Street across from the SPE house, only a block from Guggenheim Hall. Dean Burger always took the side of the students. Sometimes he was like a father-confessor, and he intervened when necessary with police, especially the Colorado University campus cops. He walked a fine line between the faculty and students, never becoming involved in dispute over grades — at least not to the student's knowledge — but was there for moral support.

When one of the authors had performed poorly on a quiz as a student and was walking dejectedly down 15th Street, Dean Burger stopped him to ask about his problem. They went into the Dean's house for a cup of coffee, and Burger listened quietly to the author's story.

"Nobody died," Burger said finally. "It's not so bad. Everybody flunks something sometime. It's God's way of reminding us we're mortal, and that we need Him in our lives. If you have to take the course over, do it. Rise to the occasion and prove to yourself that you can take adversity. I have to do it every day."

"You? You have everyone's respect," the author answered.

"I don't have what it takes to graduate from Mines, and am reminded of that fact every day. I'm just the guy holding your coat."

It was a new perspective for the author, and one that he needed. Dean Burger had to choose his battles carefully, particularly with the faculty who were so jealous of their prerogatives. But when emotions ran too high, Burger was always there to tamp things down.

The Director of Admissions, H. Dean Burdick, would also come high on a list of "good guys." Burdick held little respect for form and arbitrary rules, and many a graduate owed his admission to Mines to this fine gentleman.

Perhaps the best story illustrating the humanity of Mr. Burdick is that of Manny Robles. In Sept, 1952, Manuel (Manny) Robles, a 26-year old truck driver from California, his wife, Mary, and their baby, came to Golden with the intention of Manny matriculating at Mines. Although he was a high school dropout, he wanted to become a mining engineer. Even though it was an absolute requirement that all freshmen have a high school diploma, Manny talked Burdick into accepting him as a probationary student. He then passed the placement tests and became a regular student. Manny and Mary lived in a trailer at Prospector Park which Mary later said had "no facilities."

Although he never made the honor roll, Manny never got a grade below "C". He graduated in 1956 with an E.M. degree and three additional children, a number which would eventually burgeon to seven. Upon graduation, he joined ASARCO (American Smelting and Refining) at a mine in Mexico, then worked for a division of Kaiser Steel in Baja California, and a different Kaiser division in California before finishing his career with Exxon in Houston. His employers consistently gave Manny high marks as a valuable employee. The chance that Dean Burdick took on a high school dropout paid out handsomely for the mining industry. Although he was unable to contribute heavily to Mines at any point in his career and was never considered for a distinguished achievement medal, Manny was one of the best of the best. Starting over the horizon from the rest of the freshmen, Manny passed by 75% of them academically, and made everyone proud. Not bad for a high school dropout, and not bad for Mines.

It's one thing to start out in a wealthy Houston oil family and attend private schools before attending Mines, then graduate in petroleum and go back to Houston, increase the family wealth and contribute to Mines. It's another to start out as a high school dropout with a wife and three kids, do well at Mines, and build a competent, if not spectacular career as an engineer while also being a good father to seven children. Which one deserves a distinguished achievement medal?

A footnote is necessary here from one of the author's personal experience. One of the finest professors was in the English Department, Anton G. Pegis. He was tapped to become the Director of Development in 1964, and in 1972 was made Vice President for Development. Dr. Pegis mentored many students and taught one of the authors how to play handball. They played nearly every day while the author was in his senior year, and Dr. Pegis freely talked about his life, Mines, and the necessity of doing everything to the best of one's ability. In the 1960s, Tony Pegis was a rabid Mines supporter and one of the few professors whose door was always open to students.

Guggenheim Hall and Arthur Lakes Library

Chapter 8 - Presidents of Mines

A college consists of eight discrete human elements; undergraduate students, graduate students, faculty, administrators, college staff, alumni, trustees, and the community; but the institution's president sets the tone and direction for all activities. Others may be more important to any particular individual, particularly a department head for a student in that option, but over time it is the president who guides the Board of Trustees to its decisions, and sets guidelines for academics, enrollments, admissions, faculty recruitment, and physical plant planning.

So it has been for Mines. The school's history shows the effects of strong and effective presidents, as well as some weaker individuals. By and large, the presidents were not career academicians, and many returned to industry after their sojourn as president of Mines, several becoming wealthy in the process. A number became authors of engineering books, several were awarded patents for their inventions, and others became presidents of various private and public corporations. Other than William Loveland, however, none became active in politics and sought elective office. With the exception of President Coolbaugh's service in assisting in the creation of the Marshall Plan, none went back and forth between academia and the federal government as is so common among elite universities in the East or those that rely heavily on federal research grants for funding. Only a few came directly from an administrative office in another university (Dr. Alderson, for example), and only one, Dr. Orlo Childs, left Mines to go to another university. With only a single exception since 1883, the Mines presidency was the apex of their academic careers, providing an experience that could not be exceeded at another school.

Two presidents stand out in the history of Mines: Dr. Regis Chauvenet and Dr. John W Vanderwilt. Oddly enough, they both took degrees at Harvard; Dr. Chauvenet studied there for a bachelor of science, and Dr. Vanderwilt came away with a PhD in Geology. But there the similarity ended.

Dr. Chauvenet's father, William, was one of the founders of the US Naval Academy, having been made a professor of mathematics in the U.S. Navy in 1841. He taught on the USS Mississippi, and then at the Philadelphia Naval Asylum School where he established a rigorous eight month course of study. This short program of study was clearly inadequate, and Chauvenet proposed a four-year course of study and began pushing for the creation of a separate naval school devoted solely to academic studies. In large part as a result of his efforts, the Naval School was founded at Annapolis, Maryland in 1845, by the Secretary of the Navy, George Bancroft, with the stated purpose of achieving Professor Chauvenet's objectives. Annapolis was chosen over Philadelphia because Secretary Bancroft did not want the students subjected to the "temptations and distractions that necessarily connect with a large and populous city." William moved to Annapolis in 1845, as professor and department head of mathematics and astronomy.

Secretary Bancroft had established a five-year program, but only the first and last were spent at Annapolis in course work while the the other three were on board vessels in active service. The program was rigorous and structured as a severe ordeal, but Chauvenet was still not satisfied. He continued to push for a full four-year curriculum at the school with the on-board training coming during intensive summer cruises. Due to his efforts, the Naval School was reorganized in 1850-1851 as the U.S. Naval Academy, with a course of study of four consecutive years.

His father's design at the Naval Academy became the template Dr. Regis Chauvenet used to establish the curricula and programs at Mines. First and foremost, he wanted to toughen the course of instruction so that 100% of Mines graduates could handle literally any situation that might arise in their chosen field of endeavor. As in the Navy, a certain level of competence was required and expected at every step as one rose in rank, and Dr. Chauvenet wanted to be able to certify that its graduates could meet that level without reservations. CSM's summer programs and plethora of required industrial inspections and trips were surrogates for the Academy's summer service on board serving vessels. At Mines, the four-year program would make use of every waking hour, during the academic semesters and the summers.

For example, the mining option students took many trips to mines in order to see the varying practice and the operations and machinery described in the classroom. The trips were planned to illustrate definite operations, to develop the power of observation and the ability to report concisely such observations. Each student was to make a study of some mining district, and, whenever possible during his college courses, to apply learned principles, methods, and criticisms to that district and make recommendations through his mining professors. The following were the trips taken by mining students during Dr. Chauvenet's presidency:

Freshman Year. The Cook or Oldtown Mines at Central City, the Gem Mine and Newhouse Tunnel at Idaho Springs, and the Colorado Central Mine at Georgetown. These trips brought before the student various methods of shaft-sinking, tunneling, drifting, and stoping, and illustrated practices in haulage, hoisting, and pumping. A general report, including sketches of various assigned subjects, was required of each student.

Sophomore Year. The Cripple Creek district was visited in order to illustrate underground operations in general, and special methods of mining, timbering, and drainage. Numerous maps and modes of mines emphasize topics discussed in the lectures on mine surveying. Then came the Northern Coalfields in Colorado, which illustrated methods of mining, ventilation, haulage, and timbering.

Junior Year. More trips were made in order to illustrate local practices in shaft-sinking, tunneling, and other important operations. During the summer, an extended trip was made to South Dakota and Montana. Methods of mining and handling low-grade ore were illustrated, the equipment of mine plants studied, and available data was collected by each student in order to furnish practical examples in the study of mine plants during the senior year. Carefully prepared reports were required at the end of the trip.

Senior Year. The trips of the senior year included illustrations of mining operations, construction-work, and power machinery. Leadville, Aspen, and Breckenridge were visited to furnish illustrations of timbering, pumping, and placer mining. The course in mine examination and reports required each student to make several additional trips of his own design for the examination of properties.

This avalanche of work produced almost immediate results. Mines graduates became highly sought after by the giant London mining companies, and their efforts and competence became known world-wide, especially when their new techniques made the South African gold mines so productive. It was graduates of Dr. Chauvenet's regimen that won for Mines a "best in the world" reputation, and by 1902, when Dr. Chauvenet stepped down, the men of Mines had demolished all competition.

During the first half on the 20th century there were three schools in the U.S. that made excessive demands on their students -- West Point, Annapolis, and Mines, and all three were recognized world-wide for producing the best men in their specialties. All were steeped in engineering and the applied sciences, and none probably ever expected to graduate more than a few rare women who might show extraordinary talent in their courses of study. Two were supported by the federal government, and one by the State of Colorado. All were undergraduate teaching schools, eschewing post-graduate work and research, and they resisted progressive teaching methods, policies, and socialistic ideas for faculty welfare such as tenure and academic freedom. These "politically correct" ideas had been brought to the United States from Germany at the end of the 19th century and championed by influential educators such as John Dewey, Woodrow Wilson, and Edwin R. A. Seligman. They believed in the elitist German/European higher education model and spread it rapidly through the Ivy League and state universities, but it was rejected by the three schools listed above.

By the time Dr. Vanderwilt arrived on campus in 1947, the Colorado legislature had developed a decidedly hostile attitude toward Mines, and the school was under siege. Much of the pressure came from the Denver papers that seemed unable to countenance Golden's pre-eminence in Colorado education. The school changed its method of awarding course credit and began to lower standards under President Ben H. Parker, but the outside pressure intensified. The North Central Accreditation Association smelled blood in the water as Parker sought approval from the educational establishment. Such approval rested on scrapping the Mines of old. Parker couldn't do that, but Vanderwilt could. A deal was cut, and in 1950 Dr. Parker joined the Board of Trustees, and Dr. Vanderwilt left the Board to become the school's president.

Dr. Vanderwilt's first actions were to attack Mines traditions that he felt were out of order in a well-run institution controlled from the top. Senior Day headed his hit list. Efforts were made to mollify the North Central Accreditation Association to gain its acceptance of Mines and its programs, but whereas West Point and Annapolis could thumb their noses at such outside interference, Dr. Vanderwilt decided Mines could not. He introduced the Horizon Plan to construct an impressive physical plant to support his moving Mines from undergraduate teaching to performing research, and he replaced student self-help with administrative staff. Although the full elimination of the Professional Engineer degree did not occur during his tenure as president, it was a foregone conclusion that the degree was on the way out when he stepped down.

By 1970, the Mines of Dr. Chauvenet had disappeared, and been replaced by a regional engineering school accepting transfers from community colleges and with college entrance scores reflecting a broader, and less able and committed student body. Attendance at Mines became fun, enrollments grew, and research dollars flowed in. A new Mines had arisen on the ashes of the old one, and the presidents after Vanderwilt were all adherents of progressive education.

Probably none of them ever knew or realized what Dr. Chauvenet had constructed, why, and what it all entailed. In its place the new presidents struggled to raise enrollments, the new measure of success. They hired faculty members with terminal degrees and other people who could attract research money, construct new facilities, and create an extensive list of engineering and technical programs that would hopefully ensure the survival of Mines. One can only wish them well, while pointing out how Mines had become the World's Foremost Mineral Engineering School in days gone by. (Feel like you're reading James Thurber's *Fables For Our Time?*)

The great sin of the presidents of Mines following Parker was in believing that accreditation by the North Central Association meant something. No doubt the NCA would have found Annapolis and West Point deficient for concentrating on military and technical courses, and not producing well-rounded, sensitive, and socially acceptable military officers. Winning battles would no longer be the object, since the academies would have to concentrate on producing well-adjusted and happy officers. Their lives would be shortened, but what would the accrediting individuals care? The NCA was not seeking excellence: it was levelling university education throughout its region of the United States. For the NCA, like the federal government, one size fit all.

Presidents, Bios and Actions:

Years — President

1871 - 1875 **Edward Jones Mallett, Jr.,** Professor in Charge. Mallett studied at Columbia, and in 1871 was the owner of Solar Chemical Company in Kings County, New York. He came to Colorado as an expert on metallurgical processes, but first climbed Gray's Peak, thought to be the highest peak in Colorado. He saw the great waste in the treatment of silver ores and developed the idea of drawing the air through reverberator furnaces rather than forcing it in. His motto was: "If experiments are not directed by theory, they are blind, if theory is not sustained by practice it is deceiving and uncertain." He left Mines to become the President of the School of Mines, Denver City, which never took off. Back in New York City, he became an owner and trustee of the Control Combustion Company, capitalized on his inventions and patents, and became wealthy.

1875 - 1876 **W. A. H. Loveland**, Professor in Charge. The prominent Mr. Loveland assumed the presidential duties temporarily until a replacement could be found for Mr. Mallett. One of the most colorful of the early Colorado pioneers, William Austin Hamilton Loveland served in the Mexican War as a wagon master, and fought in the battles of Veracruz, Puebla and Chapultepec under General Winfield Scott, and was severely wounded in the assault on Chapultepec. He came to Colorado from Illinois in 1859, and quickly became Golden's foremost business person and promoter of the town. It was due to his efforts that Golden became the territorial capital of Colorado in 1861. He was one of the founders of the Colorado Central Railroad and as its president, extended a railroad network into the Rockies to service the many mining communities that produced so much of Colorado's early wealth. Loveland Pass, now on the main route west from Denver, is named for him, as was the city of Loveland. In 1870, Loveland was the driving force in obtaining funds from the Territorial Legislature for the establishment of the Colorado School of Mines. Loveland later founded the city of Lakewood in 1889, but his first and most abiding love was the Colorado School of Mines.

1876 - 1878 **Gregory Board**, Professor in Charge. Professor Board possessed a British diploma from the Birkbeck School of Science & Art, and one as a Mining Engineer from the Royal School of Mines, British Museum. Mr. Board was the superintendent of a smelter in Golden when appointed at a salary of $100.00 per month plus 50% of the receipts from assays, chemical tests, analyses of ores, etc. He was authorized to examine candidates with "gentlemen of suitable attainments" and grant diplomas. Upon Mr. Board's resignation, he became the superintendent of the Golden Smelting Works.

1878 - 1880 **Milton Moss**, Professor in Charge. PhD, University of Munich, EM, Colorado School of Mines. Dr. Moss was a practicing chemist, who used his summer vacations to augment his salary by conducting inspections as Commissioner of Mines — an office that was then attached to Professor in Charge. He established the principle of extreme specialization which would be the hallmark of Mines' curriculum. He also turned back the first attempt by CU to absorb Mines. His salary in 1879 was $125.00 per month. In 1882, Moss was awarded an honorary engineer of mines degree.

1880 - 1883 **Albert Cable Hale,** Professor in Charge & President. BA, MA, University of Rochester, PhD, University of Heidelberg, EM. Dr. Hale lengthened the course of instruction from three to four years, and instituted degrees of Engineer of Mines (EN), and Civil Engineer (CE). Hale's title was soon changed to president, a position that earned him $2,500 a year. In 1883, Mines held its first commencement ceremony for two graduates: William B. Middleton and Walter H. Wiley.

1883 - 1902 **Regis Chauvenet, President**. AB, AM, Washington University (St. Louis), BS, Harvard, Honorary LLD, Harvard. Dr. Chauvenet was a chemist and metallurgist who eschewed enrollments for excellence in curriculum & education. He modelled Mines on the Naval Academy, and built Mines into a world-class institution. He taught chemistry and metallurgy after stepping down as president, to devote attention to his career as a mining engineer. He was the author of *Chemical and Metallurgical Calculations, 1911, Chemical Arithmetic and Calculation of Furnace Charges, 1912,* and *History of the Colorado School of Mines: Origin and Early Years*, written in 1920 but never published. In 1897 the trustees over-ruled the president and faculty in a matter of scholarship and student discipline. Dr. Chauvenet resigned, but withdrew his resignation at the request of the trustees, who passed a resolution to the effect that "thereafter in matters of discipline and scholarship the action of the faculty shall be final." Five years later, in 1902, the trustees ignored their own resolution and again interfered in matters of student discipline; this resulted in the resignation of Dr. Chauvenet from the presidency.

1902 - 1903 **Charles Skeele Palmer**, President. AB, MA, Amherst, PhD, Johns Hopkins. He defined chemical terms in *Webster's International Dictionary,* 1890 edition, and translated the 1st edition of *Nernst's Theoretical Chemistry - From the Standpoint of Avogadro's Rule & Thermodynamics*, 1895. In 1900 he invented the basic process for cracking oils to gasoline, patented the process in 1907, and sold his patent to the Standard Oil Corporation of Indiana (later Amoco) in 1916. Dr. Palmer served only from September, 1902 to April, 1903 before being terminated by the Board of Trustees. In February, 1903, the entire freshman class walked out over the faculty's treatment of students. Palmer and the Board took a hard line, temporarily expelling a number of students and requiring them to re-register to continue their studies. Palmer then decided to correct the faculty problems in the classroom by creating a faculty evaluation process, and the faculty rose in protest. In April, the Board was told by a delegation of faculty members that either Palmer was fired, or the faculty would resign *en masse*. The Board fired Palmer along with the ringleaders of the faculty protest. Palmer readily found a job as the Chief Chemist of the Washoe Smelter, Anaconda, Montana, and became wealthy through his inventions.

1903 **Horace Bushnell Patton**, Acting President. BA, Amherst, PhD, University of Heidelberg. Dr. Patton came to Mines in 1893 from the Michigan School of Mines, as Professor of Geology and Mineralogy. He served as president only temporarily for a summer while the situation with the faculty and students calmed down. He remained on the faculty of Mines until at least 1912, and authored a number of works, including *Lecture Notes on Crystallography* (1896, reprint 1905), *The Geology and Petrography of Crater Lake National Park* (1902), *The Montezuma Mining District of Summit County, Colorado* (Colorado Geological Survey 1909), *Geology of the Grayback Mining District, Costilla County, Colorado*, (Colorado Geological Survey 1910), *Rock Streams of Veta Peak, Colorado* (1910), and *Geology and Ore Deposits of the Alma District, Park County, Colorado* (1912).

1903 - 1913 **Victor Clifton Alderson**, President. AB, Harvard, DSc, Beloit College, DSc, Armour Institute of Technology. When hired in 1903, Dr. Alderson was Dean of Engineering and Acting President of the Armour Institute of Technology in Chicago (now the Illinois Institute of Technology). He presided over a major building program, the founding of fraternities, and the completion of the "M". He authored *The Scientific Spirit* in 1905 and *The Oil Shale Industry* in 1920. Dr. Alderson did not support President Palmer's idea of faculty evaluations, but the campus was hardly quiet during his administration. Many faculty members were dissatisfied with his administrative methods, and ultimately enough pressure was put on the Board of Trustees to cause Dr. Alderson's termination. He was accused of failing to support the faculty in matters of discipline or of academic standing, and of irregular practices in connection with the dismissal of the members of the faculty.

1913 - 1915 **William George Haldane**, Acting President. BS (Mining Engineering), Case School of Applied Science, (Cleveland, Ohio), PhD, University of Denver. Dr. Haldane came to Mines in 1900 after working as an engineer for the American Steel and Wire Company (US Steel). He taught metallurgy at Mines, but also practiced as a mining engineer. He received patent US890584, Process of Extracting Uranium and Vanadium from Ores, with Professor Herman Fleck in 1908. Dr. Haldane left Mines in 1917 to take a position as the superintendent of a large potash plant in Antioch, Nebraska.

1915 - 1916 **William Battle Phillips**, President. AB, PhD, University of North Carolina (the first PhD earned at UNC). A consultant in mining and chemistry from 1888 to 1892, he was also professor of chemistry and metallurgy at the University of Alabama. His work was critical in the ongoing development of the iron and steel industry at Birmingham. He worked for the Tennessee Coal, Iron and Railway Company from 1892 to 1898, and from 1898 to1900 was editor of the Engineering and Mining Journal, American Manufacturer, and Iron World. Phillips was professor of field and economic geology from 1900 to 1914 at the University of Texas. In 1901, he inspected Spindletop, an oil well located in a salt-dome field that would launch the Texas oil boom. His report on the oil well received such notice that he became recognized as the state's eminent expert on mining and petroleum. He served as director of the University of Texas Mining Survey from 1901 to 1905, and of the Bureau of Economic Geology and Technology from 1909 to 1914. He was instrumental in the establishment of the Texas State School of Mines and

Metallurgy at El Paso, now University of Texas at El Paso. By 1914 Phillips had acquired an international reputation, and he came to Mines as its president in 1915. He resigned after one year, apparently after some dispute with the Board of Trustees. In 1916 he returned to consulting in Texas, where he died two years later in Houston. Phillips contributed more than three hundred scientific articles to various publications.

1916 - 1917 **Howard Coon Parmelee**, President. BS, AM, University of Nebraska, honorary DSc, Colorado College. After a short stint with the Union Pacific Railroad as a chemist, Parmelee worked for the American Smelting and Refining Company's Globe Plant as chief chemist for two years. He spent three years as a consultant, then took over the Mining Reporter which he edited for two years, followed by three years as the editor of the *Western Chemist Metallurgist*. From 1910 to 1916, he was the Western Editor of *Metallurgical and Chemical Engineering*. After being terminated by the Mines Board of Trustees, he became the editor of *Chemical and Metallurgical Engineering* in New York. He received an honorary degree of Doctor of Science from Colorado College in 1917. Primarily interested in journalism, Dr. Parmelee was hardly the best choice for president of an engineering school. His term was wracked by conflict. Matters came to a head in April of 1917. The senior class of the School declared a "Senior Day" in accordance with the annual custom, and all classes were dismissed. The day was usually devoted to various forms of amusement and sport, concluding with a baseball game in the afternoon between the students and the faculty. There was a fair amount of drunkenness among the students, and evidently some type of assault on a faculty member at the baseball game took place. Parmelee called the faculty together to consider these breaches of discipline and conduct, and suspended five students and imposed minor penalties on six others. The students threatened a strike. The trustees tried to get Parmelee to back down, but he wouldn't. The conflict ended in the dismissal of President Parmelee. Dr. Victor C. Alderson was then reappointed president of the school, although there was a great deal of opposition to his reappointment on the part of alumni and members of the faculty.

1917 - 1925 **Victor Clifton Alderson** (2nd term as President). Dr. Alderson successfully maneuvered CSM back on track after the turmoil of the preceding years, but was terminated again by the Board of Trustees. Apparently the issues were his extended absences from the Mines campus and his involvement in the shale oil industry in western Colorado. According to the charges filed against him by faculty representatives, he was using faculty and student labor to support his shale oil activities. A former editor of the *Mines Magazine* introduced a number of mining periodicals to prove that President Alderson was guilty of permitting unscrupulous oil shale promoters to use the school's experimental facilities for the installation of their demonstration plants. The American Association of University Professors filed a formal complaint listing five issues, and two of the charges were substantiated. On the other hand, Dr. Alderson was popular with the students during both stints as president, and graduates tended to give him the credit for firmly cementing Dr. Chauvenet's vision as a reality for the next fifty years.

1925 - 1946 **Melville Fuller Coolbaugh**, President. BA, Colorado College, MA, Columbia. In 1917 began his association with Colorado School of Mines as Professor and Head of its Chemistry Department. He received an honorary Law Degree, LLD, from Colorado College in 1925, and another from the University of Colorado in 1927. After doing graduate work at Colombia University and special research work at the Massachusetts Institute of Technology. Dr. Coolbaugh taught Chemistry at Colorado College, Columbia University, Case School of Applied Science in Cleveland, and South Dakota School of Mines and Technology in Rapid City, SD, and was also Vice President of Mines in 1918. During World War I he served in the Chemical Warfare service and also was director of metals research. In 1947 he accepted President Truman's personal invitation to serve on the Committee of Nineteen, the group that outlined the Marshall Plan. His administration ended the turmoil that had characterized the presidents since the retirement of Dr. Chauvenet, and restored the reputation of Mines among academicians.

1946 - 1950 **Ben Hutchinson Parker**, President. EM, MS, DSc, Colorado School of Mines. Dr. Parker was the only president who attended Mines as an undergraduate. Personally quite charming, he experienced difficulties in handling the influx of veterans following World War II. Dr. Parker entered Mines in 1919 at the age of sixteen, and graduated in 1924. For the next seven years he worked as a petroleum geologist and engineer in New Mexico, Colorado, Oklahoma, and South Dakota. In 1931 he returned to Mines and received his DSc in 1934. He worked for a short time for Gulf Oil and tried his hand at consulting, but in 1936 returned to Mines as a faculty member in the Geology Department. Following his years as President, Dr. Parker served on the Board of Trustees, where he worked closely with Dr. Vanderwilt on producing the Horizon Plan and remaking Mines into a college meeting the approval of the Colorado Legislature and educators at lesser institutions. He became the executive vice president of Frontier Refining Company in 1950, and president in the 1960s before its merger with Husky Oil. He was active in many professional associations and authored or co-authored twenty-two scholarly papers.

1950 - 1963 **John W Vanderwilt**, President. AB (Geology-Mineralogy), MS (Economic Geology) University of Michigan, PhD, (Geology) Harvard. He began the Horizon Plan, and was responsible for the elimination of many Mines traditions, its heavy course loads, and several historical buildings. He also established the CSM Foundation, obtaining an endowment of $50 million in 1951, and formalized the graduate school in 1953. After receiving his MS in 1923, Dr. Vanderwilt worked as an instructor in Geology at Colorado University for two years. He received a doctorate in Geology from Harvard in 1927, and was employed by the U.S. Geological Survey until 1934, with a one-year sabbatical as an assistant professor of Geology at CU in 1929-30. In 1934 he became a consulting mining and engineering geologist primarily working with Climax Molybdenum on the geology of its molybdenum ore deposits. This became a life-long endeavor, and he worked with Climax until his retirement in 1968. He authored some thirty-six publications, and was best known for his knowledge of the Climax ore deposits. In 1947 he was appointed to the Mines Board of Trustees, and in 1950 made president of the school. Vanderwilt also brought Mines much closer to various government agencies, serving on numerous advisory committees and councils to the Department of the Interior, National Science Foundation, Bureau of Reclamation, and many professional organizations. During his tenure, student enrollment went from 1,075 in the fall of 1950 to 1,048 in 1963.

1963 - 1970   **Orlo E. Childs**, President. BS, MS, (Geology) University of Utah. PhD. (Geology), University of Michigan. He presided over the destruction of CSM's heavy course loads, the replacement of the Professional Degree with a Bachelor of Science, the diversification of courses of study, the de-emphasizing of extreme engineering specializations, and the substitution of administrative bureaucrats for student-run orientation assistance and the major roles played by fraternities in Mines life. His career was divided among academic, industrial, and government employment. Prior to coming to Mines he taught at Weber Junior College from 1937 to 1942, the University of Michigan from 1943 to 1945, Colgate University from1946 to 1947, and the University of Wyoming from 1949 to 1950. His time in industry came next: he worked as a district geologist and ultimately exploration projects director for Phillips Petroleum from 1949 to 1962. Then he tried government, and in 1962 became the director of the research program in Marine Geology and Hydrology for the U.S. Geological Survey. It was from that position he was hired by the Board of Directors to become President of Mines. Dr. Childs was the only Mines president to later accept employment in another university as an administrator. From 1970 to 1974, he was vice president for Research and Special Programs at Texas Tech University, in Lubbock, Texas. Appointed a university professor in 1974, he taught at Texas Tech until his retirement in 1979. Not content to stay in retirement, he served from 1980 to 1985 as Director of the Mining and Mineral Resources Research Institute in the College of Mines at the University of Arizona. His production of academic publications was slight, but for some reason he was appointed to many government committees and councils from 1963 to 1985.

1970 - 1984 **Guy T. McBride, Jr.**, President. BS (Chemical Engineering) Rice University, PhD (Chemical Engineering) Massachusetts Institute of Technology. Born in 1919, Dr. McBride received a BS in Chemical Engineering in 1940 from Rice, then moved to Cambridge and worked on his PhD in Chemical Engineering while he taught various courses during World War II. He received his doctorate in 1948, and returned to Rice where he remained until 1958 as a faculty member and later Dean of Students. He left Rice to work for Texas Gulf Sulphur from 1958 to 1970, rising to become vice president and general manager. His highest priority as president was the Mines Honors Program for Public Affairs. The core purpose of the McBride Program was to bring Mines graduates with technical and scientific backgrounds into the decision-making processes in Washington. Mc-

Bride was also responsible for developing the Future Graduate Profile, stressing the following areas to be gained during a student's sojourn at Mines: technical competence, communications skills (written, oral, and graphical), ability to work in diverse teams, dedication to life-long learning, awareness of the impacts of non-technical influences, and integrity and self-discipline. To complete McBride's plethora of "New Age" programs, he introduced the Engineering Practices Introductory Course Sequence (EPICS) in 1982, a two-year sequence that became required of all freshman and sophomore students. Students worked in teams on enjoyable outside projects, usually with small government entities, businesses, or non-profit organizations, and hopefully learned to communicate with individuals of diverse backgrounds and objectives. These projects involved issues such as environmental concerns, social justice, political factors, and potential economic and societal costs. Even before they learned the basics of engineering, students learned the appropriate doctrine. The students would have been better advised to read *The Woolsey Papers*, by Mines professor Robert E. D. Woolsey, but that did not fit McBride's political agenda. Mines enrollments grew substantially during his time at Mines as standards fell and the student body diversified.

1984 - 1998 **George S. Ansell**, President. BS (Metallurgical Engineering), MS, PhD, Rensselaer Polytechnic Institute. Dr. Ansell graduated from the elite Bronx High School of Science in New York before going to RPI. He came to Mines after being the dean of the RPI School of Engineering. The student body at Mines became much more diverse during his presidency, with the number of minorities and female students rising considerably. He claimed it was his mission to graduate minorities from Mines in the same proportion they were in the general population of Colorado. He also expanded graduate and research programs across the campus and accelerated the school's development into a research university. Dr. Ansell was allegedly asked to resign due to his ineffectiveness in raising money, especially from alumni who had become increasingly alienated from the college. Dr. Ansell was also the first Jewish president of Mines. He and his wife died together in Arizona in 2013.

1998 - 2000 **Theodore A. Bickart,** President. BS, MS, PhD, (Electrical Engineering – Computer Science) Johns Hopkins University. He claimed his primary goal was to transition Mines from a period of long-term stability in the fields of applied science and engineering to an era of rapidly changing technology. He believed that to be successful as an engineer (although he had never worked as one), a student had to focus on four main areas: human systems, engineering systems, earth systems, and economic systems. His goal was to integrate all four systems into the Mines curriculum. Dr. Bickart retired after two years.

2000 - 2006 **John U. Trefny,** President. BS (Physics) Fordham University, PhD (Physics) Rutgers University. Prior to coming to Mines in 1977, Dr. Trefny taught at Cornell University and Wesleyan University. At Mines he began as an Assistant Professor in Physics, and progressed to Head of the Physics Department, Vice President for Academic Affairs, and Dean of Faculty. Completely in tune ideologically with his three presidential predecessors, Dr. Trefny was on the boards of WorldDenver and the International Center for Appropriate and Sustainable Technology (ICAST), both politically globalist, and with Agenda 21-oriented organizations. With his Trefny Innovative Instruction Center, ten percent of Mines faculty restructured courses in 2016 to accelerate the pace of innovation in education and instruction at Mines. The goal was to create a distinct and unique student experience for Mines students. He also implemented a transfer agreement between Red Rocks Community College and the Colorado School of Mines to allow

Red Rocks graduates to transfer to CSM as juniors.

2006 - 2015   **Myles W. Scoggins**, President. BS University of Tulsa, MS University of Oklahoma, PhD University of Tulse (all Petroleum Engineering). Dr. Scoggins came to Mines after 34 years in the oil and gas industry, lastly as executive vice president of ExxonMobil Corporation. He involved Mines in a ridiculous suit wherein an alumnus wanted to purchase a plate to put on a locker in the new Athletic Complex. However, the alumnus wanted to quote a verse from the Bible, Colossians 3:23, saying: "Whatever you do, work at it with all your heart, as working for the Lord, not for human masters." Scoggins decided that violated the Constitution's first amendment, "Congress shall make no law respecting an establishment of religion, or prohibiting the free exercise thereof." A suit resulted, and the school not only looked absurd to Christians in general, but to prospective students and donors as well. After Scoggins stepped down as president of Mines, he returned to the oil and gas industry as an investor and member of various boards of directors.

2015 - Pres.   **Paul C. Johnson**, President. BS (Chemical Engineering) University of California-Davis, MS, PhD (Chemical Engineering) Princeton University. His expertise is in soil and groundwater remediation, specifically, the optimization of soil and groundwater remediation systems and the monitoring and modeling of exposure pathways. Johnson came to Mines from Arizona State University where he had been a faculty member since 1994, a professor in the School of Sustainable Engineering and the Built Environment, and executive dean of the Ira A. Fulton Schools of Engineering. At ASU he greatly increased the amount of research and governmental contracts, expanded enrollments, and built the Fulton Schools into a regional powerhouse generating inventions, patents, and start-up technology companies. Like his predecessors, Johnson apparently is oriented towards sustainable development, a code word for Agenda 21 as defined at the Rio Conference in 1992 and discussed in Appendix G.

Chapter 9 – Faculty

The Old Mines Faculty During the "Golden Years":

Mines had no lack of colorful professors before the 1970s. Until the fraternities were driven from the campus's interior, professors were routinely invited to dine at various fraternity houses and generally had close contact with many students. J. O. Ball, Petroleum Professor, often lunched at the Kappa Sigma House, and E. B. Jacobs, E. G. Fisher, L. W. LeRoy and J. Harlan Johnson, were regular visitors to the ATO House for dinner. There were also the usual professors in the 1950s who generated great stories on campus.

Thomas E. Paynter, Professor of Electrical Engineering, kept unusual things in his office, including a human embryo in a jar. He also had an interesting procedure to keep the students' attention in class. If he made a mistake or said anything that was incorrect in his lecture, the student first noting it called out "BEER!" Then the student proceeded to point out what error he thought had been made. If the student was correct, Prof. Paynter owed the class a beer, but if the student was wrong, the student owed the class a beer. The score was marked prominently on the board at the front of the room. About every 5 weeks, the Prof would pay off by relocating the Friday 11 a.m. lecture to Dud's Bar and Grill (now the Buffalo Rose) on Washington Avenue where he (and any student who might also owe the class) would buy round after round, occasionally a round more than was owed.

Prof Paynter would also bring interesting things to discuss during the payoffs, so the class continued to learn while enjoying his largess. After lunch the class would repair to the EE lab on the top floor of the school Power Plant, where Professor Paynter or EE Instructor **Scott Marshall** would run the experiment while the students just watched. With the students pretty well under the influence of the beer, it was too dangerous for the students to run their own experiments.

Hildreth Frost, a Metallurgy instructor who also owned the historic Maxwell House in Georgetown, Colorado, was known for his ever-present pipe. He later became Chief Assayer at the Denver Mint. While there he became involved in the celebrated Great Gold Case of 1971 in El Paso, in which Paul and Ercell Stone, husband

and wife, were tried by the Federal Government for possessing one ounce of gold bullion. Frost did the assaying and determined that the bullion was not made from jewelry and testified to that effect in the trial. Federal lawyers suborned perjury, and the Stones were found guilty under Roosevelt's gold law passed in 1933. Paul faced a possible sentence of 20 years and a $20,000 fine; Ercell 25 years and a fine of $25,000. On January 1, 1975, it became legal for Americans to own gold bullion in any amount.

It was rumored during the 1950s that **Dr. J. Harlan Johnson**, Professor of Geology, worked at Mines for a dollar a year. It was well known that he was a consultant to Shell Oil, and that he spent a few weeks each year there for a rumored $25,000 per year, which was an astronomical sum at the time. True or not, Dr. Johnson did nothing to dispel the rumor, and was accorded great respect by his students. The idea that a person could donate the great majority of his time to the teaching of his specialty for the good of the nation and the students, simply raised Dr. Johnson to god-like status.

Edward B. Jacobs (Jake) was originally hired as an instructor in Physical Training in the 1920s and was noted throughout his career for having appeared on the cover of both *Physical Culture* and *Strength* magazines. Jake held a degree in Electrical Engineering, and while employed in the PT department also worked as an assistant in the Chemistry Department. He later became a Professor of Chemistry. Yet even in his sixties, his strength showed. On one occasion, Jake and his wife were leaving the Golden Theater on Washington at Thirteenth in an unexpected downpour. Washington Avenue was deep with water. Jake picked up his wife and ran with her to their car parked on the other side of Washington in the next block, while astounded Miners gaped.

Henry Babcock of the Civil Engineering Department considered himself quite a wit, and frequently made students the butt of his jokes. One student came back at Babcock immediately, to the laughter of his classmates. The professor asked whether the student had seen Phil Silvers in Top Banana. Since he had not, Babcock explained that Silvers had told a joke and one of his foils had told a better one. Silvers said, "You topped me."

"Yes," the butt of Silver's joke replied.

"Don't do it again!" Babcock shouted.

The student understood, but it was too late. With Babcock teaching 3 courses on the student's schedule over that and the following semesters, it cost him a letter grade in each course, or 10 quality points, which he could ill afford to lose. Babcock became "Bad cock", and his type of professor was perfect for the AAUP. But who was there for the student?

James G. Johnstone in the Civil Engineering Department suffered from some nervous problem with his eyes that caused them to continually dart left and right. No one could tell where he was looking, and as a distraction, it was off the charts. Finally, students learned to look away the whole time of his lectures in order to take proper notes. Johnstone's lectures were good, but the distraction interfered greatly with the instruction.

Donald Marsh in the Math Department was a rather queer duck with a PhD from Boulder. He liked to sit in the back of the classroom, with half of the class working on the blackboard. He would dictate problems for everyone to work, then critique the students at the board. Nobody could hide, as Marsh would then switch out the seated students for those up front. If he didn't like the class's performance, he would then either assign homework for the next day or put a pop quiz on the board. Nobody liked working at the blackboard, but nobody missed one of Marsh's classes either.

One student gave Marsh a problem his father had sent. If one started with any triangle and drew lines at thirty degrees from the sides at each point, the resulting intersections would form an equilateral triangle. The problem was to prove it. March returned the next day with the proof using the law of sines and cosines, then assigned the problem as homework to the class. That was the end of taking problems to Marsh.

Crystal Paul Keating, Geology Professor, had lost his wife in an automobile accident. Because there was conflicting testimony from witnesses, he painted his 1938 Hudson Terraplane two colors – the right half red and the left half black. He said that witnesses now only needed to know red from black, not right from left.

Prof Keating's hands shook so badly that students could not understand how he could see anything through his shaking hand lens. But he could describe everything he saw very well. When lecturing in Crystallography, he drew crystal structures on the board, his shaking hand making the chalk sound like a machine gun as it vibrated against the chalkboard, but when he actually started drawing, the lines were perfectly straight. No one could understand how he did it.

Keating also had one of the largest and best collections of rocks and minerals in the Rockies and possibly the nation. To teach

Crystallography he used his own private collection which students sometimes borrowed to augment their own collections. Regardless of specimens disappearing, Keating never complained, and his collection never seemed to become reduced in size.

In Mineralogy, Keating waylaid many unwary students. He had three special exams and each year he stunned the students with at least one. In one test he had twenty-five specimens of green mineral, his "all green" test, which looked alike but weren't, and were very difficult to identify. The second was an "all white" test, again with the specimens appearing identical. Third was his "all sphalerite" test. All the specimens were different in color, fracture, striations, and apparent crystal structure, but when hydrochloric acid was applied, gave off the tell-tale hydrogen sulfide aroma which easily identified the rock as sphalerite. These tests were designed to force the students into being extremely thorough, even when pressed for time, and the result was an abnormal number of flunks. Sometimes the upper-classmen warned the sophomores taking Mineralogy, but many didn't get the word and paid the price.

Doc (Leslie W.) Leroy was not only a frequent party-goer at the various fraternity events, but he was a force for good when it came to teaching geology. Once on a Geomorphology exam a student lost a point on one question, but then Leroy waxed eloquently in commenting on the student's answer to another question (yes, department chairman Leroy graded his own freshman exams.) The student received a score of 100, with the comment from Leroy that the exam had earned that grade, regardless of missing a point. No other Mines professor to the authors' knowledge ever did something like that or would.

One of the fixtures in the Chemistry was **Leonard W. Hartkemeir**. In 1958, Hartke was lecturing in the large interior lecture hall in Coolbaugh Hall which held several hundred students. About 10 minutes into the lecture, the lights went out, throwing the lecture hall into complete darkness. There were no emergency lights. After several minutes, Hartke said that enough time had been wasted, and continued his lecture, with the students unable to see their notebooks or their notes. The room was still in total darkness when the lecture hour was concluded, and the students fumbled their way out the door to head to their next class.

Another notable individual was an instructor in Metallurgy named **Robert O. Day**. He was referred to as "Doodeley Abba" because of the way he walked. He moved as if he had no spine, and his head went forward and backwards like a turkey's when it walks. Day usually wrote every word of his lecture on the board as he talked, but the students needed to pay close attention as his writing was practically illegible. His lectures were challenging and required creative thinking to piece together.

William H. Jurney, Associate Professor in Mathematics, was a brilliant mathematician but the terror of the department. He was so good in calculus that he could work a problem on the board while explaining it thoroughly, then notice that time was about gone, and start skipping steps going directly to the answer and leaving students mystified as to how he arrived there. A student needed roller skates to keep up with him.

Raymond R. Gutzman, Assistant Professor in Mathematics, was teaching in summer school to a group of students who were repeating the second semester of Integral Calculus. Halfway through his first lecture, he sensed that he was leaving the students behind, so gave an impromptu exam. The next morning, he told the astonished class that everyone had failed the exam, and it only covered the first semester of Calculus which all had taken and passed. Since the students clearly hadn't mastered the prerequisite material, Gutzman decided his class would cover the first semester again. In two weeks, he had finished the Differential Calculus material that the students should have known, then began the work in Integral Calculus.

Dr. Paul F. Bartunek, Professor of Physics, once took off his shirt, lay down on the table in the Physics Lecture Hall, put a large rock on his chest, and invited the strongest students to attempt to break the rock with a sledge hammer. Several jumped at the chance, thinking that he would be injured by the act. Of course, the rock just absorbed the impact without transferring it to the Professor's chest, leaving some students amazed, but most just amused. He had made his point.

Late one May evening, Assistant Professor **Albert L. Gosman** of the Mechanical Engineering Department ran into one of his students enjoying an ice cream sundae at the Dairy Bar on Ford Avenue and made a comment that he should be home studying for the next morning's final exam in Thermodynamics. When the student's exam paper was returned, the grade was 96, with the query written in red ink: "What flavor ice cream did you eat?"

Many of the faculty were irreverently referred to with pet names by their students. Professor Bartunek in Physics was always "Black Bart", Malcolm Hepworth in Metallurgy was "Boy Wonder" because he looked like a teenager, Prof Francis Smiley in Mechanical Engineering was "Fannie Smiley", Johnstone was "Shaky", Robert Osborn in math was "Unborn", Paul Fritts in Descriptive Geometry was "Fritz the Sh_ts", Augustus Houghton in Chemistry was "Bumble and Stumble," and Rudy Epis in Geology was "Round Rudy" to name a few.

Hepworth was also called many worse names, as he once referred to his lecturing Mines students as "casting pearls before swine." Fortunately for Hepworth, this was after Senior Day had been abolished. His lectures may have contained a pearl or two, but they were so convoluted as to be totally opaque to even his fellow faculty members.

Mines had no lack of colorful professors before the 1970s, but **Robert E. D. Woolsey** would be one to top the list. A math professor who came to Mines in 1969, Gene Woolsey was an arch-conservative who sported a sign in his bookcase above his desk saying "F-ck Communism." He meant it too and held no truck with progressive faculty. He stressed the marriage of practical experience with technical and communication expertise for the successful completion of anything and everything and was arguably the world's foremost practitioner in the application of management science and operations research techniques to real-world problems and situations. Always in opposition to ivory-tower theorists, Dr. Woolsey was probably CSM's outstanding personality from 1970 until he retired, and a throwback to the old Mines. Gene never solicited nor accepted any government money or grants. He believed his mission was to serve the American public by "graduating the entrepreneurs of tomorrow so socialist politicians would have someone to tax." He and his students, espousing practical operations research, had saved American companies more than one billion dollars when he stopped recording project savings in 2010.

There were others who should probably have made this list, including **Sergeant Foley** of the ROTC Department. He became the butt of many jokes and pranks, but always remained cheerful and helpful. A victim of a mid-1950s "RIF" (reduction in force), Foley was a former major who served at Mines as a sergeant to accumulate his full twenty years for retirement.

In short, there were undoubtedly many more interesting stories about faculty, but they were unknown to the students. That was a shame.

The Changing of the Faculty:

The traditional faculty of Mines was heavily invested in corporate America, teaching students to become excellent engineering employees or entrepreneurs, but in any case, entering private employment and contributing to the general welfare of the citizens of the United States through their engineering and business expertise. Until the 1950s, professors without terminal degrees were in the vast majority, usually amounting to 80 to 90 percent of the faculty. In 1956, 22% of the faculty held terminal degrees, but then hiring practices changed, and in 1961 34% of the faculty held PhD or DSc degrees, 56% of those being in the departments of Chemistry and Geology. By 2016 over 90% of the faculty would have terminal degrees, and the day of the highly skilled practitioner of engineering coming back to Mines to teach was a thing of the past.

According to Professor Emeritus Robert J. Weimer, faculty before the introduction of the Horizon Plan in 1954 suffered from many deficiencies. A Committee on Development was formed which worked out a seven-point plan for faculty improvement "in the areas of salaries, teaching loads, physical facilities, improved teaching, support staff, professional development, and academic leaves." Weimer himself was hired in 1957 under a plan calling for the hiring of PhDs from other institutions, creating time and incentives for research projects utilizing funded graduate assistants, and funds for faculty travel. This new faculty was to have interests in basic or applied scientific research, in Weimer's words, "an essential ingredient to Mines (sic) success". To Weimer, Chauvenet was just the name of a building on campus.

As a result of funding campaigns, endowed faculty chairs, normally an indicator of alumni support for a school, went from zero in 1961 to where in 2016 about one in ten professors were occupying endowed chairs. Clearly, it cannot be said that the alumni were being miserly in their support for academics at Mines. But do endowed chairs foster better instruction in the classroom? Nationwide evidence indicates that it does not: it merely provides professors with a better living without driving up costs to the state.

It is important to understand PhD programs and their objectives to appreciate the effect on Mines when the faculty goes from 10% to 90% PhDs. Depending on the objectives of the school, this can be a good thing or a bad thing. Overall in the United States, "creeping credentialism" has taken over so that college degrees are seen to be nearly mandatory for all employment above the level of manual laborer. The federal government is largely the culprit, as it now issues occupational licenses for about 30% of all jobs in the US, compared to under 5% in 1950. Skills are no longer important: it is only necessary to have the proper college degree or certificate.

Traditionally, Mines heads of departments and full professors were in evidence teaching not only undergraduate courses, but even freshman and sophomore required courses. Rarely does this happen in research universities except in cases where a famous professor lectures once per week in an extremely large lecture hall and by video to other rooms. The course is then listed under that professor's name, although the remaining two class meetings are held in normal-sized sections by graduate teaching assistants. On the student's grade report, however, is the famous professor's name, and the student can boast that he learned from the famous man.

Prior to the 1970s, the job of the Mines faculty, first and foremost, was to teach the undergraduates and produce fledgling engineers with a great deal of expertise and knowledge to work in private industry. After the 1970s, the job involved the writing of scholarly papers, and to gain respect for the school among academicians across the nation. Most important of all, the Mines faculty was to attract money for research, primarily from government agencies, and to a lesser degree from corporate America. To do that they needed to have credentials, academic publications, books, and a name recognized in their line of expertise. Teaching had to be sidelined or avoided altogether as a counter-productive use of a faculty member's time.

The pressures on untenured faculty increased dramatically as research papers became required. Formerly, faculty had to toe the line in what they taught, and how they taught it. Their job was simply to teach the material that the student would be expected to have mastered by graduation. Faculty members knew what to do, and, in the main, they did it. After the 1970s, untenured faculty had to meet research and publication demands. This required a different type of individual, in an altogether different line of work. What emerged were research-oriented faculty, often totally unsuited for teaching, and even more often, did not want to teach. Mines was not improved by the result.

The change in the faculty over time can be shown in a series of charts from data furnished by the CSM administration:

1925, Highest Faculty Degrees

Department	Dept Head	DSc/PhD	Master	BS/PE	Total
Chemistry	DSc	2	1	2	5
Civil Eng	MS	0	1	1	2
Desc Geometry	EM	0	1	1	2
Electrical Eng	EE	0	0	1	1
Geology	PhD	1	2	2	5
Language	AM	0	2	1	3
Mathematics	MS	0	3	1	4
Mechanical Eng	ME	0	2	0	2
Metallurgy	MS	0	3	3	6
Military Science	MS	0	1	1	2
Mining Eng	EM	1	0	2	3
Petroleum Eng	MA	0	1	1	2
Physical Training	AB	0	0	3	3
Physics	MS	0	1	1	2
Totals		4	18	20	42
Percent of Total		9.5%	42.9%	47.6%	

The comparison with 1961-2 is stark, and the terminal degrees (PhD and DSc) were concentrated in a few departments. Master's Degrees became the norm for teachers, but PhDs were rapidly becoming more numerous as befitting the increased emphasis on research.

1962 Highest Faculty Degrees.

Department	Dept Head	DSc/PhD	Non-Doctor	Total
Chemistry	PhD	10	5	15
Civil Eng	BS	0	5	5
Desc Geometry	MS	0	4	4
Electrical Eng	MS	0	2	2
English	MA	4	6	10
Geology	D.Sc	12	6	18
Geophysics	Geol Eng	2	3	5
Mathematics	MS	1	9	10

Mechanical Eng	MS	0	3	3
Metallurgy	MS	2	7	9
Military Science	M.EM	0	11	11
Mining Eng	EM	2	4	6
Petroleum Eng	MS	1	1	2
Petroleum Refining	PhD	2	2	4
Physical Training	MA	0	5	5
Physics	PhD	3	4	7
Totals		39	77	116
Percent of Total		33.6%	66.4%	

From less than 10 percent of the faculty having terminal degrees, in 1961 a third of the faculty had earned a PhD or its equivalent. However, a number of department heads, even with doctorates in their departments, were still in their chairs. Over 56% of the doctorates were concentrated in two departments, Chemistry and Geology, and six of the sixteen departments had none at all. Only four departments were headed by a PhD, and the replacement of Master's Degree holders with PhDs was taking some time.

By 2016, however, the conversion to an all PhD faculty body was nearly complete. If anyone doubted the importance of research money coming into the college, they needed to look no further than the mission of Mines. As released by the school in 2016: Mines was:

"...a specialized research institution with high admission standards and a unique mission in energy, minerals, materials science and engineering and associated engineering and science fields."

Its mission was stated to be *"the generation of new knowledge and educating students and professionals in the applied sciences, engineering and associated fields related to:...the discovery and recovery of the Earth's resources; their conversion to materials and energy; their utilization in advanced processes and products; the economic and social systems necessary to ensure their prudent and provident use in a sustainable global society; and the preservation and stewardship of the Earth's environment."*

First and foremost, the mission was "to be the generation of new knowledge..." In addition, the goals of Agenda 21 had been written into the mission of Mines, although Agenda 21 itself (now Agenda 2030) is not mentioned. These goals had been spelled out in great detail in a 40-chapter, 300-page document titled Agenda 21, signed and adopted by 179 nations, including the United States, in 1992 at the UN Conference on Environment and Development in Rio de Janeiro. Most Americans, if they have heard of Agenda 21 at all, still believe it is some type of conspiracy theory, but professional educators know that it is not. See Appendix G for a discussion of Agenda 21 and why it is important to Mines.

In 2016 Mines pledged to advance

> "...these areas with the conviction that future infrastructural and societal developments are dependent upon the availability of energy, the sustainable development of the Earth's resources, the synthesis of materials, and the environmental consequences of these processes and their interactions. [Mines believes that] these inherently related focus areas represent not only extraordinarily fertile ground on which to base the strategic development of the institution, but they also embrace [its] responsibility to attract, shape and provide engineering and scientific talent to help address the technological and societal challenges implied."

It became all about the graduate school and the obtaining of research money to advance the reputation of the administration and faculty of Mines.

Between the 1950s and 2016 the administration changed the faculty in order to change the direction of Mines. During the 1950s and early 60s, Mines faculty members were heavily Republican, often making no bones about their political orientation, sometimes not even in class.

For many years, Mines pursued a running battle with the highly progressive American Association of University Professors (AAUP). Essentially a union for university faculty, the AAUP supposedly championed three main ideas: academic freedom, tenure, and benefits for university faculty. It promoted the idea that an administration, governing body, or even a university's primary benefactor had no say in regulating faculty behavior, or what faculty members taught, how they taught it, where and to whom.

The AAUP was formed in 1915 following principles laid down by progressive educator John Dewey. Edwin R. A. Seligman, a Marxist political economist championing the income tax at Columbia (where Dewey then was) headed a committee to draw up the principles of academic freedom for the AAUP. Seligman wished to limit administrative interference with faculty activities, including research, teaching, and other activities. His model was that of German universities where faculty had successfully been able to limit the power of the princes and governments that paid their salaries. Throughout his life he pushed for the concept of tenure wherein a faculty member was granted lifetime employment.

The traditional relationship of the administration to the faculty remained stable until about 1969 when the AAUP began its war of conquest at Mines, although relations were becoming increasingly strained. Faculty contracts continued to be renegotiated each year until the establishment of de jure tenure in 1989. In practice, the associate and full professors had long enjoyed de facto tenure, and only the instructors and assistant professors found themselves at risk in the annual negotiations. Even then, it had been CSM's practice to notify a faculty member at the start of the spring semester that his contract would not be renewed after the following year, effectively giving the fired instructor over a year's notice. The administration was hardly the unfeeling beast the AAUP charged it with being in cases like that of mathematics assistant professor Winton Laubach.

In 1969, an AAUP chapter was established on campus, and agitation for a faculty senate and tenure, higher salaries, and various employment benefits began. The first great test of the AAUP versus the Mines administration followed rapidly in 1973 when the AAUP published a bulletin entitled *Academic Freedom and Tenure: Colorado School of Mines,* in which the union took dead aim at CSM's policies. The bulletin cited the case of Winton Laubach who was going blind from a hereditary eye disease, and had been notified in April of 1969 that his contract after the academic year of 1969-1970 would not be renewed.

Professor Laubach's problem was of long standing, and it was known that he possessed tunnel vision and couldn't drive at night during the 1950s. Unfortunately, his condition had become much worse as the disease advanced. Laubach requested a hearing before the Board of Trustees which was denied, but the Board did extend Laubach's contract until the end of the academic year 1970-1971, effectively giving the assistant professor two years' notice. That was not enough for the AAUP investigating committee. It concluded that although the school's (and trustees') decision might have been valid and correct, Mines should be censured for not affording Laubach proper due process and not granting CSM's faculty members tenure as "generally understood and accepted in American higher education." Mines needed to toe the politically correct line (a term dating from its creation in the Soviet Union to describe one's adherence to the Communist Party's dictates), and was placed on the AAUP censure list. In accordance with AAUP strategy, a compromise was not possible — a school must accept the AAUP's opinion or pay the consequences. It was not until 1992, after the introduction of a satisfactory (to the AAUP) tenure policy by President Ansell, that Mines was finally removed from the AAUP's censure list.

The AAUP also demonstrated its hostility toward all things military by agitating against the Mines ROTC program from the very beginning. Many Mines students supported the AAUP in clamoring for ROTC's removal. Even under assault from the radical left in the student body and faculty, ROTC and the tradition of Mines as the backbone of the US Army Corps of Engineers remained strong for another two decades.

By the 1990s, the faculty had become increasingly powerful and self-absorbed with its perks, graduate programs, scholarly publications, right to teach what and how they wanted, and most of all, tenure. Who cared about student evaluations that tended to be counter-productive anyway? Once Senior Day had punished poor or autocratic faculty with exposure and penalties that could not be disregarded, but it was long gone.

With the AAUP pushing all the way, the faculty eventually decided it needed a representative on the Board of Directors to make its desires known to the Board and administration. A non-voting faculty representative was therefore put on the Board, and Mines became completely co-opted to progressivism. The faculty had its union with a representative involved in the management of the school, tenure was in place, and academic freedom trumped effective student instruction.

Chapter 10 - Enrollments at Mines

Although most elite universities actively tout the quality of their undergraduate and graduate education and numbers of masters and doctorates granted, CSM was truly different. It let its alumni speak for it, and they told of earning an excellent education that no other university could match. As Mary Holt wrote in 1949, "The proof...is in the achievements of Mines alumni who occupy important executive and engineering posts in every mineral producing country in the world." She might have overstated the case for Mines somewhat, but she was essentially correct. This dominance of the small school in Golden was due to Dr. Chauvenet's vision. The experience of Mines was not a rarified two or three years in graduate work for a committee of several professors, or a wild ride for four years in non-stop socializing, but an entire immersion in an honorable engineering life. Almost every commencement address and congratulation by Mines administrators included an admonishment concerning good citizenship in addition to excellence in engineering. Never was this a fad or the isolated opinions of a few individuals; the entire tenor of Mines was structured to build men upon whom the United States and its mineral industries could depend under all circumstances.

Right from the founding of the school, Mines operated at full capacity as measured both by the number of its faculty and the size of its physical plant. Beginning with the presidency of Dr. Regis Chauvenet, Mines was forced to turn away applicants, at the time a measure of a successful school. By 1902 when Dr. Chauvenet stepped down, the undergraduate enrollment at Mines in mining engineering was greater than any other university in the United States. Its undergraduate instruction was so excellent, it was also first in the nation in attracting students with degrees from other universities, colleges, and foreign institutions to another undergraduate program.

In the early days, as reported in the Circular of Information No. 1, 1903 of the United States Bureau of Education, titled History of Higher Education in Colorado, the requirements for admission to CSM were:

- *Candidates had to be at least 17 years of age.*
- *They had to sustain examinations in English, geography, arithmetic, algebra, geometry, and zoology.*

• *Graduation diplomas from accredited high schools were accepted in lieu of examinations to entering a class.*

The 1903 Circular stated that the education was free to bona fide residents of Colorado, but that students from out of state were charged $50 per term. That was an extremely high tuition, but still students from other states flocked to the school due to its reputation. This situation continued until the boom in education following World War I.

Under Dr. Chauvenet, the school began to feature an enrollment pattern that persisted until late in the 1960s. Each year, 10 to 15% of the student body graduated from a student body in the fall of which 15 to 18% were seniors, 20 to 23% were juniors, 25 to 29% were sophomores, and 31 to 35% were freshmen. In general, less than 40% were upper division students, and that was only maintained by transferring in students from other colleges who had taken most or all of their lower division courses at other universities. Mines was forced by Colorado law to accept all qualified Colorado high school graduates as freshmen, but in practice, the fearsome reputation of the school limited the number of in-state applications. Following World War II, the president of Mines, Dr. Ben H. Parker, was forced to use a priority system to allot enrollment slots to applicants for the freshman class due to the heavy influx of veterans. He established a limit on enrollment of 1,200 in order to maintain high standards. This limit remained in place until the 1960s when the administration took active steps to increase enrollments at all costs and grow the school. Part of that push came from the increasing size of CSM's physical plant, as enrollments were needed to meet the increased costs. Tuition increased steadily during the 1950s, but that was not enough. "Growth" replaced "Excelsior" in the administration offices.

To broaden the school in the 1950's and 1960s, Mines gave out scholarships to two residents of each state in the union. Not all of them were awarded each year, as some states were without applicants. There were other scholarships granted for a variety of reasons, but Mines had learned that awarding scholarships could be a tricky business.

In 1952, CSM awarded three E-Day (Engineers' Day) Scholarships to Colorado high school graduates, based on a competitive examination. But not all applicants were dedicated engineering students. Three students from the same high school placed first, second, and third in the competition, and the scholarships were to be awarded at an E-Day presentation. The administration got involved and decided to limit a school to only one scholarship. The second and third place winners were arbitrarily moved to fourth and fifth and their scholarships awarded to others. As events unfolded, the scholarships were unused, and were quietly given to the original winners. The whole thing was a huge mess. From that day onwards, the Mines administration and the E-Day committees followed their own rules, regardless of who won a scholarship and what high school they attended.

The number of E-Day scholarships rose steadily over the years to nine being awarded to Colorado residents at the present time. Scholarships were desperately needed by many middle-class students, as by 1950, in-state tuition was $100 per semester, and out-of-state tuition $212.50. By the late 1950s, tuition had risen to over $600 per year for non-resident students. In 2016, annual tuition was $15,690 for Colorado residents, $34,020 for non-resident students, and over 70% of Mines students received some form of financial aid. Even in the late 1950s, most upper classmen were on scholarships, regardless of their residency. Mines was an expensive school, particularly for out-of-state residents.

In the 1950s Mines started requiring the Pre-Engineering Inventory Exam to be given to all entering freshmen on campus during freshman orientation. Low scores were used to counsel potential students to seek another college. Achievement tests were given in math during orientation that determined a student's placement in remedial mathematics, regular math, and advanced math. The same was done for English proficiency, but with only two possible placements, remedial and regular English. The Scholastic Aptitude Test (SAT) was also used to counsel students on whether or not to enroll at Mines. The result was an ever-improving freshman class, but until the 1960s, the flunk/drop-out rate remained extremely high.

Until the institution of new degree programs in the late 1960s to increase the breath of engineering offerings, the areas of specialization were very limited. The first two years of study were common for all Mines students. With all six options (equating to majors in other universities) in place, the upper division breakout was generally about: Metallurgical Engineering 27-29%, Mining Engineering 19-21%, Geological Engineering 18-20%, Petroleum Engineering 11-13%, Petroleum Refining Engineering 10-12% and

Geophysical Engineering 9-11%. These numbers varied somewhat over the years, with mining generally falling and metallurgy and petroleum gaining. Geophysics was generally the smallest of the options, and after World War II, metallurgy was always the largest.

According to the US Office of Education, Mines led the nation in 1960 in undergraduate enrollments in three majors, Geological Engineering, Geophysical Engineering, and Mining Engineering, and was third in Metallurgical Engineering and Petroleum Engineering when combining the two petroleum options. In fact, there was no comparable department in the United States to the CSM Geophysical Engineering Department. As late as 1954, Mines was the only school in the U.S. concentrated on engineering for the mineral industry. To say that Mines was a highly specialized school would be to understate the obvious, but it was also the hands down leader in half of its courses of study, and third in the other three. To have such leadership in all of its teaching areas was probably unmatched by any other university. In 1960, Mines could claim to be the top university in the nation in its areas of specialty, both in quantity and quality. The enrollments at Mines, along with the number of faculty and graduates are given for each year in Appendix C.

In the 1960s and 1970s, however, the siren song sung by the Lorelei was "Diversify or Die." Mines added Mineral Engineering-Mathematics, Mineral Engineering-Physics, and Mineral Engineering-Chemistry, and then went on an orgy of branching out into other disciplines. It was thought that CSM's specialty areas were declining, evidenced primarily by declining enrollments. New programs and degrees needed to be added to the curriculum not only to attract students, but to remain relevant in the modern world

In actuality, American society was changing under the avalanche of baby-boomers who were no longer willing to labor for long hours in the trenches as Mines required. The production industries that were the mainstay of Mines grads were dirty, mostly located in remote or unpleasant places, and generally without large offices, high-priced furniture, and beautiful secretaries. All this suddenly became very unappealing.

Dedication to study had previously been the hallmark of earlier generations, but many baby-boomers had been reared indulgently and avoided tough courses of study. They handed engineering throughout the world by default to students of other countries, most notably Japan, China, and India. Enrollments began to stagnate or drop, and the administration decided Mines had to diversify and dilute its requirements in order to survive.

By 2015, Mines offered a total of seventy degrees, both undergraduate and graduate, and two Non-Degree Graduate Certificates. In 1960 Mines offered the degree of Professional Engineer, a Master of Science, and Doctor of Science in the degree-granting departments.

1960:

Professional Engineer: (6)	Master of Science: (6)	Doctor of Science: (4)
Mining Eng.	Mining Eng.	Mining Eng.
Metallurgical Eng.	Metallurgical Eng.	Metallurgical Eng
Geological Eng.	Geological Eng.	Geological Eng.
Geophysical Eng.	Geophysical Eng.	Geophysical Eng.
Petroleum Eng.	Petroleum Eng.	
Petroleum Refining Eng.	Petroleum Refining Eng.	

2015:

Bachelor of Science: (16)	Master of Science: (23)
Applied Mathematics & Statistics	Applied Mathematics & Statistics
Civil Engineering	Civil Engineering
Environmental Engineering	Environmental Engineering Science
Computer Science	Computer Science
Electrical Engineering	Electrical Engineering
Mechanical Engineering	Mechanical Engineering
Economics & Business	Mineral and Energy Economics
Geological Engineering	Geological Engineering
Geophysical Engineering	Geophysical Engineering
Mining Engineering	Mining and Earth Systems Eng
Petroleum Engineering	Petroleum Engineering
Chemical Engineering	Chemical Engineering
Chemical and Biochemical Eng.	Geochemistry
Chemistry	Chemistry
Metallurgical & Materials Eng.	Metallurgical & Materials Eng.
Engineering Physics	Applied Physics
Hydrology	Engineering & Technology Mgmt
Materials Science	Geology
Nuclear Engineering	Geophysics
Underground Construction & Tunneling	

Master of Engineering (ME): (5)	Professional Masters: (3)
Engineer of Mines	Mineral Exploration
Geological Engineer	Environmental Geochemistry
Metallurgical & Materials Science	Petroleum Reservoir Systems
Petroleum Engineering	
Nuclear Engineering	

Masters: (1)
Master of International Political Economy of Resources

Non-Degree Graduate Certificates: (2)
Graduate Certificate in International Political Economy
Graduate Certificate in Science and Technology Policy

Doctor of Philosophy (PhD) Degrees: (22)

Applied Mathematics & Statistics	Civil and Environmental Eng
Environmental Engineering Science	Computer Science
Electrical Engineering	Mechanical Engineering
Mineral and Energy Economics	Geology
Geological Engineering	Geophysics
Geophysical Engineering	Mining and Earth Systems Eng
Petroleum Engineering	Chemical Engineering
Applied Chemistry	Geochemistry
Metallurgical and Materials Engineering	Applied Physics
Hydrology	Materials Science
Nuclear Engineering	Underground Constr. & Tunneling

It is to be noted that the Doctor of Science (DSc) that Mines formerly awarded was changed to the more universally accepted Doctor of Philosophy (PhD). In addition, more than half of the degree programs at Mines in 2015 were not engineering at all, marking the School not as a school of engineering, much less of mineral engineering, but of science and technology. Even more importantly, Mines now gives degrees in Economics, Business, and Management, normally given by business schools. What comes next?

Clearly, as of 2016 it was no longer a "School of Mines," but rather Colorado's Institute of Technology. The school and alumni will have to work exceedingly hard to keep the legislature from changing the name or incorporating it into the University of Colorado as "University of Colorado at Golden" (UCAG.) Perhaps CU will move its business and technology schools to Golden in a grand consolidation move.

In 1961, Mines presented 184 silver diplomas to graduating seniors earning a Professional Engineer degree (unbelievably, one student received degrees in two options), and also awarded 23 Masters and Doctorates. In 1970, the numbers had risen to 229 undergraduate degrees, and 57 advanced. The great majority of the undergraduate degrees were the new four-year Bachelor of Science rather than the Professional Engineer degree, and it was clear that the easier curricula were the students' choice for the future. The student to faculty ratio had risen from 9:1 in the late 1950s to

17:1 in 2016, and the average class size had increased from 20 to 34 students. To put the situation into perspective, 51 students were awarded the degree of Metallurgical Engineer in 1961 out of 184 total professional degrees, but by 2016, Mines awarded 835 BS degrees, but only 42 were earned by students in Metallurgical and Materials Engineering. The flagship program of study in 1961, accounting for about 28% of the graduates, had become nearly irrelevant in 2016 with only 5% of the graduates.

The data in Appendix C is revealing and speaks to a number of issues. One that it doesn't is the drop-out rate, in particular the drop of enrollments from the fall to the spring semester. From 1949 through the 1950s, data are available on fall versus spring enrollments for 1949, 1950, 1951, and 1957 as follows:

Year	Fall	Spring	% Drop
1949	1,200	1,134	5.5%
1950	1,075	852	20.7%
1951	905	835	7.7%
1957	1'127	1,027	8.9%

Assuming that 1950 is an outlier, possibly due to graduate school enrollments of around 90 students being included in the fall number (giving a new percentage drop of 13.5%,) the drop in enrollments between fall and the following spring averaged to 8.9%. The vast majority of these dropouts were freshman. Assuming that new enrollments by transfers off-set at least a two or three percentage points of the drop, and that the breakdown of the student body was approximately 16% Seniors, 20% Juniors, 30% Sophomores, and 34% Freshmen, somewhere around a third of the freshman class didn't survive the first semester.

The average enrollment at Mines by decade is somewhat difficult to pin down as apparently graduate and undergraduate enrollments were sometimes included into a single yearly figure. The following table gives those numbers and the percentage increase or decrease from the preceding decade:

Years	Ave. Enrollment	% Increase/Decrease
1876-1889	50	
1890-1899	151	202%
1900-1909	292	93%
1910-1919	264	-9% (WWI)
1920-1929	463	76%

1930-1939	636	37%
1940-1949	789	24% (WWII)
1950-1959	1,055	34%
1960-1969	1,543	46%
1970-1979	1,945	26%
1980-1989	2,235	15%
1990-1999	2,223	-0.04%
2000-2009	3,218	45%
2010-2015	4,413	37%

In essence, Mines has enjoyed steady growth throughout its history buffeted only slightly by exogenous events. The first one to depress enrollments was World War I, followed by World War II. There was no discernable effect from the Great Depression, but there certainly was as college age men were called into the army during the latter part of World War II. Then enrollments burgeoned as veterans returned to college using the GI Bill, and that effect lasted until 1958 with servicemen returning to college after serving during the Korean War.

The greatest and longest lasting drop in enrollments at Mines began in 1983, and Mines didn't recover to its 1983 levels until 1996. The cause of this sag is controversial, but has been blamed by the Mines administration on a slowdown in the oil industry. During this period there was a highly touted "glut" of oil on the world market that drove down oil prices, most notably in 1986. Supposedly that led to fewer college-age individuals being interested in oil-related employment, and therefore decreased demand for a Mines degree. There was certainly hysteria in some quarters, but during the Reagan and George H. W. Bush years, the American economy did extremely well. Oil exploration was down somewhat, but other sectors were surging.

Since Mines students had traditionally gone into a wide range of industries after graduation, the argument that the oil industry slowdown caused a huge decline in the demand for Mines graduates seems over-hyped. Earlier graduates were still experiencing a great demand for their services, and it is more probable that the direction taken by the Mines administration to stress ecological concerns and touchy-feely subjects made Mines students much less desirable to management in its traditional industries. There is also anecdotal evidence that the decline in standards and rigor at CSM caused management in mineral and petroleum industries to look at schools other than Mines for starting engineers. Nor were Mines graduates able to command premium starting salaries.

Once the news got around that newly-minted Mines graduates, with their much less rigorous BS degrees, were not getting hired, prospective students went elsewhere. Somehow, the Mines administration had forgotten that its traditional industries were rock-bottom conservative, and joining the tree-huggers, anti-pipeline, and anti-oil exploration groups was not the way to success. The alumni, also generally conservative, were shunned, and at one point, the Almuni Association was actually kicked off campus. Some alumni, tired of being treated as the dark side of Mines, no longer went out of their way to hire Mines graduates. It was a perfect storm, and mostly self-inflicted. Politics were best kept out of the boardroom, but the Mines administration got ahead of the curve and were punished by the industries that had made Mines world-renown. This is a seminal point, as the current direction of Mines indicates this same situation can be easily repeated in the future.

Mistaking why Mines had become less marketable, the administration diversified its degree offerings to rope in students like a circus barker. It worked to an extent, but continued success from this time forward depended on politicians keeping the spigot opened in Washington for implementing Agenda 21 and fighting climate change. Climate change is indeed occurring, as it has throughout the history of the earth, but there is still no irrefutable evidence that this round of climate change is man-made. Even the "hockey-stick" graph has been exposed as a scam; the program producing it gives the same graph regardless of the data being input.

Hopefully the Mines administration will re-evaluate its strategy in attracting students and once more "dance with those that brung them." There is one thing for sure: current wisdom is always wrong and going with the flow to get along does not produce great faculty, great students, great graduates, and a great institution of higher education.

Chapter 11 - Student Life? You've Got to be Kidding

There were many aspects to student life on campus in the 1950s, but orientation, testing, registration, and hazing (called Freshmen Agitation) left an indelible mark on all first-year students.

The orientation of freshmen and other new students was perfunctory. The Dean of Students welcomed the entire incoming freshman class in a large lecture hall in the Old Chemistry Building through 1952, then gave his greeting beginning with 1953 in Coolbaugh Hall. Throughout most of the decade of the 1950s, Dean Burger was fond of saying, "Look to your right. Now look to your left. Only one of you will graduate. Which one will it be?" The statistics bore out Dean Burger's comments, and it was sobering to hear.

The vast majority of students had arrived alone, and most without transportation. Many had received correspondence from the fraternities, and already made tentative plans to live in a fraternity house. Others had signed up for the school dormitories when they were built, but most simply found housing in Golden, particularly students from Denver or Colorado who were able to come to Golden during the summer and make prior arrangements. One of the authors came to Golden about a week before the start of orientation in 1952, obtained a list of rooms in Golden from the Registrar's office, and after looking at several, found a room for $15.00 per month on Washington Street. The other author arrived in Denver by train from St. Paul, Minnesota with two suitcases. He had corresponded with the ATO House and was met at the station by an ATO active. The author was driven to Golden where he was put up in the ATO house while he found a room in town. It only took a day, and he was set for orientation and rush week.

That was how the system worked back then for out-of-state freshman. Most fraternities required their actives from out-of-state to write letters of introduction to incoming freshmen from their localities or states, welcoming them to Mines and offering to provide transportation to campus and temporary housing. Not only was this impressive to the frosh, it worked to the fraternities' benefit. Arriving freshmen could be evaluated before rush week, and housing in the fraternity houses offered if the prospect looked good.

Probably ninety percent of out-of-state students (not including international students) were first welcomed by the fraternities and found housing through them, if not in the fraternity houses themselves.

Few of the entering freshmen during the 1950s possessed automobiles, certainly less than 15%. Most of the ones who did came from wealthy families, and rapidly became popular with the students without transportation. As a result, owners of cars usually flunked out in a semester or two, being unable to concentrate on their studies when a vehicle could readily take them into Denver or up to Boulder. By the spring semester probably fewer than five percent of freshmen possessed cars, compared with 15-25% for sophomores, 25-35% for juniors, and 35-50% for seniors.

In 1952, freshman orientation took up the better part of three days, mostly spent at the old Chemistry Building. In addition to Dean Burger, all of the heads of the Departments spoke along with some of the professors the freshmen would have, particularly in Geology and Chemistry. Frosh Bibles (information booklets) were passed out, and the students were told they needed to memorize the booklets' contents. There were about 360 prospective students to take the placement tests and be enrolled as freshmen, including one girl from Texas, Nancy Easley, the 13th female ever to enroll at CSM. Since there were 128 graduates 4 years later, the "one of three" prediction was clearly correct, as the graduating number included later transfers as well as students that took more than 4 years to complete the requirements.

Other speakers included the Presidents of the Barb organization and the Interfraternity Council. The IFC President welcomed the freshmen and encouraged them to take part in rush week which began that first evening, and the Barb President assured the students if they didn't pledge a fraternity, there would still be plenty of activities and the intermural program in which they could participate. A schedule was passed out for taking the four-hour Pre-Engineering Inventory test (PEI), the Mathematics, English, and Chemistry placement tests.

All lower division transfers were also required to take the Pre-Engineering Inventory exam during orientation, as well as the Math and Chemistry placement tests. The PEI essentially determined the student's suitability for a Mines education, and around the middle of the first term, all freshmen were required to receive counseling from a three-man team of faculty members. Using the

PEI as well as IQ tests and SATs, the counselors would tell a student what his expectations were with regard to success at Mines. This was compared with his performance to date, and the student would be told whether he was under- or over-achieving. Many students were counseled to consider another school. This was the only counseling session given to Mines students after matriculating, and true to engineering form, it was a cold appraisal of the situation.

Registration was another surprise for freshman. Based on the results of their math placement exam, the students were broken in three groups: those requiring remedial (dumbbell) math, regular students, and those for advanced math. English and chemistry were only broken into regular or remedial sections. In the early 1950s, freshmen were put into 20-man sections in alphabetical order. This caused Nancy Easley to spend her two years (1952-1954) at Mines with almost the same group of students throughout, including one of the authors. By 1957, when the freshmen lined up when they arrived to receive their schedules, they were handed a paper with the schedule for their section. For regular students, the first twenty in line received schedule A, the next twenty B, and so forth. The only elective was the substitution of band or intercollegiate athletics for physical training (gym), and if a student was disabled, a foreign citizen, female, or a veteran, he was exempt from ROTC.

This system continued throughout a student's four years if he remained a regular student, having either flunked no courses or made them up in summer sessions. The first two years were the same for all students, with the exception of a single elective in the English department. One could choose between a literature course and a philosophy course, both three hours credit, and both widely perceived as an easy "A" or "B".

Schedules for the junior and senior years were handed out by option. The schedules provided for one or two electives per semester, usually one in the student's option, and if a second was present, it was usually in physics or chemistry. None of the elective courses in the upper division level were easy.

Severe problems arose for non-regular students who were allowed to register only after the regular students were finished. Often needed courses were closed, and five-year programs sometimes became six unless the students attended summer sessions. All classes were limited in size, usually from twenty to twenty-four students. In addition, there were many students hovering around a 2.0 grade point average who were merely striving to reach the magic 2.0 to graduate. Even the senior class president in 1961 was in such dilemma, and he did not finally graduate until 1963. Other students took six to 10 years, and the freshman roommate of Ralph Dougherty in 1952 graduated with his brother Dave in 1961. In short, once a student got behind, it took help from the Devil himself to finally graduate.

Mines was tough from the first day of a student's arrival on campus. The placement exams were a sobering experience for many who were forced to take remedial math, English, and until 1956, chemistry. One entering freshman in 1957 from a mid-western state where his high school possessed a reputation for academic excellence, was shocked by the math placement exam. He had taken all the math courses his high school offered, easily obtaining "A" s. So, he signed up for the advanced math placement exam, fully expecting to be put into the accelerated program. He hardly knew what to do when he saw the exam. He could work a couple of problems, maybe attack a few others, but most left him completely stumped. He was placed in regular math, but firmly believed if he had taken the regular math placement test, he would have been put in the remedial course.

Still believing that he would easily excel as he had through high school, the student went through the motions in doing homework and studying. On his first math exam he earned a 78. Unbelievable! It was the lowest "C." An "A" was now almost certainly out of the question, and he would have to fight to obtain a "B" for the semester. Then he studied with Gary Gray, a student who had received advance placement. Gray studied only a few minutes each night on math, rapidly turning pages in Thomas's calculus book, stopping only sometimes to scribble a note or work a problem. Within ten minutes he was ready to do something else. And Gray never got below a 98 on a math exam. The mid-western student rapidly considered bailing out of school — the competition was too tough. But he stuck it out, and earned a 3.35 GPA in his first semester. Gray left Mines after his sophomore year with straight "A"s in math, but failing in other courses. He was a math prodigy for whom a special curriculum was needed.

At Mines, freshmen agitation was well-organized and physically brutal to help prepare students for the mental cruelty and harsh treatment he would experience in the classroom. The majority of the hazing rules were in place by 1926, but always subject to modification. The vast majority of the hazing was conducted by sophomores, as juniors and seniors were much too busy to become involved with lowly freshmen.

Freshman hazing was explained by an upperclassman:

- *Frosh had to "Button Up" and "Sound Off" whenever ordered by an upper classman.*
- *Freshmen were not allowed to enter Guggenheim or Alderson Halls by their front doors, or Stratton Hall from the campus (south) side. If caught in the Assay Lab, they would get blackened faces.*
- *The Freshman Bible, containing much Mines trivia, were to be memorized and the information disgorged when required by an upperclassman. The booklets dated from President Chauvenet's day and were modelled after what is now the Reef Points used at the Naval Academy.*
- *Freshmen were not allowed to step on the grass.*
- *Freshmen had to wear Miner's caps and run between classes with their books on their heads.*
- *De-Pantsing, was the penalty for not knowing something or not obeying an upperclassman with "alarming alacrity."*

Hazing started with the Freshman-Sophomore tug of war across Clear Creek. Overseen by Blue Key, the national honor fraternity for student leadership, the outnumbered sophomores had a D-9 Caterpillar to help make up for their lack of numbers. Usually the sophomores won, but not always. Regardless, any lingering freshmen lost their pants, and everyone went into the icy waters of Clear Creek. For the Golden citizens it was a fun outing with spectacular entertainment.

De-Pantsing was actually more of a problem than the reader might guess. Upperclassmen would jump on a wayward freshman, remove the unfortunate individual's pants and throw them up in trees. Sometimes it took a major effort to get them back down, and campus trees looked like laundry lines.

Freshmen were told that they possessed no standing to complain about Mines or its traditions. Paying tuition did not make a Miner—he had to prove himself by surviving the first year and a half. Over fifty percent of the students would be gone by that time, having shown that they did not have what it took to be a Miner. When one freshman belligerently protested the unfairness of the sophomores having a giant bulldozer on their side, one of the Blue Key men unceremoniously threw the complainant in the creek. "Life is not fair, and neither is Mines!" shouted the Blue Key member.

In order to be eligible for any of the school honorary fraternities or student positions, frosh had to run the all-school Gauntlet that was the official end of the hazing period immediately before Thanksgiving. It consisted of running a 400-yard beltline of all upperclassmen. During the late 1950s the agitation period was cut shorter and shorter until being discontinued in the 1960s, at least in the severity that had existed since the time of President Chauvenet. In 1962, the Gauntlet itself was discontinued, making a major statement for a kinder and gentler Mines. In the 1950s, however, tender rear ends burned for a week after getting hit by some 700 belts.

Mines was tradition-rich; a situation which would disappear before the end of the Vietnam War. One of the most colorful and offensive Mines traditions known by the public was the "Milk Train", a special chartered train that would take students to other colleges for football games. Leaving from the Golden station near Sena's Pizzeria (until the station was closed in 1955 and thereafter from the Coors Beer siding) the train would be awash in beer and booze for the entire trip. As expected, many students would arrive at the game in a state of total intoxication, and the rest would reach that condition before the train returned to Golden. Milk trains were normally engaged for all football games at Greeley and Colorado Springs, but under an avalanche of public outcry at the wanton destructiveness and open drunkenness, the trains were discontinued after the Greeley trip in 1958.

The milk train to Colorado College in Colorado Springs for a Saturday evening football game in 1957 was typical. The weather was atrocious: it was a steady downpour, and the Mines students drank to keep warm. The halftime show consisted of Mines band members marching up and down the field playing and challenging the CC band to come out and fight. Since the Mines band uniform was engineer boots, Levi's, red-checkered shirt and miner's helmet, the miners possessed a considerable advantage over their dandified counterparts.

The end of the game, which was lost as usual, turned into total bedlam. Miners tore down the goal posts and started roughing up CC students. Responding to pleas for assistance from the outfought CC students, the CC football team came back onto the field and joined the fracas. It became an uneven match trying to fight football players in full uniforms including helmets and the newly popular facemasks. The train was a welcome sight as the C-Springs police herded the still truculent CSM students through city streets to the station, but most would never remember the return trip.

All was not lost, however, and the steel pipes which had held the upright goal posts disappeared into four large craters following loud explosions the following night, evidently from a lightning strike. Nature was truly wonderful and had taken her revenge for the Miner's loss.

The train in 1955 to Colorado State College at Greeley was even worse. No amount of playing the Star-Spangled Banner could break up the fight, nor could Dean Burger who decked a Greeley student who sucker-punched him. Long lines of police, deputies, and state troopers with drawn guns "escorted" the Mines contingent back onto the train, and the Greeley papers screamed to ban Mines from intercollegiate athletics. Mines students were like drovers hitting Dodge City and releasing tensions — no longer an acceptable activity in polite society. Sealing off outlets for aggressive behavior and frustration bottled it for an explosion into drugs, suicide, or serious criminal violence in lesser schools than Mines, but that lesson was yet to be learned. There was a reason why the '60's became the '60's.

Colorado University and Boulder were an insult to the Front Range for many Mines students, but CU did provide a number of foxy ladies eager to hook up with the potentially high earners at Mines. Freshmen, however, tended to overlook the social bonanza available and treat CU with great disrespect. In 1952, on the weekend following orientation, about thirty freshmen piled into cars and went drinking at Tulagi's and The Sink, watering holes in Boulder. They sang the Mining Engineer, especially the verse with "to hell with Boulder", but nothing happened. So they moved downhill to the Foxhole. There they ran into a packed house of CU students who immediately took offense at the singing. The freshmen were invited outside, where the CU students took off their shirts, so the sides were clearly identified. The Miners were stunned: every CU student looked like weightlifters. As well they should have: after all they were all on the CU football team. The regular students hadn't arrived on campus yet, but the football team was in two-a-day drills. After a short time, it was clear the CSM freshmen were badly outmatched, and the CU athletes called a halt, even buying the Miners beer until the midnight closing. When the group arrived back at Mines, the infirmary totaled up the damage: numerous cuts, bruises, bloody noses, and black eyes, one broken nose, and a broken wrist. Nonetheless, the harassment of CU continued unabated. Denver University came in for its share of disrespect following certain statements in the press by DU personnel. The steps to its library were relocated by another noisy lightning strike, although the building itself was not damaged. The administration building also found its access restricted when two workers installed barricades and proceeded to dig a trench across the street with jackhammers. At quitting time, they left, never to return. And of course, one of the wagon wheels from the DU Chuckwagon hung in the ATO bar, the other having been traded to another house for a likewise suitable trophy.

Until the interurban between Denver and Golden ceased operating, a Halloween tradition was to blow up the tracks to prohibit the last train from leaving the Golden Station. There were many more such traditions, but the reader gets the idea. Mines and its student body were not to be messed with, or the West would become wild again.

The school was fully integrated with the town since the first dorms weren't built until 1954. The fraternities housed less than a seventh of the students, and the townies showed substantial tolerance towards the students, even enjoying the hijinks and often coming to fraternity parties. A Miner wasn't exactly king of the hill when he went downtown, but he was treated with respect and friendliness. The population may not have been 100% pro-Mines, but most students thought so.

In Denver, however, only reporter-columnist Jack Carberry at *The Rocky Mountain News* was pro-Mines, and he did his best to publicize and defend the institution. He was particularly helpful when the Mines soccer team routed the Air Force Academy, and the junior birdmen complained about the Hispanics on the Mines team being ill-mannered. Actually, they had shown better sportsmanship than most Miners, except that their cheers and taunts were in Spanish. Mines was also helped considerably by Alberto Charles, a world-class player from Ethiopia. The Air Force (always referred to at Mines as the Air Farce) wanted him to be considered ineligible, but he still had his amateur status and could play like no one at Mines had seen before. Finally, Mines was grudgingly granted some respect in increasingly professional intercollegiate athletics.

Mines had strictly amateur athletics; players were engineering students first, and varsity athletes somewhere down about ninety-ninth. Therefore, Mines lost most games and athletic meets in the 1950s. Mines athletics could not compete in the face of programs which recruited athletes with all sorts of inducements and did not require them to pursue academics. The one exception was soccer where the extensive foreign contingent at Mines handily defeated anything the American colleges could offer. Mines had several world class players in addition to Charles from third world countries, and Spanish was the primary language used on the field. The Denver papers pilloried Mines' soccer team, particularly when it won both the game and the fight afterwards.

The other main sport in which Mines shone was wrestling. Coach Hancock was an unbelievable recruiter, and he had to be. Some of the best wrestlers ended up on academic probation in a year or two and became ineligible for varsity competition. So they kept themselves in shape through intramurals as did varsity athletes in other sports. The wrestling team usually acquitted itself honorably against top schools from the Big Ten, Big Eight, and others; but only a few of the wrestlers remained in school beyond their sophomore year. Nonetheless, Coach Hancock kept it well-stocked from the fine Colorado high school wrestling programs, and academically the team was probably the finest in the nation during the fifties.

A lesser sport in which Mines traditionally acquitted itself well was shooting. The rifle and pistol teams sometimes competed against big schools, and several individual shooters won national and regional awards. As in all varsity sports, participation was always affected by the necessity to maintain one's GPA. One good shooter in 1959 was also a dedicated re-loader, but his real passion was mountain climbing. In the spring he fell while climbing the Flatirons near Boulder and was in the infirmary for a week with substantial injuries. The day after being released from the infirmary he went back up the Flatiron, taking the same route where he had fallen. This time he reached the top, but the interruption to his studies caused him to withdraw from school for the semester. He returned to Mines later and graduated on a six-year program.

Mines introduced hockey one year in the early 1950s, but it was discontinued after a single season. Players were few, there were no practice facilities in Golden, and Mines could not compete with hockey powerhouses like Colorado College and Denver University, both of which extensively recruited Canadians to bolster their programs. In forming the team, the coach lacked a goalie. He decided to recruit the toughest student he could find. He watched intermural boxing and approached one fellow who had been badly beaten in the heavyweight class but had stayed in to the end. The student had never played hockey and didn't know how to skate. Nevertheless, Joe Teeters became the goalie. The team learned fast but was never competitive. Against Camp Carson (Fort Carson), Mines fell behind in the first period 17-0, ended the 2nd period at 21-0, and the third at 23-3. If there had been three more periods, maybe Mines would have had a chance. The CC players were worn out, whereas the Miners were just getting started.

This was also the era of decline for many big college football programs; TV revenues were yet undeveloped, injuries were making expenses unjustifiable, and the recruitment of blacks as paid gladiators was just beginning to gain acceptance. Many schools such as DU terminated its football program in the middle fifties, but not Mines. Whatever the score, it was in the game.

Not only could Mines not recruit top student athletes, it could also not provide the time to train them. Most athletes were not free to practice or work out until 4 p.m., necessitating practice to start at 4:30. By six thirty the football team was eating supper in the cafeteria's "training table," and Mines football players barely had time to learn the plays, but, of course, they were an order of magnitude brighter than their opponents. In all sports, the best athletes at Mines were often ineligible due to their grades, and many times the intermural teams could challenge the school's inter-collegiate representatives. Mines had to win on spirit, grit, and natural talent, or it could not win at all.

It wasn't all fun for freshmen after they had successfully gotten through the hazing period — they still had to make the grade in the classroom. One individual, who only spent his freshman year at Mines, remembered his first semester in 1957 as having 20 semester hours of credit, and over 40 hours per week in lecture and laboratory work. He was also told that a mere seven percent of Miners would achieve a GPA of 3.0 or better. The 40 hours per week were probably high, but they probably felt like it to the freshman. A recent survey by the authors found the fall semester of freshman years during the fifties to have class and lab schedules more in the range of 32-36 hours, but less than five percent made the honor roll with a 3.0 or above. The first semester, freshman year, was the lightest schedule a Miner would have in his four years, in part to ease the transition from high school to college.

In his book, *All Trappers Don't Wear Fur Hats,* a former student related numerous examples of vandalism to both the CSM and CU campuses by warring students, mostly led by the Korean War vets on both campuses. There was an early-Colorado type vigilante security force at CSM led by vets that would retaliate against anyone wishing CSM, its students or faculty harm. In particular, the writer related an incident shortly before mid-terms in the fall of 1957, when miscreants from Boulder spray-painted "CU" and other graffiti on the Mines gymnasium and attempted to dynamite the "M". The retaliation was well-organized.

There were three separate points of attack: a panty raid on sorority row, an "M" would be burned into CU's football field between the 40-yard lines, and the duck pond would be set alight after being liberally supplemented with gasoline. Nearly seventy Miners in twenty-two cars traveled to CU to do the deed. Mass hysteria struck sorority row about 3 a.m., which drew off campus security and the Boulder Police. Panty raids were considered exciting but not destructive, so it was not until the smoke from the football field and duck pond rolled upwards that the police took action. Eight of the Miners at the duck pond were arrested, but all others escaped. Dean Burger somehow got the eight jailed students off with unsupervised probation, and a day later they were back studying for exams. The "M" in the CU football field would be visible for almost two years.

There is some doubt as to when this incident occurred, with some alumni saying 1956 and some saying 1957. But all agree that it happened.

The public outcry against the drunkenness, violence, and vandalism, however, brought an end to this colorful era in the 1960s. Colorado was becoming civilized through the mass of easterners discovering the untamed frontier which they rapidly trashed in the name of saving it. Boulder became the new mecca for people to the left of Lenin, and mixed with party-goers from the East, made for an explosive mix at CU. The old West was dying to be replaced with trendy continentals turning Colorado into a high-priced sports and vacation-land, and the sandal-wearing back-to-nature types would turn their portion into a dump. The frontiersman, hard-ass miner, or Clear-Creek Annie types were not even missed or lamented.

Meanwhile, there were a few social events left to brighten the Miner's day (or night.) A typical Mines event, the Barb Smoker, was held in El Dorado Springs, or wherever the Barb Council could secure friendly premises for what was patently an illegal activity. Usually three girls were hired to strip to the buff, hounded by horny Miners brandishing their combs like weapons.

Wearing beards was the exclusive prerogative of seniors, and any lesser classman with a beard ran the risk of being forcibly shaved with shoe polish and a broken beer bottle. In 1958 one student took exception to this, grew a beard, and dared the seniors to object. They did and gave him twenty-four hours to shave or face the consequences. The following day he packed a pistol to class, and when the seniors jumped him, he shot one in the stomach. The freshman was expelled, the senior lost a kidney, and Mines incurred more bad publicity. The preservation of traditions claimed casualties.

Hell Week hazing in the fraternities was awesome, and pledges normally went without sleep for four days. Christmas presents (swats from the entire fraternity house) were bad enough but receiving 200 swats during Hell week was not unusual. Pledges bought piles and piles of barrel staves that were used up by the end of the week when the class went active. The first night started for the pledges with a "function", drinking Pluto Water, swallowing raw oysters on a string, having certain sensitive parts of the pledges' bodies painted with HEET, and learning to bounce on their butts holding a raw egg in their teeth and their feet in the air. They wore various costumes all week, PJs one day (with pillow and alarm clock), women's clothes another, burlap sacks another, and funky military uniforms on the remaining day. At all times they wore a large raw onion around their necks as their "Happy Apple". Almost all made it through the week being pulled through by their brothers and the combative Mines spirit, and they took pride in being able to take anything anyone could dish out.

Unnoticed by the administration and casual observers was that fraternity pledge classes became welded together under the hazing, and these students often bonded for life with each other. Everyone recognized that groups of soldiers became "bands of brothers" under combat conditions, but Mines was only different in that the brothers didn't get killed—at least not on campus. Fifty years later, members of the same pledge class were usually overjoyed to see each other again and be able to catch up on old times.

As mentioned elsewhere in this work, being a Mines student was like being in combat, with the administration and faculty against you. Although the other students provided general support and your classmates were important in academics, it was your pledge brothers who could be counted on to help out when most needed. This was also a reason the fraternity produced most campus leaders. They were continually involved in campus activities and committed to helping their brothers get through school. This was not a day for speeches, campaigns, or promises — it was simply a time to get done what needed to be done, and in the groups of already extraordinary men, real leaders emerged.

There were no amenities for women, but there was no discernable discrimination either. It was not until the mid-sixties that Mines would actively recruit women and provide extra benefits and accommodations for them. Concomitant with the paucity of free time, there was an almost complete absence of romantic involvement during the week. Indeed, life was harried; sleep was lacking, food was marginal, hygiene was minimal, and the students' Levi's stood up by themselves. The blow-dryer had not yet made its appearance and taking more than five minutes to wake up and leave for class was unimaginable. The few girls that attended Mines during the 1950s adapted to the regimen for survival; but who wanted to become involved with something that looked that bad? Besides, during the '50's, no females graduated, and there were never more than four enrolled at the same time. Miners had to look elsewhere for feminine comfort.

During the summer, students usually learned a number of useful things; how to make bombs, set dynamite charges, dance at the Elitch's Gardens Trocadero Ballroom, trace drawings on the spike (copy) table, organize the course materials and tests files, find the fastest way to Colorado University, Colorado Woman's College (always referred to as "Cow College"), University of Denver, and the St. Luke's Hospital Nurses' dorm, and how to drive down the face of Lookout Mountain from Sam's without going over the side while dead drunk. All of these were extremely useful skills.

And then there was Senior Day. It is fondly remembered as the greatest Hell-raising day of the year by Miners from its era. As listed in the 1952 Edition of the Senior Wipe, headlining the trial and ball game, the following Senior Day activities were scheduled:

8:00   *Classes Begin*
8:30   *Boom!*
8:30.1   *Classes dismissed*
8:45   *Supreme Court of the United Seniors convenes in Steinhauer Fieldhouse (Only Mines students and faculty admitted.)*
10:15   *Give Downtown Golden a thrill*
10:45   *Field Trip*
2:30   *Annual Annihilation of Faculty in National Pastime at Rocky Field*
7:00   *Eye, Ear, Nose, and Throat Refreshments for Seniors and Honor Faculty*

Typical activities included a kangaroo court for faculty, attendance more or less arranged voluntarily or involuntarily by the seniors, followed with a short terrorizing of downtown Golden with faculty and students in various costumes and advancing state of inebriation, then a trip to Denver to tree the town and disgust the *Rocky Mountain News* to the utmost. Cow College normally received a visit as did Denver University. It was not a good day to be a policeman, nor an unpopular faculty member. In those days Miners gave real and direct meaning to student evaluations.

The Senior-Faculty baseball game restored good humor among those still walking, and the evening followed with more drinking and partying with unmentionable activities. It was not a night that participating faculty members would later discuss with their wives.

Each year the seniors would publish totally disgusting newspapers for Senior Day, including *The Senior Gas Attack*, 1923, *The Senior Butt*, 1924, *The Corn Cob, Vol XYZ*, No. 6-7/8, *The Tail Bearer*, 1930, *The Senior Roast*, 1938, *The Senior Foo*, 1939, *The Douche – We Flush the Slush*, 1941, *The Senior Challenge*, 1942, *The Rugget Nugget*, 1945, *The Outhouse News*, 1947, *The Senior Growler*, 1951, and *The Senior Wipe*, 1952. Least-favored professors were featured at length, but so were the best. Some of the papers were really inspired, again showing that human beings have the most imagination when young.

All the harassment was something the freshman class and transfers rapidly learned to endure and even give back but coping with the institutionalized cruelty as dished out by many of the faculty was something else. There was a good reason for Senior Day, and when Dr. Vanderwilt abolished it after the 1952 event through threats of expulsion—a serious matter to a senior with only a few weeks to go before graduation, often getting married and departing for an already-arranged job—some faculty members became more deserving of the day than ever. The proverbial feces flowed downhill, and the students were at the bottom. The student activists in California and the East during the 1960s thought they were the original bad dudes, but they should have been at Mines. They wouldn't have lasted a week.

The Mines administration then re-wrote or expunged history. Many years after Senior Day was abolished, the campus police were created, ostensibly to fight crime on campus, but actually to control the ever-increasing parking problem. There was little, if any, crime, and the school had gotten along for a hundred years without a campus police force. But eastern universities had them, so once again Mines copied a bad example. To sell the police, the administration said it was because of Senior Day, and the campus police was needed to keep such unsafe practices from reoccurring. But that was not enough. Logan Caldwell, a 1940 Mines graduate, returned from his 50th Class Reunion in May of 1990 with an idea. Logan had taken movies of Senior Day in 1940, and still had them. He was convinced that the film was a treasure that should be in the Mines archives. So he packaged it, and sent it to a member of the Administration, a fellow Mines grad that he knew personally. After waiting several weeks for an acknowledgment of his gift, Logan followed up with a letter to his friend, but never received an answer. Not only did Logan lose a friend, but the film had vanished.

The Stories:

Almost every student at Mines during the 1950s had his favorite story about life on campus, and many of them were even true.

Out of Money - Freshman Mines student Charlie Brewer ran out of money in November, so he needed money fast. In order to finish the semester, he went to Denver, looked over some automobile dealerships, and approached Lou Bell Lincoln-Mercury. With his great gift of gab, he made a deal with the owner that he would not interfere with the current salesmen or their prospects, yet still promised at least a sale per week. The owner was taken in by Charlie's confidence, and said he would pay Charlie $100 for each Mercury sold, and $200 for each Lincoln.

Charlie's sales technique was to loiter across the street from the dealership, and when someone walked by and slowed to admire the new cars, Charlie would approach him in a friendly manner suggesting that the car he was admiring would be wonderful to own, but was obviously above the man's means. If the man protested that he could afford the down payment, Charlie would take him to the sales manager and consummate the sale. During the 4-day Thanksgiving weekend, Charlie was able to sell four cars, which carried him through the end of the semester. He then repeated the process to provide the necessary funds for the second semester. Unfortunately, his grades were not the equivalent of his sales skills, and Charlie faded from the Mines scene.

The STOP Sign - About 2:00 a.m. one Friday night in the 1950s, two Miners were carefully removing a STOP sign from its post on East 10th Street, when their activity was noticed by a police patrol. The officer stopped and asked what they were doing with the sign, which by that time was in the students' hands. They replied they were going to put it on the wall in their room, whereupon the officer took them to jail. In the morning they were fed breakfast, taken back to the empty sign post, made to refasten the sign properly, then turned loose.

Such was the tolerance of Miners' antics in that decade. The students were glad that the policeman did not accompany them to see their room, however, for he would have found their walls sported a SLOW sign, and one that read NO PARKING.

Asbestos - Before the 1970s, the assay lab and pyro-metallurgy required the use of asbestos gloves to handle the hot tongs, crucibles, etc. Many of the students routinely removed the asbestos gloves from their hands with their teeth. Bunsen burners in geology and chemistry labs usually heated asbestos plates. Somehow students lived through all this oblivious to the dangers. A similar situation played out for a graduate in metallurgy when he became responsible for the toll rolling of molybdenum spray wire at Vanadium Alloys in Latrobe, Pennsylvania. The mill personnel refused to work the cross-country mills due to the heavy clouds of moly oxide given off by the rapidly oxidizing molybdenum. The Mines graduate put himself in the heaviest clouds of moly smoke, and the workers went back to work. Miners also knew about leadership and how to get a job done.

Old Chem - The Old Chemistry Building (1880) was last used for Chemistry classes in 1952. The fall semester found only the first few lectures given in the Old Chemistry lecture hall, then classes were suspended until the opening of Coolbaugh Hall about 10 days later. The floors in the 1880 building had myriad holes through which one could see the floors below. The stairs were so badly worn and dished out from years of students going up and down that the footing was difficult. The top floor, however continued to house the Descriptive Geometry and Engineering Drawing Department, the domain of Department Head John M. Coke. It was also the department which required the students to carry the most gear to and from class. Of course, it was located in the worst building.

The Golden Grade School -- Physics was housed in the old Golden School, and the band room was there as well early in the 1950s. However, once the Old Chem Lecture Hall was no longer in use, the Mines Band moved in and used it as its practice room until Old Chem was razed to make room for the metallurgy building, Hill Hall. The band then practiced in the auditorium on the top floor of Guggenheim Hall, where the President has his office today. The Physics department remained in the old Golden School until 1963, giving the students more practice in walking up dished-out staircases.

The Poltergeist – otherwise known as Dominick Perrigo (aka Dominic Perigo or Perico), student extraordinaire. One of the stories in which he figured prominently was featured in Wilton Eckley's *Rocky Mountains to the World*. Perrigo, an alias for a 1961 grad and significantly aided by others around him, carried on a four-year battle with the local ROTC detachment. He successfully prevailed on the student ROTC Band Leader to incorporate five of Dominick's non-instrument playing fraternity brothers in the band to escape ROTC drill. Then he used his connections to padlock the drill field to hold up the annual inspection. Earlier classes also claim Dominick, so it is possible he was on campus for as long as nine years.

Perhaps the most feared course at Mines was ROTC in the sophomore spring semester. The detachment taught American military history during the two hours of lecture every week, complete with a military history textbook that was denser than the one on historical geology. For one credit hour, the students were expected to memorize the book. Dominick had another idea. One student was already an expert on military history, so on the multiple-choice exams, Dominick organized the students to sit around and behind him. He would copy the student's answers and pass them around. Even some of the top students at Mines availed themselves of Dominick's services, after all, who had time to study for ROTC when there were Chemistry and Calculus exams coming up? Dominick's copy of the exam, of course, went into the files, so the course became a piece of cake in subsequent years.

But those achievements were nothing compared to his continual enrollment in Mines classes and earning passing grades. Since the stealthy Perrigo seemed to be bereft of worldly substance (some said he was composed entirely of beer), the administration was at a loss to graduate or expel him from campus. In the event, it did neither, and folk hero Perrigo managed to make his presence known on campus for four long years without anyone ever setting eyes on him.

Betting on the Presidential Election – One enterprising senior during the 1960 election bet heavily on Kennedy being elected. Conservative students lined up to place their bets on Nixon, and the senior made enough money to see himself through the fall semester. Known to be a Republican, he was asked why he bet against the candidate he wanted to win. "I have unbounded faith in the level of corruption in the Democrat Party," he explained. "Rayburn and Johnson own Texas and will produce more votes for Kennedy than there are voters in many precincts, and the Kennedys will do the same in Chicago, New York, Philadelphia, and other big cities to ensure Kennedy's election. Watch how those cities are slow to record their votes. They're held to the last, and then the machines create as many votes as necessary." After Kennedy won, the senior simply stated that the election was never in doubt, and later studies of the election showed that precisely what the senior had predicted indeed occurred in Illinois and Texas. And that was without the benefit of having taken a single course in political science, a true oxymoron.

Chapter 12 - Student Social Life in the 1950's

What little social life the students of the 1950s enjoyed usually revolved around their wife (if married), the Barb organization and intermural competition, some hobby such as sports cars, shooting, rock hunting, or skiing, or as a member of a fraternity. There simply wasn't time for anything else — in fact, there was precious little time for any social life.

Fraternities:

The number of social fraternities at Mines varied from none during the nineteenth century to a high of eight during the fifties. Houses were established as follows:

Founded	Fraternity	Chapter	Discontinued
1901	Sigma Nu	Gamma Eta	
1903	Sigma Alpha Epsilon	Lambda	
1904	Kappa Sigma	Gamma Gamma	
1908	Beta Theta Pi	Beta Phi	
1920	Mu Epsilon Tau		1929
1922	Eta Omega Delta	Beta	1929
1923	Sigma Phi Epsilon	Delta	
1929	Alpha Tau Omega	Epsilon Alpha[1]	
1951	Pi Kappa Alpha	Delta Phi	1965
1951	Theta Chi	Delta Lambda	1958

The fraternity system at Mines was probably unique in the nation. None of the chapters featured house mothers, and all offered relatively nominal living costs. On a per month basis, double room rent during the fifties was generally $15.00, board for seventeen meals per week was only $42.00, and chapter dues amounted to $7.00 or $8.00. The house manager was a student elected by the chapter to collect the dues and run the house. For that he received only free room and board.

Fraternities accounted for somewhat less than half of the undergraduate Mines students from 1910 to 1950, and in 1926 they reached 46 percent. But they were organized and tended to have an out-sized influence in campus activities and organizations. During the 1950s the high point was reached, when fraternity students reached a high of 56 percent of the student body according to one IFC study in 1955. Meanwhile, all non-fraternity members were automatically members of the Barb (short for Barbarian) organization

[1]Formerly Mu Epsilon Tau

for representation in the Student Council and participation in inter-mural sports.

Some fraternities allowed non-members to eat at their house, and all allowed non-members to study in their facilities. Some faculty members also ate at the fraternities, mostly at lunch time. Graduate students were noticeably absent in participation with the fraternities, but many, if not most, of them were foreign students for whom the fraternities remained a mystery. Theta Chi was the only fraternity that routinely accepted foreign members other than Canadians.

In spite of the popular conception fostered by a number of television shows and movies, fraternity members did not dress alike with little green beanies or anything like that. In fact, other than the tiny pledge pin worn by pledges, there was nothing to distinguish Greeks from Barbarians at all. Fraternity members did not necessarily come from wealthier families, and the standard dress for all students was a t-shirt or something else that didn't need ironing (25 cents per shirt at Margie's), jeans or wash pants, loafers or boots, and a jacket on cold days.

Television did not come to Colorado until 1952, and even then Denver only had one station. Most fraternities did not acquire TV sets until a few years after that, and television was simply not a factor on campus until the 1960s.

Rush week was hectic for the actives, and particularly on the sophomores who were expected to recruit most of the pledges. They organized non-stop functions, trucked in girls from CU and CWC, and collected freshmen off campus. The houses offered an open bar and entertainment every evening. Rush week took place during freshmen orientation, the week before classes started, so everyone was free to party. Various houses became famous for various lightning concoctions. One famous recipe named Luau Lite was for five gallons; two fifths of 151 proof Vodka, one fifth light rum, one fifth dark rum, one gallon white wine, one gallon red wine, half gallon Hawaiian Punch (red), half gallon Seven-Up, half gallon ginger ale, two bottles concentrated lime juice, three bottles lemon juice, one bottle grenadine, and assorted sliced or diced tropical fruits — pineapple, lemon, lime, and anything else available. Another was a Spode Odie party with a punch made up of one quart of vodka, one of rum, one of Captain Morgan's Parrot Bay Coconut Rum, one of triple sec, six quarts of Hawaiian Fruit Punch, and four quarts of 7-Up. Females couldn't withstand that concoction.

As fraternity actives, students took part in hazing pledges under the diabolical direction of a sophomore "pledge trainer", breaking barrel staves over their rear ends, supervising their housekeeping duties, and making them perform dumb stunts at mealtimes. The toughest hazing took place in fraternities' "functions" and every day "beat ass" which consisted of getting hit with a barrel stave for any infraction of rather arbitrary rules. A "function" was a malevolent all-night hazing prank of some sort; getting left in the mountains without clothes, swimming in the snow, guarding the "M", or some all-night games. Pledges would get swatted several times a week, and actives took pride in hitting hard enough to snap the heavy wooden staves cleanly in two.

On the other hand, fraternities also enforced good study habits on their pledges and others, helped in their acclimation at Mines, let them borrow cars for dates, and in general assisted them in meeting the challenge of a harsh, unforgiving system. Grades were published for all pledges in the fraternity house, and pledges got beat for a grade of "C" or less on any exam. The actives, who became pledge fathers, were responsible for helping their pledge sons along, and often the input and influence from an upper classman made a great deal of difference.

The pledges organized themselves to bedevil the actives, electing a pledge captain. Usually the pledges struck first, kidnapping an active or two, and taking them to Boulder or somewhere where drinking or other activities were carried out. This was called a "sneak" and a demonstration of the pledge class's virility and resourcefulness. The actives would retaliate with a "function" and so it would go during the semester. This mini-war would force the pledges to band together and become a cohesive group, much tighter than the freshman class, and build leadership and teamwork.

Living in a fraternity house was not all milk and honey. The conformity of living and the lack of privacy were serious factors. Study hours included all of Sunday from 11:00 a.m. onwards, and Monday through Thursday nights from 7-11:00 p.m. Any loud noises, radios, stereos, etc., were punished by $5.00 fines — a significant amount at the time. Girls were never allowed above the first floor (e.g. in the bedrooms) and were not allowed in the house at all except on Friday and Saturday evenings. Even then, their presence was expected to be limited unless they were there for a party. Pretty much, females were a limited pleasure subject to a lot of restrictions. If a frat member developed a heavy relationship with a girl, it was away from the campus and the fraternity house. Date night was Saturday, and for unmarried Mines students, intimate activities were limited to Saturday nights. Dating on week nights was a sure way to flunk out.

Except for pledge formals and the like, parties were open to all, Greeks and Barbarians alike. Most of the faculty and staff that had extensive contact with the students attended, and even some of the townspeople. Females were not allowed above the first floor, except in switcheroo parties, when the women stayed overnight in their date's rooms in the fraternity house, the males were not allowed above the first floor and forced to vacate the premises from 2 a.m. to 8 a.m.

Parties were held only on Saturday nights, and the fraternities had traditional theme parties which were open to everyone. The Kappa Sigs held a Pajama Party and Zombie Party in the fall and a Hawaiian Luau Party in the spring. The ATOs held a Gay Nineties Party, Casino Night, and Voodoo Party, SPEs had Lil's, South Sea Island Party, and another Gay Nineties Party, Beta Theta Pi hosted the Frontier Brawl and South Seas Party, Pi Kappa Alpha the Ship Wreck Party, and Little Abner, the SAEs the Basin Street Party, the Sigma Nu house had Las Vegas night, and there were also Mardi Gras, Halloween, fruit juice, and grunge parties. Drinks were twenty-five cents per shot, beer was ten cents, and the special concoction was either free or ten cents. The girls were obtained from either Colorado University, 23 miles away in Boulder, Cow College, or other places in Denver. Going to Mines for a fraternity party could be a fascinating walk on the wild side; particularly if one was unaware of the Jenson Blue in the beer which turns urine blue.

Stories about party happenings are legion, and they range from the ridiculous to the sublime. Supposedly one Golden store owner lost his store in a high-stakes poker game at a frat party—a game in which no students were taking part. Following another party, a local lovely was found in the basement of a frat house asleep with an alumnus who was visiting the campus. At still another, the Sigma Nu's Las Vegas Night, the Wheel of Fortune featured the wrong odds and payoffs, and a Kappa Sig figured it out and broke the bank.

Sometime there were complaints, but by far the best known was by a later Miss America who was a student at Colorado Women's College. She was banned from campus after she complained that the PKAs had held an unchaperoned party with underage drinking. Unfortunately for her, the Dean of the Faculty was there along with two professors from the Physics Department at the Pi Kap's "Fruit Juice" Party, and he didn't take kindly to her charges. She became "Persona non grata" on campus, and the year later when she won her title it became a status symbol to have turned down a date with her.

As at every college, Mines had its share of "Don Juans," but the best of the 1950s was probably Jerry Hanks. Jerry was just of normal height and build and reputed to be some part Indian. He rarely had to shave, looked vaguely exotic, and went by the name "Indian." Hanks moved like a cat and played up his Indian blood (if any) to anyone who was dumb enough to listen. As it turned out, there were many who listened, mostly females. Jerry loved Robert Service, and had memorized a number of his poems, most notably "The Cremation of Sam McGee" and "The Shooting of Dan Mc-Grew." His frat brothers would egg him on to recite the poems before he became totally inebriated on the local firewater (definitely not Indian-like), and the women would gather at his feet to listen. It was awesome, and some girls claimed they could feel the heat of the fire cremating old Sam. Most likely, it was something else. Towards the end, the girls would all be breathing hard from the Indian's magnificent and spellbinding delivery, and some were moved to tears almost like Hanks himself. Jerry was always the high point of the party, as couples then paired up to work off the effects of his poetry. Hanks himself could have had the pick of those at his feet. It was an entirely unintended consequence, of course, as no one could have predicted such an outpouring of emotion.

To fast-forward the Jerry Hanks saga, he married a girl from his home town of Ft. Worth that everyone called "Sweet Child", and who was drop-dead gorgeous with long blond hair and deep blue eyes. As a married man, he fell behind his class and graduated two years late, but no doubt Sweet Child was worth it. Hanks passed away prior to his 45th reunion, but his poetry recitations will be long remembered.

All School Beer Busts were held every Friday evening in the clay pits during football season and on special events. To support the team, dynamite was set off in clay pits for every Mines touchdown. This practice tended to upset the visiting team as well as some cupcake spectators, but it was all harmless fun. Pledges at several of the fraternities were responsible for storing and rotating the dynamite and turned it at least monthly. For many students, handling dynamite became simply something they did. Clearly, Mines was not located in Illinois or New York.

Not only did the miners drink, they gambled. The parties were protected by the Jefferson County Sheriff, Arthur W. (Moose) Wermuth, who had gained fame as a Captain in WWII on Bataan for killing 116 Japs. Wermuth had been made sheriff following the conviction of his predecessor, Sheriff Carl Enlow for not paying $1,271.00 in income taxes (he received three years in Leavenworth for the heinous crime) in 1957. Moose was a close friend of the Alumni Executive Secretary, Wendell Fertig, who had led the American guerrilla force on the island of Mindanao in the Philippines. Both loved Mines and the toughness and the rowdiness of the school. When forced to raid one of the parties because of the volume of complaints, Moose would always call first and give the house twenty minutes to hide the booze and get everything in order. It took him a long time to travel the two blocks from his office to the frat house.

Old Coloradans possessed a strong streak of independence and vigilante justice was commonplace. Wermuth was good to Miners, although he was removed in 1962 for petty corruption. Nobody wanted the students jailed or the parties closed down—just made a little quieter sometimes. And that he did. There probably wasn't a person over thirteen in Golden who didn't know what went on at Mines parties. They even went to the football games like another high school, drinking the free beer in the clay pits which student organizations supplied. No one checked IDs there either. If someone wanted to wear a cashmere sweater, he went to CU. Like the sign over Washington Street said, this was "Where the West Remains." The Golden city fathers can take the sign down any time now.

Before they were driven off campus onto a fraternity row, the frats performed a lot of services for the students in general.

In addition to active fraternity members writing a number of entering freshmen and welcoming them to Mines, they sometimes visited the prospects during the summer, even bringing some to school. Most of the fraternities provided this service, but surprisingly few of the freshmen receiving letters and services eventually became active members of the fraternity that contacted or provided services to them. Nonetheless, incoming freshmen were made to feel a part of the student body as rapidly as possible. It was a two-way service, but in the sixties as the administration tightened its control of student life, the ad hoc welcoming system was discontinued to be replaced by impersonal school letters and brochures. As historian and social critic Christopher Lasch said, the students had become wards of the state, and subjected to bureaucratic custody. Mines hired people to perform a lesser service than the students had provided for free.

During the 1950s, the fraternities participated in a Blood Donor program, coordinated by the IFC. The ATO fraternity was typical, sending five or six members to Colorado General Hospital every month during the school year to donate. Most frats pledged 5 or more pints a month to the program, and many committed individuals gave four or more pints per year. The frats weren't strictly social; they were also about service and forming bonds that promoted education and student cohesion. As any psychologist can attest, unit cohesion (as in the Army) is often the most important factor in the success of the unit and its members in training and in combat. And Mines was definitely combat.

SES (Seniors Eat S#*&t) days, when certain fraternities threw their seniors into Clear Creek, were sometimes rough and tough. The fights started at lunchtime, but by mid-afternoon everything was under control. The seniors were locked in car trunks and driven down to Clear Creek. The seniors went in the thirty-eight-degree water, but so did all of the antagonists. As a typical Mines happening, a sizable portion of downtown Golden came out to enjoy the spectacle.

During this decade, specifically on July 11, 1955, the first class of 306 cadets (all male) was sworn in to the Air Force Academy at a temporary site, Lowry Air Force Base, in Denver. The very first sports event that was hosted by the Air Academy as the home team was a swimming meet with Colorado School of Mines, in December of 1955. Even though all of the cadets were freshmen, and the Miners were upperclassmen, Mines still lost. After the meet, the Miners were hosted by the Falcon Swim Team at the Cadet Dinner. For that one meal, the Cadet Swim Team members did not have to eat "on the square" (making all motions in straight lines and ninety-degree angles.) On Aug. 29, 1958, the wing of 1,145 cadets moved to its permanent site at what was Husted, Colorado, near Colorado Springs, and the Academy graduated its first class of 207 on June 3, 1959. The school developed into one of Mines' main competitors in soccer and debate, but those were the only two activities in which Mines was competitive with the USAF Academy.

Upper Classmen:
The social groupings changed from fraternity members or various club groups to the other students in an individual's option during a student's junior year. For example, on Tuesday and Thursday nights in 1959 a group of about ten metallurgists would meet in the basement of the Kappa Sig house to do thermodynamics problems, and that included guys from maybe four or five different frats. The houses kept hot coffee going each night and everyone was welcome, Greek and Barb alike.

Only seniors were allowed to wear Stetsons, the traditional headgear for the mining engineer. Most seniors bought theirs at McKeehen's, the men's clothing store next to Foss's Drug Store on Washington Street, as soon as they finished their junior year. That was a neat tradition—the seniors wore their Stetsons all the time like badges of honor—which they were, of course. It wasn't easy to become a senior.

Most graduating seniors could not wait to escape the institution. There were no parties, before or after graduation. It was a rite of passage in which seniors were relatively disinterested participants. Many departed immediately after the ceremony, and most of them were out of Golden within a day. As mentioned earlier, their feelings towards Mines were often negative—after putting them through copious quantities of coprolite for four years, the administration now wanted to congratulate them for withstanding the ordeal. Mines was not a nurturing institution, it was a hostile, arrogant environment. The saving grace was that the students nurtured and supported each other. In the trials of the first freshman semester a student usually proved his willingness and capability to work with his brother freshmen to defeat all comers, including the university. Many still flunked out, but everyone pulled for everyone else. Competition was nominal, and usually limited to students from the east.

In addition to the normal flunk-out attrition, there was a certain loss from student deaths, sometimes as many as a dozen out of a student body of a thousand. Most often they were killed in accidents, such as in 1954 when two ATO fraternity actives and a prospective pledge drove off Lookout Mountain. Alcohol was sometimes involved, but most were killed doing normal things like skiing, fighting forest fires, mountain climbing, automobile accidents, and the like. Some deaths were possibly suicides, but rarely were they labelled as such. The mortality rate of Mines students was actually greater than that of servicemen in the American Army during World War Two. The US had twelve and a half million troops and a quarter million battle deaths in the war. That's two percent in four years, and Mines had about four percent in four years.

Make no mistake: it was warfare—the students against the system. It was combat against the faculty and administration. Students ended up with 200 semester hours credit and more—good enough for a PhD in liberal arts. But they completed this regimen in the prescribed four years only if they were able to do the impossible and take the hill in a frontal assault. There was no way around, and no easy routes.

It was the final two years which were expected to change a student from someone studying engineering to a professional in his chosen option. As President Vanderwilt said in the 1952 *Prospector*:

> "...*The many significant contributions to the world's mineral industry made by alumni of the Colorado School of Mines have established an enviable reputation for your Alma Mater. Each succeeding generation of alumni enjoys and benefits by this reputation and each is charged with the responsibility to strengthen and broaden it through the years to come. We are confident that your pride in your Alma Mater will continue to grow in the future.*"

In the 1953 *Prospector*, school traditions were clearly recognized as under siege from the Mines administration. The editor's remarks in his introduction are worth pondering in light of their clairvoyance:

> "*We are witnessing Mines in a surge of metamorphosis. New buildings seem to spring up before we can become familiar with recently completed ones. In addition to the renovated campus, there is the usual turnover of students and faculty. Chemistry and mathematics continue to eliminate thirty to forty percent of the freshman class while juniors still face many threats to their aspirations.*
>
> *Important too, are the changes in tradition and attitude. Senior Day and the [Sophomore-Freshman] Barbeque are no longer held. The Gauntlet has been frequently threatened with extinc-*

tion. It is not for the class of '53 to judge if this is mental evo-lution. Only the future will reveal if we are to uphold the high standards of those who have earned their silver sheepskins before our time."

Only eight years later, the editor of the 1961 *Prospector* re-fused to dedicate the book to a faculty member or someone in the administration. Instead, it was dedicated to the Seniors:

"Only a man who has traveled the arduous road from the bewil-dered awe of a freshman to the supreme self-satisfaction of a senior can truly comprehend the successes and the failures, the achieve-ments and the heartbreaks, and the anxieties and the nonchalance that have set him apart from other men.

To the men with the coveted silver diploma nearly in their grasp, the seniors, this 1961 Prospector is humbly dedicated."

Mines eventually killed the cooperative spirit in fraternities through harassment, eminent domain, forcing a formal bidding system down the IFC's throat, and constantly threatening houses with social probation for the slightest infraction or lack of coop-eration. To create an image as a benevolent and gentle institution, Mines recruited females, ran their own affirmative action program for the women, and lowered scholastic standards to make Mines socially more acceptable. The coeds didn't automatically lower the standards, but that was the effect as social life increased and educa-tion was reduced. The result is what we see today.

In 1962 the Kappa Sigma house was purchased by the school using eminent domain and converted to a woman's dorm. The building was renamed Caldwell Hall, for the first female grad-uate of Mines, Florence Caldwell, class of 1898, married name Jones. It was hailed by the administration as a notable advance for Mines, although the Kappa Sigs, who lost their house, didn't agree. Two facets were troublesome: the administration was now exercis-ing its power to pick winners and losers (winners: women and the administration's recently stated policy to promote diversity in its student body, losers: the Kappa Sigs), and secondly it was using its power punitively. The Kappa Sigs, along with the ATOs, had been in the forefront in maintaining CSM's traditions: those very same traditions that President Vanderwilt wished to see eradicated. The handwriting was on the wall, play ball or else. The fraternities' role in helping to manage student life was being assumed by the growing administrative bureaucracy, and as all anachronisms, the frats should go quietly. Using eminent domain the administration was able to pick up the houses fairly cheaply, and literally force the dispossessed frats to purchase waste land in the clay pits. The land price was only $5,000, but it was arguably the worst land in Golden. Tucked away in a tiny corner of the campus whereas they had once been mixed in with the school buildings, the frats were out of sight and out of mind.

Traditions:

To say that Mines was tradition-rich until the 1960s would be an understatement. A list of the traditions that have been expunged from Mines life or changed is long. It all began with the razing of the Old Chemistry Building and the start of the Horizon Plan in 1952 to re-make Mines in the image of an eastern college. The list would include: freshman agitation, exclusive privileges for seniors such as wearing beards, Stetsons (that started in 1926), and neckties, the Freshman-Sophomore Tug-of-War, Senior Day, the Gauntlet, the Freshman-Sophomore Barbeque, requiring freshman attendance at all home football games, shaft house parties, the Barb Smoker, birthday dunks in the irrigation canal running parallel to Maple Street, throwing all seniors into Clear Creek, plastering wars between Theta Tau and Sigma Gamma Epsilon, nighttime Scabbard & Blade tactical maneuvers up Lookout Mountain, the fall Sophomore-sponsored Flunk & Forget Dance, Hell Week by fraternities, paddling in the fraternities, Beer Busts in the clay pits, open bars and open parties (to anyone on campus) by the fraternities, milk trains, guarding the "M" and punishing vandals, Freshmen required to take a rock up to the "M" and help paint CSM's most visible symbol, blasting with dynamite when the Mines football team scored a touchdown, harassing the ROTC parades, *The Picker*, *The Prospector*, the Homecoming traditions of the float parade down Washington Avenue, house decorating, the soap box derby, cross-country race, burro race, raft race down Clear Creek, the Homecoming dance, open fraternity houses and dinner, and many more. Intercollegiate boxing was discontinued in the late 1940s, reinstated, and finally dropped in 1957, while intermural boxing was dropped in the middle 1950s. Mines life has changed over time, and become tamer.

The Mines cycle of life in the 1950s started on noon Sunday when the student began his week of study and class through

Friday afternoon, getting inebriated on Friday night, performing necessary chores and maintenance activities on Saturday, going on a date Saturday evening, and Sunday starting the cycle all over again. With the heavy workload, literally anyone going on a date (a euphemism for many activities involving social interaction with a female) during the week risked flunking out, as homework was due every day, and although the quizzes for lower division students were scheduled regularly in a "quiz hour" (usually 7 a.m. on Wednesday), there were also many other scheduled exams, and unannounced quizzes could occur at almost any time.

Homecoming was a traditional Mines event with booze, broads, contests, music, food, fights, house decorations, a soap box derby, and whatever. With typical miner ingenuity, a soap box derby racer's visibility was almost non-existent, steering tight as a bobsled, and the braking system little more than a joke. The race was down Washington Street through the center of town, and the prize was two cases of beer.

There was also the 100% student-produced *Picker* which had questionable redeeming social value. *The Picker* was the Mines humor magazine, ribald, funny, and obscene in a collegiate way. The orientation was strictly a miner's, with names named and many insider comments. The artwork was amateurish, but the sarcasm was tellingly directed. All original, *The Picker* was devastating. Some readers and the Colorado public criticized *The Picker* as pornography, but, of course, they did not understand the campus-oriented humor. Who would, who was not a miner?

The Growing Bureaucracy:

Beginning in the late fifties, the Mines administration consistently hired individuals unable to comprehend the uniqueness of Mines, and who undertook to make it over in their own undergraduate schools' images. To them should have been told the story of the reply of the Baal Shem Tov, the founder of Chassidism, when asked about the rabbis who called his teaching false. The Baal Shem Tov replied, "Once, in a house, there was a wedding festival. The musicians sat in a corner and played upon their instruments, the guests danced to the music, and were merry, and the house was filled with joy. But a deaf man passed outside the house; he looked in through the window and saw the people whirling about the room, leaping, and throwing about their arms. 'See how they fling themselves about!' he cried, 'it is a house filled with madmen!'

For he could not hear the music to which they danced."

Unable to hear the music, the non-Mines hires torched the house. The Mines spirit of self-determination and the men it produced were eliminated and replaced during the sixties and seventies by baby boomers with entirely different orientations. Golden changed too. It became a suburb of Denver, overrun by cyclists in fancy Spandex and helmets. Levis jeans for men were changed to knee-length shorts like those worn by little boys in grade school. Women showed up wearing the Levis, a reversal of roles that could hardly be missed. And, of course, there were the sandal-wearing back-to-nature types. The Dean Signer, Dean Burger, Wendell Fertig, or Ms. Tomi Bain types were gone by 1970 and forgotten by historians. Worst of all, the shootin, fightin, dynamitin, mining engineer was gone. In his place were boys and girls enjoying college as if they were at CU, Wisconsin, or Maryland. The sole holdout was Gene Woolsey in the math department, and he was viewed by the administration as an anachronism.

The beer-busts in the clay pits vanished with the pits themselves during the sixties, as the fraternities struggled to build their new houses under the watchful eyes of a hostile school administration. All of the historic houses except the Sigma Nu house next to Coolbaugh Hall and the Beta Theta Pi house off campus, succumbed to the wrecker's ball, the last being the beautiful Georgian style ATO house after Mines threatened to revoke their charter.

The older school buildings were torn down. The old Golden High School, converted to use by the Physics Department, the huge Old Chemistry Building, the Integral Club, and other landmarks disappeared to make way for new construction. Only intervention from the Alumni Association saved Stratton and Chauvenet Halls. The State of Colorado seemed intent on destroying the relics of Mines' rough and tumble past.

Influences: Masons, Faculty, and ROTC:

Masonic influences were strong at Mines until World War II, and an active chapter of Square and Compass was present on the Mines campus until after the war. In 1926 the masonic fraternity numbered twelve faculty and thirteen students. It was not unusual for Mines students to be raised at Golden City Lodge #1 after their twenty-first birthday before they graduated. Until the 1960s Mines undergraduate students tended to be older than normal collegians; the 1926 senior class, for instance, ranged from twenty to thirty-five with an average age of twenty-four.

Cornerstones of early buildings were laid with masonic ceremony, Stratton and Guggenheim Halls being examples. In those days the example of George Washington laying the cornerstone to the US Capitol wearing a masonic apron and following masonic ritual was held out as an example for all right-thinking Americans to follow.

The faculty often gave long service to Mines, twenty, thirty, and even forty years of association with Mines not being uncommon. This occurred even without tenure, raising the question as to whether tenure was really needed. Indeed, the faculty aided immeasurably in maintaining the school spirit of Mines by supporting the athletic programs, serving as volunteer coaches in minor sports without monetary compensation, sponsoring various clubs and organizations, advising fraternities, and taking part in almost all social events. In many ways the dedicated faculty members were super-students, playing roles as stern older brothers, but willing to take abuse as well as dish it out.

Mines concentrated on preparing undergraduates to enter a world of mineral industries, acquit themselves honorably, and overcome every obstacle. A graduate school was present, squired by top quality faculty like Clark Carpenter, Ivan Hebel, Francis Van Tuyl, John Hollister, Lesley Leroy, and others, but its numbers were small. Ranging from three to six percent of the undergraduate enrollment, graduate students were hardly a significant force on campus until the seventies, and many, if not most, were foreign students. Then came the push to change Mines into a research-oriented institution, and the effect was stunning. By 1993 the graduate school was approaching thirty percent of the total enrollment. In 2016, approximately 1,565 out of a student body of 5,714 were graduate students, a number over 30 times the average graduate enrollments in the 1950s. At the same time, undergraduate enrollments only increased by a factor of around 3.5.

The ROTC Program had been an integral part of the Mines curriculum since Congress passed the National Defense Act in 1916 providing for a Reserve Officer's Corps and the organization of the Reserve Officers' Training Corps. A Student Army Training Corps unit was organized on October 1, 1918, forty-two days before World War I ended, with 162 students, and it was followed in January of 1919 with a 70-man unit of the Engineer Reserve Training Corps. The initial ROTC enrollment in December of 1919 was 117

Basic Course students, and in the school year of 1941-1942, over half of the student body was enrolled in ROTC courses. Since 1926 the Mines ROTC Detachment consistently earned the highest possible rating at its annual inspection by the War Department and Department of the Army and was a source of pride to the Mines community as a whole. It rated "Excellent" twenty-three times by the end of the Korean War.

Over 2,000 alumni and former students at Mines served in the US Army during World War II of whom 99 or nearly 5% (not counting foreign students) were killed in action. Most went into the Corps of Engineers. 847 were commissioned officers, and Mines produced more officers for the Corps of Engineers through ROTC than any other university in the United States. Had anyone understood Dr. Chauvenet's design and the history of Mines, there would have been more than one reason for calling Mines "The West Point of the Rockies."

During World War II, Mines graduates served in all officer ranks from 2nd Lieutenant to Brigadier General. Colonel Wendell Fertig became famous for his successful guerrilla operations on Mindanao, and was the subject of a book, *They Fought Alone* by John Keats, and two books by W.E.B. Griffin, *The Fighting Agents* and *Behind the Lines*. After retiring from the Army in 1950, Colonel Fertig was awarded an honorary Doctor of Engineering from Mines. From 1960 until his death in 1975, he served as Executive Secretary of the Alumni Association, although most students treated him as the Director. The high participation during World War II continued through the Korean War into Vietnam, and until the advent of the all-volunteer Army in the seventies, Mines continued to provide a heavy stream of patriotic men into the Corps of Engineers through its ROTC program. According to Norman Zehr '52, assistant editor of *The Encyclopedia of the Korean War*, 391 ex-students of Mines took part in the Korean War.

The largest Advanced Course enrollment was in the 1951-1952 year with 197 students at the height of the Korean War. By the end of 1951, well over a thousand reserve officers had been commissioned in the Corps of Engineers after completing the Mines' Advanced ROTC Course. In 1961, 44 miners were commissioned as 2nd Lieutenants in the Army, all but three or four in the Corps of Engineers. That was out of a class of 183, with 14 foreign students, 10 veterans, one woman, and about forty-five to fifty that were married. In percentage terms, nearly 40% of the unmarried graduates eligible for military service went into the Army as officers from ROTC, a truly amazing number, most likely the highest in the nation. As one '61 graduate said when asked about serving in the military, "I never considered not serving." Times were soon to change.

Ten-cent Beer and Life-long Friends:

One day a few miners gathered in mourning as workmen boarded up the door and window of a downtown business establishment that had come to mean so much to them over the past couple of years. They removed their narrow-brimmed Stetson hats in reverence for the passing of a spiritually and socially significant symbol of their soon-to-end collegiate years—like the loss of a sacramental outward and visible sign of an inward and spiritual grace—the closing of the Golden Nugget Saloon.

The year was 1961, and the closing of the Golden Nugget ended an era. At the time, Mines prided itself on being an internationally renowned, small, compact, intimate, and coeducational academic campus with only 1,100 students. The coeducational part was a bit laughable in those days, as only four female coeds were present from 1957 to 1961. Mining, petroleum, metallurgical, geophysical and geological engineering were neither welcoming to females, nor were they sought-after career pathways for women in the late 1950s.

Mines demanded more of its undergraduates than any other college or university in the country. The curriculum was five years of fulltime course work crammed into eight semesters and at least two six-week summer sessions—a grueling grind that broke the will, and even the sanity, of many a young man. It was definitely a work-hard/play-hard environment. The Golden Nugget was one of the places where the miners played to escape the grind.

Weekends saw the alcohol flowing like a cool, clear stream out of the mountains—virtually everyone indulged, regardless of age. Many became accepted as legitimate patrons of the Golden Nugget Saloon when only eighteen or nineteen and without resorting to a fake ID. The Nugget was what many might call a real dive—dark, dank and smoky—with a stale atmosphere that reeked of testosterone, yesterday's beer, and neglected urinals. Female patrons were non-existent. The Nugget was a perfect escape for many, and most of the clientele were Miners. The local "respectable" adult professional and middle-class folks who wanted a place to stop in for a drink after work wouldn't be caught dead in the Nugget — they preferred the upscale Holland House Hotel lounge or one of the other more "regular" old-fashioned bars on Washington Street — those establishments which were not frequented by rowdy Miners.

The proprietor of the Golden Nugget was a quiet Filipino man named Santos. Santos stood about 5-foot 4 and was as wiry as a Charlie Brown Christmas tree. He couldn't have tipped the scales at more than 120 pounds, reflecting his former life as a ranked bantam-weight professional boxer. He never seemed to be interested in talking about his boxing career.

Santos was one of the reasons Miners gravitated to the Nugget. He treated them well, didn't ask too many questions, and occasionally gave them a pitcher of beer on the house. He also had the cheapest beer in town — ten cents a glass and seventy-five cents a pitcher. Well, it wasn't really the cheapest beer in town because the Coors Brewery courtesy lounge made free beer available some of the time. Unlike other beer-vending pubs, the only beer available at the Nugget (or the Coors Lounge) was Coors Banquet, on tap, or in bottles.

The Saloon was spartanly furnished with old wooden tables and chairs, the requisite long hardwood bar, complete with brass foot rail, and three well-worn, naugahyde upholstered booths. One of the booths was one of those large ninety-degree corner booths in the front of the Saloon, in the corner away from the entry door. It would accommodate 10 to 12 guys. Mines students planted their flag on that booth and claimed it for their very own.

It was during the spring of 1960 that a group of Mines juniors steadily became a more bonded brotherhood of friends — more than just drinking buddies — and began gathering in a more regular basis at the Nugget. At the end of that school year, they made an informal pact to regroup in the fall, during the first week of their senior semester.

This is where that second well-known institution of Golden — the Coors brewery — came into play. Coors prided itself on beer made with "Pure Rocky Mountain Spring Water", and it loved to show off its only brewing plant to visitors. At the end of a plant tour, visitors would be escorted to the beautifully appointed and gracious hospitality lounge to be rewarded with a free sample of Coors Banquet beer (they only brewed one product at that time). The irreverent Miners referred to it as Colorado Kool-Aid. Until the middle fifties, the courtesy bar was on the ground floor in the Coors brewery, in two tiled rooms, one of which featured a pool with a running fountain. There were no chairs, and there was no limitation on how many glasses a visitor could drink. Then the bar was moved upstairs, and the rules changed. Remarkably, a visitor could park in the yard within sixty feet of the door, walk across the railroad tracks, and not pass through any security at all. It was a different age.

Well, of course, free beer was a strong gravitational force attracting mostly poor, stressed, struggling, and vulnerable college guys, including our group of seniors. When their fraternal order of Coors topers came together again in the fall of 1960, they agreed to have their first gathering at the Coors courtesy tap room to start the academic year off right with a free round or two.

But then their scheming, calculating, problem-solving minds started to kick in, and not surprisingly, they figured out ways to "work" the system. Patrons of the hospitality lounge were normally required to meet certain prerequisites before they could imbibe in the nectar of malt and hops:

- *Participate in a 30-minute tour of the plant*
- *Be at least 21 years of age*
- *Be allowed no more than one or two refills after the first free draft*

The combined intellect of this enterprising group figured out ways around each of those three house rules. The plant tours took place on a fixed regular schedule, so they merely made sure to arrive at the entrance to the lounge when the last tour was ending about 4:00 p.m.. They sauntered right into the lounge as if they were part of the tour, and quickly laid claim to their favorite corner, out of sight of the bar. They then dutifully retrieved their first sample draft and retreated to the corner. After the first round was finished, they dispatched one guy with three or four glasses to fetch refills. This process was repeated, again and again, using different runners. The bar tenders were too busy to keep close track of how many refills any one of the students had. Eventually, of course, one of them would wise up and proclaimed, "I think that's all for you boys. Don't try to push a good thing."

That being the case, the group would adjourn its meeting to the other venue, the Golden Nugget Saloon, where they took possession of their stammtisch—the large corner booth. Because most of them had a relatively light class load on Fridays, maybe only five or six classroom hours, this gathering became a regularly scheduled social event every Thursday afternoon and evening. One of the members named Jack, however, had a two-hour optical mineralogy lab at 8:00 o'clock Friday mornings. Peering through a microscope at thin slices of various rock types with blurry, beer-washed eyes did not work so well, but, Jack was nothing but resourceful.

At the start of the fall semester, Coors tightened up its rules, and the Nugget became the group's location by default. The first evening back together at the Nugget, someone declared, "You know, this has become a really important aspect of my weekly routine here at Mines—one of the few things I really look forward to—gathering together with you guys for a few beers, some good laughs and some bitch sessions about our work load and profs. It really helps me through the pressure and stress of the week." There were some enthusiastic nods of agreement. Then someone else said, "Yah, this is the most important group I'm involved with on campus. We should call ourselves something!" More nods of agreement.

"What do you think we should name this motley crew?" someone asked.

"How about 'Motley Crew?'" answered another.

"Naw, that's too obvious," Dave suggested. "How about something a little more serious and official sounding? I've got it! The Seniors' Serious Drinking Club!"

"Hey, I think that fits us to a tee!" Larry proclaimed.

Without further debate they unanimously agreed on that name. But then Jack spoke up and warned, "We need to be careful and not get too formal or organized, lest we start drafting bylaws, establishing club officers, recording meeting minutes, taking on service projects, etc."

That caution was received with whole-hearted approval. They agreed that there would be no organizational structure, no bylaws, no officers, no meeting minutes, and no stated mission, purposes or objectives, other than to meet regularly to enjoy the comradery over a few brews.

The club did establish one policy in the beginning, however. Because most of its members were relatively poor, one of its first rituals had to address financial matters. As members showed up to the Thursday afternoon meeting, each was required to empty all his loose change from his pockets onto the booth table. That became the beer money for the night.

Santos appreciated the club well enough to keep the corner booth reserved for it every Thursday afternoon. There was usually enough change on the table to cover the cost of three or four 75-cent pitchers. It was the honor system—no one was concerned about how much or how little any member put on the table. If anyone was still thirsty when the pool of loose change dwindled to less than 75 cents, one or more Seniors' Serious Drinking Club (SSDC) members would usually suggest "Aren't we about due for a round on the house?" in a voice loud enough for Santos to hear. If Santos felt that they weren't abusing that tactic, a pitcher of free beer would promptly arrive at the table.

One of Jack's talents at the time was arm wrestling. He had developed a strong right arm with varsity wrestling training and strenuous summer jobs. One of the other SSDC members would pretend to challenge him to a contest at the Nugget's bar. They would engage in a very competitive-looking contest that Jack would eventually win. Then the SSDC members would invite other non-club patrons in the bar to challenge him for a pitcher of beer. Playing on male egos, they were usually able to get a taker or two. Several free pitchers of beer were enjoyed using that tactic, and Jack lost only one contest.

Another fund-raising gimmick involved Dave Dougherty. He possessed an arm exerciser with five springs and had developed his arms so he could pull the exerciser fully out across his chest starting at arm's length. He was a little guy, but somehow no one took into account his lack of reach, which meant the moment of force required for him was much less than for a long-armed big guy. Sometimes the bets went to fifty dollars, and Dave was a sure-fire money-maker.

When the club adjourned each Thursday meeting, there was usually some of the loose change remaining on the table. That presented a problem to be dealt with—what to do with the residual coins? Out of necessity, it was agreed that the club would break its prime rule (not to have any rules or officers). Bruce Henry spoke up with his observation, "The residual coins should be set aside and saved for the next meeting because they are community property of the Club. We need to appoint a trustworthy member to take on this weighty responsibility." For some inexplicable reason, several members turned and stared at Jack through bleary eyes.

"Jack has the most honest-looking face in the group. Let's let him do it!" It was sort of like the popular ad on TV: "Let Mikey do it."

By acclamation, Jack was appointed SSDC "Keeper of the Kitty," a title he still bears today—the only office and the only officer ever appointed for the club. He happened to have one of those small flexible plastic coin purses that opened when squeezed, embossed with the 1960 Oredigger football schedule. The purse became the SSDC safe deposit box for the kitty coins. Jack still has the purse and some residual coins from 1961.

Outside of bitching about the injustice of the Mines administration and the work load, the primary activity of the SSDC was playing whale's tails. The members became experts, and visitors usually paid the price of their incompetence with inebriation. The SSDC also entered a soap box derby racer in the Homecoming race and came in a respectable fourth. But the tour de force was winning the kayak race down Clear Creek since the prize was several cases of beer. The club even decorated the Nugget as their frat house and entered it in the contest for best house decoration.

The SSDC flourished the rest of the academic year and went on to become a continuing unofficial, but revered, institution at the School of Mines. Unfortunately, due to health concerns, Santos was forced to close down the Golden Nugget in the spring semester of 1961. The SSDC then had to seek a new venue, and it chose the Big M Lounge immediately south of the Golden Theater.

In the spring at the Club, one of the members careened into an argument with a graduate from 1941. The alumnus bemoaned the loss of most of the traditions he had known and chided the club members for having such an easy academic schedule. Freshman agitation had lessened considerably, but the worst in the alumnus's opinion was that the school was succumbing to outside pressures to make the school "easy", at least in his opinion. He had earned the equivalent to 238 semester hours of credit, whereas only one member of the SSDC had broken 200. It was sobering to think the load was once tougher.

Everyone knew of the adjustments made in 1956 when a number of courses had lowered the credit hours given with no change in classroom instruction hours, and the SSDC member tried to argue the load hadn't changed. Organic Chemistry had previously been a five-hour course, for example, four hours of lecture and three hours of lab. Now the course was only four hours of credit for four hours of lecture and three hours of lab. But the alumnus was not having any such rationalizations. He believed Mines was on its way out as the world's foremost engineering school. Maybe he was already right at the time, but within another decade he would be absolutely proven correct. All things were relative, and the 1961 graduates did not like to be told that their degrees had been won more cheaply than those in 1941.

One might think that the membership of the not-so-august SSDC organization consisted primarily of the underbelly portion of the class of '61 student body — those who might be candidates for the least-likely-to-succeed honors in the yearbook. Nothing could be further from the truth. The Club had an amazing array of individuals with outstanding achievements at Mines, and who would achieve even greater heights after graduation. Consider these examples from the twenty-six members:

One was academically second and another fourth in the class.

Three were named to Who's Who in American Colleges and Universities.

Four were members of Tau Beta Pi, scholastic honor fraternity.

Three were members of Blue Key, national honor fraternity.

Five were members of Scabbard and Blade (national military honor fraternity.)

Two were members of Sigma Gamma Epsilon, national earth sciences honorary society.

Four were members of Theta Tau, national engineering honorary fraternity.

Three were members of Kappa Kappa Psi, national band honor fraternity, including the president and vice president.

One was the President of the Student Council and five were members (out of a total of 15 Student Council members.)

One was Interfraternity Council President and two were members.

Four were members of the Board of Publications.

One was the Business Manager of the Prospector, the student yearbook.

Seven were members of the Press Club, the student honorary for work on student publications, including the president.

One was the Barb Council President.

One was the Prospector Park (married student housing) Council President.

Thirty-nine memberships were held in various professional organizations on campus (some were in two or three organizations.)

Far from being a discontented minority of poor students, the SSDC was a power on campus, represented everywhere. The feelings of the group, their hostility toward the administration and the arbitrary and unreasonable rules promulgated by the faculty, were par for the course. But SSDC members were not looking for a soft touch, and certainly not desirous of lowering the standards of Mines. They were not looking for better student recreation facilities, a *Student Union*, or anything that was common to other universities. They wanted the uniqueness of Mines to continue along with the toughness of Mines. But there was a difference between tough and harsh. And Mines was harsh and punitive.

Even the grading system took a turn for the worse in 1954. Going to a four-point system did not add to a student's credits but subtracted from them by creating a greater penalty for failing. On the three-point system, if a student made a "B" the second time he took a course, the grades averaged to 1.0 or a "C". Under the four-point system a "B" changed the average to 1.5, effectively lowering the average by half a point—still not sufficient to graduate. A student was not allowed to take a course again after making a passing grade, so an "A" was needed the second time to achieve a passing average. The system at Mines was constructed to hurry the departure of students who did not rapidly master course material.

Using a strategy of ignoring a course to concentrate on others was rarely employed due to the automatic "F." Probably more than half of the SSDC members had flunked a course during their time at Mines, but usually under circumstances where the professor refused to weigh later or final exams greater than early scores. With most engineering courses being cumulative in nature—that is later work depends on a mastery of earlier material—early exams were little more than progress indicators. Yet they counted. More than one student received an "A" or the highest grade in his class on a final exam in a cumulative course only to find that he still flunked. Mines required excellence at all stages, not merely when looking at the final product.

Student Backgrounds:

Other than students from Texas and Oklahoma oil families, Mines had a definite lack of students who came from money. In the freshman class there was a goodly number, but it was precisely the rich kids that flunked out the fastest. Another group that flunked out rapidly was the lower division students who owned cars, but they were also usually kids from wealthy families. At Mines wealth made no difference, and the kids weren't accustomed to brutal and arbitrary treatment. At home they were special, but as a freshman at Mines, they were nothing.

College kids in the 21st century enjoy portraying themselves as behind the eight ball financially, with enormous tuitions, fees, and living expenses, including birth control. At Mines in the fifties it was worse. Typical was one fraternity member who lived from hand to mouth and counted pennies. In his senior year his father became unemployed shortly after fall registration, and the student was on his own. He held a position for a Mines publication paying $40.00 per month, and he also received subsistence pay of $27.88 per month as a member of advanced ROTC. Other than his spotty winnings at bridge, poker, and euchre, that was his total income. He lived in Golden in a double room with another student for $17.50 per month, had no vehicle, skipped breakfasts, ate lunch in the fraternity house for 45 cents per day, six days a week, ate supper at Sena's Pizza for 90 cents a day, six days per week, and paid chapter dues to his fraternity of $11 per month and assessments of $5.00 every two months. Altogether that came to $39.10 per month. The storm on the horizon was that he had to save money for the spring semester, as tuition, fees and books in late January would be over a thousand dollars. He still had many normal expenses to cover, such as eating on Sunday, laundry, haircuts (he learned to cut his own hair), and other essentials. He figured his total expenses could be kept at about $68.00 per month, but that precluded dating, any social life, new clothes or literally anything that college students today would consider as base necessities. And, of course, there was only one type of birth control generally in use at the time, and it was the male's cost — condoms. At the time they cost a quarter apiece and had the consistency of ten-ply tires.

The solution to his spring registration problem came in two forms: Dr. Anton G. Pegis, later Vice President for Development, and Colonel Wendell W. Fertig, executive secretary of the Alumni Association. Tony Pegis was an ardent handball player, and he taught handball to many students, including our destitute senior. Tony mentioned that the Alumni Association sometimes loaned money to students in financial distress, so the student went to see Colonel Fertig. To make a long story short, both Colonel Fertig and the student were interested in military history and got along famously. The colonel immediately loaned the student enough money to register, and then a week later arranged another $400.00 loan to help with the student's living expenses during the semester.

Life-long friendships were cemented between the student and his two promoters, Tony Pegis and Wendell Fertig. Later in the spring semester, Dr. Pegis personally loaned the student enough money to purchase a five-year old used car, and with a high-paying job already waiting, the student's financial situation was finally looking up. As it transpired, he was able to pay back everything before going into the Army the following year.

Another student graduated from Mines in the middle 1950s, with only $30.00 to his name. He went to the bank in Golden and obtained thirty silver dollars, since they were in common circulation in the Denver area at the time. He then left for Chicago, where he was due to start work at a steel mill. In Nebraska he stopped for a meal and gas, and using his silver dollars, bargained the meal down to only one dollar. The attendant only took two silver dollars in payment for a fill-up although gas was twenty-four cents per gallon, and repeating this technique again twice again, arrived in Chicago with half of his stash intact. There were no interstate highways at the time, and the trip was about 1,050 miles. He moved in with two other Mines grads and was able to live on his remaining fifteen dollars until his first payday. Not all Mines graduates were flush with money, but they did possess resourcefulness.

To the modern reader, all this might sound implausible, but banks did not make student loans at the time. Part-time work was hardly an option for a Mines student given the heavy course loads (there were no work-study students at the time), and some students were forced to drop out of school for a year to earn enough for the next year. Another option was marriage, and a goodly number of students were supported by working wives. A silver diploma meant its holder would be a high earner in the vast majority of cases, and Mines students were good marriage risks. Out of sixteen graduates of one fraternity in 1961, only one remained unmarried twenty-four months after graduation. Even more astounding was the success of those marriages. Almost all were still going strong fifty years later.

Amenities provided by the State on campus for students were minimal to non-existent, but they were hardly missed. There simply was no time to use them, and even the handball courts were more often than not unused. The Olympic-sized swimming pool mostly experienced use by faculty, and even the weight training rooms were seldom visited except by varsity athletes. The Integral Club, the old gym next to Guggenheim Hall, was a hang-out for a handful of students during free periods, but freshmen usually returned to their dorm rooms and upper classmen to fraternity houses to sleep or study with friends.

Even in the best of times, however, Mines took its toll of the students. Sports and drinking were the main outlets. Mines touted student participation in sports, but the devotion to physical activity was actually much higher than what was officially reported. The two hours from 4 to 6 p.m. were crammed with physical activities, intermural competitions and "pick-up" games of various types.

Married students, attempting to lead normal lives with their families, were at a disadvantage in coping with the stress. This sometimes led to bizarre incidents of absent-mindedness or the suppression of natural instincts. In 1954, one miner and his wife and baby drove from Golden to Nevada with another Mines couple. They had a baby bed that hooked on the back of the front seat, and the guys rode in the front and the girls in the back. They made a rest stop at Grand Junction, then headed west again. The baby started crying so the father warmed a bottle with the cigarette lighter socket, fed the baby, and put him back to sleep in the baby bed. Just as they were about to cross into Utah, they were stopped by a Colorado State Trooper.

"Are you missing something?" he asked.

"No, the baby is fine."

"Look further back."

There were no wives. A return to Grand Junction found the girls, but the guys had no peace the entire rest of the trip. Nor did they deserve it.

Another student in the 1950s used sex to relieve the enormous stress of being at Mines, and he had worked out a slick technique for picking up women. He would go into a bar, find the homeliest girl there, and treat her like a queen. It never failed until he woke up one morning and found that he had not only gotten drunk, he had gotten married. Several days later he was found wandering along a highway, and it took months before he remembered his name. Another Mines casualty was a student who put in a magnificent performance and missed a 4.0 for his freshman year by the closest of margins. He spent the summer in a rest facility. Both of these stories resulted in happy endings, but there were those that didn't.

Burnout was a common malady, and often good students lost their interest in engineering under Mines' regimen. Sometimes they were able to recover and graduate, sometimes not. Often it took years, and students receiving their silver diplomas after seven, eight, nine, and ten years from the time they were entering freshmen were present in almost every graduating class.

In spite of all the above, or maybe because of it, Mines students in the 1950s were surprisingly religious. There was the Newman Club for Catholics, the Wesley Foundation for Methodists, and many other Protestants attended services in the Golden churches. They even attended Easter services at Red Rocks. In 1954, one student visited the Park Hill Congregational Youth Fellowship in east Denver and obtained a car pass for the Red Rocks Easter Service. About 4:30 on Easter morning, he jammed eight fraternity brothers into his two-door Oldsmobile and headed for Red Rocks Amphitheater. It took about 45 minutes to arrive at the parking lot, then they walked about a half mile. The service began promptly at 6 a.m. Just as the sun began to rise a couple of minutes later, a trumpet sounded. As the sun continued to rise in the east, right in their faces, they began to see an empty tomb. What a moving service! All of the brothers talked about the service all week long to everyone who would listen.

Perhaps the single most obvious feature that defined an engineer or a Mines Student in the 1950s was the ever-present slide rule. The one used by miners was no ordinary rule: it was a log-log-duplex rule, with twenty-three scales, including the LL0, LL1, LL2, and LL3 scales. These were necessary for making stoichiometric calculations in physical chemistry and metallurgical problems. In the 1950s, no one wore a backpack, but rather carried a clipboard or notebook for notes, on which were piled the books necessary for the morning's or afternoon's courses. The slide rule was often suspended from a belt loop, but sometimes just carried on the notebook. The rules were generally Keuffel & Esser (K&E), but sometimes Pickett & Eckel or others. Hand calculators were unknown, although a Monroe hand-cranked calculating machine was used for surveying problems due the requirement for great accuracy. It required skill and both hands to operate.

Electric calculators did not become popular until after 1963, when the Friden Calculator Company produced a desktop model using Reverse Polish Notation, and by 1968 was marketing it at a price of only $550.00. By 1975, Japanese calculator manufacturers like Sharp were producing engineering hand-held calculator models for under $100.00, and the slide rule became history.

With the advent of portable calculators and computers with application programs able to solve a great number of standard calculations, engineering education changed dramatically. Whereas linear programming was taught in the 1970s using the manual simplex method, by 2000, the solving of linear programming problems involved only learning how to input the data into an application on a handheld device. Students were taught how to set up the problem, and not how the solution was obtained. Later as consultants, engineers would be dependent on canned programs to be accurate, for they no longer knew how they worked. Worse of all, the technique of always making an engineering estimation of the correct range for a problem's solution was discarded, and engineers began to make catastrophic errors when software or hardware failed.

A college student in most technology schools today is like the tank commander Oddball in the movie Kelly's Heroes. When asked by Kelly if he shouldn't be helping to repair the tank, Oddball says, "No, Man, I just use 'em, I don't know what makes 'em work."

Mines students formerly knew how everything worked, and hopefully this is one tradition that will be restored at some point. One miner programmed a Less-Than-Truckload trucking system in the 1990s and computerized the rating of freight. When challenged in a meeting by the manager of the rating department at a large trucking company—a department that would be eliminated by the miner's programs—the miner quickly went through the steps to calculate the proper rate without resorting to a single note or document. The manager quit the next day. He had believed the miner didn't know how to calculate rates, especially under the complex conditions in his example. That would have worked with most upper-level software managers, but he had run into a Mines graduate. Somebody should have warned the poor fellow.

Chapter 13 - Academics & Administration

Originally conceived to grant degrees in mining, metallurgical, and geological engineering, Mines included civil engineering before the end of the nineteenth century. It was soon dropped, Petroleum engineering added in 1922, geophysical engineering in 1927, and petroleum refining engineering in 1947. Prior to the 1960s, Mines granted only the Professional Engineer degree (PE) in its six options (majors at most universities), the Master of Science (MS), and Doctor of Science (DSc.) The Bachelor of Science (BS) was felt to be below the level of a Mines graduate.

Although required semester hours for graduation fluctuated over the years between 168 and 200 hours, normal loads brought students credit in a minimum of 175 semester hours during the fifties. Compared to liberal arts colleges requiring 120 or most engineering schools with 128-138, Mines demanded a heavy academic load indeed! Taking advanced engineer ROTC added another twelve hours to bring the load to 187, and since the above did not include electives other than those selections fulfilling requirements, students often supplemented their curricula with six to twelve hours of other courses. In addition, band and varsity athletics often added another 6-8 credit hours to the 193 to 199 hours commonly scheduled. Two hundred semester hours in four years was fairly normal even after the two-hundred-hour requirement was discontinued in 1947.

A modest number of graduate degrees were conferred over the years before the 1960s. In addition to masters and doctorates in the standard six options, Mines sometimes granted a few degrees in civil, chemical, electrical, and mechanical engineering. Whereas the first professional diplomas were granted in 1883, no graduate degrees were issued until 1913.

The growth of CSM academically until 1970 can be seen from the dates each department was established. Prior to 1880 the designation "Professor in Charge" was utilized for each specialty, and academic departments as such did not exist.

1880	Chemistry, Civil Engineering, Geology, Mathematics, Metallurgy, Mining, and Physics.
1891	Electrical Engineering
1893	Descriptive Geometry
1902	Mechanical Engineering

1903	English
1922	Petroleum Engineering
1925	Economics
1927	Geophysics
1947	Petroleum Refining Engineering

Although advanced degrees had been awarded since early in the school's history, a Graduate School with a Dean was not created until 1953.

The first round of curriculum diversification in the 1960s brought three other degrees into existence; Mineral Engineering-Mathematics, Mineral Engineering-Physics, Mineral Engineering-Chemistry, but no new departments. In 1968 the Professional Engineer degree was withdrawn as the school's primary focus, and a Bachelor of Science was substituted. Forty-two required semester hours in engineering courses along with two in business and four in ROTC were deleted from the four-year curriculum while liberal arts gained eleven and a half. This was on top of the reductions made in the 1950s, eliminating twelve hours in engineering, one in business, and adding five in liberal arts. But that was not all: the 1950 requirements significantly differed from those in 1905-09. During the first fifty years of the 20th century, Mines had lowered the required hours in engineering by 34 hours, business by two, and added thirteen in liberal arts.

The intent of this "dumbing down" of the Mines requirements was to ease the educational experience and to raise enrollments. In 1968 the Professional Engineer degree was retained as a five-year program, but as expected, few students were willing to perform the additional coursework for what they perceived as offering no material advantage.

Previously the Professional Degree had been offered by several world-famous schools including MIT and California Institute of Technology but fell into disuse as academic standards declined across the nation following World War II. In 1968, Mines followed this trend as a marketing strategy. The cherished silver diploma was properly eliminated for CSM's four-year bachelor's degree, but it was retained for those few students pursuing the five-year program. Masters programs (with and without theses) producing degrees Master of Engineering and Master of Science were stressed in lieu of the old Professional Degree program. They were eminently more marketable and acceptable to the general public, and enrollments increased accordingly.

Before the 1960s, Mines assumed that students were dedicated to engineering, and already had chosen an option. In Metallurgical Practice, a six weeks summer course after the sophomore year for students going into metallurgy, a research project was required in which the students would work in teams of three. Midway through the course, the professor announced that the students needed to formulate their research plan on a metallurgical problem of their choice or interest and submit it for approval. This was a stunner for those students who were taking the course but hadn't really decided which option was best for them. Their metallurgy knowledge was slight, after all, that was why they were taking this course, and they certainly had not formulated any research interests. Surprisingly to the undecided students, most of their classmates in the course did have such interests already and had decided on an area of specialization; ore dressing, production metallurgy, or physical metallurgy. Somehow, all the teams worked up something, but the lukewarm metallurgical students quickly found themselves at a disadvantage.

The students that came from oil families in Texas and Oklahoma knew where their careers in petroleum engineering or refining would lead them, but other students were not so dedicated. Geological engineering took a number that were still finding themselves, geophysics took the math whizzes, mining the hard rock enthusiasts, and metallurgy the rest. The first two years were all common engineering with a geology slant, but then a decision had to be made. One student took the Kuder Preference Test as a junior and found that his interests were evenly spread across a wide range of fields, most of them not involving engineering. When the director of student affairs asked him why he was at Mines when his interests were so broad, he answered, "I didn't think I could teach myself engineering—everything else I could." When he checked with the Dean of Students just before graduation, he found that only three students had taken the preference test by that time, and the other two had been freshmen. Mines left little time for students to contemplate what they wanted out of life.

Until the 1970s, Mines also took a somewhat different view of examinations than most universities. In general, there was no curving of grades, and each course grade was comprised of various elements that were defined the first day of class. For example, all mathematics and calculus course grades were based on five one-hour exams making up 50% of the student's grade, 25% in homework and unannounced quizzes in class, and 25% on the final exam. If a student missed a pop quiz or homework assignment, he received a zero for that quiz or assignment. The only saving grace was that the professor threw out the two lowest quizzes or homework assignments. Inevitably they were zeroes. Missing an exam also resulted in a zero, and there was no opportunity for a make-up and none were thrown out. The only acceptable excuse was to be physically in the school infirmary, and in that case the remaining four exams each went from 10% of the grade to 12.5%.

The emphasis in most engineering courses was on getting the right answer, regardless of how one got there. For example, in civil engineering's fluid mechanics course (junior year), the scheduled exams had four difficult problems to solve. If you missed getting the correct answer on just one, you received a grade of 75 percent (a "D"). You did not get partial credit for using all the right methods to calculate the answer. The instructor emphasized that in the real world, getting the right answer to a civil engineering design is all that counts. A wrong answer could spell disaster, even if you used all the correct technical approaches. As a result, fluid mechanics was the most feared course at Mines. The second was a junior math course that was required of everyone in geophysics.

Some courses, such as plane surveying, featured a point system with 1,000 points possible if a student completed everything perfectly. In surveying there were five one-hour exams and field proficiency tests for a various number of points, five maps due on Mondays for 10 points each, a number of field problems with one hour of expected work representing 1 point, and a final exam of 300 points. 940 points or better was an "A", 939 was a "B". There were no make-ups except for the field problems that could be repeated for credit.

Students helped each other as much as they could, and in surveying, the team members became close. One time a student drew a map for one of the other members of his three-man surveying crew and earned the slacker ten points while only receiving nine for his own map. Even worse, the student ended up with 937 points in the course while the other crew member earned 941. The student who did the two maps received a "B", while his team member got an "A". Life was sometimes not fair, and Mines never was.

Final exam week was usually four days. It was intended that a student would have no more than two finals in one day, but frequently for students taking seven to nine courses, three finals were scheduled on a single day. Nobody bothered to complain—it wouldn't do any good. No professor ever rescheduled a final exam for any reason, nor were there any make-ups. As had been explained in freshman orientation, it was a requirement in engineering that problems be solved as rapidly as possible or when scheduled, and the convenience of the engineer was never a factor. If there was a hardship, one just rose to the occasion. Nor was anyone ever excused from a final exam because of prior performance in a course. Everyone had to do everything.

Examination and course grades were always posted by name on the professors' doors or outside on building doors. Exams were piled on tables for students to pick up at their leisure. This was a different day and age, and the Federal Government's Buckley Amendment of 1974 was not yet in force. Everyone knew where everyone else stood, and students routinely picked up their friends' or fraternity brothers' exams for them. There was no privacy or secrecy, but a lot of openness and cooperation. Normally a student would write down the grades for all his friends or fraternity members and spread the word as soon as possible. Exam grades for fraternity pledges were posted in a prominent place in the fraternity house, and each pledge had to announce his grade at lunch or dinner as soon as it was posted. The idea was to give the pledges incentive, as bad scores automatically earned a student swats.

Normally, once a grade was posted, it was cast in stone, and impossible to change. There were a few times, however, when the impossible happened. One grade for a student in the class of 1960 was posted as a "C" on the door to Engineering Hall (mathematics), but the grade showed up as a "B" on the student's grade card, much to everyone's surprise. No one clued in the administration that they had made a mistake.

Another student finished calculus and differential equations with a 94.3 average on exams but only 89.5 on homework. The course was in a summer session, and although the student had achieved the best point count in the class, his grade was "B". When he approached the instructor, he was simply told he hadn't worked up to his potential and deserved the "B." The instructor knew the student as both played the same instrument; the student in the CSM band, and the professor in the Golden Orchestra. So much for personal relationships, and so much for the idea of "curving" the grades.

A more telling example was supplied by a student taking a physical metallurgy course during the late 1950s. As taught at the time, it was a totally cumulative course which was easy or difficult depending on the student's ability to visualize lattice structures of metals.

The student received a 48 on the first exam and was lucky to get that. On the second exam, he began to see what was going on and scored a 68, still flunking. But most of his class was in the 60s and 70s, and it seemed as though he was gaining ground. He talked to his professor, Douglas Bainbridge, who assured him he would still pass if he performed well on the final since the knowledge was cumulative and the last part depended fully on mastery of the first. The lightbulb of understanding flicked on and the student discovered how to work Bragg's equation and lattice structures with ease. On the final exam he took top honors with an 88, even though there were several Tau Beta Pi students in his class. But his course grade was posted as an "F".

Barely able to control his anger, the student went to see Professor Bainbridge again. Bainbridge cut the irate student short and recalculated the grade. A 48 plus 68 plus 88 averaged to a 68. The student needed a 92 on the final to pass the course. That the final exam encompassed problems and subject matter from the entire semester and that the student had achieved the highest grade in the class was not relevant. The student then pointed out that 10% of the grade was supposedly determined by his performance in the laboratory. Dr. Bainbridge answered, "Oh, everyone does more or less poorly in lab, so I don't count it." The "F" stood, and the student was waved away. So much for talking to a Mines professor.

This incident also caused the student to lose out on a $1,000.00 scholarship, a significant amount of money at the time. The only remaining metallurgy student not receiving scholarship money of some kind, he had applied for a $1,000 grant from Carnegie-Mellon that was given each year to a Mines metallurgy student. The scholarship specified that it could not be awarded to a student receiving any other assistance, so the student was the only applicant. At the time he had a 2.78 GPA and was even eligible for Tau Beta Pi. The metallurgy department chairman, H. Gordon Poole, commonly referred to as "Cess," called the student in to say he could not recommend the student for the scholarship. The stated reason was that the student had flunked a metallurgy course. When the student related the circumstances, Poole blithely stated that was between the student and Professor Bainbridge, and that he would not interfere. No one received the money, and the student had to wait until the following spring to re-take the course.

Of the fifty or so Miners contacted during the research for this work, only two knew of an instance where a Mines professor changed a grade when a student complained. One occurred in 1961, when a student was taking Physical Chemistry II in the spring semester of his senior year. Alerted by one of his friends that his posted grade was a problem, the student rushed to Coolbaugh Hall to find out for himself. He thought he had aced the final and expected a "B" in the course. The friend was correct: opposite his name on the hallway wall was the grade of "F." In a rising panic as he was due to graduate within days, he located his exam in the pile on the table, and saw a grade marked as 68.

Impossible! The student hurriedly checked his exam and saw he had received full credit on most problems. He added up the score, and it came to 92, but the front page showed 68. Examining the test carefully, it was apparent Professor Williams had not added the scores on the third page of the four-page exam and missed adding in 24 points.

The student ran to Professor Williams's office, but the door was closed and locked. Taped to the door was a note wishing everyone a good summer, and that the professor would be back on campus in the fall. In total panic, the student raced to the department office, and showed the exam to Professor Dumke, chairman of the Chemistry Department. He looked at it skeptically and said he could do nothing to help. The student would have to take up the situation with Professor Williams.

At that very instant, Professor Williams walked into the department office. The student practically assaulted him with the problem, and Williams said frostily that he would have to re-grade the entire exam, he could not just add a number to the grade. They repaired to Williams's office, and the professor quickly went through the exam. Finally, he commented on the student's fine performance, and said, "It seems like I overlooked the third page when I added up your score." He changed the grade on the exam, and pulling out his grade book, briefly looked at the student's grades in the course. "Looks like you should have gotten a 'B' or a 'C,' he said. "I'll have to study this. I gave you an 'F' because I don't believe anyone who flunks a final exam should be allowed to pass the course."

At this point the student wasn't going to get fussy even though the professor had arbitrarily given him a grade based on unannounced criteria. The student's graduation depended on Williams's good graces. "A 'C' will do just fine," the student said.

"You sure? You might squeak over to a 'B.'"

"I'm only interested in graduating, and I need the change put in as soon as possible."

Professor Williams changed the grade to a "C," and the student graduated. A story like this one was extremely rare in the annals of Mines. Such things simply weren't done, regardless of the circumstances. Had the student's friend not alerted him to his posted grade, the student would not have graduated that year. He would have lost the job offer he had already accepted and been forced to return to Mines the following spring to retake the course. Yet in the second known case, three grades were adjusted under bizarre and somewhat similar circumstances, and in the same course as above, Physical Chemistry II. About twenty students were taking the course in Summer School in the mid-1950s, and three students decided to form a study group, made up of two Seniors — Bill Bowie (a descendant of Jim Bowie), Hollis Sawyer, who needed only credit in the course to graduate, and a student we will call Harding, who was completing his junior year. The three studied diligently, but the result of the first hour quiz had the three each scoring below 50, while the other students scored between 65 and 77. The three redoubled their study efforts. In class, they asked Dr. R. Thomas Myers whether they could have the low grade expunged if they all received a passing grade on the remaining two exams and the final. The answer was a resounding negative.

They then asked if he would expunge the grade if the three took turns each receiving the highest grade in the future exams and none of the three received a grade lower than 75 on the remaining exams. Myers laughed, and said, "Sure, if you do that, I'll throw out the first quiz." Like everyone else in the class that heard the offer and acceptance, Dr. Myers didn't believe such a performance was possible.

Against all laws of probability and straining everyone's credulity, Sawyer achieved the highest grade (about 87) on the second hour quiz, Bowie achieved the highest grade on the third hour quiz (again in the high 80s), and Harding achieved an 89 on the final, again the highest grade. Myers, however, posted a grade of "D" for each, using the first low quiz grade in the calculation.

Harding saw the grades and ran to Dr. Myers' office to see him, but, alas, he wasn't there. The department secretary had more disquieting news: she said the good doctor had left on vacation. Despondent, Harding waited in the office wondering how to get the grade raised to a "C," when the secretary took a telephone call. Lo and behold, it was Dr. Myers, telling the secretary he would be stopping by shortly for some things. She related the news to Harding who kept a sharp lookout for the arriving professor. When Dr. Myers entered the office, Harding asked him why only one person achieved a "C" in the class. He said that was the result of his grade calculations. Harding asked if he remembered the agreement that was made in class regarding the three students. Dr. Myers acknowledged the verbal agreement, and confessed that he hadn't even checked the grades, so improbable was the possibility that the three students had achieved what they promised. He opened his grade book and examined the scores.

"You did it!" Myers exclaimed. "I never thought it was possible." He immediately called the Registrar and changed the grades.

It would have been a wonderful ending to a typical saga of Mines students versus the Mines faculty, but shortly thereafter, Hollis was killed in a Montana mine cave-in where he had already started his full-time employment as a Mining Engineering. He never knew the grade had been changed.

On the other hand, stories like the following one, also involving Harding, abound from the 1950s. In it, graduation was actually denied him, although he had completed all the course requirements. It concerned Dr. N. Cyril Schieltz, who taught X-Ray Diffraction, an optional course for Ore Dressing or Production Metallurgy students in the final semester of their Senior Year. Harding had earned a solid "C", but when grades were submitted to the Registrar, his was an "F".

Immediately, Dean Burger called him (Burger literally knew all the prominent students on campus, and Harding had been president of the ATO fraternity for two years.) The Dean informed him there was a problem, and that he would not graduate. The Metallurgy Department Chairman, H. Gordon Poole, had not given him the required recommendation of the Metallurgical Department for granting the degree although he had achieved the requisite GPA and passed all required courses. Harding raced over to the department office.

Poole stated he was withholding his recommendation until a passing grade was achieved in X-Ray Diffraction, because a Metallurgical Engineer should pass every metallurgy course attempted. Harding argued that his grade should have been a "C." Dr. Schieltz was called to Poole's office.

In his heavy German accent, Schieltz admitted that the reports Harding and his partner had submitted had earned them an "A" in lab, but he said to the incredulous student, "You get an 'F' because I never saw you in the lab."

Schieltz had no proof of his allegation since he never took roll in the lab, but that didn't matter. What had happened was that Harding's lab partner was a favorite of the professor's, always standing at his elbow, asking many questions, and devouring Schieltz's explanations and answers. Harding, who like most of the students, generally stayed over by the equipment or in the darkroom, doing the work that his partner wrote up. In the end, it was appearances and apparent interest that counted. Dr. Poole denied Harding the right to call in his lab partner, and upheld Dr. Schieltz as within his rights to issue the "F." Harding did not receive his silver diploma and would not receive it until he obtained a passing grade in X-Ray Diffraction.

After contacting many other schools teaching X-Ray Diffraction, Harding was unable to find one offering it in summer school. He discussed his problem with Metallurgy Professor Douglas Bainbridge who offered to teach the course if Harding could find nine other students to take it. No one was interested in X-Ray Diffraction. The story had spread through campus like wild fire, and the usual response was, "Don't you know what happened to some senior who took it?" Harding reported this to Bainbridge, who laughed and said he would teach it as a graduate course. Bainbridge then told Harding to check out all the books that could be found at the library on X-Ray Diffraction and read the first chapter of each book. The first day, Bainbridge solemnly took roll, marked it in his roll book, then walked around the lectern and took a seat. After a minute of silence, he turned and said: "Well?"

"Well, What?" Harding replied.

"Get up there and teach. You've had this course, I haven't." So, Harding did.

The following week, Bainbridge took over the lecturing. When Harding asked about lab, he was told he had already passed the lab portion, and that everyone in the Met Department was well aware of what Dr. Schieltz had done to him.

After the final exam, Harding went to Bainbridge's office to get his grade, sure that he had earned a "B."

"Since there was only one student in the class," Bainbridge said, "It is obvious that whatever you earned will be the class average, so a "C" is the only grade warranted."

It is difficult to reconcile the two stories recited in this work about Professor Bainbridge (who later taught X-Ray Diffraction on a regular basis), but Bainbridge was a character, well-known to be arbitrary, capricious and punitive. Students avoided him when possible, like the plague.

In another recorded case, a professor structured an exam to weed out those students unwilling to go above and beyond. At the last class before the last hour quiz in organic chemistry, the professor passed out a take-home quiz. He stated the exam was totally optional homework, but to work it could be to the students' advantage. A group of about 10 students gathered at the ATO House on Friday night to discuss the quiz and found that every question was extremely difficult. The group broke into teams, with each team assigned to wrestle with certain questions. The work went on until Sunday evening, when all the teams gathered together to discuss their results. By the end of the evening, the group had decided on solutions to all problems, except one, to which there were two schools of thought. Monday, the professor was asked to explain the one problem before passing out the test. He refused but collected the take-home quizzes from the ten students who had worked it, then distributed the actual exam, which was identical to the take-home quiz. The ten students received high grades, but the others were blown out with poor grades, mostly below 50, with the lowest being 22.

And then there was the Physics Department, known to be consistently off the wall. One physics quiz in 1954 was so difficult that most students were highly perplexed. One student read the entire exam of 4 questions without seeing anything he recognized. Since all Physics seemed to stem from the basic formula "$F = MA$", he wrote that formula under each question, then spent the rest of the hour determining parts of these parameters for each question, never reaching an answer on anything. Expecting to have failed, he was astounded to receive the grade of 80 on the quiz with a notation that he had attacked each question properly. Evidently, this time just simply attempting to solve a problem was good enough for a "C".

The reader should understand that these examples are the tip of the iceberg when relating stories from class and the faculty's grading. Probably every student from the old Mines has a favorite story of his own, and as unbelievable as they sound, it is likely that most are true. Very often a "C" was a very good grade and difficult to obtain, to say nothing of "A"s and "B"s. The quest for obtaining good grades took an enormous toll on many students. In 1959, the student graduating with the highest-grade point average — only a single "B" marred his record — ended his life shortly after graduating in a Dallas hotel room.

The academic rigor at Mines, if that can be said what it was, colored the experiences by Mines graduates at other universities when they pursued advanced degrees. Both authors earned advanced degrees and found the requirements relatively easy after surviving Mines. One became an attorney, passing the bar on his first attempt, and the other took top honors in the MBA program at Case Western Reserve University, and advanced to candidacy for a PhD in two different specialties, Information Systems Management, and Management Science and Statistics at the University of Maryland. It was a piece of cake compared to Mines.

One ex-Mines student took a General Systems Theory seminar in a doctoral program at another university. A paper was required each week on subjects that the professor passed out, and after the papers were collected, each subject was discussed. After six weeks the professor blew up at the class. The ex-Mines student was the only one who had turned in a paper on every assignment: several students had done just one or two, and a couple hadn't done any. The ex-Mines student received an "A", while the others were all given "B"s. Mines undoubtedly would have washed most of those students out of the program.

It is difficult to apologize for the rigor of Mines and the life lessons learned on campus. Often a Mines education paid off, sometimes in surprising ways. In 1957, a recent Mines graduate living in the Calumet Area of Indiana visited the Calumet Campus of Purdue University to see if there were any advanced courses in metallurgy of other engineering disciplines that might be advantageous for him to take. The Director of Admissions met with him and asked why he wanted to take such courses. Upon learning the potential student was a Mines graduate, the director reached into a drawer, produced a document, and said, "Fill this out and bring it back by the end of the week." He then talked about the need for a teacher of a specific math course.

It was an application to teach mathematics at Purdue as an adjunct professor. The miner protested that he had never taught at any level and was unfamiliar with the math course the director had mentioned.

The director said, "If you graduated from Mines, you are just what we need. No other qualifications are necessary."

CSM's regimen was also in line with the "Great Man" theory concerning the progress of mankind. Born leaders were attending Mines, and they were taught to shun committee structures and concentrate on individual excellence. The operative rule in industry management of technology was to hire the smartest man available, give him enough money and support to do the job, and then **get the hell out of his way**! A plethora of behavioral research supports this as the best approach, but only when the employee is not only smart, but also driven, innovative, tireless, and professionally competent. Mines could assure an employer that a Mines graduate possessed the last four attributes, even though the grad might not be the brightest bulb around.

For example, in 1985 a Mines graduate programmed an entire Time Accounting System for CPA firms from scratch over the 3-day Memorial Day weekend, to the immeasurable satisfaction of his client. In 1986, he worked for five weeks at Silver Eagle Transportation in Portland, Oregon, and programmed an entirely new and eminently successful freight billing and rating system, eliminating manual rating and fifty-seven jobs. The Teamsters Union wasn't happy, but the owners were. During the day Silver Eagle management met with the programmer to outline their needs in some part of the system, and in every case, the programmer was ready to demonstrate the solution in the morning. It was a job on which other software vendors would have used a team of twenty to fifty programmers and multiple designers, analysts, and managers, and might have completed it in two years. Great men are everywhere, not just in high political office — and many of them are Mines graduates.

In another example, A US Army Training Center was in the throes of expanding to meet the needs of the Vietnam War. The Center's G-3, having worked on the problem with experts sent from the Pentagon for several weeks, finally declared it unsolvable without building new facilities. A Mines grad, a captain in one of the training brigades was told by his commanding officer to find a solution, since the trainees were slated to be arriving in two weeks. He did, and the next morning presented it to the Center Staff. Without a single change or a dime of new cost, it was adopted.

Guggenheim Hall

Chapter 14 - Academic Policies

CSM academic policies were harsh and unforgiving in spite of a student-teacher ratio which was one of the most favorable in the United States. The policies were often pleasant surprises to new faculty coming from more lenient institutions. Courses with multiple student sections were subjected to departmental exams, and students were responsible for the required material whether or not covered by an instructor in class. As was so often stated by CSM administrators at the time, Mines was certifying its graduates possessed a certain body of knowledge and abilities, not that someone graduated after taking various subjects and courses over four years.

Mines insisted upon a strict rule concerning holiday breaks which undoubtedly would be a cause for a Civil Rights case today. If a student was absent from his last class before the break or his first class afterwards he automatically received an "F" in that class. The only valid excuse was to be sick and physically present in the Mines infirmary. It was not unusual to see students driving all night to arrive at their first class before the period was over. The sick rule also applied to all exams; the only excuse which kept a student from receiving a zero on an exam was verification from the school doctor confirming the student's sickness and confinement in the infirmary. Even with an acceptable excuse, a student was not allowed to make up the exam; it just didn't count in determining the grade. No one could afford to miss an exam because a relative died, either.

Attendance in class was not required, and professors only took roll on the Wednesday before Thanksgiving, the Fridays before Christmas and Spring Break, and the Mondays following. As everyone had classes scheduled on those days, there was no need to take roll on any other day. Under student and parental outcry as unreasonable, the policy was discontinued. Obviously, student commitment to excellence had declined.

By 2015 attendance in class was required, and students were subject to professors lowering their grades for what the instructor's thought were excessive absences, regardless of the student's performance on exams. Supposedly this was because without attendance, the student would be unable to receive the "flavoring" from the faculty member. This argument, of course, is specious — instructors are afraid that poor student attendance at the lectures will be noticed by other instructors and negatively impact their reputations. Making attendance part of the grading process was actually an insult to the students and made them little better than education students in courses where there was no other criterion.

Other than for enforcing the school's policy on breaks, requiring attendance in the 1950s would have been considered a childish measure. Mines students were men, and such paternalistic bureaucratic measures would have served no purpose. Miners rarely missed class as they were too important to miss. There was always a mass of information and explanation put forth in class that was necessary to master so a student could pass the next examination. Notes from other students didn't cut it, and to miss many classes was to flunk out. That attendance has now become required, suggests the instruction is poor or unimportant.

In another sense, Mines has apparently moved away from class attendance being important at all. From 1952 to 1961, instructors rarely missed classes, and when they did, substitutes were provided by their departments. No classes were ever cancelled due to weather, and instructors were rarely, if ever, late to classes. In 2015, the entire School of Mines was closed due to "snow days" three times, something that would have been unthinkable during the 1950s. Nor was there such a thing as "Fall Break", amounting to a weekend and two days starting the week. Clearly, the necessity of instruction has been replaced by the bureaucratic imposition of taking class attendance.

In the 1950s, Christmas break was two weeks long, Thanksgiving was two days, and no other fall or winter holidays were observed. Final exams took place in the middle of January. In the spring, the only holiday was Spring Break that was one week long.

The school calendar underwent adjustment so that Christmas Break would not break up the fall semester. Classes now start in August, two weeks before Labor Day, rather than a week after Labor Day, which has now become a holiday. Fall Break consists of four days, Thanksgiving has been expanded by a day to become three days plus the weekend, and there is a dead week of no exams prior to final exam week of five days. With most students taking only five substantive courses, few students have to take two final exams on the same day, much less the three that had frequently occurred earlier. Winter Break (not Christmas Break, as that is politically incorrect) lasts three weeks. The spring semester also underwent substantial revision. The campus is closed for Martin Luther

King Day, two days for President's Day, a week for Spring Break, and once again, preparation time is given for the final exams that occur over five days, and school is out before the middle of May.

Under this academic schedule, not only has the course load been reduced, but the hours of instruction have been lessened. In the 1950s instruction was a full sixteen weeks long, today it is fourteen weeks and three days. This is a drop of seven days of instruction or a reduction of almost nine percent.

Grades followed a strict numerical system and were rarely, if ever, subject to curving, rounding, or any adjustments such as weighting later exams more than earlier ones. After 1947, the scale was as follows:

Grade	Numerical Scale	GP[1]	GP[2]	Explanation
A	94.0 – 100	4	3	Superior
B	86.0 – 93.99	3	2	Very Good
C	78.0 – 85.99	2	1	Good
D	70.0 – 77.99	1	0	Poor
F	below 70.0	0	0	Failing (Un satisfactory)

According to the CSM Registrar at the end of the fifties, grading was as follows:

"The semester hour in the Colorado School of Mines represents one hour of lecture or recitation per week for one semester, or the equivalent in laboratory or field work. Prior to June 1, 1947, the number of credits assigned to a course indicated the number of periods that a student was expected to devote to that course each week for one semester. To translate credits (earned before June 1, 1947) to semester hours, multiply the number by .41.

....The number of grade points earned in any course is the number of semester hours assigned to that course multiplied by the numerical value of the grade earned in the course....

Prior to June 1, 1947, the number of quality points earned in any course was the number of credits multiplied in accordance with the grade received as follows: grade H equaled 4, grade A equaled 3, grade B equaled 2, and grade C equaled 1. The method of grading was as follows: H - superior work, initiative, leadership; A - excellent work; B - average work; C - below average work; D - conditional; E - failure."

---

[1]Grade points after September 1954
[2]Grade points June 1947 to August 1954

Graduation Requirements:

For graduation a student had to complete all the requirements of the option he elected and meet a minimum scholastic requirement of a 2.0 grade point average. This average was calculated by dividing the total grade points earned by the total semester hours attempted. After June 1947 but before September 1954 a student had to complete all of the requirements of the option he selected and meet a minimum quality point average of 1.0. Before June 1947 a candidate for graduation was required to complete all the prescribed work of the option he elected, plus additional work to make a total of 500 credits (205 credit hours) and earn a minimum of 1,000 quality points. Prior to September 1940, the required credits and quality points fluctuated from a low of 480 credits (197 credit hours) to a high of 540 credits (221 credit hours).

Grades were reflections of a student's performance as measured by the appropriate yardsticks. Except for a very few electives which probably made a negligible effect on overall grade point averages, students could not select courses or instructors who could be relied upon for easy grades. Even if easy electives had existed, most students would have been unable to take them due to their heavy load of required courses. And, of course, such courses were not offered in summer sessions.

CSM did not have student evaluations of instructors in the 1950s and 60s, and professors rarely attempted to win student favor under any circumstances. In many universities where student evaluations were used as the primary determinant of an instructor's teaching effectiveness, faculty often bribed students with high grades for good evaluations. This didn't happen at Mines; indeed, instructors seemed to vie with one another for reputations as being tough graders.

Examples abound of legendary faculty toughness, but a few will suffice to set the proper tone. In plane surveying one student received 289 out of a possible 300 points on his final exam (96.3%), bringing his total to 937 for the course. There were a thousand points overall, and when the student received the "B" he expected, he did not think to argue for an "A". There was no rounding off in Professor Kelly's department.

Lest anyone think a student could withdraw from a course without penalty during the first twelve or fifteen weeks like so many do today (including Mines), it should be remembered that Mines allowed withdrawals only during the add-drop period which was the first week (5 days) of each semester. Most universities allowed students to stay for half a semester or longer before withdrawing from a course, effectively allowing a student to make multiple runs at the same material until he obtains the best possible grade. Not so at Mines. A student made his decision in the first week and had to stick it out.

This policy later changed as Mines sought to be more student-friendly after 1970. By 2015, a student could withdraw from any course through the twelfth week of a semester for any reason with a grade of W (Withdrew-no penalty.) Freshmen and transfer students in their first and second semesters were permitted to withdraw from courses through the Friday prior to the last week of classes. Students could take a course any number of times without affecting their GPA like at most universities. With the course loads reduced, it became possible for students to pursue a leisurely pace, drop courses at the last minute as appropriate, and earn very high GPAs.

Another common feature of grading policy in universities as grades were inflated during and after the Vietnam conflict, is allowing students to take courses a second and third time, replacing their earlier grades with those earned later. A student might earn a "C" the first time he took a course, a "B" the second, then finally achieve an "A" the third. Many universities today do not count the first two attempts, and simply record the course as an "A" in calculating the student's GPA. Mines required all three attempts to be averaged in, and any grade earned remained forever in the student's average.

From 2007 to 2011 Mines adopted this "highest grade only" policy, but thereafter returned to counting all attempts at a course to determine a student's GPA. Mines also expanded the grades given to include plus and minus designations, and the strict numerical value of a grade was discontinued. Only time will tell what effect this will have on student GPAs. However, with the average female GPA at Mines being 3.0 and the male average not far behind, it is clear that grading rigor is nowhere near what it was in the 1950s. Grade averages at Mines have become inflated by almost a full grade over the usual 2.05 all-student average in the 1950s.

Most universities have adopted a numeric scale of "A" 90-100, "B" 80-89, "C" 70-79, "D" 60-69, below 60 is an "F." This was not officially adopted at Mines as standards relaxed, probably because it would show a decline in numeric standards that would be difficult to defend. Instead, grading standards became fluid, and up to an instructor's discretion. Under this system, an exam earning a score of 90 might be an "A" in one course, whereas a 80 might be an "A" in another. On this basis alone, it has become impossible for Mines to certify that a student has mastered any certain amount of knowledge. No one knows what level of knowledge a specific grade represents. Everything has become subjective according to a professor's opinion and subsequent decisions. Mines also introduced an appeals process for a student to contest a grade. In the 1950s, such a process would have been unthinkable and considered as violating a faculty member's right to give grades as he saw fit. The scale in 2015 was at follows:

Excellent	A	4.00	A-	3.70		
Good	B+	3.30	B	3.00	B-	2.70
Satisfactory	C+	2.70	C	2.00	C-	1.70
Poor	D+	1.30	D	1.00	D-	0.70
Failing	F	0.00				

One of the traditions CSM could have eliminated without any decline in standards was the double jeopardy of freshman English. One of Mines' greatest cruelties occurred to seniors when they were required to repeat the same English grammar course they had taken as entering freshmen. In theory this was to insure all Mines graduates would have presentable English capabilities and repeating the lessons of three years earlier would be a handy refresher. In practice it worked out otherwise. Often the most brilliant engineering students had limited verbal interests, and English courses were their poorest subjects. But the most terrifying aspect of English grammar was its spelling test; students were given the list of the 1,000 most commonly misspelled words and tested with 100 chosen at random. Ten or more misspellings was a flunk, nine or less a pass. Flunking the exam twice caused an automatic 'F' in the course. Talk about pressure! Consider the case of a graduating senior, with job and bride waiting for a silver diploma, taking the spelling test for a second time (with a different set of 100 words); if he gets ninety words correct he graduates and lives happily ever after, eighty-nine and he faces abject disaster.

Once a student flunked a course, he was usually relegated to a five-year program, or at least an extra summer school, to graduate. Most upper division courses were offered only once a year, and scheduling a re-take was a major problem. The scheduling was set up under the assumption that no one flunked anything, and the students were expected to complete the four years in lockstep. Having to take remedial math as a freshman necessitated taking advanced calculus and differential equations in summer school, as the course was a prerequisite for many junior and senior courses. Chemistry sequences were similarly affected if an entering freshman was required to take remedial Chemistry.

Having done well in prerequisite lower division courses was essential to academic success. A student was expected to apply earlier knowledge gained in lower division in subsequent courses. For example, it was impossible to get through physical chemistry without being able to apply advanced mathematical techniques, and expertise in engineering drawing was critical to earning a good grade in plane surveying.

In a discussion in 2001 at a class reunion, several students claimed that professors never graded on the curve while others said they sometimes did. Notably, those that said curving existed were all in the mining and geological engineering options. Curving, if it existed, was apparently present only in those two departments. No one maintained it existed in the lower division, and none of the metallurgists or petroleum engineers contacted for this work believed any of their courses were curved.

There was also the tyranny of departmental exams, particularly in lower division courses. The math department, for example, was very uneven in the quality of its instructors. Some professors routinely were slow and failed to cover material that showed up on the departmental exams. According to Ivan Hebel, math department chairman and a very good lecturer, the student was responsible for the material contained in the math or calculus book, regardless of whether or not the instructor covered the material in class. Hebel officially confirmed the principle discussed previously: Mines was certifying that the student possessed a certain amount of knowledge, and it was the student's responsibility to obtain that knowledge. The professors were there only to help.

There was only one way to fight that concept, and that was to find out in advance of an exam what the department considered important. The answer lay in the fraternity files of old exams. The tests were always different, but the similarities were important. Students worked the previous exams in preparation for theirs, and the payoff was often at least a full letter grade.

Several fraternities also possessed "spike" tables for copying maps, charts, and drawings. Various courses required the submission of maps or drawings as homework. In the summer surveying course, this was a weekend project starting after the weekly test on Saturday morning. Each map was to be turned in Monday morning and represented ten points on the student's final grade. The problem was time: measurements had to be taken, and then the drawing itself would take anywhere from four to eight hours. With three-man teams, each member of which had to produce the same drawing, the stage was set for one student to do the work, and the other two to copy. Yes, it was good practice in engineering drawing to do the work oneself but copying required some skill in itself.

One of the most feared aspects of math courses were the pop quizzes given in class and which, with homework, constituted 25% of a student's grade. Attendance was not compulsory, but with two or three unannounced quizzes per week, a student could not take the chance to be absent. Although the worst two quizzes were eliminated, a student who did not do his math homework every night could lose two letter grades by performing poorly on just the quizzes. Math was five days a week, and required study and problem solving every night. Cramming was an unworkable and ineffective strategy. Like most Mines courses, daily or almost daily study and work was required. Cramming was also not effective during final exam week, with the exams over four days, and the students taking seven to nine courses. Nor were there any exemptions to taking final exams.

Chapter 15 - Course Schedules

A typical schedule during the first semester, junior year for a student studying metallurgical engineering in 1960 who was also in Advanced ROTC looked like the following:

	MONDAY	TUESDAY	WEDNESDAY	THURSDAY	FRIDAY
8:00	Thermo	E E I	Thermo	E E I	Thermo
9:00	Mechanics	Mechanics	Mechanics	Mechanics	Mechanics
10:00	Met I	Mil Sci	Met I	Mil Sci	Met I
11:00	Phy Chem	Min Dr I	Phy Chem	Min Dr I	Phy Chem
12:00	Lunch	Lunch	Lunch	Lunch	Lunch
1:00	EE Lab	Met Probs	P Chem Lab	Free	Met Probs
2:00	EE Lab	Met Probs	P Chem Lab	Mil Sci	Met Probs
3:00	EE Lab	Met Probs	P Chem Lab	Mil Sci	Met Probs
4:00				Mil Sci	

Legend: Thermo – Thermodynamics
E E I – Electrical Engineering I
Met I – Production Metallurgy I
Mil Sci – Advanced Military Science & Tactics (ROTC)
Phy Chem – Physical Chemistry I
Min Dr I – Mineral (Ore) Dressing I
EE Lab – Electrical Engineering Laboratory
Met Probs – Metallurgical Engineering Problems
P Chem Lab – Physical Chemistry I Laboratory

The time was scheduled for 35 hours in the week for 25 semester hours credit although most advanced ROTC students delayed taking Mineral Dressing I until the spring semester. For someone wishing to take an elective like German, it would be a three-hour course scheduled at 4 p.m., Monday, Wednesday, and Friday. The courses were as follows for the above schedule:
Fall semester, Junior year, Metallurgical Engineering

Course	Credit	Description & Comments
CH333	3	Physical Chemistry, 3 hrs lecture, 3 hrs lab
MS305	3	Military Science (ROTC), 3 hrs lecture, 2 hrs parade
CE311	5	Analytical Mechanics, 5 hrs lecture
MT311	3	General Metallurgy, 3 hrs lecture
MT313	2	Metallurgical Probs, 6 hrs lab (4 hrs used as lecture)
MT321	2	Mineral Dressing I, 2 hrs lecture

EE301	3	Electrical Engineering I, 2 hrs lecture, 3 hrs lab
ME303	3	Thermodynamics, 3 hrs lecture
Total:	24	25 hrs lecture, 10 hrs lab: 35 hours in class per week.

The above did not count athletics, band, or student activities such as working in organizations, on the school paper, etc.

Supposedly Mines gave one hour of credit for each weekly hour of lecture or recitation, and one hour for each three hours of laboratory work. In practice the departments cheated: in the case of Metallurgical Problems, a course for two credit hours with supposedly two three hour labs, the professor lectured for four hours while students sat at drafting tables taking copious notes, After finishing his lecture, the prof was available for questions while the class starting working on its assigned homework problems.

Thermodynamics was arguably the hardest course at Mines, and was required of all students to graduate, regardless of degree option. It was apparently designed as the final "wash-out" course to separate those who had the mettle to graduate from those who could not come up to Mines graduate expectations. Each period, students were assigned from six to ten problems due at the beginning of the next class session as homework. That in itself wouldn't have been so bad, but the material covered by homework problems was never discussed until after all papers were turned in - and homework accounted for one-third of a student's grade. Assignments often took over an hour per problem to complete, so students formed groups and each man did two problems and copied the remainder from his other study group members. There was never enough time for a student to attempt everything himself, and cooperation was required if one wished to graduate.

According to the Mines administration, students were to study three hours for each hour of recitation. For a student with the above sample schedule, this meant a minimum of 75 hours of study per week. Coupled with class and laboratory time, the minimum was 110 hours per week without counting time to study for exams — in other words the student was in school or studying nearly 16 hours per day including weekends. If a student took an hour each morning to get up and eat breakfast, two hours each day for lunch and supper, and six hours per night to sleep, he ran a weekly deficit of seven hours. Desiring to maintain some semblance of a social life, miners obviously were forced to cut corners to survive.

The pressure was enormous, but that was what made Mines Men out of boys.

By the middle seventies, most universities had adopted academic loads unrecognizable as college standards to Mines graduates from the 1950s. Lecture coverage was reduced, and twelve to fifteen hours were considered normal loads, eighteen extremely heavy, and no undergraduate was allowed to take more than nineteen hours. Professors were not allowed to assign homework without covering the material in class first, and the Mines technique of requiring a student to submit homework prior to the professor lecturing on its concepts had become unthinkable. In the 1950s at Mines no professor would discuss material assigned as homework prior to collecting the actual work. It was incumbent upon students to try first by themselves—and have that attempt affect their grade—before professors would cover concepts germane to the problems.

Another change in the seventies was that students as well as the general population began to refuse to do anything for which they had not been fully and properly trained by some accredited authority. A professor could assign homework only as an exercise to cement knowledge by giving the student practice using techniques that the professor had already taught in class. This was the learning by rote, and it has made undergraduate American students inferior to those of other countries. Thinking for oneself became a thing of the past—it allowed for too much independence of thought and made the general population difficult to control by the governing elites.

Some students elected to transfer to Mines after taking easier lower division courses at other universities to avoid those same "flunk-out" courses at Mines. Probably fifteen to twenty percent of those who graduated did not start at Mines, further reducing the percentage of survivors from entering freshmen. The transfer procedure might sound devious and immoral, but it was often the only possibility for many students to graduate in four or five years.

Marginal students began to do the same thing in the seventies, but they went to community colleges. As these institutions grew, they provided a cheap and easy way for students to avoid difficult lower division courses at major universities. They transferred in their credits and stretched out their academic career taking twelve hours each semester until they graduated. Since tuition generally covered only a fifth of the cost of an education in community and state-supported schools, society paid an enormous price to warehouse an individual who should never have gone to college in the first place.

Schedules and Contact Hours:

To compare the historical trend at Mines from its opening to 2016, the tables below show the courses required for a degree in Metallurgical Engineering. The credit hours for 1905-09 are computed on the official Mines methodology of calculating course credits to credit hours established in 1947. The 1952-56 and 1957-61 schedules are those actually taken by the two authors with minor deviations for summer school work and reflect the true picture of schedules at the time. The courses include the electives taken by the authors in Metallurgy, so schedules in other options might reflect heavier or lighter loads. Contact hours reflect the time a student spent in class, laboratory work, or other required activities. Students active in intercollegiate athletics, for example, endured much greater contact hours due to practicing for their sport(s). The "Total Contact Hrs" are weekly hours spent attending lectures, in recitation sections, or in laboratories—the actual time spent on campus in classes.

1905-09 First Semester Freshman

Subject	Credit Hrs	Lecture Hrs	Lab Hrs	Total Contact Hrs
College Algebra	5	5	0	5
Trigonometry	3	3	0	3
Chemistry I	5	5	0	5
Chem Qual Analysis	4	1	9	10
Desc Geometry	3	2	6	8
Geology	3	3	0	3
Totals	23	19	15	34

1952 First Semester Freshman

Subject	Credit Hrs	Lecture Hrs	Lab Hrs	Total Contact Hrs
Mathematics	5	5	0	5
Chemistry I	6	5	3	8
Engineering Drawing	3	2	4	6
Geology	3	2	3	5
English	3	3	0	3
ROTC	1	2	2	4
Physical Training *	0.5	0	2	2
Totals	21.5	19	14	33

* Students opting to play in the Band received one hour of credit in PT, and had an additional 4 contact hours weekly. Those participating in a varsity sport received one hour of credit in PT, and had additional contact hours of from 5 to 15 per week. Anyone playing in the band as well as being on a varsity team still received only one hour of credit.

1957 First Semester Freshman

Subject	Credit Hrs*	Lecture Hrs	Lab Hrs	TotalContact Hrs
Mathematics	5	5	0	5
Chemistry I	5	4	3	7
Eng. Drwg	2	2	4	6
Geology	3	3	0	3
English	3	3	0	3
ROTC	1	2	2	4
Physical Training*	0.5	0	2	2
Total	19.5	19	11	30

* The credit hour decline in Chemistry and Engineering Drawing did not reflect any change in the amount of material covered — it was simply a lowering of the amount of credit given. Band and participation in varsity sports remained as in the first semester of 1952. In 1961, an hour of credit (without a grade) was given for the orientation week prior to the start of the regular semester, but it was meaningless and not counted.

2016 First Semester Freshman

Subject	Credit Hrs	Lecture Hrs	Lab Hrs	Total Contact Hrs
Nature/Human Values	4	4	0	4
Chemistry I	4	3	3	6
Fresh. Success Seminar	0.5	0	1	1
Earth & Environment	4	3	3	6
Calculus	4	4	0	4
Physical Activity*	0.5	0	2	2
Totals	17	14	9	23

* Participation in varsity sports or the band earned one hour of credit and substituted for Physical Activity. Veterans and transfers were exempt from the Physical Activity requirement.

1905-09 Second Semester Freshman

Subject	Credit Hrs	Lecture Hrs	Lab Hrs	Total Contact Hrs
Analytical Geometry	5	5	0	5
Analytical Calculus	3	3	0	3
Chemistry II	5	5	0	5
Chem Qual Analysis	3	1	6	7
Machine Design	2	2	0	2
Engineering Drawing	3	0	9	9
Surveying	2	2	0	2
Totals	23	18	15	33

1953 Second Semester Freshman

Subject	Credit Hrs	Lecture Hrs	Lab Hrs	Total Contact Hrs
Calculus I	5	5	0	5
Chemistry II	6	5	3	8
Engineering Drawing	3	2	4	6
Geology	3	3	0	3
English	3	3	0	3
ROTC	1	2	2	4
Physical Training*	0.5	0	2	2
Totals	21.5	20	11	31

* Band and varsity sports participation remained the same as in the first semester of 1952.

1958 Second Semester Freshman

Subject	Credit Hrs	Lecture Hrs	Lab Hrs	Total Contact Hrs
Calculus I	5	5	0	5
Chemistry II (Qual)	5	4	3	7
Descript. Geometry	2	2	4	6
Historical Geology	3	3	0	3
English Comp	3	3	0	3
ROTC	1	2	2	4
Physical Training*	0.5	0	2	2
Total	19.5	19	11	30

* Band and varsity sports participation remained the same as in the first semester of 1952. The lower credit hours versus 1953 does not reflect any reduction in the material covered.

2016 Second Semester Freshman

Subject	Credit Hrs	Lecture Hrs	Lab Hrs	Total Contact Hrs
Chemistry II	4	3	3	6
Physics	4.5	2	4	6
Calculus II	4	4	0	4
Design I	3	2	3	5
Physical Activity	0.5	0	2	2
Totals	16	11	12	23

Summer, Between the Freshman and Sophomore Years

Year & Course	Credit Hrs	Amount of work
1905-09		
Plane Surveying	6	4 full wks
		(assume 6 hrs credit, 18 contact hrs)
1953		
Plane Surveying	9	6 weeks,
		Approximately 456 hrs, 27 contact hrs
1958		
Plane Surveying	8	6 weeks,
		Approximately 456 hrs, 24 contact hrs
2016	0	No Summer requirement

1905-09 First Semester Sophomore

Subject	Credit Hrs	Lecture Hrs	Lab Hrs	Total Contact Hrs
Diff & Integral Calculus	5	5	0	5
Physics I	5	4	3	7
Quant Analysis	4	1	9	10
Tech Chemistry	2	2	0	2
Crystallography	4	2	6	8
Mine Surveying	2	2	0	2
Totals	22	16	18	34

1953 First Semester Sophomore

Subject	Credit Hrs	Lecture Hrs	Lab Hrs	Total Contact Hrs
Calc & An Geom	5	5	0	5
Chemistry (Quant)	5	3	6	9
Crystallography	3	2	4	6
Physics I	6	5	3	8
English Literature	3	3	0	3
ROTC	1	2	2	4
Physical Training*	0.5	0	2	2
Total	23.5	20	17	37

*Band and participation in varsity sports remained as in the first semester of 1952.

1958 First Semester Sophomore

Subject	Credit Hrs	Lecture Hrs	Lab Hrs	Total Contact Hrs
Calc & An Geom	5	5	0	5
Chemistry (Quant)	4	2	6	8
Crystallography	2	2	4	6
Physics I	5	5	0	5
Tech Exposition	3	3	0	3
ROTC	1	2	2	4
Physical Training*	0.5	0	2	2
Total	20.5	19	14	33

*Band and participation in varsity sports remained as in the first semester of 1952.

2016 First Semester Sophomore

Subject	Credit Hrs	Lecture Hrs	Lab Hrs	Total Contact Hrs
Chem. Thermo	3	3	0	3
Calculus 3	4	4	0	4
Physics 2	4.5	2	4	6
Engineered Materials	3	3	0	3
Physical Activity	0.5	0	2	2
Totals	15	12	6	18

1905-09 Second Semester Sophomore

Subject	Credit Hrs	Lecture Hrs	Lab Hrs	Total Contact Hrs
Integral Calculus	3	3	0	3
Mechanics	2	2	0	2
Physics II	5	4	3	7
Quant Analysis	4	1	9	10
Tech Chemistry	2	2	0	2
Mineralogy	4	2	6	8
Mine Surveying	2	2	0	2
Totals	22	16	18	34

1954 Second Semester Sophomore

Subject	Credit Hrs	Lecture Hrs	Lab Hrs	Total Contact Hrs
Adv Calc & Diff Eq	5	5	0	5
C.E. 202	4	4	0	4
C.E. 204L	1	0	3	3
Physics II	6	5	3	8
Mineralogy	3	2	4	6
C.E. 208F	4	3	6	9
ROTC	1	2	2	4
Physical Training*	0.5	0	2	2
Totals	24.5	21	20	41

*Band and participation in varsity sports remained as in the first semester of 1952.

1959 Second Semester Sophomore

Subject	Credit Hrs	Lecture Hrs	Lab Hrs	Total Contact Hrs
Adv Calc & Diff Eq	5	5	0	5
Organic Chemistry	4	3	3	6
Physics II	5	5	0	5
Mineralogy	3	0	6	6
Indus. Psychology	2	2	0	2
History of West Civ	3	3	0	3
ROTC	1	2	2	4
Physical Training*	0.5	0	2	2
Totals	23.5	20	13	33

*Band and participation in varsity sports remained as in the first semester of 1952.

2016 Second Semester

Subject	Credit Hrs	Lecture Hrs	Lab Hrs	Total Contact Hrs
Differ. Equat.	3	3	0	3
Technical Elective	3	3	0	3
Statics	3	3	0	3
Design II	3	2	3	5
Economics	3	3	0	3
Human Systems	3	3	0	3
Physical Activity	0.5	0	2	2
Totals	18.5	17	5	22

Summer, Between Sophomore and Junior Years

Year & Course	Credit Hrs	Amount of work
1905-09		
Mine Surveying	4	4 full weeks (assume 4 hrs credit, 12 contact hrs)
1954		
Metallurgy 202	6	6 weeks, 8 hrs per day (18 contact hrs)
1959		
Met Practice	6	6 weeks, 8 hrs per day (18 contact hrs)
2016		
Particulate Met	3	3 weeks, 6 hrs per day (9 contact hrs)

1905-09 First Semester Junior

Subject	Credit Hrs	Lecture Hrs	Lab Hrs	Total Contact Hrs
Geo, Stratigraphy	4	4	0	4
Metallurgy I	5	5	0	5
Mining I	3	3	0	3
Eng. Mechanics	3	3	0	3
Eng. Construction	3	2	3	5
Machine Design	2	1	3	4
Metallurgical Chem	2	0	6	6
Electric Power Trans	3	2	3	5
Testing Lab	1	0	3	3
Metal. Trips (req)	0	0	0	2
				extra weeks
Totals	26	20	18	38

1954 First Semester Junior

Subject	Credit Hrs	Lecture Hrs	Lab Hrs	Total Contact Hrs
Physical Chemistry	4	3	3	6
Civil Eng. 301	2	2	0	2
Civil Eng. 303L	4	3	3	6
Electrical Eng 301L	3	2	4	6
Metallurgy 307	4	3	3	6
Metallurgy 309L	1	1	2	3
Civil Eng. 205	2	2	0	2
Intercolleg. Athletics	1	0	5	5
Advanced ROTC	3	3	3	6
Totals	24	19	23	42

1959 First Semester Junior

Subject	Credit Hrs	Lecture Hrs	Lab Hrs	Total Contact Hrs
Analytical Mech.	5	5	0	5
Physical Chem I	4	3	3	6
General Metallurgy	3	3	0	3
Mineral Dressing I	2	2	0	2
Metall. Problems	2	2	4	6
Direct Current EE	3	2	3	5
Thermodynamics	3	3	0	3
Band/Physical Training	1	0	4	4
Advanced ROTC	3	3	3	6
Totals	26	23	17	40

2016 First Semester Junior

Subject	Credit Hrs	Lecture Hrs	Lab Hrs	Total Contact Hrs
Structure of Mtls	4	3	3	6
Met Thermo.	3	3	0	3
Phase Equilibria	2	2	0	2
Mech. of Materials	3	3	0	3
Elect, Hum & Soc St	3	3	0	3
Free Elective	3	3	0	3
Totals	18	17	3	20

1905-09 Second Semester Junior

Subject	Credit Hrs	Lecture Hrs	Lab Hrs	Total Contact Hrs
Lithology	3	2	3	5
Met, Lead & Zinc	5	5	0	5
Mining II	3	3	0	3
Mechanics of Eng	3	3	0	3
Mill Construction	3	2	3	5
Steam Eng. & Boilers	2	1	3	4
Electric Power Trans	2	2	0	2
Assaying	4	1	9	10
Metall. Trips (req)	0	0	0	2
				extra weeks
Totals	25	19	18	37

1955 Second Semester Junior

Subject	Credit Hrs	Lecture Hrs	Lab Hrs	Total Contact Hrs
Metallurgy 312L	3	3	3	6
Phys. Chem 333L	4	3	3	6
Alt Curr. (EE 302L)	3	2	4	6
Metallurgy 324	3	3	0	3
Mechanical Eng 303	3	3	0	3
Mining 210	2	2	0	2
Mining 314L	1	0	3	3
Intercoll. Athletics	1	0	5	5
Advanced ROTC	3	3	3	6
Totals	23	19	21	40

1960 Second Semester Junior

Subject	Credit Hrs	Lecture Hrs	Lab Hrs	Total Contact Hrs
Physical Met I	3	3	0	3
Physical Chemistry I	4	3	3	6
Alt Current (EE)	3	2	3	5
Production Met I	2	2	0	2
Strength of Materials	4	3	3	6
Modern Physics	3	3	0	3
Advanced ROTC	3	3	3	6
Totals	22	19	12	31

2016 Second Semester Junior

Subject	Credit Hrs	Lecture Hrs	Lab Hrs	Total Contact Hrs
Chem Proc of Mtls	4	3	3	6
Microstructural Dev	4	3	3	6
Met Kinetics	3	3	0	3
Elective, Hum & Soc St	3	3	0	3
Free Elective	3	3	0	3
Totals	17	15	6	21

Summer, Between the Junior and Senior Years

Year & Course	Credit Hrs	Amount of work
1905-09	0	Class Trips for 2-4 weeks, but no credit
1955	0	Advanced ROTC students often took Summer Camp at this time, representing six weeks in engineering training.
1960 Met Practice	1	Report of summer employment or one week lab work.Advanced ROTC students often took Summer Camp at this time, representing six weeks in engineering training.
2016	0	Nothing

1905-09 First Semester Senior

Subject	Credit Hrs	Lecture Hrs	Lab Hrs	Total Contact Hrs
Economic Geology	3	3	0	3
Ore Dressing	5	4	3	7
Electro-Metallurgy	4	3	3	6
Power Plant Design	2	1	3	4
Hydraulics	3	3	0	3
Compressed Air Mach	2	2	0	2
Hyd. & Cement Lab	1	0	3	3
Steam Lab	1	0	3	3
Mining III	2	2	0	2
Mine Exp & Rep	2	2	0	2
Thesis	2	0	6	6
Metallurgical Trips (req)	0	0	0	2 extra weeks
Totals	27	20	21	41

1955 First Semester Senior

Subject	Credit Hrs	Lecture Hrs	Lab Hrs	Total Contact Hrs
Metallurgy 322	3	3	0	3
Metallurgy 441	3	3	0	3
Metallurgy 447	3	3	3	6
Adv Tech. Exposition	2	2	0	2
Metallurgy 531	3	3	0	3
Business Law	3	3	0	3
Senior Trips	1	0	3	3
Intercollegiate Athletics	1	0	5	5
Advanced ROTC	3	3	3	6
Totals	22	20	14	34

1960 First Semester Senior

Subject	Credit Hrs	Lecture Hrs	Lab Hrs	Total Contact Hrs
Physical Met II	3	3	0	3
X-Ray Diffraction	4	3	3	6
Met Thermodynamics	3	3	0	3
Philosophy of Science	2	2	0	2
Scientific German	3	3	0	3
Economics	5	5	0	5
Advanced ROTC	3	3	3	6
Totals	23	22	6	28

2016 First Semester Senior

Subject	Credit Hrs	Lecture Hrs	Lab Hrs	Total Contact Hrs
Mech Prop. of Mtls	4	3	3	6
Process Ctl & Design	3	3	0	3
Transport & Reactors	3	2	3	5
Metallurgy Elective	3	3	0	3
Hum & Soc St Elective	3	3	0	3
Totals	16	14	6	20

1905-09 Second Semester Senior

Subject	Credit Hrs	Lecture Hrs	Lab Hrs	Total Contact Hrs
Econ. Geology II	3	3	0	3
Met, Gold, Silver, Cop.	4	4	0	4
Met, Alum., Nickel, Etc.	3	3	0	3
Met Lab	2	0	6	6
Met Practice	1	0	3	3
Met Plant Design	2	1	3	4
Contracts & Specs	2	2	0	2
Mining IV	2	2	0	2
Mine Economics	2	2	0	2
Thesis	2	0	6	6
Metallurgical Trips (req)	0	0	0	2
				extra weeks
Totals	23	17	18	35

1956 Second Semester Senior

Subject	Credit Hrs	Lecture Hrs	Lab Hrs	Total Contact Hrs
English 402	2	2	0	2
Economics 405	3	3	0	3
Mechanical Eng 404	4	3	3	6
Metallurgy 412	2	2	4	6
Metallurgy 450	3	3	0	3
Metallurgy 424	2	2	3	5
X-Ray Diffr. (Met 448)	3	2	3	5
Senior Trips (Met 414)	1	0	6	6
Intercollegiate Athletics	1	0	5	5
Advanced ROTC	3	3	3	6
Totals	24	20	27	47

1961 Second Semester Senior

Subject	Credit Hrs	Lecture Hrs	Lab Hrs	Total Contact Hrs
Adv Tech Exposition	2	2	0	2
Mechanics of Fluids	4	3	3	6
Ceramics	3	3	0	3
Met Plant Design	3	2	4	6
Prod Met III	3	3	0	3
Phys Met III	3	2	3	5
Scientific German	3	3	0	3
Advanced ROTC	3	3	3	6
Totals	24	21	13	34

2016 Second Semester Senior

Subject	Credit Hrs	Lecture Hrs	Lab Hrs	Total Contact Hrs
Elec Props & Apps Mtls	3	3	0	3
Materials Design	3	3	0	3
Metallurgy Elective	3	3	0	3
Metallurgy Elective	3	3	0	3
Metallurgy Elective	3	3	0	3
Free Elective	3	3	0	3
Totals	18	18	0	18

Total credit and contact hours for all four curricula:

Years	Credit Hrs	Decline from 09	Contact Hrs	Decline from 09
1905-09[1]	201	0%	323	0%
1952-56	199[2]	1.0%	322	0.3%
1957-61	193	4.0%	309	4.3%
2012-16	138.5	31.1%	173	46.4%

The decline of Mines with respect to being a very demanding engineering school between 1961 and 2016 is readily seen. But even more astounding is the reduction in the requirement for engineering hours. From 1909 to 2016, 46% fewer credit hours were required in Engineering, Science, and Technology.

---

[1]Note: credit and contact hours for 1905-09 are understated due to class trips not being counted for either category. Metallurgical trips probably amounted to another 20 weeks of trips that do not show up, easily representing another 26 hours of potential credit.

[2] The 1952-56 example student in Metallurgy competed three years in intercollegiate swimming, incurring 6 credit hours and 36 contact hours for six semesters plus senior trips (8 contact hours) that were not included in the above numbers.

Redquired Credit hours by Departmental Group:

Years	Engineering/Sci	Business	Liberal Arts	PT	ROTC	Total
1905-09	192	8	0	0	0	200
1952-56	158[3]	6	13	2[4]	4[5]	183[6]
1957-61	146	5	18[7]	2	4	175[8]
2012-16	104	3	29.5	2	0	138.5

This chart clearly shows that if a student took a Liberal Arts elective for two semesters such as German like the example student did in the 1961 class, the gain in Liberal Arts and Business was only 3.5 hours of credit from 1961 to 2016. Yet the amount of Engineering and Science or Technology courses dropped 42 credit hours, representing 1-1/2 years' work. Technical subjects dropped from over 83% of a student's course load to only 75%, and on a much reduced schedule of instruction. the school lowered its requirements for undergraduates, and the bachelor degrees given out by Mines starting in 1969 were not comparable to the professional degrees given out earlier.

---

[3]The drop in credit hours required from 1952 to 1957 resulted in giving less credit for the same material (attempting to fool the North Central Association) rather than eliminating courses or subjects.This is the same for 1957-61

[4] Assumes taking Physical Training for four semesters. Varsity athletics and band earned 1 hour per semester, making a possible total of 8.

[5]Two years (4 hrs) of ROTC was required. Advanced Engineering ROTC (12 hrs) was elective. The requirement for ROTC was eliminated in the 1970s.

[6]With Advanced Engineering ROTC, 195 credit hours were required

[7]Six hrs for German in the example not included. Only 18 hours were actually required.

[8] With Advanced Engineering ROTC, 195 credit hours were required.

Chapter 16 - Summer Sessions & Field Work

As every miner knows, CSM enriched their educational experience through extensive laboratory and field work appropriate to each student's option.

Although requirements and facilities varied over the years, all options required plane surveying up to the 1960s. It was taught by the Civil Engineering Department before a student's junior year, and the vast majority of students successfully negotiated the six weeks course in one of two summer sessions following their freshman year. The plane surveying course ran from seven in the morning to dark, five days each week, with Saturday morning reserved for field and classroom examinations, Saturday afternoon remaining available for repeat work on field problems and Sunday to draw the homework problem's obligatory map. Plane Surveying was a 9-credit hour field course given during the Summer of 1953, but by 1957 the school had reduced it to only 8 hours credit for exactly the same amount of work.

Each morning there was a one to two-hour class at 7 a.m. to introduce the new concepts for the day. Then the students headed to the surveying field west of Highway 6 and south of Mines Park in 3-man teams to conduct their field problems. Saturday morning, there was a written exam, followed by a field exam where the students demonstrated what they had learned during the week. Saturday afternoon, they ran "repeats." In 1953 if a team had gotten anything lower than full credit on a field problem, they could draw a substitute one from the professors, and run that one to improve their grade. By 1957 that policy had changed. A field problem was accomplished correctly or not. If not, the surveying team could repeat the problem on Saturday afternoon, and submit a new result before 6 p.m. The problem was an all or nothing proposition, and the team either received a zero or the number of points the problem was worth. On Sundays, each student drew his map for the week, usually about 18" by 24" in size and covering an area surveyed by the team in problems during the week, which was turned in at 7 a.m. Monday. The maps could not be late, and after the start of class, no maps were accepted. That was student life for 6 weeks. Surveying also levied the requirement on the students that each three-man team have a car. That was a major problem for the students when they formed their teams since only a few students owned cars. Often three students wanted to form a team together, but none of them had a car. Nobody cares what a car looked like, but it had to get the team around. Every summer some students would buy junkers, just for the six weeks course.

One enterprising team in 1953 didn't have the $50 or $60 to buy a car, so they got the bright idea to ask the dealers if there was any work they could do to float the down payment. The owner of Golden Motors (a Ford dealer) told them they could dig a sump for him, and he would apply their wages toward a car. After the students worked all day, the dealer said they had earned $20 between them, and the cheapest car he had was $50. Somehow they borrowed the remaining $30.00, and got the title to a 1936 Chevy coupe with a large trunk. They were in business for surveying, and fortunately the car lasted all six weeks without an incident. Mines students were resourceful.

As another example, a three-man team in the summer of 1958 (Class of '61) had no car but had $100 between them to contribute for one. After visiting two or three Lakewood used car lots and pleading poverty and hardship, they found a sympathetic salesman who agreed to sell them an ugly 1946 Plymouth 4-door sedan for $95 ($33 apiece). The car lasted all summer and most of the next school year.

Students would not easily forget "Repeat Hill" in the field area at the base of Lookout Mountain, the requirement to keep a field book with a 6H or harder pencil, and the terror of dropping a chain or forgetting to tighten a transit properly. For only eight semester hours credit, plane surveying was probably the course at Mines requiring the most work for the least credit for all students. It was not unusual for students to put 425 to 460 hours of work and study into the course. A normal 8-hour course during a regular semester would represent only about 360 hours of class, work, and study.

Other summer course requirements were particular to each option:

Metallurgical Engineering:

The Department of Metallurgy required completion of a summer session before enrolling in metallurgy courses which meant that Metallurgical Practice was to be completed between the sophomore and junior years. The six weeks course consisted of an early morning lecture followed by working on various problems and assignments in the pyro-metallurgy and ore dressing labs. This went on for eight to ten hours a day, five days a week, and did not count homework and the Saturday tests, for eight hours credit. Students learned how to conduct assays for silver and gold in addition to standard hydro- and pyro-metallurgical techniques for ore concentration and refining. The work included elements of unit operations and processes for the preparation of ores, smelting, refining, foundry, welding, and physical testing of materials. It was this course that required a research project and a report, even while the students were receiving their very first taste of what metallurgy was all about.

The second summer course was between the junior and senior years and it required either a report on industrial employment for the summer in metallurgical engineering or a second metallurgical practice course where the students worked in one of the metallurgical labs on campus. For example, one of the authors spent his summer working at US Steel's South Works in Chicago as a metallurgical technician in the plant's applied metallurgical lab. The work included polishing samples for grain analysis, testing for hardness and ductility on ultra-high strength steels such as 300-M and 4340 steels, and working in the 54" blooming mill as a recorder at the breakdown shear. One of his projects was to analyze the losses in the mill before finish rolling, and he was responsible for making the appropriate report to the mill's general foreman. Professor Wichmann judged the student's report as fulfilling the course requirements, but not until after receiving photos of some of the student's lab work and an evaluation of his employment by his supervisor. The student also had to pay tuition for the summer course as if he had taken it on campus.

Mining Engineering:
The mining department required mine surveying in the summer between a student's sophomore and junior years, and mine practice on Saturdays throughout a student's junior year. Initially, the school negotiated a contract with the Stanley Mine near Idaho Springs, and taught mine surveying there until after World War I. Subsequently, CSM obtained the use of the Edgar Mine in Idaho Springs. In the Edgar Mine students learned mining techniques such as mucking and drilling in addition to surveying in a much-expanded course. This course greatly increased the load on Mining students by effectively taking away their Saturdays, so that not only was dating out of the question, they had no time for per-

sonal maintenance.

The Edgar Mine on the north side of Idaho Springs might have been just one of the thousands of abandoned ghost mines which dotted Colorado's mountainsides if not used as a laboratory for practical work by students. Located high above Clear Creek about twenty-three miles west of Golden, the Edgar lay (and still lies) south of Central City near the mouth of Virginia Canyon, in the heart of the Gilpin and Clear Creek county mining districts.

The Edgar Mine taps into the Edgar vein, a crushed schist wallrock in the Idaho Springs formation, somewhat silicified with disseminated pyrite, and containing quantities of gold, silver, lead, copper, and zinc. The vein strikes north 65 degrees east, dips from seventy to eighty-five degrees to the northwest, and intersects Hukill Gulch at 8,215 feet. Apparently an eastwards continuation of the Centennial-Two Kings vein, the Edgar vein varies from several inches to several feet in width.

Total gross production of the mine was estimated at half a million dollars, and the North American Mining Company of Denver continued operations until the late 1930s. The Edgar vein stoped out and is no longer economical, but student work on potentially economical sub-veins has caused minor excitement from time to time. Early production records showed averages of one-half ounce of gold and eighty ounces of silver per ton of ore. The ore contained a very high percentage of lead, averaging forty-five to fifty percent, and supposedly silver ranged as high as 165 ounces, but that might have been due to supergene enrichment. By the twentieth century the high-grade ore had played out, and although gold remained in the half ounce region, silver declined to fifteen to twenty ounces per ton. Lead dropped to under forty percent, zinc accounted for percentages in the middle teens, and copper fluctuated between two and seven percent.

The first major gold strike in Colorado was made less than three miles from the Edgar Mine on the junction of Chicago Creek, a small tributary of Clear Creek, and the South Fork of Clear Creek. In January 1859 Kit Carson's cousin, a miner and Indian trader named George Jackson, panned a sand bar and recovered a half ounce of gold dust. He had been wintering with two friends in a cabin where Golden is today and wandered up Clear Creek prospecting in a week of relatively mild weather. The ground being frozen from the winter's cold, Jackson marked the spot, and kept his discovery secret until the spring. Then he returned in May with a group of men originally from Chicago, Illinois, (thus naming Chicago Creek), and panned out several thousand dollars' worth of gold.

The rush that followed established the town of Jackson's Diggings at the mouth of Chicago Creek. The thriving settlement soon changed its name to Sacramento City, then Idaho City, and finally Idaho Springs. There was no shortage of names at the time as political power changed hands as rapidly as mining fortunes were made and lost.

Jackson's strike was followed almost simultaneously by John Gregory's fabulous discovery on the North Fork of Clear Creek at the present-day boundary between Blackhawk and Central City, only nine miles to the north (by road -- maybe five miles by air). He too had actually made his find in January, but driven out by a blizzard, had not returned until grubstaked by several men from South Bend, Indiana. Nevadaville, Gregory's Gulch (renamed Central City because it was in the center of the mining camps), Gregory Point, Mountain City, Missouri City, and Blackhawk sprang up, with Russell Gulch on the road between Idaho Springs and Central City. Gregory mined only nine hundred dollars from the outcrop he staked before selling his claim for twenty-one thousand. But the gulch bearing his name produced over seventy million dollars in gold, many millionaires, and became perhaps the primary reason for establishing the Colorado School of Mines and locating it in Golden.

The Glory Hole is located on Quartz Hill between Russell Gulch and Central City west of Highway 279 near the ghost town of Nevadaville. As a monument to the early miners' industry, this huge pit is unsurpassed. Over a thousand feet long, several hundred feet wide, and four hundred feet deep, the Glory Hole baffles modern imaginations when one considers it was dug by hand.

Central City is the seat for Gilpin County and was joined to Golden by Berthoud's Colorado Central Railway running through Clear Creek Canyon. Road access was more roundabout until 1950, travelers primarily ascending Golden Gate Canyon northwest of Golden on Route 58. After the railroad was removed, US 6 was pushed through Clear Creek Canyon to join US 40 at the foot of Floyd Hill, thus providing ready access to both Central City and Idaho Springs from Golden. The big attraction then was the Central City Opera House, and its season of opera and musical presentations drew much of Denver society. Today, with the construction of a number of gambling casinos in the Blackhawk and Central City area, a new highway, just to handle the casino traffic, connects to the area from I-70.

In 1921 the Stanley Mine at Idaho Springs was closed, and Mines lost the use of its facility for teaching mine surveying. A champion for a new facility was found in Dr. James Underhill, an Associate Professor of Mining at Mines. Like his associates Pi Warren and Joe O'Byrne, he was a member of Square and Compass and an ardent Mines supporter in spite of having taken his PhD work at CU (or maybe it was because his undergraduate degree was from Harvard). On behalf of Mines, he approached the North American Mining Company which was continuing to operate the Edgar Mine at a relatively low level of activity. The Company agreed to grant a ninety-nine-year lease to CSM on the upper works which were no longer in use.

Dr. Underhill also negotiated an agreement for the later use of the mine's lower portions and especially the Big Five tunnel which ran under the mine for over 8,000 feet. Somehow, the Colorado Legislature was influenced to appropriate twenty thousand dollars for equipment, buildings, and mine repairs, and the Edgar went into service immediately as a teaching laboratory for mine surveying.

Along with the long-term lease, CSM purchased a number of lots in Idaho Springs at the base of the Edgar's access road. An office building with drafting facilities was constructed on the lots, lending an air of permanence to the site.

In 1935 CSM began actual mining operations in the Edgar with the purchase of a compressor from the Gardner-Denver Company. As part of the agreement for the compressor's purchase, Gardner-Denver began using the mine for drill testing, and research activities took a giant leap forward. The entire mine became available with the cessation of North American Mining's operations, and Mines began an aggressive program of equipment and supplies acquisition. In addition to mine surveying, student instruction was expanded to include actual mine operation, drifting, stoping, blasting, and all mechanical engineering aspects of mining.

The Edgar facility was further enhanced in 1949 when CSM purchased the Goodyear, Sunnyside, and Newton claims from North American Mining for a price of $5,000.00. President Ben Parker was instrumental in obtaining these properties, and construction of a change house, machine shop, and new portal to the

Edgar followed.

The unique facility had become a showplace by the fifties, and public tours were begun in the summer of 1953. Students were hired as guides, and a veritable avalanche of visitors descended upon the Edgar. CSM's policy of prohibiting advertising kept tourists to a manageable number, but the Edgar Experimental Mine as it was then called became a noteworthy addition to Colorado's list of points of interest. Mines had done itself proud with an excellent facility to train mining engineers and give them experiences far beyond what they could obtain in other schools. No other mining school possessed such a facility, and Mines shot past Columbia University in importance to the mining industry since Columbia could only teach mining in urban classrooms.

Geological Engineering:

The geology department maintained two camps for summer course work: one at Wild Horse Park fifteen miles northwest of Pueblo between Pueblo and Colorado Springs, and another near Ouray in the San Juan Mountains. The Wild Horse facility was used for a six weeks summer course required of petroleum-oriented geologists. Camp Bird, the facility near Ouray on the Western Slope, was used by mining-oriented geologists and geological engineers for a six weeks course to give them a contrasting picture of the geology in Colorado after all the emphasis on the Front Range. The students learned to map igneous, metamorphic, and sedimentary terrain using air photos, topographic maps, and other methods, and studied the application of mining geology techniques to the prospecting for and development of ore bodies. Students were presented with many kinds of problems in mining geology, engineering geology, structural geology, and stratigraphy, and formal reports were required.

Camp Bird included the Camp Bird Mine, the second richest gold mine in Colorado, producing $25 million from 1895 to 1915. Thomas F. Walsh, owner of a smelter in Silverton, sampled the dumps of the Camp Bird Mine which had been worked for lead, zinc, and silver, and found gold. Where others had failed, he succeeded.

Although these two courses were normally taken between a student's junior and senior years, a substantial number took them as the last remaining course before graduation at the end of their senior year summer session. Students were also required to make extensive field trips to various sites in Colorado and Utah during the junior and senior years emphasizing regional geology as well as mining, petroleum, and engineering projects.

Geophysical Engineering:

The geophysics department operated a four-week summer field program at various sites, usually in western and southern Colorado, but sometimes in South Park, and which was normally taken between the junior and senior years. The students conducted geophysical field investigations in which they began with a geological study of the camp's surrounding area. They learned field techniques of recording and interpreting data coming from deep and shallow seismic, magnetic, gravity, electromagnetics, self-potential, resistivity, and ground penetrating radar data collection technologies. Following their field work, the students returned to Golden to further process and interpret the data. At the conclusion of the summer program a thorough report of the area studied was produced that was normally made into a monograph of the studied area and its geophysical characteristics for public consumption.

Petroleum Engineering:

Petroleum production held its summer camp at Rangely, Colorado, on the Rangely Anticline, and in the center of several oil fields. The six-week course allowed the students to study the various techniques of oil field production in a real-world setting. They were required to map the producing horizons, learn how to use oil production equipment, and gather data for various studies. The course was also supplemented with two weeks of trips to various oil production fields to broaden the students' backgrounds. Through the summer camp and trips, the PE students became familiar with the equipment and techniques they would be using as petroleum engineers after graduation. Such "hands-on" experience would give Mines graduates a leg-up on the competition.

Petroleum Refining Engineering:

The petroleum refining department conducted its six-week long summer course in its Oil Testing and Analysis Laboratory in Alderson Hall. The course includes a study of A.S.T.M. and other methods for testing and analyzing petroleum materials. Like the students in petroleum engineering, the students were required to go on a number of field trips to refineries in Colorado and other western states to see how crude oil was turned into gasoline and other products through a variety of processes.

The key aspect of the summer courses at Mines was to prepare graduates who could be immediately productive in industry. They knew the theories and how things worked through classroom study, but the summer gave them familiarity with the equipment and how to do things in practice. Time and again, Mines graduates would be shown a piece of equipment by their new employers that they already knew how to operate as if they had been working in the industry all their lives.

Senior Trips:

The students in each option participated in senior trips, for which they received one hour of credit for each week of the trip (upon submission of a lengthy report on the trip, on which the grade was based). The trips were appropriate to each course of study.

For example, the Metallurgy Class of 1956 took two senior trips to industrial sites, for one week in the fall, and for two weeks in the spring. The fall trip, which was only to facilities in Colorado, included the Colorado Steel and Iron mill in Pueblo, the cement plant at Portland, the mines around Victor, the lead smelter at Leadville, and the molybdenum mine and ore dressing plant at Climax. The spring trip included the Westvaco lime plant at Green River, Wyoming, the Monsanto chemical plant at Soda Springs, Idaho, Bingham Canyon copper operations at Tooele, Utah, American Smelting and Refining (ASARCO) and United States Smelting and Refining (USSRCO), near Salt Lake City, US Steel's Geneva Works on Utah Lake near Provo, the uranium processing plant at Moab, and the Redcliff Mine at Minturn, Colorado.

These trips introduced Miners to a wide variety of industries in their fields of study, and the operation of manufacturing facilities similar to those that they would soon be operating.

By 1962 these trips were curtailed by the administration as not being an appropriate part of collegiate study. It was a mistake, as Mines graduates had previously earned instant respect for their knowledge of industrial practices and machinery, and this had enabled them to rise more rapidly than graduates of other universities in many corporations.

A Mines grad from the 50s reported for his first day of work at a mid-western steel company, and was asked by the personnel officer, "Do you want a tour of the mill, or do you want to start work?"

"I've seen steel mills, let's go to work," he answered.

A year later, the Miner received orders to report for active duty in the Army. In the process of clearing the mill and insuring that his job would be waiting upon his return from service, he again visited the personnel officer.

" You are the only one of your trainee class that never complained about the conditions in the mill. All of the others have, especially those from Purdue, Notre Dame, Illinois, and Northwestern." It was the senior trips, later abolished, that had caused him to stand out above his contemporaries.

The elimination of industrial involvement in education was all part of a national push by educators to separate college study from actual practice. The primary object of progressive education was to teach an individual how to live, not how to do a job. Many academicians felt that engineering per se was not a subject that should be taught in universities — it should be separated and taught in trade schools or in post graduate facilities like law and medical schools. Such beliefs were frequently behind criticisms of Mines and its curricula and are one of the reasons Mines later pushed so hard into research and graduate studies. Yet America needed and still needs more Mines graduates from the old school, as Mines Professor Gene Woolsey would say, "To generate corporations, products, and wealth for socialist politicians to tax" (the author's rendition of Woolsey's statement.)

The Mines approach and its interaction with industry is perhaps best illustrated from an incident in the spring of 1955. Coors was developing the extruded aluminum can, and Metallurgy professor Arthur Wichmann arranged for the head of the Coors project to discuss it with his class in Production Metallurgy. The students asked many questions, all of which were answered candidly, despite the fact that the project was still a proprietary secret. There were a number of unsolved problems that were openly discussed, and this was long before the advent of confidentially agreements and the like. Coors management trusted the Mines students to protect their interests and were never given cause to regret their close relationship with Mines.

The Payoff:

One of the authors was employed for several years by Chase Brass and Copper, a subsidiary of the Kennecott Copper Corporation. He was selected for Chase's Executive Management Training Program, a group of about a dozen individuals who had been tagged as candidates for various upper management positions. Part of the program was to visit not only all Chase facilities and interview the present management, but also to visit all the major Kennecott locations, including all Kennecott's subsidiaries, in the domestic US. After visiting New York City and talking with Frank Millikin, the President of Kennecott, the group went to visit the Kennecott Refining Corporation in Baltimore. There it was met by a manager, about 35 years old who posed a question as soon as he finished introducing himself.

"Anybody here from Mines?" he asked.

"I am," the author said, introducing himself.

For the remainder of the introductory session, the manager spoke mostly to the author, and afterwards continued to show him special deference. It turned out that the manager was a Mines graduate from 1952, but that was never mentioned to the group. The other group members were nonplussed over the attention being given to the author. There were three Harvard MBAs in the group, one from Wharton, one from Chicago, and one from Northwestern. The author's MBA from Case Western Reserve didn't count for much in such august company, and the other MBAs had no idea what "Mines" was. The next day the author told them, but they just shook their heads. The situation soon got worse.

The next trip was to St. Louis to visit Peabody Coal, a Kennecott subsidiary like Chase. At the opening meeting, the Peabody Coal Public Relations Manager was talking when another man burst in and shouted, "Which one of you is from Mines?"

When the author identified himself, the second man said loudly, "Well, you come with me." The Peabody employee turned out to be another Mines graduate and the manager of two of the Illinois coal mines. The author received a private tour of the offices in St. Louis, meeting a whole bunch of people, and two of the mines in southern Illinois. He only rejoined the group for dinner, and, of course, everyone wanted to know what had happened. The Harvard MBAs were visibly ticked off, as they felt themselves to be superior to anyone from some school named "Mines."

But the worst was in Utah when the group visited the Kennecott mine at Bingham Canyon, and the associated ore concentrating, fire refining, and electro-winning facilities. The group was met by two Kennecott representatives, and the first one asked for the author by name. He then said, "Come with me," and told the rest of the group to remain with the other guy. Once again, the author received a personal tour and special attention, this time from a 1955 graduate who knew his brother.

There was a sequel to this story. The author was selected to produce the Chase 5-Year plan for presentation to Kennecott the following year, and was slated to be the President of the Chase Foundry Division in Waterbury, CT. All three of the Harvard MBAs left Chase during the next two years, apparently thinking that the cards at Kennecott were stacked against them. They were, but the MBAs didn't understand why. None of the three possessed any engineering expertise. They had taken business or liberal arts degrees before their MBAs, and thought they were trained to be managers and executives of major companies. Maybe that would have worked in the East, but not in corporations populated by Mines graduates.

Hill Hall - The Metallurgy Building

Chapter 17 - School Organizations in the 1950s

Athletics:

Mines featured a number of inter-collegiate varsity sports during the 1950s: Football, Soccer, Basketball, Skiing, Wrestling, Rifle, Tennis, Swimming, Boxing, Baseball, and Track. Other sports made their appearance for a year or two, either as clubs of official sports such as Pistol Shooting, Hockey, Judo, Weight Lifting, Cross-Country, and Golf. Most of these sports were also played in the intermural sports program (along with softball, volleyball, and bowling) between multiple Barb teams and the social fraternities. There was a long history of excellence in sports, including Russell "Rut" Volk who won the RMC championship in heavyweight wrestling and light-heavyweight boxing on the same day in 1925, Leroy T. Brown who won a silver medal in the high jump at the Olympics in 1924, and Bill Henry who consistently scored well in swimming from 1959 to 1962, even though he had only one leg!

Rut Volk became a legendary figure at CSM, earning fourteen letters in five sports, football, basketball, baseball, wrestling, and boxing. He won football letters from 1923-1925 and made all-conference center in his last two seasons. In four years of competition, three on the varsity team, Volk wrestled in the heavyweight class and never lost a match. In boxing it was the same story, but there he competed as a light-heavyweight (175 pounds). He was the RMC conference champion in boxing in 1924 & 1925, played basketball in 1924 and 1925, and on the baseball team in 1926 was voted to the all-conference second team. As a college athlete, Volk ranked up with the immortal Jim Thorpe and others of his caliber. Of course, none of the others completed an engineering degree from Mines in four years at the same time they were competing in athletics.

Varsity football at CSM in the 1950s had fallen a long way from 1890 when Mines beat Colorado University on November 22 by the score of 103 to zero. Three weeks later, Mines defeated CU by 50 to 4. Supposedly, CSM began fielding a football team in 1888 and won the state championship in 1889, but the authors have been unable to confirm such a championship. Mines was a member of the Colorado Football Association which was one of the earliest football conferences in the US, operating from 1890 through 1908. CSM won the first four championships in the Association, the 1898 championship, and another four in a row from 1904 through 1907.

In the early days, colleges often played good high school teams, and many major colleges still carry these scores in their media guides. The highest score ever achieved by Mines was 106 to 0 against Longmont High in 1903. The last high school opponent of the Orediggers was North Denver in 1912.

In 1909, the CFA members formed the Rocky Mountain Faculty Athletic Conference, which was considered a major football conference until 1938, when Colorado University, Denver University, Wyoming, and Utah University left to form the Skyline Conference. CSM is the only school that has been a member of the Rocky Mountain Athletic Conference (its current name) from its inception to the present day.

Mines was a powerhouse in the early days, winning the RMC championship in 1912, 1914, and 1918, not the least because of Dr. Chauvenet's regimen and the esprit de corps manifested by Mines teams. Mines won the Rocky Mountain Conference title four more times after the big schools departed, in 1939, 1942, 1951, and 1958, but after that became increasingly uncompetitive. Universities and colleges of all sizes across the country began to recruit athletes who were students only in the broadest sense, and sports such as football and basketball became big business and important sources of revenue. Students at Mines were full-time students and part-time athletes, not full-time semi-professional athletes as at schools with major football and basketball programs. By 1960, Mines could only compete with small colleges.

In 1926, for example, Mines played Utah A & M (later Utah State), Colorado Aggies (Colorado State University), Denver University, Wyoming, Colorado University, BYU (Brigham Young University), Colorado College, and Colorado State College (now Northern University of Colorado). These were formidable opponents, but Mines held its own in spite of the handicap of its student athletes being drawn strictly from engineering majors. One would wonder what would happen to Colorado University if only its engineering students could play football.

To make up for the loss of the large universities, the Rocky Mountain Conference added Montana State College and Western State College (Gunnison) in 1937, and later Idaho State College and Adams State College (Alamosa).

In 2016, Mines was still in the Rocky Mountain Athletic Conference but facing a very different group of schools. The conference was spread out over five states, and included Colorado

Mesa at Grand Junction, Black Hills State at Spearfish, Dixie State at St. George, Utah, South Dakota Mines at Rapid City, Fort Lewis at Durango, Chadron State at Chadron, Nebraska, Adams State at Alamosa, and New Mexico Highlands at Las Vegas, NM. None of these schools are household names, and none have pretentions of academic excellence. Against this group, Mines has become competitive once again, winning four championships between 2004 and 2016.

It must be understood that big-time college sports are a national scandal of corruption and mendacity, and many, if not most, recruitments of high school star athletes involve all sorts of chicanery and even illegal activities. Once in school, the athletes are coddled academically, and often great pressure is put on faculty to give athletes respectable grades for the good of a university's athletic program (and gate revenues.) Nonetheless, few football and basketball players actually graduate from the major athletic powers, and those that do often concentrate on taking physical education courses such as "Theory of Basketball" and the like. Football players take spring training, summer football camp, and schedules of training during the fall that run from morning to evening. They live in athletic dorms, eat special food, and are supplied by the athletic department with everything they need, sometimes including social amenities.

In addition to athletic departments recruiting football players with various emoluments, alumni often work to attract athletes their universities. They shower the athletes with gifts, funds, trips, and all sorts of amenities, none of which have anything to do with academics. Nor does this largess disappear unless the player becomes injured and ineligible to play. In those circumstances, the player is dropped from the program, and left on his own. University inter-collegiate sports are simply semi-professional, without a doubt.

Mines has never done any of the above and suffers athletic obscurity as a result. But rather than feeling shame, Mines students should wear their cross of defeat as a badge of honor. In the old Mines, winning the fight after a football game was almost as important as winning the game itself. It was the student body that was tough, not just the football team. Mines could hire athletes too, but not if they had to take engineering and be in class 35 hours per week.

Athletic Council – The athletic council set the athletic policy of the school. It was comprised of two alumni, two faculty members, two students, two coaches, and a secretary from the school administration. It also approved the schedule of all inter-collegiate athletic events, all varsity letters, and sponsored the athletic awards dinner.

"M" Club – All athletes who have won varsity letters were automatically members of the "M" Club. Band members earned a letter for 2 years of participation in the CSM Marching Band, which qualified them as members of the "M" Club. Very active in campus affairs, the club sponsored the annual Homecoming Dance, and the sale of Mums for homecoming.

Honorary Fraternities:

A monument in front of Berthoud Hall and to the southeast of Guggenheim Hall has three sides, each of which displays three keys of the following nine honorary fraternities. Polishing its key was always included in the initiation rite for each honorary.

Tau Beta Pi – At the top of the first side of the monument, Tau Bate was the oldest of the honorary fraternities at Mines, having established its Colorado Alpha Chapter on campus in 1905. The main scholastic honorary, Tau Beta Pi's purpose is: "To mark in a fitting manner those who have conferred honor upon their Alma Mater by distinguished scholarship and exemplary character as undergraduates in engineering, or by their attainments as alumni in the field of engineering." This last clause has generally been overlooked by the Mines chapter, as no alumni from the 1950s or 1960s have been elected to Tau Beta Pi.

Sigma Gamma Epsilon – Sig Gam was a professional engineering society which became established on campus in 1922 with the installation of its Lambda Chapter. Founded at the University of Kansas in 1915, Sig Gam selected its members based on high scholarship and activities in the earth sciences, mining, metallurgy, and geology.

Theta Tau -- Established at Mines in 1907, it was the oldest of Mines' professional engineering societies. The Gamma chapter was founded at CSM only three years after the national organization came into being, and selected its members based on scholarship, personal worthiness, and potential engineering ability. At Mines, Theta Tau tended to add another basis for selection — that of participation in intercollegiate athletics.

An annual burro race took place between Sig Gam and Theta Tau during Homecoming, normally after appropriate insults had been traded. The challenge and answer in 1951 were as follows:

THE CHALLENGE

"Be it know that the worthy, honorable and virile men respected far and wide as the noble brotherhood of SIGMA GAMMA EPSILON does hereby recognize the pathetic existence of an emasculated species of biped called theta tau.

We do hereby order your presence at Brooks Field homecoming at halftime, in order that you may be publicly exposed and defeated in a burro race. Have for once the decency to use a burro, though you chose to ride one of your own number, few could detect the difference.

And bring one keg of beer, with which the victorious men of SIGMA GAMMA EPSILON may wash from their throats the sickening stench with which you will permeate the atmosphere."

THE ACCEPTANCE

"One score and eight years ago, there came forth on this campus a crude and obnoxious monster, dedicated to the proposition that some men can live more lowly than others.

This monster, called sig gam, has been getting too big for its scales and has had the audacity to defy the MEN of THETA TAU and to challenge these great intellectuals to a burro race. The almighty THETA TAUS will be present at the stated time should any of the scurvy scum that be sig gam have the courage to appear.

If you have a soul, give it to your maker, for the only other part of your body, as well as your beer, shall belong to THETA TAU."

The two honorary fraternities carried on their rivalry throughout the year, but the most notable aspect beside the burro race was the plastering of the rival fraternity's pledges. What and how it was done was discussed in Chapter 3.

Scabbard & Blade – At the top of the second side of the monument is the key for Scabbard & Blade, the honorary fraternity for Advanced ROTC students. The honorary was noted for its strenuous initiation rite that consisted of running a military operation from the Mines campus to the top of Lookout Mountain at night during the winter and usually in heavy snow. As always with such initiations, it was looked upon by the selectees as being nothing special and performed without regard to safety or injuries. Today, such an initiation could not take place.

Kappa Kappa Psi – A national band fraternity, KKP was composed of outstanding bandsmen as voted by their contemporaries. It was the backbone of the Oredigger Band and coordinated its functions and promoted its interests on campus and in the community. Working with the director of the Golden Symphony who was also the band director, it promoted band and music participation at all Mines events. It also staffed a dance/jazz band that rode in the homecoming parade in addition to the regular marching band and provided a band leader to the ROTC band for ROTC parades.

Blue Key – An honorary service and leadership society, Blue Key came to Mines in 1926, a year after its first chapter was founded at the University of Florida. The purpose of Blue Key was to unite campus leaders into an effective group which would promote the interests of the school and assist in solving campus problems. It was committed to cooperation with the faculty and the stimulation of school spirit. Members were chosen based on a combination of scholarship, student activities, leadership, and general service to CSM. The founder of Blue Key at Mines, John H. O'Conner, was killed in a Bolivian miner's strike in 1949, leading the relatively hazardous lifestyle favored by so many CSM graduates. Usual Blue Key activities ranged from conducting student rallies and school elections to campus improvements, freshman agitation, and painting the "M."

Press Club – On the third side of the monument was the most honorary of honoraries. Press Club selectees came from the *Oredigger* and *Prospector* staffs. The purveyors of the *Picker* and other non-official publications could also be initiated into the mysterious rites of the august Press Club, and while Senior Day was still a hallowed event, the Press Club donated its expertise each year to the publication of whatever that year's Senior Day newspaper was called. Activities mostly centered around the regular meetings at Dud's, draining pitchers of Golden's finest, and chowing down on baskets of French fries.

Octette – This was an honorary key for excellence in the Mines Chorus. There was no actual organization, merely an honor.

Sigma Delta Psi - the most mysterious key on the monument. In the middle 1950s, several students wondered about this key and determined to obtain one if at all possible. Sigma Delta Psi turned out to be an athletic fraternity founded at Indiana University in 1912 to promote the physical, mental, and moral development of college students. Candidates for membership must successfully pass fifteen tests, and there was a scholarship requirement. Three students, Harlan Brown, Chuck Daugherty, and Rob Roark successfully met the requirements, and became members of Sigma Delta Psi, the only Miners ever to do so. Today there is no national organization, but chapters exist in a few colleges, notably The Citadel and Stanford.

Student Representative Organizations:

Student Council -- The Student Council was composed of representatives elected by the various student organizations on campus. Normally, the Barb Council had three representatives, and there was one from each social fraternity, as well as the Interfraternity Council, M Club, Blue Key, Theta Tau, Sigma Gamma Epsilon, Alpha Phi Omega, Scabbard and Blade, Press Club, International Council, E-Day Committee, Prospector Park Council, and Board of Publications. The council's purpose was to act in the interests of the student body of Mines, coordinate and regulate of campus activities and organizations, enforce the rules and regulations of the student body, defend the traditions of Mines, and help maintain the good reputation of the school. The Student Council functioned well and was generally respected throughout the campus by the Administration, faculty, and students, even by the more truculent and recalcitrant individuals.

Inter-Fraternity Council – Made up of two members from each social fraternity, the IFC represented the interests of the eight and then seven fraternities. The fifties were a time of trial for the frats, as the Vanderwilt administration increasingly clamped down on fraternity activities and sought to marginalize the influence of the houses on campus. The fraternities were in a very large sense the campus police, and they defended the "M" and other Mines facilities, meting out frontier justice as of old. Crime on campus was literally unknown.

On the other side, however, whatever unrest there was on campus, particularly that which upset the administration, originated from the fraternities. After the 1950s, the administration repeatedly threatened various houses with being placed on social probation, and when that failed to obtain the desired result, threatened pulling a house's charter at Mines. Rather than the IFC, however, the major factors holding President Vanderwilt in check were several highly placed, prestigious administration and faculty members who were pro-fraternity, such as Dean Signer, Dean of the Graduate School, Dean Burger, Dean of Students, and Dr. Leroy, chairman of the Geology Department.

Vanderwilt hired a "Director of Student Affairs" in 1959 in an attempt to neutralize Dean Burger and bring the campus organizations to heel. Bill Pugh was the new hire, but his tenure was short as he saw little to change. The next young man hired to this position, Chauncey Van Pelt, was completely new to the world of engineering, but determined to make his make in academic administration. He immediately put in a formal system of bidding for pledges at a designated time at the end of rush week, ostensibly run by the IFC, but actually operating under Van Pelt's control. This system was what Van Pelt had seen at several eastern universities that featured highly exclusive fraternity systems, completely unlike what existed at Mines. The relationship between the IFC and Van Pelt rapidly became strained, and the administration took reprisals where it could without stirring up substantial student resentment.

Towards the end of the 1950s, for example, the administration began electing various students to "Who's Who in American Colleges and Universities." These students were not elected by the student body for their leadership, but by the administration on its own secret criteria. The presidents of the IFC were not named to this perceived honor, and one finally approached Van Pelt in the early 1960s to find out why. The answer was that both he and the IFC had refused to accept administration direction, so he could not be considered for "Who's Who." This particular IFC President had the last laugh: the Student Council President and the IFC President received the two highest employment offers that year; at salaries higher than many faculty at Mines or van Pelt himself were making.

Vanderwilt was upset with the fraternities' continued truculence because the Horizon Plan called for the fraternity houses to be moved off campus. The 21st century reader must understand that the fraternity houses were literally scattered throughout the center of the Mines campus. The SAE house was located on the corner of Illinois and 15th Street, directly across from Guggenheim Hall, and five others were within two blocks of the President's office. All of the houses except the ones owned by Beta Theta Pi and Sigma Nu were in the way of future building plans, and none of the fraternities had indicated a willingness to move. Financial induce-ments were offered, and when that didn't work, President Vander-wilt became angry and threatened both administrative and legal actions. Ultimately, eminent domain was the answer, and the first to fall were the Betas and the Kappa Sigs.

The Betas leased their house to the Kappa Sigs in 1963 and moved onto what would be Fraternity Row, and the Kappa Sigma house became a dormitory for women. One by one the fraternities were forced to move onto Fraternity Row, a state-owned area made up of clay pits immediately north of 19th Street and west of Elm. At the time, that area was not considered as part of the campus.

The last of the fraternities to knuckle under the administra-tion's demands was the ATOs. They lost their bitter eminent do-main fight in the 1980s and leased a small home opposite where the former Kappa Sigma house had been. The Trustees refused to pay compensation as ordered by the Court, and ultimately the chapter received only $95,000 for one of the most beautiful structures on campus. While the administration unleased the wrecker's ball on the distinctive Georgian structure, the ATOs struggled to survive in a house unfit for a fraternity and became very weak. It was saved by the action of a group of ATO alumni who provided the funds to build a suitable house on the hated, eastern style, segregated frater-nity row. The other former fraternity houses were destroyed by the administration, and eventually, only the Beta house on Arapahoe and 17th, and the Sigma Nu house across from Coolbaugh Hall at Cheyenne and 14th would be left standing.

Barb Council – consisting of twenty-one members elected from all classes, the Barb (short for Barbarian, or non-Greek) Coun-cil primarily organized the non-fraternity students together for in-termural athletics and social events like the Barb Smoker.

Prospector Park Council – The governing board for the married student housing area, it was made up of seven council-men and a mayor for the park. Altogether, the Student Council, Inter-fraternity Council, Barb Council, and Prospector Park Coun-cil made up the organizations recognized by the administration as representing the students in their respective housing and activity sectors.

International Council – Consisting primarily by foreign students and their wives, this group was made up of various indi-viduals interested in promoting better relations between students from all countries at Mines. It hosted an annual International Day and enjoyed the support of the Mines administration and some of the faculty. This Council was slated to grow and become more important due to the very active recruitment of foreigners as graduate students.

Board of Publications – This was the governing board for all student publications, acting under the direction of James Sankovitz, Director of Publications for the school. It established the budgets for *The Oredigger* and *Prospector*, the two official student publications. The publications staff consisted of three women in addition to Mr. Sankowitz, all of whom were extremely competent. The office also contained the most beautiful woman in Golden, the wife of one of the students who eventually graduated in 1961, much to the disappointment of most males on campus.

Publications:

The Colorado School of Mines had a long tradition in publications, administrative, scholarly, alumni, and student. In 1870 Jarvis Hall began publishing *Annual Reports*, and the *Scientific Quarterly* was produced from 1892 to 1899. *The Bulletin* followed in 1900 and was superseded in 1905 by the *Colorado School of Mines Quarterly* which has continued since that date. *The Mines Magazine*, the monthly alumni journal, was begun in 1910, and *Information Circulars* were published at irregular intervals.

The Oredigger -- the completely student-run newspaper, "The Voice of the World's Foremost Mining School" was first published in 1921. Published weekly, it contained items of student interest and was the basic media through which the majority of the student body could be reached.

The Prospector -- the student yearbook first published in 1912 and discontinued after 2001. *The Prospector* was always in high demand by earlier graduates as a souvenir of arguably the toughest time in the life of many Miners.

The Picker - The student humor magazine was first published in 1954 by an enterprising upper classman to make money and poke fun at faculty members and the administration now that Senior Day had been abolished. The rarest and most coveted of all the student publications, the definitely bawdy ones by Homer Burrows and Pat Rice probably are the ones most in demand. The last *Picker* known to the authors was produced in 1961.

Religious Organizations:

In the 1950s, the impact of the Supreme Court decision of 1947 in the case, *Everson vs. the Board of Education*, was still slowly making its way through American governmental institutions. The effect was to expunge the worship of God, particularly the majority Protestant God, from all government property and property that in any way receives government money. Of course, that included the Colorado School of Mines. The Square and Compass, the masonic fraternity which required faith in God and had been a part of Mines life for over fifty years, became inactive. Nonetheless, two religious organizations still functioned at Mines into the 1960s.

Newman Club – the campus affiliate of the National Newman Club Federation, the Newman Club was comprised of Catholic students and was intended to promote the spiritual, intellectual, and social development of the students according to the tenets of Roman Catholicism.

Wesley Foundation - a fellowship of students and their wives professing the Methodist Faith, the Wesley Foundation held weekly meetings designed to combine serious religious discussion and thinking with Christian fellowship.

Other Organizations:

Band – The CSM marching band was always short of members, but nevertheless displayed great enthusiasm. Surprisingly, there were a number of very good musicians at Mines, proving to many observers that engineering and music talent was a good mix. Band uniforms were unique for an American college, consisting of engineer boots, Levis, a red plaid shirt, silver miner's helmet and a brass carbide lamp. This uniform was adopted in 1921. Membership in the band was worth an hour's credit per semester, for four hours of practice, plus attendance at all events requiring the band.

Glee Club – a volunteer organization with no course credit being involved, the club was under the direction of a Mines faculty member for most of the 1950s, Math Professor Vic Bauman. The Club sang for various local civil and business organizations and put on an annual Christmas Concert along with the Mines Band.

Debate Club – Although the Debate Club did not have official intercollegiate status, it functioned under the direction of an English Department coach and received a budget from the school. It regularly participated in intercollegiate debates on the yearly debate question, and faced Colorado University, Denver University, Colorado State, Adams State, The Air Force Academy, Wyoming, Brigham Young, Utah, Utah State, Western State, Colorado College, Colorado State College, Texas Tech, Kansas State, and others. It participated in radio programs featuring abbreviated debates with local colleges such as Loretto Heights and Regis. No college credit was given for this activity, as it tended to disprove President Vanderwilt's contention that Mines was only producing technically competent graduates.

Alpha Phi Omega – A national service fraternity, it established a local chapter, Mu Pi, on the CSM campus in 1958. It was founded on the principles of leadership, friendship and service following the Boy Scouts of America, and provided its members the opportunity to develop leadership skills as they volunteer on their campus, in their community, and for the nation. Members helped at registration, painted the new Presbyterian Church in Golden, conducted swimming classes at the State Industrial School for Boys, and other such activities.

Veterans Council - Although veterans and the Veterans Council were important from the end of World War II through the Korean War armistice, by 1958 the Council had been dissolved. Mary Paddleford handled Veterans Affairs from Guggenheim Hall, and the number of veterans had dropped precipitously. Veterans had been a major factor in rowdiness early in the 1950s, as they rejected authoritarianism on the part of some professors and were much less willing than other students to put up with unfairness either by the faculty or administration. They tended to treat a Mines education as something they had earned while the faculty and administrators had been hiding in an ivory tower. They were also quick to defend Mines against raiding by students from other universities and took little mercy on either DU or CU when extracting revenge.

The Student Chapters of National Professional Societies – there were a number of professional engineering societies on campus, and various faculty members actively recruited students into student chapters. Included were the American Institute of Mining, Metallurgical, and Petroleum Engineers (AIME), broken into two sections, AIME-Mining and AIME-Petroleum, American Society of Mechanical Engineers (ASME), American Society for Metals (ASM) which later became ASM International, Mines Society of Engineering Geologists (MSEG), the Petroleum Club, Society of Exploration Geophysicists, Society for Sedimentary Geology (SSG), and the American Institute of Chemical Engineers (AIChE). These groups met regularly, and chapter members also attended society meetings in Denver and other places to make industrial contacts.

Radio station KCSM – this was the student-run Mines radio station that functioned throughout most of the 1950s, becoming discontinued for lack of interest by 1960. The call letters were subsequently assumed by a San Mateo, CA radio station.

Pershing Rifles – Run by the ROTC detachment on campus, the local chapter of the National Society of Pershing Rifles was formed in 1951. It maintained a precision drill team which performed at football game halftimes and held meetings twice a month featuring speakers or films on various military campaigns and other subjects of military interest. No college credit was given for this activity.

Dames Club - One of the more important clubs on campus, at least for the married students, the Dames Club automatically included all student wives. A chapter of the National Association of University Dames, it held a regular schedule of meetings with speakers on various topics, and also provided a number of social functions for the husbands and wives on campus. In addition, it participated in charity and welfare work, and was active in helping students make industrial contacts for post-school employment.

Other Clubs – Beginning in 1923 there was a Russian Club on campus, containing the ten or so Russians that attended Mines. It disappeared around the beginning of World War II. There were also state clubs, such as the Ohio and New York clubs. These rarely lasted for more than a few years as the students vastly preferred the cohesiveness offered by the fraternities or options. Special interest clubs such as the Sports Car Club and Parachute Club sprang up from time to time, but never attracted substantial memberships.

Engineer's Day Committee - Toward the end of April each spring Mines would host a two-day Engineer's Day conference complete with industrial exhibits in Steinhauer Fieldhouse, speakers on a variety of subjects, and engineering events such as hard-rock drilling and mucking contests. A committee composed entirely of students planned and conducted the event, which was generally held to be the high point of the spring semester.

Each option sponsored speakers in their profession as well as arranging the presentation of technical papers of interest. Outstanding students in each option were honored, and with this event students moved one step closer to becoming more like professional engineers than engineering students. The late date normally prevented Engineer's Day from being used by students and recruiters alike for employment discussions, but often those with waiting jobs could showcase their talents to their later employers.

Since its beginning in 1927, Engineer's Day rose steadily in importance as an annual event. It was originally sponsored by the Colorado Engineering Council, but CSM students took over its management in 1937. During World War II Engineer's Day was suspended, but it was reestablished in 1946. The general program has remained the same since that time. In addition to providing student-industry contacts, Engineer's Day sought to acquaint Colorado high school student with Mines and the mineral industry. Tau Beta Pi sponsored an E-Day examination throughout the state, and top scorers received scholarships to Mines.

Various contests enlivened the event, most notably the mucking and hard rock drilling contests, the Clear Creek raft race, the Theta Tau -- Sig Gam pushball contest, and the judging of the best E-Day beard.

Theta Chi House Fraternity House (c. 1960)

Chapter 18 – Goodbye Old Mines

The change of Mines to a baccalaureate-granting college competing against standard American engineering colleges was not an event that occurred in 1968 as is viewed by so many alumni, but a process that can be dated from 1950 to 1968 and even to the present day. The loss of Senior Day could be considered as the first step in this process. Although President Coolbaugh had fought to shut down Senior Day in the 1940s, it was President Vanderwilt who eliminated it along with the Sophomore-Freshman Barbeque in 1952. From that point onwards, Vanderwilt sought to remake Mines in the image of his alma mater, Yale University, focusing his main energies on greatly expanding the physical plant, and raising funds to put Mines on a par with the eastern universities with respect to attracting research grants and projects.

In Golden, the Mines administration hastened to cast off its "hard rock" image in the 1960s, and in one edict after another, eliminated the policies that had made Mines great. The idea that students could run their own lives and organizations disappeared as the administration hired bureaucrats to provide services the students and townspeople had formerly furnished for free. Enrollments and graduation rates became the measures of success, not the expertise of CSM's graduates. Diversity became the great watchword, and one president even stated that CSM's goal was to graduate students in proportion to Colorado's ethnic, gender, and racial percentages.

In 1952 President Vanderwilt gave his vision of the future, one that denied the greatness of Mines under the academic system at the time. At graduation he said:

> "...Technical engineering training, alone, does not make the successful engineer. Character, integrity, and individual effort are essential for happiness and real success. These qualities have been demonstrated by Mines Men in the past and we are confident that it will be said of each member of this graduating class that he is not only an engineer, but a man as well.
> ...You must, to be a successful engineer, acquire a broad knowledge in the related fields of finance, law, and labor, and every community interest; appreciate cultural values, resort frequently to searching self-appraisal, avoid arrogance, and maintain a proper degree of humility."

The reader will note the complete conformance to the doctrine of progressive education, that education is not to teach a person a skill (unless it's for employment in academia.) All this was in line with the sentiments expressed in his first well-wishes to the 1951 graduating class. But he was already on record for desiring an overhaul of Mines. In 1950 Vanderwilt wrote:

> "...*However, more is expected of you than development of professional activities. Active and intelligent participation in local, national, and world affairs is essential to good citizenship whether you are living in the United States or some other country. As engineers you are trained to use only facts as a basis for the honest and logical thinking that is necessary to solve engineering problems. The same approach is vital for solving the economic, social, and political problems of the day. Engineers like anyone else must accept these responsibilities to attain a balanced success and personal satisfaction through the years.*"

In 1955 he still touted the theme of general education over that of the specialist when he wrote to the graduates:

> "...*The purpose of your training at the Colorado School of Mines has been to develop [an] understanding of fundamental values and sound judgment.*"

Strange words indeed from the President of an engineering school.

In the end, Dr. Vanderwilt was not well respected by the alumni, particularly after one incident in the 1960s began making the rounds. For many years he maintained a relationship as a consultant for American Metals Climax and its successor, AMAX, as perhaps the world's foremost authority on molybdenum and other refractory metals. This relationship continued after he stepped down as President, and representing AMAX, he visited the General Electric Refractory Metals Plant in Cleveland in 1966. AMAX was interested in purchasing the facility — which it ultimately did — where GE rolled and fabricated molybdenum and tungsten products for space-age applications. Dr. Vanderwilt was stunned by the processes and remarked that the metallurgy involved had moved a great distance from his day. In short, the great molybdenum expert wasn't an expert in molybdenum at all, unless strictly in its mining. One of his guides was Larry Goetz, Met Eng '56, who was fond of telling the story of Vanderwilt's ignorance in the metal that had made his reputation. In Goetz's words, "He was a charmer, but he wasn't an engineer."

Clearly, President Vanderwilt did not understand Dr. Chauvenet's reasoning in constructing his Engineering Academy. It was there for all to see, yet few understood. The graduates of the three military service academies all understood that rigor in instruction and a re-molding of an individual's attitudes and abilities to attack problems and situations in a way that gave a high probability of success was necessary to achieve excellence. The service academies taught honor, cooperation, critical and rapid thinking, and how to simplify the most complex problems into a manageable number of variables. That was precisely what Mines taught, and its traditions, like the service academies, were there to mold those capable of withstanding the school's demands into truly exceptional engineers and leaders of the country.

Can anyone imagine West Point or Annapolis turning out superior army and navy officers without hardening them with hazing, requiring a course schedule and regimen that takes more hours per week than there actually are, and demanding their students solve problems without having been given the "school solution" first? That was what Mines did, at least until Vanderwilt arrived on the scene.

Some believe the introduction of female students at Mines contributed to CSM's loss of excellence; but in fact, it played no part at all. Only seven women had graduated from Mines out of about forty that had entered as freshmen through 1968 when the new curriculum was announced. Additionally, the three service academies have all successfully integrated women into their programs without compromising the demand for excellence. Mines could have done the same.

The problem lay with the administration. Stripping out 46% of the required credit hours in engineering, science, and technology from 1909 to 2012 was bound to have a negative effect on the obtaining of excellence. Mines was turned into a fun school for students, as evidenced by the reports from many students concerning the "fun" they experienced in obtaining a Mines education. The Engineering Academy disappeared with the new degrees in 1968, and no amount of public relations propaganda could put the genie back into the bottle.

Dr. Weimer, in his address to the faculty senate in 1999, made a number of statements that require re-examination. He stated that "*In the mid-50's, the number of hours required for undergraduate degrees changed from about 212 to 175.*" Outside of being somewhat inaccurate as shown in Chapter 15, he apparently did not understand how that reduction in credit hours was accomplished. The credit hours were lessened, but the material covered remained the same and usually even the number of class hours. He also admitted that the most controversial change was the reduction of credit hours for graduation from "*175 to 145 in the late 60's*". But then came a severe error. He stated, "*Previously this degree was called a Professional Engineer Degree (PE) which took* **THE MAJORITY** *of students five years to finish.*" Actually, the majority of students never attained their degree, and of those that did, **MOST** took only four years to do it. Among the SSDC members mentioned in Chapter 12, ALL but two listed as juniors in the "Sources" received their PE in four years. That was the mark of excellence. Would the good Dr. Weimer want to sail on a navy vessel under officers that took five or six years to graduate from the Naval Academy?

Then Dr. Weimer employed a classical Tavistock propaganda trick: he said that "*Many alumni,* **BUT NOT ALL***, were incensed [at the reduction in credit hours for graduation]; their claim was that their degree had been cheapened, a charge* **NOT** *substantiated.*" Well, maybe a few who graduated with a PE were not bothered, but the overwhelming majority was. And, anyway, how would he know? Did he take a poll of all alumni? And the PE was cheapened. The Mines administration itself left the PE holders out in limbo. The degree was not good enough to be changed to a Master of Engineering, so of course it was not better than a BS. 200 hours of credit was no different than 138.5. The administration never "grandfathered" in the PE holders by changing their degrees to a Master of Engineering although their credit hours exceeded the new requirements for the Master of Engineering (without thesis.)

Current students also have reason to be worried about their own degrees. Mines apparently feels that it can change requirements at will. As Dr. Weimer stated under his "*Lessons For The Future*":

> "*When a described four-year program takes a full-time student five or more years to complete, then the faculty, administration, and BOT [Board of Trustees] must make adjustments* **IN REDUCING** *curriculum and in designing new programs...*" Then he throws in a sop to excellence: "*...while at the same time being mindful of maintaining excellence in traditional internationally*

recognized fields."

Taking 46% of the engineering, science, and technology hours out of a curriculum is not being mindful of the need for excellence. If the students can't cut it with a current curriculum, then two options are present: get better students, or require prerequisite program completion in high schools and community colleges.

The administration touts the current student body as being the best ever. But the administration's focus is on the continuation statistics and is proud of the high percentage that graduates in four years. Of course, lowering requirements will increase that percentage. Clearly, according to Dr. Weimer, holders of the BS may soon see a reduction in credit hours to 120, and all of it coming in the difficult engineering courses. This is classic "levelling" that is the hallmark of progressive education, and apparently Dr. Weimer was in full agreement with this ideology. Such levelling will hardly make America great again. And, of course, Weimer made his remarks only to faculty. Maybe they weren't intended for a larger audience like the students and alumni.

What the series of presidents starting with Vanderwilt have not understood is that true greatness comes from being very good **at something**. Until recently, they railed against extreme specialization, but it was precisely that specialization that normally gave a person the confidence and ability to expand into different areas and be competent, if he possessed sufficient wherewithal, in many different fields or as a generalist. Herbert Hoover was an expert in ore dressing, and he built on his reputation as a great engineer to go all the way to the presidency. Dr. Ben Carson specialized in pediatric brain surgery and was able to become a national leader as a result. Becoming a generalist in college is self-defeating and dooms the individual to mediocrity unless he later specializes. Majors such as women's studies, general studies, black studies, and general liberal arts prepare the graduate to do nothing in particular and finding a job after graduation often becomes a nightmare.

One of the Mines graduates in Metallurgical Engineering in 1961 decided in 1979 to obtain his Registered Professional Engineer certificate from the State of Texas. He found that he qualified under no less than four classifications, Metallurgical Engineer, Computer Systems Engineer, Industrial Engineer, and Electrical Engineer. He decided to process his application as an Electrical Engineer, and readily passed. After all, a Mines graduate could do anything.

In a larger sense, it is definitely true that an engineer needs to have knowledge outside of his narrow specialty. For most engineers, that knowledge comes as he applies his critical thinking and engineering methodology to problems as he runs into them outside of his specialty. Mines trained men to recognize and solve problems of all types as a by-product to confronting the very tough problems he was expected to handle in his specialty. That's why Mines graduates have been able to be successful in all walks of life.

Few Mines graduates have remained in their narrow specialties for their lifetimes — most have moved over into other disciplines or into management where their engineering backgrounds and approach to problem-solving, have stood them in good stead. Mines didn't teach solutions — it taught critical and innovative thinking, and trained men to run the world from an engineering perspective. Most have been successful beyond the administration's expectations. Many have sought advanced degrees such as an MBA, while others have moved into law. The combination of a Mines background with an MBA has been particularly devastating to the competition, and Mines graduates have often excelled when taking the non-stressful courses in business departments in universities that believed they set the standard. They didn't and never have: Mines did — at least until 1968.

One Miner with a 2.5 GPA at Mines moved to a prestigious MBA school, earned the highest score ever recorded at that institution on the ATGSB (Admission Test for Graduate Study in Business), and earned the highest graduate GPA in his class. For him the MBA was a piece of cake compared to Mines. He then moved on to another university to work on a PhD in Operations Research and found the course work there fairly easy also. Of note was that he was only given a probationary admission for the MBA due to what the university thought was a poor undergraduate performance. The Mines graduate was only admitted when the admissions officer noted the heavy course load on Mines transcript, unbelievable, and far higher than he had ever seen before.

Outside of the influx of easterners like Vanderwilt into the faculty and administration, there were several outside influences that pushed Mines into giving up its rigorous course load and high requirements. The North Central Association of Colleges and Schools refused Mines application for accreditation in the early 1950s, claiming that Mines was producing intellectual barbarians. The fields of study were far too narrow, and the course load much too heavy. Of course, the bureaucrats making those statements were mediocrities themselves, and would have been unable to graduate from Mines. In the opinion of the accreditation commission, **the learning pace was too rapid to be absorbed**, and the lack of humanities and liberal arts courses tended to produce a graduate limited in scope. He could not hope to understand modern society and its times to be of much use to the world. The commission demanded the inclusion of more humanities and a lowering of the credit hours in order to be re-accredited.

There has never been a more damning indictment of the John Dewey-oriented educational establishment than the actions and words of the North Central Association in dealing with the accreditation of Mines. The Lilliputians in the Association were like the deaf man in the Bal Shem Tov story, and they were incapable of recognizing greatness. All they sought was for the blanks to be filled in, and the required topics to be listed in the curriculum. That a school and its student body might dare to be great, was beyond them.[1]

There had been no complaint from the industries Mines served, but progressive education and its tenets had arrived and were to be universally applied or else. For Vanderwilt, this gave him institutional backing and the legitimacy he needed to put through his program of easing requirements.

In 1952, mandatory course loads were supposedly limited to twenty-one hours per semester, with freshman and sophomore curricula only requiring 18-1/2 and twenty hours per semester, not counting summer work that was required after both years. In practice these standards were ignored, and students routinely took twenty-two to twenty-four hours and more in a semester, even though twenty-four was supposed to be the absolute limit.

The North Central thought the academic load was excessive, maybe because it put all other schools to shame. But worse was that the Association wanted to dictate what courses were taken. Liberal arts courses were to be substituted for engineering ones to make the students well-rounded. That such a curriculum might reduce the ability of a graduate to perform as an engineer was not their concern. "Fitting in" and becoming a happy, well-adjusted cit-

[1] One day a deaf man passed by a house where a wedding celebration was taking place. The celebrants were singing and dancing with great enthusiasm. The deaf man looks in and declared to his companion: 'Look, this house is full of mad people. See how they fling themselves about.' Of course, that was how they appeared, for the deaf man could not hear the music.

izen was. Excellence was not in the equation.

Having not been accredited by the North Central Association since 1937, the administration decided it had no choice but to accede to the NCA's demands. It lowered the amount of credit given in courses, leaving the required material intact. After the adjustments were finished in 1956, schedules for the freshman and sophomore years were as follows:

Freshman Fall Semester:

General Chemistry	4 hrs lecture, 3 hrs lab	5 hrs credit
Engineering Drawing	2 hrs lecture, 4 hrs lab	2 hrs credit
English Grammar	3 hrs lecture	3 hrs credit
Geomorphology	3 hrs lecture	3 hrs credit
Math Analysis I	5 hrs lecture	5 hrs credit
Military Sci (ROTC)	2 hrs lecture, 2 hrs lab	1 hr credit
Physical Training	2 hrs lab	1/2 hr credit
Totals:	19 hrs lecture, 11 hrs lab	19.5 hrs credit

Freshman Spring Semester:

Chem Qual Analysis	4 hrs lecture, 3 hrs lab	5 hrs credit
Descriptive Geometry	2 hrs lecture, 4 hrs lab	3 hrs credit
English Composition	3 hrs lecture	3 hrs credit
Calculus I	5 hrs lecture	5 hrs credit
Historical Geology	3 hrs lecture	3 hrs credit
Military Sci (ROTC)	2 hrs lecture, 2 hrs lab	1 hr credit
Physical Training	2 hrs lab	½ hr credit
Totals:	19 hrs lecture, 11 hrs lab	20.5 hrs credit

Summer Session: (not counted in the following analysis)
Plane Surveying   6 weeks, 6 a.m.-6 p.m. M-F,   8 hrs credit
Tests Sat a.m., large drawing due Monday. Ave wk 25 hrs lecture, 51 lab Semester equivalent: 10 hrs lecture + 23 hrs lab/wk

Sophomore Fall Semester:

Chem Quant Ana	4 hrs lecture, 3 hrs lab	4 hrs credit
Physics I	5 hrs lecture	5 hrs credit
Calculus Ana Geom	5 hrs lecture	5 hrs credit
Technical Exposition	3 hrs lecture	3 hrs credit
Crystallography	2 hrs lecture, 4 hrs lab	2 hrs credit
Military Sci (ROTC)	2 hrs lecture, 2 hrs lab	1 hr credit
Physical Training	2 hrs lab	½ hr credit
Totals:	21 hrs lecture, 11 hrs lab	20.5 hrs credit

Sophomore Spring Semester:

Organic Chem	4 hrs lecture, 3 hrs lab	4 hrs credit
Calc & Diff Equ	5 hrs lecture	5 hrs credit
Physics II	5 hrs lecture	5 hrs credit
Mineralogy	2 hrs lecture, 4 hrs lab	2 hrs credit
West Civ (elective)	3 hrs lecture	3 hrs credit
Psychology (elective)	2 hrs lecture	2 hrs credit
Military Sci (ROTC)	2 hrs lecture, 2 hrs lab	1 hr credit
Physical Training	2 hrs lab	½ hr credit
Totals:	23 hrs lecture, 11 hrs lab	22.5 hrs credit

Total required credit 1st two years: 91 credit hours.

Total credit based on credit of 1 hour for each hour of lecture and 1 hour for each three hours of lab during the fall and spring semesters: (82 hrs lecture, 44 hrs lab) equaled 97 credit hours that should have been awarded. Mines used two metrics for studying, both unreasonably low, 2 hours for each credit hour, or 3 hours for each hour in lecture or recitation, for 194 and 246 hours respectively. Using an average of 220 study hours for four semesters, Mines expected students to study 55 hours per week and be in class or studying 86 hours per week for the first two years—if the courses had represented their proper amount of credit. In actual practice, students who expected to graduate studied six to seven hours per day, Monday through Thursday, raised hell on Friday night, took care of personal maintenance and dating on Saturday, and studied ten to twelve hours on Sunday.

That regimen involved 37 hours per week in study in addition to the 30 to 34 hours in class, an average total of 70 hours, or much less than the 86 hours the school expected. According to the school's expectations, about 51% of a student's time was to be taken up in class and study, or over 12.3 hours per day, seven days a week, but in actuality, students only devoted 41% of their time to school and studying. Some studied more and some less, but that was probably the norm. After 1970, no school in the United States expected anywhere near that much from its students, Mines included. Most hoped for about 25% of a student's week to be devoted to school and study or about 45 hours in total. Mines in the 1950s expected to receive over twice as much of a student's time than a normal university from its students.

To silence the critics who maintained that Mines flunked out an inordinate percentage of students to build the school's reputation for excellence, H. Dean Burdick, Director of Admissions, addressed the retention rate in 1953. According to statistics developed by the Educational Testing Service, only 35% of freshmen in engineering colleges graduated in four years, while Mines was 42%. The numbers and analysis contained severe problems, as many students in universities started out taking engineering, but soon switched to other, easier, degree programs even when not at risk of flunking out. So the graduation rate in engineering colleges was not an indication of the "flunk out" rate, merely a continuation or retention rate in engineering.

The figure at Mines was woefully overstated, as the ratio was a simple one between students enrolling as freshmen in 1948, and the number graduating in 1952. That failed to take into account transfers coming into Mines as sophomores and even juniors and graduating in 1952. Moreover, there was no way to separate out students who had taken five, six, or more years to graduate, and were included in the class of '52. Probably fifteen to twenty percent of Mines graduates during the 1950s did not start at Mines as freshmen. Mines did flunk out an enormously high percentage, actually as high as two-thirds, and that was of students with high engineering aptitude in the first place. The Mines Librarian, Mary E. Holt, noted in 1949 that approximately 11,000 students had enrolled at Mines to that time, but only 3,245 had graduated. Allowing for the students still in school, her numbers indicated a graduation rate of less than 34%. Dean Burger reported that only a third would graduate in four years, and when looking at anecdotal data of fraternity pledges and those going active and completing their degrees, the number is even less.

Mines applied for accreditation again in 1957 based on a 200-page study called the "Colorado School of Mines Self-Survey Report." This document did not achieve its objectives. The North Central examining committee focused on faculty qualifications as expressed in graduate degrees and faculty salaries and compared the curriculum to liberal arts and general education offerings. The Mines faculty was deemed to show insufficient competence in their areas of expertise by not obtaining the necessary graduate degrees required to conduct research and guide graduate students in their chosen fields. That the faculty might have been excellent in teaching was not considered. Supposedly, the faculty salaries were too low to attract highly qualified research-oriented PhD faculty, and it was expected this situation would get worse without the necessary funding for research to generate academic publications. But stripping everything else away, at the core of the North Central's analysis was that Mines did not offer sufficient liberal arts, business, and general education courses to produce a well-rounded individual according to the North Central's arbitrary standards.

In desperation, Mines produced a curriculum revision to appease the North Central. Required courses in the humanities and social sciences were increased from 21 to 27 hours. Starting in the early 1960s, lower division math requirements were lowered from 20 to 17 hours while lower division physics was increased from ten to thirteen hours. Lower division chemistry was reduced from 18 to 16 hours but included Physical Chemistry, formerly two upper division courses due to their dependency on high-order math. With the necessary math no longer available as prerequisites, the Physical Chemistry courses were watered down substantially, and bore no resemblance to the earlier offerings. Lower division geology was reduced from 10 to 7 hours, and renamed as "earth science," a change considered to be a major improvement. Six hours of free electives were added to the upper division, so the number of easy courses increased, hopefully resulting in higher GPAs.

According to Dr. Vanderwilt's 1958-1959 Annual Progress Report, it was noted that:

> *"The Mines graduate...should be able to reason cogently and to deal with the abstract as well as the concrete and should have intellectual integrity. The Mines graduate should be able to express himself effectively both in speech and in writing...he should have some knowledge of the economy and the place of his society in civilization. He should have moral integrity, accompanied by a sense of obligation to individuals, groups, and nations. As a well-developed human being, he should have some appreciation of the cultural — preferably an appreciation sharpened by an awareness of aesthetic criteria."*

In short, the Mines graduate would become one of John Dewey's minions, taking his place in humanity as a happy and appreciative cog in society. Whether or not he could contribute anything due to some specialized expertise was not important. Based on this obeisance to the gods of humanistic government, the North Central Association re-accredited Mines with reservations in 1960, an event that President Vanderwilt considered a great victory. More lowering of standards and additional liberal arts courses were needed, but that would wait until the later 1960s.

There were two other problems, both with faculty, that the Mines administration had to solve: upgrading the faculty and meeting the demands of the AAUP. As noted previously, the Mines faculty was deficient in the eyes of the North Central Association due to the low number of PhD holders in its ranks. Colleges were rated by the percentage of PhD holders in the faculty, and Mines fell short by every metric. The emphasis on practical knowledge and experiences rather than research work was what drove Mines, but that was precisely what held it back from high evaluations by the North Central. The saying of "publish or perish" had never been applicable for Mines faculty, but all that was about to change. In order to make a major move into research — and the money it attracted — Mines needed PhDs. Initially, however, it was the chicken or the egg problem: high research funding attracted PhDs, and PhDs were necessary to attract research funding. In CSM's case, the school had to lift itself up by its own bootstraps and replace its faculty with PhDs.

The requirements of the AAUP affected a critical aspect that was not fully recognized at the time: it espoused academic freedom whereby faculty were not to be controlled by college and department administrations in what they could teach or how they taught. Academic freedom, therefore, meant that Mines would not be able to guarantee that its graduates possessed a certain level of engineering knowledge — merely that they had passed a certain number of credit hours.

Senior Day had definitively identified bad instructors, and some professors undoubtedly felt insecure in their positions. As a result, there was a push for going mainstream. That meant adopting the standards for students as determined by the North Central Association, and standards for faculty following the demands of the NCA and the precepts of the AAUP. Eventually, Mines capitulated to both.

The last president of Mines to lack a PhD was Melville Coolbaugh. He received an honorary Doctor of Laws from Colorado College when he was named to head Mines, and another followed two years later from Colorado University. Ben Parker was only barely acceptable with a DSc from Mines as president, and this may have been a factor in his trading positions with Dr. Vanderwilt when Parker went on the Board of Trustees and Vanderwilt left the Board to become president of the school.

Dr. Vanderwilt wanted to take Mines into this new age of a research institution, awash with money for research, the production of scholarly papers and reports, graduate students, and terminally-degreed faculty. To do so, Mines needed to be restructured from top to bottom. Money was the key, and Vanderwilt entered the school into the federal grant sweepstakes, becoming more of a salesman and fund-raiser than an academic.

The Mines administration never looked back or even questioned the correctness of its new course. In 1963, Orlo E. Childs became president of Mines, and in his 1963-64 Annual report, "We Look Ahead," he defined the miner he wanted:

"Preparedness for engineering and science careers cannot be made solely in engineer- and science-oriented curricula but through the liberal arts and the other intellectual and spiritual disciplines. Mines must become a place where students will have freedom to seek, to explore, to find out for themselves, to experiment, to learn by error, to change their minds and their beliefs upon a more perfect revelation of the truth, and to hold fast to these beliefs without external molestation."

The "Me" generation of the 60s had arrived, and the hard disciplines of engineering and science were on their way out. Childs was the perfect successor to Vanderwilt.

Enrollment that had been flat for a decade began to increase, helped immeasurably by increased financial aid and, to some extent, three new undergraduate degree programs in engineering, physics, math and chemistry. But the main reason was the national plea by President Kennedy for more engineers to help the nation meet the challenges of the space age. For a brief moment in American history, engineering had become sexy.

Bolstered by increased enrollments, Dr. Childs went for the gold in 1964 and proposed changing the name from Colorado School of Mines to Colorado Institute of Technology. Almost as a single voice, the alumni howled its disapproval, and Childs withdrew his idea.

But other factors were at work to stifle the continued excellence of Mines. Anti-war faculty helped students avoid military service during the sixties by inflating grades to qualify students for deferments. The national grade inflation epidemic did not leave Mines untouched. Average grades increased by half a grade, then a full grade, and the 2.05-2.1 GPA all-men's average in the fifties crept upwards to 2.9. By the 1970s class averages in many liberal arts and education colleges became 3.3 to 3.5. During the fifties at Mines, Tau Beta Pi took members with GPAs as low as 2.7, whereas by 2000, most schools limited Tau Beta Pi candidates to 3.7 and higher.

Nor was Mines immune to drugs starting in the late sixties. Marijuana made its endemic appearance, and Mines administrators chronicled a drop-in student goal-directed behavior. By the mid-seventies complaints were rife that students lacked dedication, and drugs were usually blamed for decreasing student interest in academics. That school policies were a factor seem to have been entirely disregarded.

Additional forces pushing the lowering of standards in the mid-sixties included the need for increased enrollments to combat acquisition pressure from Colorado University, and agitation for the recruitment of women and minorities as students. Through 1963 only six women had graduated from Mines, and CSM was reputed to discourage females from applying. In 1952 Life Magazine had featured "Lone Co-ed Attends School of Mines" as its lead article, but the lady portrayed lasted less than two years.

Only a handful of women registered before 1952, but only four had graduated, one each in 1898, 1903, 1920, and 1949. One transferred to Mines in 1957 after earning credits at three other universities and was awarded a degree in 1961. Of the one to three females who started Mines as freshmen each year during the fifties, only Mary McGill graduated, in 1962 on a five-year program. During the 1960s before the introduction of the Bachelor of Science degree, only three more women graduated from Mines, but then the population exploded. In 1982, no less than seventy-four women were included in the graduating class, a number that represented almost 15% of the graduates.

Although foreign students including Africans were prominent on campus more or less constantly after World War One, an examination of *The Prospector* showed few American blacks attending Mines until after 1968. Hispanics, Asians, and other nationalities and races, however, were abundant both inside and outside social fraternities and apparently not experiencing on-campus discrimination. The composition of the Mines student body changed dramatically as standards were lowered and women and minorities began to be recruited in great numbers. The standards of Mines were not lowered to attract women and minorities, but apparently had that effect.

Before the introduction of the BS, women accounted for about 0.1% of the graduates, with only five earning professional degrees in the 1960s, afterwards, they rapidly rose to being 25-27% of the undergraduate student body, and experienced higher graduation rates than the men (74% as compared with 64%) as reported in 2010. These percentages, of course, both compare very favorably with the pre-1969 graduation rate average for all students of about 25% in four years, and about 33% in six years. Women also rose to be over-represented (by 100%) in student leadership positions, with even a higher percentage being elected as officers in student organizations.

But most interesting is that the women achieved a higher GPA (3.0) than males (2.9) in the 21st century. There is an answer that one of the authors has developed in his years of teaching computer science. He discovered that women, in general, made much better programmers than men. The reason is not flattering to the males. The women have less personal ego tied up in their product, and more readily acknowledge that they might have made a mistake. If a program doesn't work correctly, the male programmer says it can't be that his program has an error, so fails to address the problem in a timely fashion. The woman looks at her program with the assumption she has an error, finds it, and learns from her mistake. As in lots of engineering situations, dogmatic certitude stands in the way of the solution. Men simply do that more than women. This situation is exacerbated in mixed groups where women are present, and the men will do anything to avoid loss of face. In an all-male group, the males solve problems as well as females because their masculinity is not threatened. Separation of classes by sex has always facilitated learning by students, but alas, that has now become politically incorrect.

None of the new GPA numbers, however, like the SAT scores and other major test results, are comparable to the old system when the all-student average barely exceeded 2.0. By 2010, at least 60% of Mines students would be eligible for Tau Beta Pi if the standard for eligibility had remained the same as in the 1950s. Even at Mines, we have reached the point that no child is left behind.

Meanwhile, the administration continued to flounder about looking for new mountains to climb. A large number of studies were made of Mines, its situation, and about how to meet the future. None of them, however, seemed to be aware of Dr. Chauvenet's original design or why the old Mines existed as it did. In 1967, the Colorado Commission of Higher Education commissioned a task force headed by Carl Borgmann, Advisor on Science and Technology at the Ford Foundation, to examine the situation at Mines and make a report. The Borgmann Report was a bombshell. Borgmann concluded that if Mines continued to concentrate on undergraduate education as it had formerly, its days as the foremost mineral engineering school in the world were numbered. Mines had little support from the federal government, the faculty was only fair to good as measured by the number with terminal degrees, the student body only fair to good as measured by its grades, and graduate programs needed to be vastly expanded. The report was lightweight propaganda and easily refuted, but it carried great weight with President Childs.

In 1968 Mines set about de-emphasizing undergraduate instruction and started on the long road to become a major research-oriented technological institute. For openers, Childs recognized that Mines could not continue producing professional degree graduates and develop the necessary new programs, a student base, and funding opportunities for a world-class research organization at the same time. The professional degree had to go, and it did. It was changed into a five-year program in which the last year was moved to the graduate school and made a Master of Engineering (without thesis.) Beginning in 1969, Mines granted Bachelor of Science degrees in Engineering or Science which eventually required only 138.5 semester hours that were laced with non-rigorous courses in liberal arts and general education. New graduate degrees were introduced such as Master of Science in Chemistry, Mathematics, Physics, and Mineral Economics, and PhDs in Engineering and Science. The day of completing 188 semester hours which should have been 212 hours within four years was gone forever. Henceforth Mines would be nurturing, kind, fun, relaxing, and very politically correct.

Graduation itself became scheduled twice a year, and almost immediately, the move to de-emphasize undergraduate education became apparent. As the Mines Magazine reported in 1970, Mines awarded diplomas to 171 Bachelor of Science degrees, 58 Professional Engineer diplomas, and 58 advanced degrees to graduate students. The sterling silver diplomas were given out for 7 Doctorates, 23 Master of Science degrees, 5 Master of Engineering degrees, and the 58 PE degrees while the BS recipients received their diplomas on parchment. The new PE degree represented the completion of a four and one-half-year program with lighter credit loads than formerly. In the January ceremony, there were 57 bachelor and Professional Engineer degrees awarded, and 22 non-PE graduate degrees. Overall for 1970, the graduate school represented 25% of the degrees granted, whereas in 1956 it had produced under 6% and in 1961, only 10%.

At the same time a chapter of the AAUP was installed on campus, and in 1973, the AAUP came out swinging. Given that there was no academic tenure at Mines, the AAUP censured the school. The hiring of high-quality research faculty screeched to a halt as the AAUP lambasted Mines at every opportunity.

To add to the school's misery in 1974, the North Central Association once again raised its ugly head and conducted an evaluation review of Mines. The evaluating team reported thirteen concerns, including a substantial drop in the school's reputation in Colorado (no surprise there!), an unclear vision for the future, little to no improvement in the integration of humanities and social sciences into the degree programs, and all of the complaints of the AAUP. As expected, the newly-formed faculty senate approved of the findings.

The changes so far had all been for naught. With each concession, additional demands were presented of which there was no end. The bell could not be un-rung. The school continued to become involved in more and more progressive research experiments. For a while, enrollments continued to increase due to the expanded degree offerings, but then came the 1980s.

As discussed in Chapter 10, the Mines administration was shocked when enrollments began to decline. The oil industry was under siege, and although pressure certainly came from OPEC, more permanently, it came from environmentalists seeking to eliminate all fossil fuel use. Oil-related jobs began to vanish, and the Mines administration panicked. It moved forward with a vengeance seeking research dollars and expanded degree programs to anything that even remotely sounded technical. The graduate school picked up, and the administration doubled down on its long-term strategy. Mines had to go forward and win the research funding battle or die.

It was up against a lot of competition: literally every university now included in its mission statement that it wanted to become a nationally recognized research institution with nationally-known research faculty. For example, the president of San Diego State University, hardly known for its excellence in education, was congratulated in 2011 for his success in improving graduation rates and transforming SDSU into a research university. Sound familiar?

The undergraduates now became a semi-necessary evil to maintain enrollments to satisfy the legislature. And the students themselves had changed. As one Mines professor, a Mines graduate himself, said in 2006, "*Make no mistake. The students today are nothing like the students in the 50s. Education has to be fun, or else they're not interested. It is doubtful that more than a very few could handle the workload we had in the 50s.*"

A footnote should be added to this discussion. In 1997, the CSM Retention and Management Committee, distressed by a retention rate of only 60%, authorized a study of Mines students by Dr. James H. Banning of the Campus Ecology Service at Colorado State. Dr. Banning's survey revealed that the student complaints were remarkably similar to those in the 1950s. He recommended the number of credit hours required for a degree be further reduced, that students should be given more free time, on-campus activities be increased, and that an academic ombudsman's office be established.

All this came after reducing student loads by over 46%, establishing a stunning *Student Union*, creating a student recreation center as the largest building on campus, installing free medical treatment, building dormitories to meet various student needs, and adding untold counselors and bureaucrats to aid the students in every endeavor. What more could the school do? Maybe put them in teams to work on high profile projects helping the environment and give everyone the same grade? They were already doing that. How about stressing reports and presentations and eliminate tests? Or let students take classes by computer from off campus? These students were supposed to be the engineers of the future, and they will represent Mines. But how many of them would have lasted past Thanksgiving as entering freshmen in the 1950s?

Gone was the Mines graduate of the 50s who, within a year of joining General Electric, developed the process for producing large diameter fully wrought tungsten bar and put GE into a new market. Gone was the Mines graduate of the 50s who never took a computer programming course in his life, but over a twenty-year period produced more computer code than anyone else in the world. Mines graduates built large companies by virtue of their technical expertise, the basis of which was their Mines education. Where were these people going to come from when 16 hours of class time per week is simply too much? China or Japan?

Mines became the poster boy for the decline of American technical expertise. Even in computers and software, we see large numbers of foreigners occupying slots for which there are no Americans available. It is not a "brain drain" to some foreign location that the United States is suffering; it is the destruction of the Protestant work ethic and the ability to innovate. This phenomenon can be directly attributed to the American education establishment. The AAUP looks after the welfare of its faculty members. College administrations chase funding. Students want a useable education, while the citizens want a return on their investment. Neither the students nor citizens should be paying for a system destroying the nation.

Coolbaugh Hall

Chapter 19 – The New Mines

In 1990 the average CSM student was in the top 10 percent of all college-bound students nationally in math ability and in the top 20 percent in verbal ability as determined by SAT (Scholastic Aptitude Test) scores. About 60 percent of each freshman class during the 1980s ranked in the top 10 percent of their high school class.

It should have been expected that ALL CSM students would be in the top two percent in math and somewhat less in verbal. The SAT test scores used in the 1980s were a national disgrace, and with the greatly increased number of students with marginal abilities taking the tests since the early sixties, those individuals who might have scored in the top ten percent in 1962 would now be in the top two or three percent. That only 60% of the entering freshmen at Mines were in the top ten percent of their high schools was extremely troublesome. It was a correctable situation, however. Those low achievers accepted during the 1980s should have rapidly flunked out and unburdened the system by seeking less rigorous institutions.

That did not happen as the administration stressed retention as a policy. 65% of the entering Mines students in the late 1980s eventually graduated. The conclusion was inescapable. Mines was starting with weaker students than formerly, and more of them were graduating. Hence, the Mines graduate of the 1980s could not be expected to have the consistently high quality of bygone years. Placement figures were quoted to show Mines graduates were still successful, but such statistics were truly meaningless. What is meaningful is the graduates' professionalism and contributions in their fields of endeavor, not whether or not a graduate was able to find a job. A 1957 graduate believed he could do anything; the 1990 graduate could qualify only for an entry position and further training.

For an elite school only two options are available to insure top graduates: have extremely high entrance standards or eliminate the weaker students through draconian educational standards of excellence. In the 1950s Mines did both. Since 1968, Mines has not done either. It has accepted low quality students and worked hard at keeping them in school—apparently to maintain high enrollments.

Enrollments dropped drastically during the 1980s and 1990s, and the administration misread the problem and instituted an even worse solution. Student placement information indicated increasing difficulties for students seeking employment in the traditional mineral and oil industries, and the administration assumed the job loss was permanent because the United States was moving into a new age of information and computerization. Apparently believing that diversity was an institution's strength, a concept debunked by literally every measure and socio-metric except political propaganda, Mines broadened its course offerings and programs to attract students interested in ecology, environmentalism, and many other "new age" programs. Standards remained low, and Mines avidly sought federal money and support.

What was missed was that the graduates until 1968 were mostly hired by manufacturing and conglomerate corporations interested in obtaining problem solvers, men not afraid to tackle new projects, and men who could think for themselves. Companies like GE, Polaroid, Boeing, Procter and Gamble, Haliburton, Coastal Energy, and the like, wanted high producers, men who could work long hours, and were not afraid to go into areas where they had only rudimentary knowledge. The Mines concept of specialty training produced experts in those fields, but the harshness of the programs produced graduates also able to sink the proverbial "ten-foot shaft to Hell" or build a "Bridge to Mars."

The administration also perpetuated another mistake that almost destroyed the school. When it converted the old PE degree programs to Master of Engineering (without thesis) degrees, alumni naturally asked to be grandfathered in and have their professional degrees changed to the new masters. The administration refused in no uncertain terms, almost as if they were at war with the alumni. Vice-President Tony Pegis stated the programs were "in no way comparable" due to new technologies, and this to graduates that had been out of school for less than a decade. Sadly, one of the authors and Dr. Pegis ended their relationship in 1973 after a number of contentious discussions concerning the elimination of the Professional Engineer degree and its replacement by a Master of Engineering. The primary issue was that Dr. Pegis refused to even consider a program whereby holders of the PE could swap their degree for an ME. His logic was tortuous, even stating that the two were not equivalent. Clearly Tony Pegis was speaking for the administration rather than personally, and the disrespect for earlier graduates by the administration became formalized.

Converting previously earned professional degrees into Master of Engineering would finally have legitimized the former Mines program for what it truly was: a six-year Master of Engineering curriculum taken in four years. Yet to this day, the school refuses to consider such a step. Maybe the memories of Senior Day were previously too strong for CSM's faculty and administration personnel, but that should have been dispelled by now. One wonders how many millions of dollars in contributions from alumni were lost through the administration's short-sighted stance. Much worse happened in the marketplace. Alumni stopped hiring graduates with the new bachelor's degrees, and stopped recommending the school as a good place to find new employees.

The administration apparently recognized that placement in industries populated by CSM alumni fell off, but thought it was simply due to a lack of demand in CSM's specialties. It wasn't: it was due to two self-inflicted wounds. The Mines administration had lowered the school's standards and alienated the school's alumni. The Alumni Association was kicked out of the top floor of Guggenheim Hall, moved to unimposing offices in Chauvenet Hall, then to the Weaver Towers on 19th Street, then to the basement of the Jefferson County administrative complex, then to Coolbaugh House, and finally to the Welcome Center. To say that the Alumni Association has been a red-headed step-child would be kind.

The Alumni Association was and is the best ambassador to the world that Mines could have, even with representatives from the new school. But concerns over lowered standards and graduates with decreased capabilities are real. Can the clock be turned back? Probably not in today's political climate, but at some point, the nation will be become interested again in producing well-trained engineers with great leadership capabilities. In the interim, the Student Recreation Center is a stunningly bad sign: its purpose is to make a student's sojourn at Mines fun instead of a survival course in learning engineering. It certainly does not impress a prospective employer that a student spends many hours per week in a recreation center.

One father of a 1990 graduate even stated that his son had enjoyed his education at Mines — it seems impossible that any graduate in the fifties would have made that statement. But it shows the impact of the "Me" generation and the gospel that life must be fun. History has taught us that success comes from extending individuals beyond the norm, even beyond what they expect of themselves, weeding out those who lack the ability or dedication to succeed, and making the movers and shakers readily identifiable. Once upon a time, the silver diploma had done that for an elite group

One graduate, who was a university professor and Army veteran, stated the case succinctly in a 1990 letter to Nordy Jenson, Director of Public Relations. The letter was in response to an article announcing the creation of a student counseling center on campus, staffed by three young ladies, all in their twenties. In the graduate's time at old Mines, there were no counselors on campus. The only semblance of counseling a student received occurred in the fall freshman semester, which was a critique on his performance in relation to his SAT, IQ, and Pre-Engineering Inventory exams. It was helpful in convincing marginal freshmen to quit, but counseling it was not.

Dear Mr Jensen:

It was with interest that I read Gene Tafoya's article on the Student Development Center. It appears someone has convinced the powers at Mines that the current Mines students are as neurotic as the kids hiding from the work force in liberal education institutions.

The typical Mines student of the fifties would have laughed at the idea of a counseling center. Almost universally we were committed to making a contribution with our lives, and we recognized the necessity of acquiring discipline and knowledge to accomplish that contribution. Many of us left engineering for other pursuits – I for one studied engineering to gain discipline, and because it was something I would not teach myself.

Although I am a registered Professional Engineer, the habits and discipline learned at Mines enabled me to acquire substantial knowledge in other areas. Today I have fulfilled Dr. Vanderwilt's fondest wish by becoming proficient in a number of disciplines and acceptable in society.

Mines during the fifties was like combat with the students battling the system. In my fraternity's pledge class of thirty-one, five left at Thanksgiving, and only fifteen achieved the necessary 2.0 to go active in January. None of the students flunked from lack of intellectual ability – they lacked the dedication to discipline and achievement to survive. Like most entering freshmen, I too had no idea of how to study. High school had been a social experience with little challenge. But we soon found ourselves faced with two options: learn to study immediately or flunk out. It was like the first time on patrol in Vietnam – you learned overnight or died. There was no time for remedial education, and Mines certified its graduates as survivors under the harshest of condition.

I graduated in four years with enough semester hours for a PhD in liberal arts. But then Mines changed its system, reduced the workload and made strenuous efforts to provide a more comely social atmosphere for the students.

With lowered scholastic loads came the time to develop the neurotic behavior normally associated with the '60s and '70s. Apparently, students are like soldiers, and we know that idle troops readily disintegrate into undisciplined rabble. In my teaching life, I have found that student personal problems are inversely related to their course loads and the demands placed upon them by their professors. Mines went in the wrong direction and decided it was necessary to hire these three young ladies as surrogate mothers for the student body.

My era ended in the sixties. The Professional Degree was changed to a Master of Engineering, although no grandfather clause was inserted for the earlier graduates. The war continued — the Administration was happy to take our money as contributions, but otherwise seemed ashamed of its former, non-liberal educated graduates. The Administration only seemed able to feed increasingly at the public trough and generate products indistinguishable from those of the University of Colorado or Denver. The curriculum was watered down to appeal to a broader range of students. The sterling silver diploma was discontinued. The beer-busts in the clay pits vanished with the pits themselves.

The State of Colorado seemed intent on destroying the relics of Mines' rough and tumble past. Mediocrity always fears greatness, and no better example presents itself than the sad story of the treatment of Mines by the Colorado Legislature and its own Administration. Mines had once been unique — the world's foremost mineral engineering school. Now it is being reduced to just another state college with socially-oriented students in need of counseling by three young mothers raising their young children.

So now we have a cute little counseling center set up to assist the young men or ladies who don't know how to find themselves. Not to denigrate the qualifications of the three female counselors, but the center's head says Mines students are similar to college students of other campuses. Is that true? Are there no differences between the kids at Colorado State College, where if your body is warm you can graduate, and the CSM engineers-to-be What a terrifying state of affairs!

But maybe the counseling center is needed. We've staffed it with three young ladies, none of whom have pursued a successful career, to tell the students how to be happy. Are they also going to tell the students how to achieve excellence in engineering? Is there no chance to return to a system of excellence? Has no one in the Administration read Bob Waterman's book?

You need to provide less counseling and more work requirements to achieve more capable graduates. I learned in my doctoral work in Or-

ganizational Behavior that the goal of counseling is not to help produce a productive individual, but someone "happy" and "well-adjusted." Is that what Mines has become? Is it an institution oriented to generating happy graduates? The counselors should be able to tell you that true happiness comes through the self-actualized process of successful creation and contribution, not sitting around in a support group rapping about your personal problems.

Mines formerly produced men able to create and contribute having passed a brutal and thorough curriculum. Now, I expect to see Mines graduates in analysis blaming their broken homes, drugs, alcohol, or sexual problems for their failures to contribute – or students seeking counseling to handle their anxiety problems. The Administration has brought this situation on itself by choosing to be paternalistic towards its students. Mines might as well keep the boys and girls there safe from harm by the outside world by moving them all into research and advanced degree programs. That way they can stay in the protective cocoon of academia for the rest of their lives and receive excellent pensions. Woops, I just described the faculty.

And stop asking for contributions to an institution espousing trendy, "current wisdom." One thing history has taught us is that "current wisdom" is always wrong. Schools like the old Mines generated the contributors who overthrew "current wisdom," not ones like the new Mines. Evidently my Mines has gone to the Tower of Silence – stripped naked, laid out for the vultures to pick clean, and its desiccated bones were tossed absently into the lime pit so that nothing remains. There will be no more leopards close to the western summit of Kilimanjaro – not from Mines, at any rate.

Sincerely yours, A Mines graduate from the 1950s.

Rather surprisingly, Mr. Jenson actually responded to this letter, but failed to address any of the issues contained therein. Instead he concentrated on the standard PR statistics: that enrollments were up, graduate programs were flourishing, new buildings were being built, and more research money had been obtained.

The response necessitated a second letter from the disgruntled Mines alumnus, one that no one in the administration deigned to answer.

Dear Mr. Jensen:

Thank you for your letter of May 29, 1990. It gives me a much clearer appreciation of the values presently considered important by the Mines administration.

Your statistics are startling and disturbing. You may attempt to quote placement figures to show your graduates are successful, but such statistics are truly meaningless.

Obviously, Mines has changed from my day. You are touting your expanded appeal and increased numbers. No doubt that will lead to a larger school, more state money, and increased compensation for the administrative bureaucracy. My point is that it is leading to graduates of lower quality. I hope the best for your son, [a student at Mines] and trust you have shared my letters with him and the remainder of the students so that they can have a basis for understanding my concerns.

What is required is excellence in CSM's undergraduate school. The German Army accomplished incredible feats during World War II with inferior numbers through excellent staff work, planning, and leadership. It was all due to the excellence of the graduates of its Kriegsakademie at Berlin who survived a dropout rate of over two-thirds. The Japanese flyers from the misty lagoons lost four-fifths of their school chums in training, and then startled the world with their prowess until attrition ended their supremacy in the air. But Mines has eschewed excellence to attract federal money. Gene Woolsey would not have approved.

Not that I'm in favor of litigation, but I wonder how many of today's Mines students realize how badly they've been cheated. They expected to receive a top education from the world's foremost mineral engineering school (if they survived), but instead are enduring four years of bureaucratic custody and obtaining a standard education.

I hope your son does not come to blame you when he discovers Mines is no longer an elite institution and his educational experience was sacrificed in order to expand a bureaucracy. No doubt he will ultimately be employed by the Japanese who, like the Germans, have raised elitist education to the highest plane. Mines formerly competed with them, but no longer. How far the Gods have fallen!

Please feel free to share my feelings with anyone you wish. I noticed your reply did not address any of my earlier points. Instead you pointed out that Mines was doing well – it was growing in numbers and appeal. Community colleges are also growing in numbers and appeal.

Sincerely yours, a Mines graduate from the 1950s.

The new school of Mines mirrored the nation's spiral downward in competence, leadership, and education. Educators observed the negative trend but failed to understand its underlying causes. Politicians threw money at the problem, and President Carter created the Department of Education. The result was an acceleration of the downward spiral. Educators stressed certification and licensing to ensure expertise, and the nation went from licensing about 10% of the jobs in America in 1950 to over 38% in 2000. A whole new industry sprang up as schools were created to teach courses leading to certifications and licensing. Bureaucracies were created, but very rapidly the public discovered that just because a person possessed a degree, license, or certification, it didn't mean he was competent.

Responding to all sorts of government programs designed to produce high school graduates or those who passed an equivalency test, K-12 education pushed students through from one grade to another even when the student had not mastered the required subject matter. Perhaps the outstanding example of this policy occurred at a California state-supported university, but it could have happened in any number of football and basketball factories. A group of basketball players had used up their basketball eligibility and the university suspended them for failing to maintain a minimum GPA. In fact, several of the players were illiterate. It came as no surprise to many observers that one could graduate from high school without learning to read or write, but it was stunning that they were accepted at a college, and after four years in school, that deficiency had not been remedied. Although the students themselves were ultimately responsible for remaining illiterate, it was equally clear that the university did not care if they were illiterate so long as they could play basketball.

Since the 1980's a basic college degree has lost much of its luster and most manufacturing and technical industries increasingly look to applicants with a master's degree for supervisory positions. Better yet s the person with a PhD. He has shown that he possesses the necessary social and organizational skills to negotiate the academic maze and satisfy diverse personalities on his dissertation committee. That most PhD dissertations have little intrinsic value in furthering knowledge is not relevant.

As a result of these trends, colleges provide undergraduate programs as a requirement to maintain public support, rather than a choice. Undergraduates in the 21st century normally pay for about 20% of their schooling in public institutions through tuition, and schools are left to find funding for the remaining 80 percent. Until the 1960s, Mines was a notable exception to this rule as student tuition and fees covered nearly their entire education. The rule changes in graduate schools where students provide a wealth of low-paid or unpaid services to the school such as teaching, grading, laboratory help, research assistance, and so forth.

For students, becoming a graduate student is often quite appealing, particularly if someone else is paying, and 25-30% of Mines graduates are currently going on to graduate school. Maybe they don't feel ready for industry, maybe they can't find a reasonable job, or maybe they've figured out the credentials game. Costs are often defrayed through research grants and teaching assistant-ships, and one can delay his entry into the cold world of the private sector for two or three years. For faculty, graduate students are essential to a professor's well-being. The prof can off-load part of his teaching and all of his grading responsibilities onto graduate teaching assistants. Graduate students can even help write a faculty member's academic papers.

For the school administration, graduate students mean money. They are titled "research associates" in grant applications, with billing hours often in the $60.00 to $120.00 per hour range, while actually being paid only ten or twelve dollars per hour. Most university take 65% or an appropriate high percentage off the top for "overhead," and federal research grants often make a huge difference to a college's bottom line.

Perhaps the most important question today is "How good a school is the New Mines?" The answers are controversial to say the least. Parents of college aged students and school administrations often point to the various rankings of engineering schools by *USA Today*. Unfortunately, there are many such rankings, with varied criteria that is often difficult to understand or assess for relevancy. On one such ranking in 2017, Mines was at the top, but in others is it well down in the pack, even behind Colorado University and engineering schools in New Mexico and South Dakota. In the important factor of initial salary after graduation, Mines was clearly not outstanding, and behind schools that in the 1950s would have been considered inferior to Mines. All this reflects the fact that Mines is now producing graduates with a BS in engineering rather than a PE. Excellence in one's education is considered difficult to measure, and various opinions are substituted for an analysis of a school's curricula.

In 1984, a mid-sixties alumnus in Texas hired two recent Mines graduates, one male and one female. He found them unable to work more than thirty-five hours per week, and their primary concern seemed to be their after-hours social activities. Neither showed any special aptitude. The two students belonged to the tail-end of the baby-boomer generation and were exhibiting many of its negative characteristics, including self-adsorption and neurotic behavior. What they didn't know was always someone else's fault for not teaching it to them.

Attitudes such as self-adsorption and refusing to take responsibility have become typical in college graduates matriculating since the 1970s, but should not be present in Mines graduates. If present, these attitudes should not be allowed to continue. It was as though college graduates in general have caught a disease, but treatment for that disease is already at hand. Simply re-institute a heavy load of instruction and re-establish extremely demanding standards.

Part of the changes that faced Mines and other institutions coincide with the increased enrollments of women but cannot be blamed on them. The drop-in course load and standards have resulted from actions by the faculty and administration, not the students.

The socio-economic forces driving women to college have been exhaustively studied by sociologists. Three groups of women began enrolling in college during the 1960s and 1970s: women desiring a career as an alternative to marriage, married women whose family needed a second income, and divorced women who had learned not to depend upon a male for their economic security or on their children's father for support. Education was seen as critical to be successful in the post-Vietnam workforce, Pressures built on universities to make the necessary adjustments for the accommodation of females in all fields, and Mines was no exception.

Almost all of the hallmarks of the old Mines that made it what it was were gone by the 21st century, most of them by 1970. Only two survived the 2001 demise of *The Prospector*, the "M" on Mt. Zion and the name of the school itself. Both were under attack. The "M" has consistently been deplored by environmentalists who considered it to be environmental vandalism, a defacement of nature, and a mark of man that should be eliminated. Various efforts to change the school's name either to "Colorado Institute of Technology" or incorporate it under the University of Colorado and eliminate its independent status have been made since the early 20th century. The most serious challenge took place in 1964, and the Colorado Institute of Technology very nearly became a reality. It took massive alumni and citizen protests to rescue Mines and finally the Mines administration and the Colorado Legislature backed off.

The loss of the *Prospector* itself denoted the change in Mines from a small college with devoted alumni to a large, faceless institution in which undergraduates had become merely numbers.

The freshman class was no longer welded into a cohesive group through hazing, leadership in such an amorphous body no longer had any meaning, and mementos of their time at Mines were no longer prized by graduates. Why the *Prospector* was discontinued is controversial, but its loss was symbolic of what Mines sacrificed for growth. All growth is not necessarily good, as American politicians are finding out with the nation debt now exceeding 20 trillion dollars in short-term borrowings, and 245 trillion in known and obligated debt that is yet to be put on the books to avoid terrifying the citizenry.

Today there are new initiatives to change the school's anachronistic name that makes Colorado so proud. According to the environmentalists, it invokes the image of despoiling the land by lauding the extraction of the Earth's resources: an activity to be eliminated in favor of living in harmony with the land and only using renewable resources. The Mines administration has attempted to obfuscate such efforts by stressing Mines' commitment to "sustainability" and "sustainable development," code words for Agenda 21 that is a program discussed in Appendix G that is still unrecognized by the vast majority of American citizens.

The struggle for survival in the coming years by Mines may be a short one unless the school is able to convince the federal government that it is fully committed to sustainability in all its programs. That is now a requirement to obtain federal grants and contracts, and the school is pursuing those funds with unrestrained vigor. Fearing only the federal government, Mines dived into this program with all the fervor of a reformed prostitute.

The administration seems to be casting about for answers to CSM's survival, but is hampered by an apathetic alumnus, a vision little different from many other engineering schools, and a legislature dominated by the graduates of a competing school (CU). Clearly, Mines is heading for another succession of life-threatening pressures, and since the 1950s, the trustees and the administration have failed to exhibit the necessary skills in meeting the school's challenges. At this point, the rate of societal changes are accelerating, and the "new" Mines may rapidly go the way of its predecessor if it does not carve out a niche in higher education that it can proudly maintain and exploit to the benefit of Mines, Colorado, and the nation.

Chapter 20 - The Physical Plant

The development of Mines' physical plant can be divided conveniently into four stages after moving from the Jarvis Hall facility; the 1880-1894 complex, 1902-1910 expansion, 1921-1950 consolidation, and 1951 Horizon Plan.

A) 1880-1894 Complex: located between 14th and 15th streets mostly west of Arapaho.
1880 Building. The southern wing of what became known as the Old Chem Building.
1882 addition. Expanded the 1880 Building towards 14th Street. The library was moved from the 1st floor of the 1880 building into the new addition.
1890 northern wing. Finished the Old Chem (also Old Main) Building as a single large, red brick building constructed in three distinct phases. The northern wing was called the Executive Building. A gymnasium was in the basement. The building was completed in 1889 and occupied in 1890.
President's House. Located on 15th Street at the end of Cheyenne Street, the house was completed in 1889 and used by the President until 1926. A beautiful home with distinguished architecture until demolished under the Horizon Plan, it was occupied after 1947 by the Dean of Faculty until 1956, and then afterwards by the Dean of Students. Before being demolished to make way for the Kadafar Commons in 1964, it was used as a women's dormitory.
Engineering Hall. Constructed in 1894, it was used for organic chemistry and called the Hall of Advanced Chemistry until 1953 when it became home to the mathematics department. This is the oldest building remaining on the Mines campus. It was designed by Colorado's first licensed architect, Robert Roeschlaub, and is constructed of red brick from the Golden kiln and has a rhyolite foundation and sandstone trim.

B) 1902-1910 Expansion: between 14th and 15th streets westwards to Maple.
Stratton Hall. Built in 1902 from $25,000.00 donated by Winfield Stratton of Colorado Springs in 1900. Mr. Stratton had studied chemistry and mining at Colorado College, and in 1891 discovered one of the richest gold deposits in Cripple Creek District on Battle Mountain. In 1899 he had sold his "Independence" Claim

to English interests for ten million dollars. Stratton Hall housed civil, electrical, metallurgical, petroleum, and mechanical engineering until 1954. Since then it housed mechanical and electrical engineering.

Assay Laboratory. Built immediately west of Stratton Hall in 1902 and enlarged in 1906, it housed the metallurgical laboratories until 1958. At that time it was turned over to the mining department and remodeled.

Simon Guggenheim Hall. Donated by Simon Guggenheim and constructed in 1906, it houses CSM administrative offices. Guggenheim was a senator from Colorado, scion of the Guggenheim family, and president and chairman of the board for American Smelting and Refining Co. (ASARCO). The donation of Guggenheim Hall was the largest private grant ever made to a state institution up to that time. From 1906 to 1955 the library occupied one half of the first and second floors. After the Lakes library building was completed in 1955, the publications department moved into the Guggenheim basement from a remodeled frame house northeast of the Integral Club on 14th Street. The mining department was housed in Guggenheim until moving into a purchased red brick structure on the site where Berthoud Hall was later built. The alumni office occupied part of the top floor of Guggenheim until moving to Chauvenet Hall around 1978, after which it was relocated to the campus's edge in a dormitory called Twin Towers.

Power House. Later remodeled and dedicated as Chauvenet Hall in 1951, the power house was completed in 1906.

Gymnasium. Named for the Integral Club it housed before 1926, the Old Gymnasium was finished in 1907. A basketball court occupied the second floor, and a small, 18 yard long swimming pool was located in the basement. Student facilities and athletic department offices were on the first floor, and following construction of the new gymnasium in 1959, the Integral Club housed student offices and various service facilities. One of the most beautiful and interesting buildings on campus with many student memories, it was razed after the Student Union was built in 1964.

The "M". Not a building, but perhaps the most prominent structure belonging to CSM. Built in 1908 by Mines faculty and students, the "M"'s lighting was added in 1932.

Experimental Plant -- CSM Research Foundation. Funded by an appropriation of the State Legislature in 1909, the Experimental Plant northwest of Brooks Field housed ore dressing and metallurgical research facilities. The main building was constructed in 1910, and equipment and other facilities have been added during the years. The complex was razed in 2002 to provide space for the new athletic facilities at Brooks Field.

C) 1921-1950 consolidation:

Edgar Experimental Mine. Acquired in 1921 and located in Idaho Springs, the Edgar is used for practical mining courses.

Brooks Field. Built in 1926, Brooks Field is Mines' football and track facility located north of the clay pits on 12th Street and east of the Experimental Plant. Originally named Athletic Park from 1893 to 1922, it was named after Mines trustee and benefactor Ralph D. Brooks in 1922, and subsequently renamed Campbell Field in 2010. The stands seat 4,000 spectators. In the same spot as Athletic Park, the field was the oldest football field west of the Mississippi River, and the fifth oldest college football field in the nation. The first football game there was held on October 7, 1893.

Publications Building. A private home on the north side of 14th Street opposite the Integral Club, it was purchased in 1928. In 1957 it was razed to make way for construction of the new gym.

Physics Building. Acquired from the Golden School District in 1936, the structure on the hilltop opposite Stratton Hall north of 14th Street was Mines' oldest building. Built in 1873 as Golden's elementary school building, it housed the physics department until razed under the Horizon Plan.

Steinhauer Field House. Not dedicated to Mr. Steinhauer until 1947, the Field House on 13th Street between Illinois and Maple was completed in 1937 as an indoor sports facility.

Mines Park. Faculty housing area was constructed in 1939 below the entrance to Lariat Loop, now immediately west of the intersection of US Hwy 6 and 19th Street.

Berthoud Hall. Built in 1938 and dedicated to E. L. Berthoud in 1940, Berthoud Hall houses the departments of geology and geophysics as well as the Mines Museum. The building was designed by the noted architect Temple Buell.

President's House. Purchased in 1947, the house at the corner of 18th and Illinois was first occupied by President Ben Parker. It was originally the Sigma Nu fraternity house and built in 1927 by the noted architects Burnham F. and Merrill H. Hoyt.

Cafeteria Building. Built as a temporary wooden structure in 1947, it was placed opposite the end of 14th Street on Maple.

Petroleum Refining Complex. Built in 1947, this structure on Maple was an "H" Shaped single-story wooden building for temporary use.

Prospector Park. Built of single-story wooden barracks-like structures, Prospector Park provided married student housing east of US Highway 6 on the south side of 19th Street. It was opened in 1951 and razed sometime after 1964 to make room for the improvements to the intersection of 19th Street and US Hwy 6.

New Power House. Placed into service in 1948, the new power house on 13th Street houses the electrical engineering laboratories in addition to providing power to all campus buildings.

Chauvenet Hall. Dedicated to former CSM President Regis Chauvenet in 1951, the old power house was renovated to house the civil engineering and the mining departments during 1949 and 1950. Since the construction of newer facilities, Chauvenet has been relegated to miscellaneous services and functions — a sad tribute to CSM's greatest president.

D) Horizon Plan: Although not formally presented to the public until 1954, all construction beginning with the new chemistry building, Coolbaugh Hall, was accomplished under the general outlines of the Horizon Plan as conceived by President Vanderwilt and one of the trustees, Dr. Ben H. Parker, and approved by the Board of Trustees headed by Lester. C. Thomas, President.

Coolbaugh Hall. Completed in 1952 at a cost of $1,050,000 and dedicated in 1953, Coolbaugh Hall honors former President Melville Coolbaugh and houses the chemistry department.

Alderson Hall. Named for the very controversial President Victor Alderson, the building was completed in 1953 and dedicated in 1954. It houses the departments of English, economics, descriptive geometry, petroleum refining, and petroleum production, and cost $1,000,000.

ROTC Complex. These were temporary buildings obtained from Buckley Naval Air Station in Denver after World War II, and erected on the drill ground on Maple Street, at the end of 14th. The buildings housed the petroleum refining department initially, and after Alderson Hall was completed, the complex was remodeled. It was occupied by the ROTC department in 1954 which formerly had used the Armory facilities on Arapaho and 13th Street for thirty-four years. The northeast wing housed the school nurse and infirmary. A building to the south on Maple became the school cafeteria. The complex lies between Maple and the clay pits between 14th and 13th streets. Tennis courts were built immediately to the north along Maple. ROTC also received the open area immediately west of Brooks Field in 1956 for parades when the married student housing was razed on that site.

Bradford Hall. A $300,000 dormitory, Bradford Hall was named for its donor, A. Hartwell Bradford, and completed in 1954 to provide rooms for 84 students. It is located behind Maple Street west of Guggenheim Hall.

Arthur Lakes Library. The new library was located northeast of Guggenheim Hall on the corner of Illinois Avenue and 14th Street and completed in 1955 at a cost of $750,000.

Randall Hall. Completed in 1957 as a mirror of Bradford Hall and located immediately to its south.

Publications & Band Buildings. These were formerly two private homes located on Illinois Avenue between the KS and ATO houses (16th and 17th street corners), purchased in 1957. The former building occupied by the CSM publications department and student publications on 14th Street was razed to make way for construction of a new gymnasium. These two buildings in turn were leveled in 1964 under the Horizon Plan.

Metallurgy Building. Completed in 1958, the new metallurgy building was constructed in the area where the historic 1880-1890 building (Old Chem or Old Main) had been located. It was demolished in 1956 rather than being renovated because it did not fit the architectural scheme of the Horizon Plan. The new building was named Hill Hall, and a major addition was added on its west side in 1998 where the former residence of the Dean of Students had stood.

New Gymnasium. Connected to Steinhauer Field House, the new gymnasium was completed in 1959. It was later named Volk Gymnasium for Russell Volk, a student in the 1920s who won the Rocky Mountain heavyweight wrestling and heavyweight boxing championships on the same day.

Woman's Dorm. Actually, the Kappa Sigma fraternity house, the structure was acquired by eminent domain to house an expected influx of female students in 1963.

Fraternity Row. The Kappa Sigs constructed a new facility as ordered by the CSM administration in compliance with the Horizon Plan. It was located in a fraternity row called "West Campus" at the extreme southwest corner of the projected campus, seven blocks from Guggenheim Hall. From 1962 to 1965 CSM acquired the SPE and SAE houses on 15th Street, and the PKA house on Illinois and 16th. All fraternities were required to relocate to the planned fraternity row and build new facilities as a condition for retaining their CSM charters. The PKA and Theta Chi chapters closed, and only the ATO's fought the school administration in court until forced to capitulate in the 1980s. The Sigma Nu house located on 14th Street and Cheyenne Street, and the Beta house on 16th Street and Arapaho were not acquired by CSM since they were not located on land designated to be purchased under the Horizon Plan, but the fraternity chapters were still required to relocate to fraternity row. Henceforth, the fraternities would be wards of the administration.

Meyer Hall. Completed in 1963, it became the home for the physics and geophysics departments and is located opposite Alderson Hall on the corner of 16th Street and Illinois Avenue, on the site formerly occupied by the Pi Kappa Alpha fraternity house. This building was razed in 2016 to make way for the CoorsTek Center.

Ben H. Parker Student Center. Initially called the College Union when it was completed in 1964, the building was expanded through several additions in the 1990s and 2000s. Located on Maple Street immediately west of Berthoud Hall, it was later joined to the walking campus when 15th Street was eliminated from Illinois Avenue to Elm Avenue, and Maple was torn up from Guggenheim to 17th Street. One of the additions was a new school cafeteria on the west side of the Union.

Dormitories. Two additional student dormitories were constructed and connected on the east side of Bradford Hall in the 1960s, as the administration increased its paternalistic attitude towards Mines students.

Sororities. Three sororities came into being with the rise of female enrollments, and they were located close to campus a block west of Elm Street between 15th and 17th streets. It was at least six blocks from the fraternities to the center of campus, four blocks from the sororities, and 1-1/2 from the dormitories.

The Green Center. The first privately funded building since Guggenheim Hall in 1906, the Green Center was completed on 16th and Arapahoe Street in 1971. Initially constructed to house the geophysics department, its use was expanded to house many college functions.

Weaver Towers. Twin towers connected by walkways, Weaver Towers was built in 1979 at the corner of 19th Street and

Elm Street. It houses a number of administrative functions.

Brown Hall. Housing the mining engineering and basic engineering departments, Brown Hall was finally built in 1980 after CSM successfully evicted the ATOs from their fraternity house. Brown took the entire block on the west side of Illinois Avenue from 16th to 17th streets, and necessitated the razing of the women's dorm, formerly the Kappa Sigma House, the ATO house, and the band and publications buildings between them. Brown Hall underwent a 78,000-square-foot expansion in 2011 that nearly doubled the building's size.

During the 1980s and 1990s, slumping enrollments curtailed substantial new construction, but a number of buildings received additions and renovations. Two small public safety buildings on Illinois Avenue near 19th Street were open to house the newly-formed campus police. Both crime and police-imposed order had arrived at Mines.

The Center for Technology and Learning Media. Opening in 2001, it took the space formerly occupied by the Jefferson County Sheriff and other county departments on Arapahoe Street between 16th and 17th streets.

The General Research Laboratory. This large structure was built on the site of the former ROTC complex on Maple in 2002. ROTC was reduced to two small buildings on the newly constructed West Campus Road immediately north of Bradford Hall and the other dormitories. The Geology Museum was moved from Berthoud Hall to the new building, and greatly expanded. The idea was to attract thousands of visitors to campus to see the museum and research facilities and boost public appreciation of Mines' role in the future.

Student Recreation Center. The largest building on campus, the 150,000-square-foot behemoth opened in 2007. The intent was to provide space for recreational and social activities on campus, further isolating Mines students from the community of Golden.

W. Lloyd Wright Student Wellness Center. This Health center is located on the southeast corner of Elm and 17th streets and was opened in 2010.

Maple Hall. Located on the east side of Maple Street between 17th and 18th streets, Maple Hall was completed in 2011. It consists of a 291 bed semi-suite housing unit with social lounges, study rooms, a music room, conference room, large community kitchen, common area computers, living room with a piano, and bike and ski storage rooms.

Marquez Hall. A nearly 90,000-square-foot-facility to house the petroleum engineering department, Marquez Hall opened in 2012. It features stunningly modern architecture, completely out of character with the traditional Mines architecture, but projecting Mines into the next century.

Elm Street Residence and Dining Hall. Located north of Weaver Towers between Elm and Maple streets, the 200-bed residence dormitory opened in 2014. The Dining hall has a capacity of 500 diners.

Welcome Center. Located on the northwest corner of 19th Street and Illinois Avenue, the Welcome Center open in 2015. It houses the Alumni Association and a number of administration functions, including admissions and public relations.

Clear Creek Athletic Complex. Opened in 2015, this extensive new athletic complex contains state-of-the-art athletic facilities for football, baseball, soccer, track and field and other sports. It features the 5,000 seat Marv Kay Stadium at Campbell Field (formerly Brooks Field), locker rooms, training facilities, and sports medicine. Perhaps the best indicator of the growth of the Mines physical plant is its approach to transportation. In 1961, there were no parking lots on campus, nor any parking meters or restrictions other than several spaces marked behind Guggenheim Hall for the President and the Dean of Faculty. By 2015, substantial acreage was devoted to gated parking or restricted parking lots, in addition to restrictions to on-street parking. No fewer than 29 restricted or gated parking lots adorned the campus, not counting those at the Athletic Complex. Parking for visitors had become a nightmare, and an extremely large parking garage would be necessary for future growth. For some reason, structures for parking had been overlooked in the Horizon Plan. The Mines administration officially recommended not parking on streets, even if a parking space could be found. As late as 1985 a visitor could park alongside Berthoud Hall, but no longer. Campus Police were necessary, whereas there were none at all in 1961. Mines had become a city unto itself, no longer a part of Golden.

Chapter 21 - Life After Mines

If you went to the Colorado School of Mines you were a Miner, and you came from a school known all around the world. So, there's a certain esprit de corps we had: we were proud of having gone to that school. It opened a lot of doors being a Miner, it really did.

Stewart M. Collester, Petroleum Engineer, '50

At his 40th Class Reunion, one alumnus from the 1950s brought a check for the first large donation he had been able to make to Mines and wanted to present it personally to President George Ansell. At a reception for his class, he talked with a fellow alumnus who was retiring as Executive Vice President of a large oil company in New Jersey, who mentioned that he had given his largest donation to Mines the previous year, but that it would be his last. At that point, President Ansell walked up. When the alumnus with the check addressed Dr. Ansell, he was pointedly ignored. President Ansell actually walked around the man trying to give him a check and pursued the oil executive. After attempting to talk to Dr. Ansell three times and being brushed off repeatedly, the alumnus went to Guggenheim Hall to find someone interested in receiving his donation. He found a person who would accept it on behalf of the school, and the donation was made. A few weeks after returning home, he received a school tie and a short note apparently signed by Dr. Ansell in acknowledgment of the gift, but it would be his last one while Ansell was president.

The attitude exhibited by the arrogant, yet servile Dr. Ansell showed his terminal disrespect of Mines graduates, even when substantially successful in life. Obviously, Dr. Ansell failed to understand the principle that alumni were important to the school's health.

Ansell also failed to understand Dr. Chauvenet's vision, and that the School of Mines had produced capable professionals much in the same way the US Navy has produced Navy Seals. The training was highly specialized, brutal, uncompromising, and demanding. A student had to rise above his limitations, open himself up to the road less traveled, and think outside of the box. He was taught that all problems have a solution, and although sometimes it could be found through brute force and ignorance, more often the path to success lay along the fault lines of logic and the extension of creative thinking. Like the Navy Seal, the Mines graduate believed in himself, after all, he had survived everything Mines could throw at him. Limits were for others.

The 1961 class in particular showed the way as to what could be done. The SSDC members featured earlier paid society and Mines back a hundred-fold for their education at the "Engineering Academy." After graduation, the twenty-six members produced the following:

A late-blooming polymath who excelled in many fields

The executive vice president of Polaroid

A prominent orthopedist

The founder and Chairman of Canadian Oil Sands, a $5 billion corporation which holds 37 percent of Syncrude, one of the world's largest producers of synthetic oil from oil sands

The founding chairman of Matrix Solutions, a large Canadian environmental consulting and engineering company

A prominent career army officer

A professor and department head of the Geology Department of a major university

A full-time Episcopal priest

A pioneer in client-server networks and cloud processing, arguably the world's most prolific computer programmer with about thirty major application systems to his credit (such as LTL trucking, materials requirements planning, all major accounting systems, inventory control, and retailing) writing over three million lines of computer code

A professional staff member for the United States Senate

An appointee as a White House intern

A well-known and respected historian who has published nine books

A prominent lawyer in Southern California

An executive vice president for Amerada Hess Oil Company

The founder and prime mover behind HydroGeoLogic, Inc., a company with 250 employees

A very successful securities and financial expert

The President and CEO of PanAmSat Corp, a 4.5-billion-dollar corporation in 2004

An inventor of oil field equipment and international consultant in oil recovery

One of the two most successful spymasters in Europe during the Cold War

A successful entrepreneur in the Nevada Mining business
A much-respected airplane designer for Boeing
Three Distinguished Achievement Medal Recipients from
Mines by 2000.
Three university professors, and others were successful engineers for a variety of companies. Probably half became Registered Professional Engineers, and no doubt others became prominent and accomplished feats that were not mentioned to the authors.

The 1961 class was studded with individuals in the various Marquis *Who's Who, in the West, South, America, and the World*. One became a partner at Booz, Allen, and Hamilton, was Director of OMB under President Reagan, and the President and CEO of Pan-AmSat Corp, a 4.5-billion-dollar corporation in 2004. Others in the class of 1961 became university professors, a number took MBAs from Harvard and went on to distinguished careers in business, and at least eleven became lawyers. Clearly, the specialist education the class received stood them in good stead, and refuted President Vanderwilt's contention that CSM's regimen needed to be loosened and broadened for Mines graduates to become well-rounded individuals ready to take their place in society.

The 183 graduates in 1961 went into all walks of life, and in the main, were astonishingly successful. They became doctors, lawyers, college professors, corporation presidents, entrepreneurs, high government officials, members of the Mines Board of Trustees, authors, computer experts, farmers, ranchers, real estate developers, army officers, and yes, engineers. Their Mines education proved not to be limiting but enabling. It may not have been fun, but it inured them to hardship, setbacks, and trials, and gave them the skills they needed to succeed at whatever they attempted. With their silver diplomas they went everywhere, in the United States and foreign lands, and everywhere they went, they did Mines proud.

There was also another entire component of a miner's education that was understood through the 1950s, but then lost on the faculty and administration sometime in the 1960s. In a word, it was "leadership."

The American service academies, including Mines, taught leadership by demanding the impossible, and making the achievement of the impossible routine. After all, military officers were and are expected to lead their men (and women) to act against their own self-interest to achieve their goals, leading by example at all times. Until Vietnam changed the concept of leadership, military leaders were hardened in combat, and learned to lead from the front. That began to change in Vietnam: leaders became corporate managers, able to build teams that could bring various resources together to address demanding situations, usually by the simple expedients of throwing money, equipment, and manpower at the problems, handling the media effectively, and hoping for the best. This transformation of military leader to corporate manager was eloquently exposed by Thomas E. Ricks, in his work *The Generals* in 2012.

It wasn't until after World War II that the US Army developed adequate tests for leadership to go along with training programs. These tests had been designed and used by the German *Wehrmacht* during the war and had proved spectacularly successful. Officers were divided into six-man teams, then given a number of problems to solve, sometimes with a designated leader, and others without. All of these problems were essentially unsolvable under ordinary circumstances. To produce a solution, teams had to become sufficiently motivated to go beyond their normal capabilities. A typical example was the ammunition cart problem. The ammunition cart weighed 1,000 pounds, and the team had to get the cart and themselves over an obstacle within five minutes. There was a bar with a pulley over the obstacle, and a length of rope on the ground. The solution, however, was to ignore the pulley since it would leave insufficient room below for the cart to clear the obstacle. The cart was manhandled to a height where it would clear the obstacle, then one by one the men would jump over the obstacle and hold the cart until all were over and it could be lowered to the ground. Of course, the solution required each man to lift at least 200 pounds, since while the men were crossing, only five men would be holding the cart. The weight was staggering. Normally this was impossible. Everyone needed to get every bit of adrenaline going, and that required motivation and belief in oneself and the team. Perhaps surprisingly, about one team in ten completed the test successfully. That took real leadership and devotion to getting the job done!

Prior to the mid-1960s, Mines ROTC students going through officer basic training facing these tests were often able to complete them successfully: after all, THEY WERE MINES MEN. One wonders what the success rate would be today, but, of course, ROTC participation on campus is now minimal.

There is another metric to be considered. Mines graduates worked on the building of Hoover Dam from 1931 to 1936, but when the bypass bridge was constructed from 2005 to 2010, it was built by the Obayashi Corporation, a Japanese company, as the general contractor. Mines graduates were only present in the monitoring function within the federal government. This anecdotal item nonetheless indicated that both Mines and American engineering was falling behind other countries. Yes, it is time to worry. The US may well become dependent on foreign companies and engineers for its well-being. It doesn't have to be that way.

Graduates tended to look upon themselves as special, having accomplished something that few undergraduate students in the United States could. One CSM grad from 1956, working as a lawyer in Washington, D.C. in 1961 was given tickets to the Kennedy Inaugural Ball by his mother, a labor union leader. When he spotted Robert McNamara, Kennedy's pick for Secretary of Defense, he strolled over and introduced himself, saying, "It looks like we are the only Republicans in the room." Yes, a Mines grad could do anything, in this case, with unmitigated chutzpah.

Mines was not just about teaching excellence in a host of subjects: it was always about leadership. Most students today would consider 200+ credit hours of which 192 were engineering, technical, and science courses to be successfully completed in four years to be an impossible regimen. It probably is, unless the student is highly motivated and willing to devote the time and resources necessary to get the job done. And it will take a great deal of cooperation with other students, probably more than is allowable in the current environment where a student's grades and test scores are more secret than the information on Hillary's Clinton private server. But this is how to train the leaders for the future. The requirements of leadership have not changed—just the willingness to pay the price in becoming a good leader.

An example of the leadership required in industry occurred at US Steel's South Works in Chicago, where the wearing of hard hats had become increasingly mandated throughout the mill to meet federal safety requirements during the 1950s. In 1962, the mandate was extended to all Roll Shop employees, and everyone knew that a protest, possibly even a fight, was coming. The roll shop foreman, a Mines graduate, was assigned to obtain compliance from the steel workers. He grabbed a bunch of hard hats and ventured forth into the shop. All activity stopped, and everyone watched the Mines man. He walked up to Ziggy Stasiak, a very large and highly belligerent worker known for his hatred of company managers and foremen. The foreman told Ziggy that wearing a hard hat was a condition of employment since he had clocked in that morning and held out a hat for him to take. There was a long moment of silence while Ziggy stared down the grad. Finally, he tossed his own soft cap into the chip bucket, and took the proffered hard hat. The other United Steel Workers personnel put on their new hats without protest, one saying that if Zig wasn't going to fight the foreman over the hat, no one would. The Mines graduate had taken the challenge head on and succeeded, but as he later explained to the author, he undoubtedly would have taken a different line of attack if he hadn't have gone to Mines.

Another testimony to Mines training was made in 1976 by a holder of a professional degree from the early 1960s. While a PhD candidate at a DC area university, he was asked by the Dean of his college to help out a good friend. The Dean had noted that the Mines grad had completed a $300,000 contract with the US Navy to design its BUPERS teleprocessing system in three days and was reputed to be some sort of wizard. The friend was the president of the area's largest office supplies provider, with large contracts with local financial institutions and many of the beltway bandits.

Of course, the Mines grad was happy to help out, and soon discovered the office supply company was the proud possessor of a McDonnell-Douglas Microdata computer featuring a Reality system. It ran the Pick Operating System and a post-relational data base management system, reputed to be the world's most advanced DBMS. The Miner knew nothing about this technology, having only used GE, IBM, Burroughs, UNIVAC, and DEC systems previously, none of which offered a relational DBMS.

Nonetheless, the Miner took on the job to speed up the Microdata and add an accounts payable module to the applications furnished by the third-party vendor supplying the application software. He soon discovered there was a great deal of unused software on the system, and there was no feature for archiving or deleting data out of the active portions of user data storage. Files sizes were not being adjusted for quicker access as they grew, and it was not uncommon for a READ command to use fifty-disc accesses to retrieve or store data. In short, the system required maintenance to limit normal READs and WRITEs to no more than a half-dozen disc accesses, and normally only two or three. Storage was totally random, all files, data names, and data fields were variable length, and data fields were unlimited in size. There was no data typing, and no data formats. To a large extent, there was no need for system analysts or designers, only programmers.

By three AM on Sunday morning, the Miner had completed his work, and re-booted the system. To his utter astonishment, the system crashed immediately. Here he was, with a dead system, and in twenty-five hours the pickers had to be cut for the warehousemen to start pulling inventory and load the delivery trucks. There was no one he could call for help, and he was already exhausted, having already worked for nineteen hours without a break.

He went home for a nap but couldn't sleep. Four hours later he was back in the computer room. The Miner had an idea that the problem might have been caused by his deletion of a file on the system for each port. He had scanned the application software, and there was no program opening or using those files. They were tiny files of 512 bytes in size, and apparently had no function. But his immediate problem was to bootstrap the computer through the switches on the front of the computer, manually bypassing the normal boot-up software. Fortunately, the Miner had worked in BAL and SLEUTH, both assembler languages, and was familiar with bootstrapping, and working at the machine level in addition to compiled languages. Against the odds, he was successful in bootstrapping the machine, and restored the port files. He then re-booted the computer, completely out of ideas as to what to try next if the boot failed.

It didn't, and the Miner was showered with kudos on Monday for restoring the system to normal operating speed. Yes, Mines graduates could do anything, even in technologies not taught at Mines.

The Reality system made extensive use of firmware, and unhampered by poorly sized files, was truly an impressive system. Years later in 2001, the Miner's son took a data base course at the University of Illinois, Urbana-Champaign. The boy unwisely took on the professor citing the capabilities of the Pick System he had used while working for his dad. The professor curtly told the class the boy was mistaken – no data base management system in 2001 possessed the feature the boy related. The Miner contacted the professor and offered to demonstrate the Pick System to his class, but the full professor, a well-known "expert" on data base, refused the invitation, and once again said that no such system existed.

Another example involved a 1950s Mines graduate who had become a lawyer for US Steel. In 1970, Big Steel opened a new plant in Baytown, Texas, and the following year, the Miner visited the plant. The Superintendent of Steel Production was talking with the Miner, when he suddenly received an urgent call. He turned to his visitor and said: "We have an emergency! I'll see you on your next trip."

"What's the problem?" the Miner asked.

"Open pour." This meant that while pouring molten steel from a ladle, something had failed, and molten steel was pouring out of control.

The Miner politely said he would wait for the Superintendent's return. After the crisis had passed (at a significant cost to US Steel), the Miner explained to the Superintendent how to utilize a porous ceramic plug and sliding gate system on both the molten metal ladle and the tundish (intermediate pouring vessel) to prevent nozzle blockage as well as open pours when the stopper rod broke. The Superintendent was astonished at the metallurgical knowledge exhibited by the Miner. He immediately called the two engineers the Miner recommended, and using the Miner's name as an introduction, arranged for them to install the slide gate system the following week. There were no more open pours at the Baytown plant, and the Superintendent had new respect for lawyers that had graduated from Mines.

At the same time Mines graduates knew they didn't know everything, never took themselves seriously, and never forgot where they came from. SSDC members, for example, always took themselves with a grain of salt and good humor. Life was a series of defeats and successes, to be endured and enjoyed with a good wife and family to the maximum benefit of all; family, friends, engineering, and nation. They planned a reunion in 2011, and it was a great success. Afterwards the SSDC became involved in the planning for a permanent facility to function as its home. The correspondence and events are covered in Appendix F.

In 2016, the 1961 SSDC did not hold a reunion, in part to protest the movement of the reunion time to coincide with Homecoming and the football game. Mines was never about football or Homecoming in the fall, and not having been consulted in the change, the '61 SSDC felt abused and neglected once again. Nothing came from the Alumni Association, there was no poll of alumni, and October didn't fit into many schedules. The reunions were a time for the graduates to get together, relive old times, and renew old friendships, not sit in Brooks Stadium and cheer a bunch of kids they don't know, and who are not living the alumni's experience at Mines.

That experience is gone forever, and the '61 grads are dinosaurs, to be trotted out only if they open their wallets. Or at least, that's the way it seems. They still have their humor, maybe a little rough for today's day and age, but they can still meet the morning sun with a smile. Mines was a cataclysmic time in their lives, beyond the ability of today's Mines students, faculty, or administration to comprehend. They did everything asked of them, climbed every mountain, met every challenge, and bore every hardship.

The world has moved on, and today universities espouse multiculturalism and globalism in lieu of excellence. American academia is perhaps more politically correct than any other segment of the economy or American society, and it forces its beliefs and ideology on its students with an intensity that defies credulity. There is little or no dialog in American universities: students are to hear and believe. College administrations no longer tolerate dissent from any quarter, particularly the alumni, and progressivism is the new religion of the educated, or better said, those who think they are educated.

The world is the lesser for the passing of the old Mines, and it remains to be seen how the new Mines will evolve to meet its existential challenges.

Alpha Theta Omega Fraternity House (c. 1960)

Chapter 22 - The Future of Mines

There is no way to un-ring the bell that changed Mines from Dr. Chauvenet's Engineering Academy to an institution hardly different than dozens of technological institutes in the United States. Mines is continuing on its present course; expanding the graduate school, pursuing research as a means to fund the school, and attracting well-known or talented researchers. Maybe that will be a successful strategy for the future, maybe not.

In 2016 the school published a statement of its mission that was issued from the graduate school, but applied equally well to its undergraduate program:

"When you attend Colorado School of Mines you become an integral member of a specialized research institution with high admission standards and a unique mission in energy, minerals, materials science and engineering, and associated engineering and science fields. You can be part of a community that interprets its mission through its dedication to generating new knowledge and educating students and professionals in the applied sciences, engineering and associated fields related to:

- *the discovery and recovery of the Earth's resources*
- *their conversion to materials and energy*
- *their utilization in advanced processes and products,*
- *the economic and social systems necessary to ensure their prudent and provident use in a sustainable global society*
- *the preservation and stewardship of the Earth's environment.*

Together we advance these areas with the conviction that future infrastructural and societal developments are dependent upon the availability of energy, the sustainable development of the Earth's resources, the synthesis of materials, and the environmental consequences of these processes and their interactions. At Mines, we believe these inherently related focus areas represent not only extraordinarily fertile ground on which to base the strategic development of the institution, but they also embrace our responsibility to attract, shape and provide engineering and scientific talent to help address the technological and societal challenges implied.

Our renowned reputation, attained through the tremendous work of our students, faculty and staff, our high admission standards, and our alumni network combine to give you an edge in the job market. Mines boasts strong master's and professional degrees that are valued as more than simple stepping-stones to a doctoral degree. You are able to pursue degree offerings including: Master of Engineering; Master of Science; Professional Master; and Doctor of Philosophy. More than 96 percent of the recipients of Mines' master's and professional degrees find employment by graduation...

With an annual research budget of more than $55 million and a faculty that has pioneered numerous advances in a wide range of technical fields the opportunity for you to conduct innovative research is virtually unlimited. You are able to work hand-in-hand with researchers at Mines and from around the world on both applied and academic research problems. Close proximity to a number of governmental research facilities such as the U.S. Geological Survey, the National Renewable Energy Laboratory, the U.S. Bureau of Reclamation, and the National Institute of Standards and Technology provides you unparalleled access to a wide variety of scholars, facilities and research opportunities." (Retrieved 7/24/2016 from http://www.mines.edu/graduate_academic)

Of course, the undergraduate program produced only professional degrees before 1969, clearly indicated that Mines has introduced a whole new school giving bachelor's degrees with much-reduced courses of study. CSM moved its previous professional degrees into the graduate school and turned the graduate programs into producing strictly research-oriented degrees. The sharp-eyed reader will note a glaring omission in the above mission statement: leadership. There is no emphasis on producing leaders for the United States, in the above listed technical areas or elsewhere. "Fitting in" and working in a cooperative manner with other is stressed instead. There are also significant insertions: a commitment to Agenda 21 is implied by the importance of government institutions partnering with Mines, *the creation of economic and social systems necessary to ensure a sustainable global society*, and the preservation and stewardship of the Earth's environment. These insertions are political statements, incompatible with a reasonable mission statement by an institute of higher education. As is now forecast by an increasing number of individuals and think tanks, private property will be abolished in the United States within the lifetimes of those attending Mines at present (2017).

This mission statement from the graduate school was developed from the statutory mission of CSM, and the general statement of CSM's mission, vision, and values issued by the Board of Directors in 2013.

Mission:

As written into the Colorado Statutes: "*The Colorado School of Mines shall be a specialized baccalaureate and graduate research institution with high admission standards. The Colorado School of Mines shall have a unique mission in energy, mineral, and materials science and engineering and associated engineering and science fields. The school shall be the primary institution of higher education offering energy, mineral and materials science and mineral engineering degrees at both the graduate and undergraduate levels.*" (Colorado Revised Statutes, Section 23-41-105)

As adopted on December 12, 2013, by the CSM Board of Trustees as part of its new strategic plan with a statement on values: "*[CSM's mission is to provide] education and research in engineering and science to solve the world's challenges related to the earth, energy and the environment... Mines empowers, and holds accountable, its faculty, students, and staff to achieve excellence in its academic programs, its research, and in its application of knowledge for the development of technology....*

*[Mines is] a student-centered institution focused on education that promotes **collaboration**, integrity, perseverance, creativity, life-long learning and a responsibility for developing a better world.....*

*The Mines student graduates with a strong sense of integrity, intellectual curiosity, **demonstrated ability to get a job done in collaborative environments**, passion to achieve goals, and an enhanced sense of responsibility to promote positive change in the world...*" (Retrieved 1/28/2017 from http://www.mines.edu/Mission)

The key to the success of a college will be the obtaining of federal subsidies and research funding, and that is becoming increasingly dependent on an institution's adherence to progressive political dogma and political correctness as shown by the above mission statement, rather than excellence in education or the performance of critical research.

This situation cannot continue much longer, especially with "Common Core" coming on-line. Inevitably, low cost community colleges will be called upon to provide the remedial education, teaching such things as cursive writing, elementary math (like counting back change), reading, English grammar, history before 1898, and other subjects formerly considered part of the K-12 curriculum. In addition, the same community colleges will offer lower division courses for a fraction of the costs at universities, making many community colleges into four-year schools, containing two years remedial education plus two years of basic college. These degrees will become bachelor's degrees, indistinguishable from regular college bachelor degrees, and possibly even more desirable since many graduated will have learned trades and become highly employable.

At this point, a consolidation of state institutions will be necessary to hold taxes at a sustainable rate, and institutions such as the University of Colorado can be forecasted to turn all their outlying campuses into community colleges and consolidate in a single university location. This consolidation trend will sweep the nation, and in twenty years, few colleges other than community colleges will exist with enrollments under 15-25,000 students. Since Mines will probably fail to meet this threshold on its current track, CSM's future looks grim.

So, the question is, "How can Mines survive?"

Ideas for the Future:

At this point, Mines may be forced to look at options other than simply being another engineering emphasizing research and graduate programs. For the moment, very few individuals in the Mines administration and Board of Trustees are personally invested in the current educational philosophy and educational trends at Mines, but this is rapidly changing with the times. The current situation may not be entirely their fault, but with every passing year, they assume more ownership of the problem. Without a major change in CSM's long-term strategy, however, it is difficult to see Mines surviving as an independent school. Smart money is definitely on a consolidation with CU. CSM's ROTC program is already part of CU's, and the rest of the school be far behind?

There are at least three long-range strategic options for possible consideration by Mines to break out of the pack:

(1) Becoming an elite school specializing in providing the technology and technical leadership for the implementation of Agenda 21.

(2) Re-inventing excellence by returning to the many of the features of the old Mines.

(3) Creating a true engineering school by working with community colleges to handle pre-engineering curricula, and only offering Master of Engineering and Doctors of Engineering.

Nonetheless, any reluctance in implementing some strategy to make Mines increasingly unique raises the specter of CSM's adsorption by CU. If for no other reason, that is why the reader should study the information contained in this work, even if some of it is somewhat unpalatable. The current administration at Mines did not create this situation, but it must address the situation and find a solution. Presidents Vanderwilt, Childs, McBride, and Ansell made huge mistakes, possibly even terminal ones, and it is now up to those today who care about Mines to find ways to regain CSM's glory and reputation.

With respect to the Agenda 21 specialist school, the main inducement is that the US and other governments have committed themselves to spending trillions on research to combat climate change and enacting Agenda 21, and Mines is one of the best situated institutions in the world to reap the funding bonanza. Its only drawbacks are a lack of national presence, and a large enough research base, faculty and graduate students. No doubt the administrative planners for Mines are quietly working on these problems, and their efforts are at the foundation of the growth of CSM's research orientation.

Everyone is now tentatively on board with the program; the Board of Directors, the administration, faculty, and students, but there is a long way to go before Mines can become the dominant Agenda 21 institution. And it will have to hurry, as other schools already hunger after the money and political power behind the program.

The rewards of winning the Agenda 21 sweepstakes are incalculable, but they will require a major suppression of everyone's morality and ethnics. At the bottom, Agenda 21 must create an international elite that will rule the world, and individual liberty and the American way of life must go the way of the dinosaur. Even more important, all religions must accommodate the new autocratic, global state.

There may not be any middle ground, but there is a minute possibility that an institution might be able to do the handmaiden's work for the elites while still avoiding any responsibility for the policies put into place. If Mines is able to remain independent from the policy makers and rulers, it might – just might – be able to generate knowledge equivocal or deleterious to the political ideologies implementing Agenda 21 and come out of the resulting upheaval with its reputation and existence intact. Nonetheless, there is a definite danger of losing one's soul -- not everything is worth doing for money, regardless of the amount.

Returning to some semblance of the old Mines is probably little more than a fantasy in the eyes of its aging alumni. Everyone is against it: The Board of Trustees, the administration, faculty, students, and even the general public. The Board doesn't want to deal with the upheavals such a change would bring, the administration doesn't want to fight the accreditation battles all over again, the faculty does not want to lose its benefits and spend most of its time teaching undergraduates, the students aren't willing to work that hard and put in seventy hours per week in class and study, and the citizens like lower standards because it allows their children to attend college even after blowing off K-12 learning.

All the cute and trendy programs in team building, diversity, "interactive learning", and citizen involvement would have to be jettisoned since they are more "eyewash" than substantive. In the Engineering Academy, leadership training took place as a by-product of the highly demanding academic program. Attempting to create separate entities to teach leadership on the cheap and easy just doesn't work. Students need to challenge themselves, develop problem-solving techniques before they are taught the school solution, and learn how to extend themselves to go beyond what is normally required. Developing programs that minimize personal development toward excellence is going in the wrong direction.

On the other hand, there is a market for a Mines of the old type and studded with excellence, particularly due to its location. Until recently, Denver could boast the 2nd highest number of non-military federal employees in the US. Denver features a high number of offices for federal departments, mostly to give high-level bureaucrats a reason to travel to Colorado in the summer and winter to coincide with their summer and winter vacations. Federal employees refer to Denver as "Washington West" and "Little DC", and Mines could target the families of federal bureaucrats for prospective students, giving the DC, Maryland, and Northern Virginia denizens another reason to come to Colorado. Showing the necessity for an engineering background in today's and tomorrow's management of federal bureaucracies, major corporations attempting to stay abreast of technological advances, technological-based entrepreneurial companies, and as an undergraduate requirement for political office (as a forerunner to a law degree) are strategies that can maintain enrollments with aggressive, ambitious students.

Mines could start preparing for all eventualities by introducing additional course requirements over the next several years, like thirty-six credit hours of required work in engineering, science or technology over four years. The program could be called the Honors Master of Engineering, and the students could be issued a silver diploma. The diploma could state it is being issued for superior performance in Engineering with the type of engineering being the student's specialty.

It would take some salesmanship to sell this program to entering students, but the term "superior" should be given to all graduates of Mines in the "Honors" program regardless of a student's GPA. It would definitively set the Mines graduate well above all holders of bachelor's degrees, regardless of where those degrees were earned.

One of the harder problems Mines would face would be to re-introduce stricter grading standards to eliminate the effects of the grade inflation during the Vietnam War. An average grade should be a "C", and the all-student GPA should be less than 2.5. Grades could be changed back to numeric scales as they were in the 1950s, and departments should closely scrutinize professors that give high numbers of "A"s and "B"s.

The problem employers face with an all-student GPA of 3.0 or greater is that there is little to differentiate good students from the bad. There is also little to go on when the course load is so light, and there are so many student organizations with leadership positions. Few of these positions are truly leadership positions, and with so much free time available for students to engage in non-academic activities, there is little impact on the time necessary for studying. In short, the student has received little, if any, leadership training, and looks the same on paper as a student at the University of Colorado or at Greeley.

In the old Mines, the curriculum made the Mines graduate a hot property compared to someone from CU—190+ vs. 124 hours—but now the requirements of 138.5 vs. 128 hours (for Chemical Engineering) are not significantly different, especially when CU touts its programs as superior to anything else in the state. Even the student-faculty ratio is similar: CU reports a ratio of 18:1, and Mines 17:1. In costs, CU reports $29,215 for in-state, and $52,763 for out-of-state. Mines is higher at $32,684 for in-state and lower at $51,014 for out-of-state. For Mines to survive, it must out-class CU in every particular. CU has long been considered the "play school of the Rockies," but is Mines now so different?

The difference between Mines and all other schools must come in its graduates, and their ability to assume leadership positions in industry and government. The question is: are the reduced requirements sufficient to prepare Mines students to out-class their contemporaries from other colleges in leadership and dedication in getting a job done? And as said before, "How can a prospective employer tell?"

There are many answers to this question, starting with the re-institution of senior trips and extensive practical field work. Grades need to be adjusted based on course load, years in attendance, and type of course. For example, assume the Mines course load to be 170 hours in four years, versus CU's of 128 hours. That's a ratio of 4:3. For a student who achieved a GPA of 2.5, Mines could publish an "Honors Adjusted GPA" of 3.33. Other schemes might be to ratio engineering hours or hours per week in class, or by some scale of class difficulty versus standard engineering schools. Numeric class scores could be on the old Mines basis, (94-100=A, 86-93.9=B, 78-85.9=C, and 70-77.9=D), but then Adjusted letter grades be put on today's normal 90-100=A, 80-89.9=B, 70-79.9=C, and 60-69.9=D. As shown in Chapter 15, the mid-50s curriculum should have reflected 222 semester hours credit in 4 years, Versus CU's 128 hours, the Honors Adjusted GPA for a 2.5 should have been 4.33 or higher than any current graduate could achieve. All GPAs higher than 4.0 could be simply reported as a 4.0. In short, there are many schemes that could be used to promote Mines graduates in comparison to graduates from other school, but in any case, SOMETHING SHOULD BE DONE. Many other schools adjust GPAs to reflect various factors in courses, and this is one case in which Mines should be no different. Mines **must** give prospective employers a reason to hire Mines graduates over those of lesser schools, whether or not the school returns to some semblance of the old Mines.

There is a third solution (other than continuing on the current road) but it requires some background discussion. A major problem for the United States is that its universities are only looking at graduate programs and research money, while high schools under "Common Core" are producing graduates at the tenth and a half grade level. There is a huge gap to be filled between those orientations to be filled. Enter the community college as the solution. In some states, community colleges have to regularly assign high school graduates to remedial math, which starts out teaching the students the commutative, associative, and distributive laws of mathematics - something taught in 2nd grade. This may sound extreme, but sooner or later community colleges will be needed to provide two years of college preparatory courses for all prospective college students. Almost certainly this will be needed for students in technical curricula such as engineering and science.

With community colleges providing two years of preparatory work, undergraduate schools will most likely have two main programs. The first will be the traditional four-year college degree - fun, but not preparing the student for any lifetime employment. Second, and much more important, colleges will offer four years of "pre" studies: pre-law, pre-med, pre-engineering, and "pre-"a number of other specialties. The pre-engineering could produce students going into three years of advanced engineering — essentially finishing the last two years of CSM's former Professional Degree, a Master of Engineering, or three years to a doctorate. At any rate, it may take up to nine years of schooling after high school (2 years community college, 4 years pre-engineering, and three years of advanced engineering) to produce the competent engineer that Mines generated during the 1950s in four years. The US is slowly making education a permanent fixture in a person's life and splitting the society into two classes based on their education alone: those with a 4-year college degree or less to work in the world in non-specialized functions, and the ruling/managerial/professional classes with two or more years, sometimes many more, in academia after four years of college.

There is a place for Mines in this new system of education, and it is not too early to begin preparing Mines for its eventual role. In fact, Mines can be a leader in the new trend, and carve out an entirely new program for engineering students as only Mines can.

Mines needs to team up with community colleges like it already has with Red Rocks, but CSM could also open a pre-engineering community college in Golden on the Mines campus, calling it something like CSM College. Mines professors and graduate students could teach many of the courses like other universities do in their community college off-shoots. A good example is the University of Maryland that operates University College as a community college not only on the College Park campus, but also off-campus at various sites such as government buildings and the various military bases around Washington, DC. Mines could do the same in Golden, Denver, and offer the courses also on-line.

The puff courses in the humanities, business, and liberal arts could be put in the community college curricula as pre-requisites to enroll at Mines. A year of such pre-requisites, including elementary math, typing, writing, and computers could make a world of difference, and lower the costs substantially for students and their parents. All this may happen anyway as the nation sinks under Common Core, but Mines could get a jump on the competition. When the pernicious effects of Common Core become evident in the next few years, Mines could then expand its prerequisites to a "Pre-Engineering Associate Degree" from a Mines accredited community college for a special engineering program at Mines that would lead to a Master of Engineering degree with three years of residency at Mines.

The authors have been unable to find any other school offering a similar program, and there is still time, still an opportunity, for Mines to get a jump on its competition. In a very large sense, such a program would allow Mines to return to its roots, do what it did best, and what no other schools except the service academies did. There is still a market for a program demanding excellence, and if it must coexist with research and PhDs, so be it. Mines should make the new program tough, demanding, and elitist. It should require 200 hours in the five years. If Mines must, it could put a thesis in the summer between the fourth and fifth years, but it should forget about teaching all the trendy garbage other degrees feature to produce a well-rounded graduate. Let the community college program do that.

The result should be an engineer who can innovate, think for himself, inside the box or out, but in any case, establishing excellence wherever he goes. That would be the really "new" Mines needed by Colorado, the United States of America, and the world. It even opens up the possibility for granting a DE – Doctor of Engineering – for five years at Mines after the first two years of pre-engineering study at a community college. That would approximate the current seven-year programs at most universities, four to a bachelor's degree, and three more for a PhD. The key would be the return of excellence in the engineering curriculum, which would be possible to re-institute since the generalist courses would be handled in the pre-engineering programs. If there must be change, it should be change for the good, and for CSM's future students, it should come at low cost.

The DE would be an entirely new degree, and a specialty doctorate as defined by Mines as the trend-setter. It would be a new degree for engineering, but similar to all the other non-PhD degrees (of which there are many) such as those in engineering (D.Eng, D.Engr, Eng.D, Dr.Eng, or Dr.-Ing), MD, DDS, JD, EdD, and the many medical specialties. The PhD given currently by Mines could continue to be a basic research degree, and the new DE could be for applied research. It would focus more on the candidates gaining expertise in the implementation of relevant engineering and scientific principles to realistic or actual problems in American industry. It is possible that Mines could establish itself as the leading institution in the nation, eschewing a BS degree, and only offering a ME, DE, and PhD degrees. This would be a change that would put Mines on the map and allow it to regain its former emphasis on excellence.

Two other small changes should be mentioned before closing. Mines would be well advised to institute the same regulations (modified for civilians) that are in effect at the Naval Academy for texting and cell phone use. Cell phones may have earned the current generation the distinction of being the "most connected generation," but this connection tends to destroy a student's social skills and his use of the English language. With respect to the physical plant of Mines, by far the most pressing need is to build parking garages for up to two thousand cars in advantageous locations on campus.

The authors wish the best for Mines and hope it will be around for another 142 years. The nation needs men and women like the Miners in the 1950s; graduates that made a difference wherever they went. Students now and in the future are out there who can get the job done, but they will need the tools and confidence to do what others have not done.

Final Note:

The authors have been criticized for writing this book, and in answer they wish to offer the poem, "The Bridge Builder" by Will Allen Dromgoole. It says it all, but only if others eventually use the bridge:

> *An old man going a lone highway*
> *Came at evening, cold and gray,*
> *To a chasm vast and wide and steep,*
> *With waters rolling cold and deep.*

The old man crossed in the twilight dim,
The sullen stream had no fears for him;
But he turned when safe on the other side,
And built a bridge to span the tide.

"Old man," said a fellow traveled near,
"You are wasting your strength with building here.
Your journey will end with the coming day,
You never again will pass this way.
You've crossed the chasm, deep and wide,
Why build you this bridge at eventide?"

The builder lifted his old gray head,
"Good friend, in the path U have come," he said.
"There followeth after me today,
A youth whose feet must pass this way.

The chasm that was as naught to me
To that fair-haired youth may a pitfall be:
He too, must cross in the twilight dim --
Good friend, I am building this bridge for him."

Semper Mines!

Beta Theta Pi Fraternity House (c. 1960)

Appendix A - CSM Boards of Trustees

The following are the Boards of Trustees for Mines throughout its history. Appendix B contains the current by-laws of the Board. The reader must remember that all board members are appointees by the Governor of Colorado and are therefore political appointees made for a variety of reasons.

Years   Trustees

1874 - 75 William Austin Hamilton Loveland, President, Edward L. Berthoud, Secretary, Nathaniel P. Hill, W. W. Ware, Alpheus Wright, and C. C. Davis. Loveland the leading citizen in Golden, Berthoud a prominent surveyor and engineer in Colorado, and Hill was a US senator, founder of the Argo Smelter and the creator of the first successful smelting process to produce precious metals from complex sulfide ores. Loveland and Berthoud were from Golden, Hill from Blackhawk, Gilpin County, Wright from Boulder, Davis from Arapahoe, Ware from Georgetown on Clear Creek, and C. C. Davis worked at the US Mint in Denver. Two others were apparently temporarily on the Board, L. Marshall Paul of Fairplay, and William Amsbary of Canon City.

1876 William A. H. Loveland, President, Edward L. Berthoud, Secretary, Capt. James T. Smith, Adair Wilson, J. H. Yonley. Captain Smith lived in Denver and was an editor of *The Colorado Transcript*, General George West's competing newspaper with *The Rocky Mountain News*. He was continuously on the board until 1921 and acted as secretary from 1879 to 1921. Wilson was from San Juan County, Yonley from Summit.

1877 - 78 William A. H. Loveland, President, Edward L. Berthoud, Secretary, Francis E. Everett, Treasurer, B. F. Hall, James T. Smith

1879 - 80 John R. Eads, President, James T. Smith, Secretary, Francis E. Everett, Treasurer, Edward L. Johnson, Frederick Steinhauer. Dr. Eads was the pastor of the Golden Methodist Church. Eads moved from Golden in 1879, and J. T. King of Golden replaced Eads in December 1879. Steinhauer, who graduated from Mines in 1899, then became President. Johnson was the US District Attorney for Colorado. Eads, Smith, and Everett were from Golden, Steinhauer and Johnson from Denver.

1881 - 82 Frederick Steinhauer, President, James T. Smith, Secretary, Francis E. Everett, Treasurer, Edward L. Johnson, R. C. Wells

1883 - 84 Frederick Steinhauer, President, James T. Smith, Secretary, Francis E. Everett, Treasurer, Edward L. Berthoud, Pietre Heinrich van Diest. Everett died in 1884 and was replaced by Charles C. Welch. Welch was a local businessman who contributed land to the Episcopal Church that was eventually deeded to the Colorado School of Mines.

1885 - 86 Frederick Steinhauer, President, James T. Smith, Secretary, Edward L. Berthoud, P. H. van Diest, Charles C. Welch.

1887 - 88 Frederick Steinhauer, President, James T. Smith, Secretary, Edward L. Berthoud, A. A. Blow, P. H. van Diest, Charles C. Welch. Blow was a mining engineer from London, England.

1889 - 90 Frederick Steinhauer, President, James T. Smith, Secretary, A. A. Blow, Edward F. Browne, Dr. James Kelly. Dr. Kelly was a territorial legislator and physician.

1891 - 92 Frederick Steinhauer, President, James T. Smith, Secretary, A. A. Blow, Edward F. Browne, Dr. James Kelly.

1893 - 94 Frederick Steinhauer, President, James T. Smith, Secretary, A. A. Blow, Dr. James Kelly, Henry Paul.

1895 - 96 Frederick Steinhauer, President, James T. Smith, Secretary, A. A. Blow, Dr. James Kelly, Henry Paul, Louis S. Noble. Blow resigned, and Louis Noble filled vacancy; Noble resigned and Frank Bulkley filled vacancy. Frank Bulkley received an E.M. from Mines in 1876, after having accomplished most of his work in Michigan universities. He was prominent in Colorado mining companies for many years, extracting gold, silver, sulphur, coal, and literally anything that could be mined.

1897 - 98 Frederick Steinhauer, President, James T. Smith, Secretary, Frank Bulkley, Dr. James Kelly, Tingley S. Wood.

1899 - 1900 Winfield S. Stratton, President, James T. Smith, Secretary, Edward L. Berthoud, Frank Bulkley, Henry Paul. Paul filled the unexpired term of Wood who had resigned.

1901 - 02 William S. Stratton, President, James T. Smith, Secretary, Edward L. Berthoud, Frank Bulkley, Otto F. Thum, W. S. Montgomery. Stratton died in 1902, Frank Bulkley became President, Montgomery filled vacancy)

1903 - 04 John Perry Kelly, President, James T. Smith, Secretary, James F. Cone, Joseph S. Jaffa, Otto F. Thum. J. P. Kelly was the son of Dr. James Kelly, Jaffa was a Denver attorney, and James F. Cone was a pioneer miner in the Cripple Creek District.

1905 - 06 John Perry Kelly, President, James T. Smith, Secretary, Frank Bulkley, James F. Cone, Joseph S. Jaffa, William B. Lewis. Cone deceased 1906, Lewis filled vacancy.

1907 - 08 John Perry Kelly, President, James T. Smith, Secretary, Frank Bulkley, Harry M. Rubey, Treasurer (non-voting), Joseph S. Jaffa, William B. Lewis.

1909 - 10 John Perry Kelly, President, James T. Smith, Secretary, Frank Bulkley, Joseph S. Jaffa, William B. Lewis.

1911 - 12 Frank Bulkley, President, James T. Smith, Secretary, William J. Bennett, Franklin Guitermann, Frederick Steinhauer, Edmond Cornelius van Diest. Guitermann resigned 1912, Edmond C. van Diest replaced. Van Diest was a Mines graduate of 1886, and the son of P. H. van Diest.

1913 - 14 Frederick Steinhauer, President, James T. Smith, Secretary, William J. Bennett, Edmond C. van Diest, Frank G. Willis. Willis was a mining engineer from Cripple Creek.

1915 - 17 Frank G. Willis, President, James T. Smith, Secretary, Howard C. Parmelee, Jesse W. Rubey, Orville R. Whitaker. Rubey was a two-term mayor of Golden and President of the Woods-Rubey National Bank in Golden. Whitaker was from Denver.

1918 - 19 Frank G. Willis, President, James T. Smith, Secretary, A. E. Carlton, Jesse W. Rubey, Orville R. Whitaker. Carlton was from Colorado Springs.

1920 Lewis Bailey Skinner, President, James T. Smith, Secretary, Jesse W. Rubey, William DeWitt Waltman, Frank G. Willis. Waltman was an 1899 graduate of Mines, and the recipient of the Distinguished Achievement Award in 1942. Skinner and Waltman lived in Denver.

1921 Lewis B. Skinner, President, James T. Smith, Secretary, Rodney J. Bardwell, Jesse W. Rubey, William D. Waltman.

1922 William D. Waltman, President, Ralph D. Brooks, Vice-President, Rodney J. Bardwell, Secretary, Jesse W. Rubey, Treasurer, Lewis B. Skinner.

1923 - 24 William D. Waltman, President, Ralph D. Brooks, Vice-President, Rodney J. Bardwell, Secretary, Jesse W. Rubey, Treasurer, Lewis B. Skinner.

1925 Rodney J. Bardwell, President, Dr. William H. Smiley, Vice-President, Max W. Ball, Secretary, Jesse W. Rubey, Treasurer (non-voting), Robert H. Sayer, Horace F. Lunt. Max Ball was a Mines graduate in the class of 1906 and a petroleum engineer. Dr. Smiley was the former superintendent of the Denver Public Schools and a highly respected educator in Colorado. Sayer was a graduate of Harvard and a mining engineer.

1926 Dr. William H. Smiley, President, John E. Little, Vice-President, Max W. Ball, Secretary, Jesse Rubey (non-voting), Robert H. Sayer, F. C. Vertrees.

1927 Dr. William H. Smiley, President, Benjamin F. Hill, Vice-President, Max W. Ball, Secretary, Edward A. Phinney, Treasurer, Robert H. Sayer, William A. Way.

Benjamin Hill was a graduate of Columbia, a geologist, and instrumental in CSM adding English composition to the required curriculum. Way was a respected Denver lawyer.

1928 - 30 Dr. William H. Smiley, President, Benjamin F. Hill, Vice-President, Max W. Ball, Secretary, Robert H. Sayer, William A. Way.

1931 - 32 Dr. William H. Smiley, President, Benjamin F. Hill, Vice-President, Robert H. Sayer, Secretary, Frederick C. Steinhauer, Assistant Secretary, William A. Way. Steinhauer was an 1899 graduate of Mines and the son of Frederick Steinhauer, the former President of the Board of Trustees.

1933 Dr. William H. Smiley, President, Frederick C. Steinhauer, Vice-President, Robert H. Sayer, Secretary, Fred Farrar, Assistant Secretary, John T. Barnett. Farrar was the general counsel for Colorado Fuel and Iron Corporation.

1934 Robert H. Sayer, President, Frederick C. Steinhauer, Vice-President, Fred Farrar, Secretary, H. Fleet Parsons, Assistant Secretary, John T. Barnett.

1935 - 38 Fred Farrar, President, John T. Barnett, Vice-President, Frederick C. Steinhauer, Secretary, H. Fleet Parsons, Assistant Secretary, Edward C. Hanley.

1939 - 40 John T. Barnett, President, Frederick C. Steinhauer, Vice-President, H. Fleet Parsons, Secretary, Thomas S. Harrison, Assistant Secretary, Edward C. Hanley. Harrison was a 1908 graduate of Mines and received the Distinguished Achievement Award in 1951.

1941 John T. Barnett, President, Frederick C. Steinhauer, Vice-President, Edward C. Hanley, Secretary, Thomas S. Harrison, Assistant Secretary, C. Quinby. Schlereth. Schlereth was a 1896 graduate of Mines.

1942 John T. Barnett, President, Frederick C. Steinhauer, Vice-President, Edward C. Hanley, Secretary, Thomas S. Harrison, Assistant Secretary.

1943 - 44　Frederick C. Steinhauer, President, Thomas S. Harrison, Vice President, Edward C. Hanley, Secretary, William Henry Leonard, Assistant Secretary, W. M. Alter.

1945 - 46　Frederick C. Steinhauer, President, Thomas S. Harrison, Vice President, William Henry Leonard, Assistant Secretary, Lester C. Thomas, W. M. Alter. Thomas was a 1912 graduate of Mines, a wealthy and prominent automobile dealer (Thomas -- Hyer Motor Company) in Denver and received the distinguished Achievement Award in 1954.

1947　Thomas S. Harrison, President, Lester C. Thomas, Vice President, William Henry Leonard, Secretary, Dr. John W Vanderwilt, Assistant Secretary, Max W. Bowen. Max Bowen was a 1924 graduate of Mines, and the Vice President and General Manager of the Golden Cycle Corporation. Dr. Vanderwilt was a consulting mining and engineering geologist with The Molybdenum Corporation of America, the U.S. Bureau of Reclamation, and the Chicago, Burlington, & Quincy Railroad.

1948　Thomas S. Harrison, President, Lester C. Thomas, Vice President, Dr. John W Vanderwilt, Secretary, Max W. Bowen, Ted P. Stockmar. Stockmar was a 1943 Mines graduate, and an attorney for Holme, Roberts, More and Owen in Denver.

1949　Lester C. Thomas, President, Max W. Bowen, Vice-President, Dr. John W Vanderwilt, Secretary, Ted P. Stockmar, Assistant Secretary, Thomas S. Harrison.

1950 - 52　Lester C. Thomas, President, Thomas S. Harrison, Vice President, Max W. Bowen, Secretary, Ted P. Stockmar, Assistant Secretary, Dr. Ben Hutchinson Parker. Dr. Parker was President of CSM from 1946 to 1950, a 1924 Mines graduate, and received the Distinguished Achievement Award in 1952. After being replaced as CSM president in 1950 he became Vice President and Director of Frontier Mining Company.

1953 - 54 Lester C. Thomas, President, Max W. Bowen, Thomas S. Harrison, Dr. Ben H. Parker, Ted P. Stockmar.

1955 - 56 Lester C. Thomas, President, Max W. Bowen, Kenneth R. Fenwick, Dr. Ben H. Parker, Ted P. Stockmar. Mr. Fenwick was a 1936 Mines graduate, and a mining engineer for municipal and civil engineering in the Rocky Mountain area.

1957 - 58 Dr. Ben H. Parker, President, Joseph Coors, Secretary, Kenneth R. Fenwick, Ted P. Stockmar. Coors was an owner of the Coors Brewery in Golden.

1959 - 60 Dr. Ben H. Parker, President, Ted P. Stockmar, Vice-President, Joseph Coors, Secretary, Kenneth R. Fenwick, David C. Johnston. Johnston was the Mayor of Golden from 1953-1954, a Colorado state representative and senator, and the Mines athletics business manager.

1961 - 62 Dr. Ben H. Parker, President, Ted P. Stockmar, Vice-President, Joseph Coors, Secretary, Kenneth R. Fenwick, David C. Johnston.

1963 - 64 Dr. Ben H. Parker, President, Ted P. Stockmar, Vice-President, Joseph Coors, Secretary, Kenneth R. Fenwick, David C. Johnston (1963), Edwin J. Eisenach (1964). Eisenach was a 1939 Mines graduate, and Vice-President of AMAX Exploration.

1965 - 66 Dr. Ben H. Parker, President, Ted P. Stockmar, Vice-President, Joseph Coors, Secretary, Kenneth R. Fenwick, Edwin J. Eisenach.

1967 - 68 Dr. Ben H. Parker, President, Ted P. Stockmar, Russell "Rut" H. Volk, Edwin J. Eisenach, William A. Alexander. Volk was a 1926 graduate of Mines, who later earned his master's degree in petroleum engineering, and was one of the founders of Plains Exploration Company.

1969 - 70 Dr. Ben H. Parker, President (1969), Ted P. Stockmar President (1970), Russell H. Volk, Edwin J. Eisenach, William A. Alexander, Leo N. Bradley (1970). Bradley graduated from Mines in 1949, filled the vacancy made by Parker's death and was general counsel to Coors

Brewing Co.

1971 - 72 Ted P. Stockmar, President, Russell H. Volk, Edwin J. Eisenach, William A. Alexander, Leo N. Bradley.

1973 - 74 Ted P. Stockmar, President, Russell H. Volk (1973), Edwin J. Eisenach, William A. Alexander, Leo N. Bradley, John A. Reeves, Sr. Reeves, President of Mid-Continent Minerals Corporation, filled the vacancy left by Volk's resignation.

1975 - 76 Ted P. Stockmar, President, John A. Reeves, Sr., Edwin J. Eisenach, William A. Alexander (1975), Leo N. Bradley, William K. Coors, J. Robert Maytag, Charles F. Fogarty (1976). The Board was expanded from five trustees to seven. Fogarty graduated from Mines in 1942, and was Chairman and Chief Executive Officer of Texasgulf, Inc. Coors was the President and Chairman of the Coors Brewing Company.

1977 - 78 Ted P. Stockmar, President, Edwin J. Eisenach, John A. Reeves, J. Robert Maytag, Charles F. Fogarty, Jack J. Grynberg, William K. Coors, Conrad Parrish, student rep (1976-1977), Joey V. Tucker, student rep (1977-1978). Grynberg graduated from Mines in Petroleum Engineering in 1952, and was president of Oceanic Exploration Co.

1979 - 80 Ted P. Stockmar, President, William K. Coors, Charles F. Fogarty, Jack J. Grynberg, J. Robert Maytag, James C. Wilson, Fred R. Schwartzberg, D. Monte Pascoe. Douglas A. Aab, student rep (1978-1979), Steven A. Ruehle, student rep (1979-1980). Schwartzberg was a Mines grad in 1953 and Principal at Rocky Mountain Engineering and Materials Technology, Inc. Pascoe, a major player in the Democrat Party, was a partner in the Denver law firm of Ireland Stapleton Pryor & Pascoe P.C.; Executive Director, Colorado Department of Natural Resources 1980-1983; Commissioner, Denver Board of Water Commissioners 1983-1995; Chairman, Colorado Democrat Party 1973-1977; and Chairman, Colorado Water Quality Control Commission, 1980-1981.

1981 - 82 William K. Coors, President, James C. Wilson, Fred R. Schwartzberg, D. Monte Pascoe, Jasper N. Warren, Don K. Henderson, Jack J. Grynberg (1981), Russell L. Wood (1982) June L. Fuller, student rep (1980-1981), Sandra J. Hollenbeck, student rep (1981-1982). Warren was a Mines grad of 1950, the owner of Goldrus Drilling, and a close associate of President Jimmy Carter, Wood was a CSM grad of 1949, senior vice president of New Jersey Zinc, president of Gold Fields Mining, Copper Range, and Asamera Minerals. Henderson was a grad of 1961.

1983 - 84 William K. Coors, President, D. Monte Pascoe, Don K. Henderson, Russell L. Wood, James C. Wilson, Fred R. Schwartzberg, Jasper N. Warren, Lon E. Rosenzweig, student rep (1983-1984). Wilson is a PE and lawyer involved with various companies and a leader in global environment and sustainability.

1985 - 86 William K. Coors, President (1985), Sally Vance Allen, Vice-President, Fred R. Schwartzberg, D. Monte Pascoe, Russell L. Wood, Don K. Henderson, Jasper N. Warren, James C. Wilson, Cheryl A. Hissong, student rep (1984-1985), Dr. Heidi Linch Reynolds, student rep (1985-1986). Allen is vice president of administration and government affairs for Gary-Williams Energy Corp.

1987 - 88 Sally Vance Allen, Vice-President, Fred R. Schwartzberg, D. Monte Pascoe, Russell L. Wood, Don K. Henderson (1987), Jasper N. Warren (1987), James C. Wilson, Donald E. Miller (1988), Charles E. Stott, Jr., (1988) Secretary, Frederick H. Earnest, student rep (1986-87), Brian A. Warren, student rep (1987-88). Miller was a Mines grad from 1953 and president of the Gates Corporation, and Stott was a Mines graduate from 1956, and is Chairman of the Board of Apollo Gold Corporation.

1989 - 90 D. Monte Pascoe, President, Charles E. Stott, Jr., Secretary, Russell L. Wood, Sally Allen, James C. Wilson, Donald E. Miller, Dr. Terence P. McNulty, Anthony L. Joseph, David C. Lawler, student rep (1988-89). William M. Powers, student rep (1989-90). McNulty earned his PhD at Mines in 1967, and is president and CEO of Hazen Research Inc.

1991 - 92 D. Monte Pascoe, President (1991), Donald L. Miller, President (1992), Charles E. Stott, Jr., Secretary, Russell L. Wood, Sally Allen, Anthony L. Joseph, Dr. Terence P. McNulty, Joe Coors, Jr., Rich V. Rosser, Jr., student rep (1991), Janelle Jeanperrin, Student Rep, (1992).

1993 - 94 Russell L. Wood, President, Sally Vance Allen, Vice President, Donald L. Miller, Treasurer, Charles E. Stott, Jr., Treasurer, Anthony L. Joseph, Joe Coors, Jr., Jeffrey S. Odenbaugh, student rep (1993), Troy E. Stucky, student rep (1994-95). Coors was the President of Coors Porcelain, later CoorsTek.

1995 - 96 Donald L. Miller, President, Russell L. Wood, Sally Allen (1995), Charles E. Stott, Jr., Joe Coors, Jr., Anthony L. Joseph, Randy L. Parcel, F. Stephen Mooney (1996), Karen Krug, (1996). Krug was a Mines graduate in 1984, on the board until 2006, and a lawyer with the international firm SNR Denton, encompassing all aspects of energy and mining, Mooney graduated in 1956 and headed Mooney Enterprises. Parcel was a Denver lawyer and Director of the Colorado Mining Association.

1997 - 98 Joe Coors, Jr., Russell L. Wood (1997), Frank Erisman, Hugh W. Evans, David D. Powell, Jr., F. Stephen Mooney, Randy L. Parcel, Karen Krug, Anthony L. Joseph (1997), Shannon Miller, student rep. Evans was a Mines graduate from 1949 and mining consultant, and Erisman graduated in 1965, and is a partner in Holme Roberts & Owen LLP of Denver.

1999 - 2000 F. Stephen Mooney, President, Frank Erisman, David J. Wagner, Karen Krug, Hugh W. Evans, David D. Powell, Jr., Joe Coors, Jr. (1999), Dr. John K. Coors, Randy L. Parcel (1999), Erica R. Leigh, student rep (1999-2000). Wagner was the Chairman and CEO of David Wagner & Associates, P.C., and John Coors received his PhD from Mines in 1977 and was the CEO of CoorsTek, Inc.

2001 - 02 Frank Erisman, President, David J. Wagner, Vice-President, Terrance G. Tschatschula, Secretary, F. Stephen

Mooney, Dr. John K. Coors, Karen Krug, Hugh W. Evans, David D. Powell, Jr. (2001), Dr. Michael S. Nyikos, Matthew H. Hutchinson, student rep (2001-2002). Tschatschula was the secretary of Blue-Sky Energy, and Nyikos was formerly the Dean of Student Affairs and Vice President of Student Affairs and External Relations at Mines.

2003 - 04 F. Stephen Mooney, President, Dr. Michael S. Nyikos, Vice-President, Terrance G. Tschatschula, Secretary, Karen Krug, David J. Wagner, Dr. John K. Coors, Hugh W. Evans, L. Roger Hutson (2004), Dr. DeAnn Craig (2004), Justin H. Carlson, student rep (2002-2003), Kale J. Franz, student rep (2003-2004). Hutson, a 1982 graduate of Mines, was the president and chief executive officer of HRM Resources LLC. Dr. Craig earned two BS degrees from Mines, and served as President of Phillips Petroleum Resources, and Manager of Worldwide Drilling and Production for Phillips Petroleum.

2005 -06 Dr. Michael S. Nyikos, President, Terrance G. Tschatschula, Secretary, L. Roger Hutson, Hugh W. Evans (2005), David J. Wagner, Dr. John K. Coors, Dr. DeAnn Craig, Frank DeFilippo, Joseph Gross, student rep (2004-2005), Laurie R. Derrick, student rep (2005-2006). DeFilippo graduated from Mines in 1972.

2007 - 08 Dr. Michael S. Nyikos, President, L. Roger Hutson, Vice-President, Terrance G. Tschatschula, Secretary, David J. Wagner, (2007), Dr, John K. Coors (2007), Frank DeFilippo, Vicki J. Cowart (2008), Dr. DeAnn Craig, James R. Spaanstra (2008), Dr. John R. Dorgan, faculty rep (2008), Justin C. Chichester, student rep (2006-2007), Aprill M. Nelson, student rep (2007-2008), Spaanstra was a partner in the law firm of Faegre & Benson LLP. Mr. Spaanstra has one of the largest and most diverse environmental practices in the Rocky Mountain region.

2009 - 10 Dr. Michael Nyikos, President, L. Roger Hutson Vice-President, Terrance Tschatschula (2009), Vicki J. Cowart, Frank DeFilippo (2009), Judge M. Terry Fox, Dr. Mohan S. Misra (2010), Stewart Bliss (2010), Admiral Richard H. Truly (2010), Francis M. Vallejo, Dr. John

R. Dorgan, faculty rep, Amy D. Goodson, student rep (2008-2009), Damian A. R. Illing, student rep (2009-2010). Fox was a 1989 graduate of Mines and an attorney in the US District Attorney's office in Denver. She was active in the Colorado Hispanic Bar Association, and the Colorado Women's Bar Association. Misra, born in India, received his PhD degree in Metallurgical Engineering from the Mines in 1986, and is the founder and chief executive officer of ITN Energy Systems and founder, chairman and chief strategy officer of Ascent Solar Technologies. Hutson was a graduate of Mines in the class of 1982. Bliss was a senior consultant in business with a specific emphasis on energy, technology, energy and industrial distribution corporations, and works out of the offices with Faegre & Benson LLP. Truly was a former astronaut who piloted the space shuttle Columbia commanded the space shuttle Discovery and lives in Golden. Cowart has a MS from Mines in Geophysics (1977) and was president and CEO of Planned Parenthood of the Rocky Mountains, Vallejo was a CSM grad of 1987.

2011 - 12   James Spaanstra, Chairman, Kirsten Volpi, Treasurer (non-voting), Judge M. Terry Fox, Stewart A. Bliss, Mohan S. Misra, Vicki J. Cowart, Admiral Richard Truly, L. Roger Hutson, Dr. John R. Dorgan, faculty rep, Jesse R. Earle, student rep (2011-2012), Stephanie L. Bonucci, student rep (2012-2013). Volpi was the Mines Senior Vice President for Finance and Administration.

2013 - 14   James Spaanstra, Chairman, Admiral Richard Truly, Vice-Chairman, Vicki J. Cowart, Secretary, Kirsten Volpi, Treasurer (non-voting), Thomas E. Jorden (2014), Stewart A. Bliss, Frances M. Vallejo, Timothy J. Haddon, Dr. Mohan S. Misra (2013), Dr. Tissa Illangasekare, faculty rep, Sydney E. Rogers, student rep (2013-2014), Gerald J. Miller, student rep (2014-2015). Haddon was a CSM grad from 1970, and Jorden from 1980.

2015 - 16   James Spaanstra, Chairman, Thomas E. Jorden, Vice Chairman, Richard Truly, Vicki J. Cowart (2015), Stewart A. Bliss, Timothy J. Haddon, Frances M. Vallejo, Patricia K. Starzer (2016), Dr. Wendy Harrison Faculty rep,

Tyrel L. Jacobsen, student rep (2015-2016), Sarah J. Steers, student rep (2016-2017). Harrison received her PhD from Mines in 2005, Starzer graduated from Mines in 1983.

2016 - 17 James Spaanstra, Chairman, Thomas Jordan, Vice Chairman, Richard Truly, Patsy Starzer, Stewart A. Bliss, Timothy J. Haddon, Frances M. Vallejo (2016), Wendy Harrison, faculty rep, Sarah Steers, student rep.

Kappa Sigma Fraternity House (c. 1960)

Pi Kappa Alpha Fraternity House (c. 1960)

Appendix B – Colorado School of Mines Board of Trustees Bylaws

The following Bylaws serve as the Board's operating rules and, unless mandated by statute, may be changed by the Board at any time.

I. Principal Office

The principal office of the Board of Trustees of Colorado School of Mines shall be the administrative office of Colorado School of Mines in Golden, Colorado.

II. Officers

A. The officers of the Board shall be: Chairman; Vice Chairman; Secretary; and Treasurer. Officers shall be elected in the odd numbered years by the Board and shall hold office until their successors are appointed. A vacancy in any office may be filled at any regular meeting of the Board or at any special meeting of the Board if notice of the intention to fill such vacancy is included in the notice of the special meeting. The Chairman and Vice Chairman shall be chosen from among the voting membership of the Board, in odd numbered years after the newly appointed and qualified board members have been administered the oath of office. The Secretary and the Treasurer are not required to be Board members, but if either position is elected from the Board membership, such election shall occur at the same time and in the same manner as the election of the Chairman and Vice Chairman.

B. In the event of an officer vacancy, the Chairman may appoint an officer to serve until the next meeting of the Board, at which time an election will be held to fill this position.

C. The Board may, in the exercise of its discretion, remove any officer at any time for any reason by vote of at least five of the voting members.

III. Duties of Officers

A. Chairman

The Chairman shall serve as the chief executive officer of the

Board and shall perform all duties customarily delegated to the chief executive officer of a governing board of an institution of higher. The chairman shall serve in the role of president of the Board, as contemplated in §23-41-109, C.R.S. The chief executive officer of Mines is also titled "president." To avoid confusion, the working title of this position on the Board shall be "chairman." Education as well as such other duties as may be specifically assigned by the Board from time to time.

B. Vice Chairman

The Vice Chairman shall perform all duties incident to the office of Vice Chairman as well as such other duties as may be assigned by the Board or the Board Chairman from time to time. The Vice Chairman shall perform all Chairman duties in the absence of the Chairman.

C. Secretary

The Secretary shall: (1) attest to the accuracy of the minutes of each meeting of the Board; (2) ensure that all notices are properly given in accordance with the provisions of these Bylaws and as may otherwise be required by law; (3) ensure that all Board records, books, reports, statements, certificates, and other documents required by law are properly filed and maintained; (4) if the Secretary is a Board member, perform all Chairman duties in the absence of the Chairman and Vice Chairman; and (5) perform all other duties incident to the office of Secretary as well as such other duties as may be assigned by the Board or the Board Chairman from time to time.

D. Treasurer

The Treasurer shall: (1) have custody of and responsibility for all funds of Mines which shall be deposited in banks, trust companies, or other depositories selected in accordance with the provisions of these Bylaws and applicable state laws; (2) ensure that all Mines financial records, reports, statements, and other documents required by law are properly filed and maintained; (3) exhibit the financial records of Mines to the Board upon the provision of reasonable notice; (4) submit a statement of the financial condition of Mines at all regular meetings of the Board and a complete financial report on an annual basis; and (5) perform all other duties incident to the office of Treasurer as well as such other duties as may be assigned by the Board or the Board Chairman from time to time.

IV. Advisory Members

As authorized by §23-41-104.6(5)(a), C.R.S. (2001), no fewer than nine and no more than fifteen non-voting, advisory members of the Board, as may be appointed by the Governor of Colorado from time to time, shall serve staggered, four-year terms. The advisory members, who need not be residents of Colorado, shall be representative of national and international industries as well as research and academic institutions. The advisory members, whose role shall be to provide advice to the Board in their areas of expertise and contribute to the development and enrichment of Mines, including but not limited to its academic and research programs, shall meet with the Board at least once per year.

V. Emeritus Trustees

Emeritus Trustees shall consist of a class of individuals who have previously served as Board members. Any person appointed by the Governor to serve as a Trustee of Mines, or elected to serve as a Student Trustee of Mines, shall become an Emeritus Trustee upon completion of the term or terms to which he or she was appointed or elected, regardless of whether his or her period of service as a Trustee shall have consisted of less than a full term. The term of service of an Emeritus Trustee shall be for life, unless the holder of such appointment shall resign. It shall be the right of Emeritus Trustees to continue their support of Mines' mission and programs through participation in Mines events and public representation of Mines.

VI. Committees

The Board may create standing and ad hoc committees, as the Board deems necessary to assist the members in performing their duties and responsibilities. The Chairman shall have the authority to appoint and remove members of such committees. Committee members shall serve two-year terms, and until their successors are appointed and qualified. Generally, only voting members are eligible to serve on committees. The Chairman may, at his or her discretion, make changes to this structure as circumstances warrant.

VII. Regular Meetings

Regular meetings of the Board, which shall be open to the public, shall be held at least four times per calendar year in accordance with a public schedule that shall be revised and updated from time to time. Public notice of the time and place of such regular meetings shall be provided in accordance with applicable Colorado law. Regular meetings shall take place in the William K. Coors Board Room on the Mines campus in Golden, Colorado or such other place within the State of Colorado as may be specified in the meeting notice. Once a regular meeting has been convened, a majority of voting Board members in attendance can vote to adjourn or cancel the meeting.

VIII. Special Meetings

Special meetings of the Board, which shall be open to the public, may be held at any time and place within the State of Colorado at the call of the Board Chairman, three Board members, or the President of Mines. Public notice of the time, place and purpose of such special meetings shall be provided in accordance with applicable Colorado law. Once a special meeting has been convened, a majority of voting Board members in attendance can vote to adjourn or cancel the meeting.

IX. Quorum

At all meetings of the Board, any four voting members shall constitute a quorum for the transaction of business, and the vote of a majority of those present shall govern, but less than a quorum may adjourn a meeting at which a quorum is not present. A voting Board member shall be deemed present for the purpose of determining a quorum and conducting Board business if such Board member can hear Board proceedings and be heard by other Board members by means of a telephone conference call hook-up or other appropriate electronic method. If a Board meeting is held at which no officer is present, the quorum shall elect one of the present Board members to preside over the meeting.

X. Motions, Seconding and Voting on Actions

Only voting Board members may make and second motions, and vote on Board actions. Proxy voting is not permitted. If a non-voting Board member desires to bring to the Board's attention a particular motion or action item, the non-voting member is encouraged to solicit voting members to introduce or second a motion on his or her behalf.

XI. Executive Session

At any regular or special meeting, the Board may convene an executive session in conformity with all requirements prescribed by applicable Colorado law. Public notice of the time, place and purpose of such executive sessions shall be provided in accordance with applicable Colorado law. Executive sessions will be conducted in compliance with Colorado's Open Meetings Law, § 24-6-401, C.R.S. et seq., and limited to the voting Board members and those parties expressly invited by the Board Chairman to participate in the sessions. Non-voting, advisory Board members will participate in executive sessions at the invitation of the Chairman. Once an executive session has been convened, a majority of voting Board members in attendance can vote to adjourn or cancel the session.

XII. Execution of Documents

All contracts, vouchers, warrants, orders for the payment of funds, or other documents requiring execution by the Board of Trustees shall be executed by the President of Mines and countersigned by the Board Chairman or Vice Chairman.

XIII. Fiscal Year

The fiscal year for the Board shall correspond to the fiscal year of Mines and shall commence on the first day of July of each year and end on the last day of June of the following year.

XIV. Amendment Procedure

These Bylaws, or any portion thereof, may be amended or repealed and new Bylaws enacted by a majority of the Board at any regular or special meeting, provided that notice of intention to consider revision of the Bylaws is given to each member of the Board not less than seven days prior to the meeting at which such action is to be considered.

XV. Repeal of Prior Bylaws

All previous Bylaws adopted by the Board, or any portions thereof, which may be in conflict herewith are hereby repealed.
Adopted March 5, 1942
Amended May 9, 1947
Amended November 8, 1957

Amended September 7, 1973
Amended October 10, 1975
Amended December 9, 1977
Amended December 14, 1990
Amended October 11, 2002
Amended June 8, 2006
Amended March 7, 2008
Amended October 24, 2008
Amended, January 29, 2010

Sigma Alpha Epsilon Fraternity House (c. 1960)

Sigma Nu Fraternity House (c. 1960)

Appendix C - Student Enrollments at Mines

The enrollments given below are for fall semesters while graduates are those of the following spring. "NF" stands for "Not Found", meaning that the researchers were unable to find reliable numbers for that year and category. Blank items are actually zero, but the fields were left blank for easier reading. Prior to 1954 and with the exception of 1951, the undergraduate enrollments are actually total enrollments.

Enrollments starting with 1962 are based on "full-time equivalents (FTEs)" a metric used by the state for determining state aid. An FTE represents a student taking 15 hours in a semester for a 4-year total of 120 hours. A lecture or recitation hour is counted as a full hour, technical laboratory is assigned a credit of one hour for every 1.5 hours of lab, and all non-technical lab hours receive one hour for every two hours of lab. In 1962, the enrollment numbers increased dramatically due to part-time and summer students being counted to accumulate additional FTEs.

Prior to 1962, students could take from fifteen to twenty-six credit hours in a semester and pay the same flat rate for tuition and fees. With the exception of summer school, part-time students were rare and admitted only under special circumstances. The statistics therefore highlight a dramatic anomaly. From 1905 to 1947, a regular student completing his curriculum in four years earned FTE 292 hours, from 1952-56, 279 hours, and from 1957 to 1961 273 hours. In other words, a student in the above three groups was 2.43, 2.33, and 2.28 FTEs respectively, or well more than twice that of standard Colorado students. No better metric illustrates the severe demand put on students of the old Mines.

The abnormally high graduation rates from 1948 to 1952 are due to students finishing their education after having it interrupted by World War II. In 1961, according to official sources, 174 Professional Degrees were earned. Of this number, at least 45 were students that had taken 5 or more years to graduate, 23 finished after the 1961 summer sessions, and 8 were transfers that did not take their freshman year at Mines. Of a freshman class in 1957 of 340, only 98 (28.8%) graduated on time in four years. The drop-out rate was truly draconian.

(See Appendix H)

Sources: Colorado School of Mines, President's Annual Progress Reports, Mining History Archive, Arthur Lakes Library, TN 210, C67; Jesse R. Morgan, A World School The Colorado School of Mines, Denver, CO, 1955; Mines Magazine, (CSM Alumni Magazine), Various editions; Colorado School of Mines Office of Institutional Research, CSM, Guggenheim Hall.

Prior to 1955 the total graduate degrees by option were as follows:

Option	MS	DSc
Geological Engineering	78	22
Geophysical Engineering	27	14
Metallurgical Engineering	64	11
Mining Engineering	57	6
Petroleum Engineering	11	4
Petroleum Refining Engineering	19	5
Civil Engineering	1	0
Chemical Engineering	7	2
Electrical Engineering	1	0
Mechanical Engineering	1	0
Totals:	266	64

The ratio of students to faculty for representative years are shown in the following table:

Year	Students	Faculty	Ratio (S/F)*
1876	26	6	4:1
1883	49	9	5:1
1899	220	17	13:1
1911	266	27	10:1
1919	432	27**	16:1
1924	503	40	13:1
1929	463	64	7:1
1953	948	116	8:1
1961	1,046	117	9:1
1962	1,271	119	11:1
1969	1,655	161	10:1
1978	2,377	205	12:1
2010	5,105	338	15:1
2015	5,809	363***	16.1***

* Rounded to the nearest whole number.
**Plus 26 Special Lecturers for specific subjects not used in calculation.

***Controversial figures, as number of faculty were also reported as 253 and 287. Official payroll reports give 69 Professors, 61 Associate Professors, 56 Assistant Professors, 56 Instructors, and 11 others for 253. There are also research faculty carrying titles such as Associate Professor – Research, and a large number of graduate assistants. Of the 5,809 total students, 1,038 are graduate students. The ratio of only undergraduate students and the school-reported faculty of 287, is 16.6 to 1. Various publication use 16:1 as the Mines student/faculty ratio. The worst case of 5,809 divided by 253, which may be correct, gives 23:1. Mines itself reports a ratio of 17:1.

In discussing with various administrative personnel, the actual numbers of faculty that should be counted to calculate the student/teacher ratio, it was apparent that, within limits, the number of faculty was almost whatever a person wanted to report. The course loads on faculty are highly variable, and by 2016, the vast majority of graduate students were titled as "graduate assistants" and some number were involved in teaching or laboratory assistant duties.

It must also be noted that throughout the generation of statistics, there is the question of what should be included in student enrollments. Apparently, for most of the years prior to 1962, the number of graduate students was included in total enrollment numbers, and the table of enrollments for any given year may include or exclude the graduate school. Generally speaking, it appears that graduate students were included until the graduate school became a separate entity in 1953, and that was how the enrollment numbers were treated in this work.

There is, however, a huge problem with the enrollment numbers that cannot be resolved at this time. Fall undergraduate enrollments were usually about 10% higher than in the following spring, but the various publications that recorded enrollments and were used in this work failed to mention whether their numbers represented the fall, the spring, or an average between the two. The assumption made throughout is that they represented fall enrollments only. Nor were summer school enrollments apparently factored in before 1962, and the current statistics, starting in 1962, supposedly exclude summer enrollments.

Even the number of degrees granted is controversial. For example, in 1961, there were 183 recipients of the silver diploma as given in the commencement proceedings and bulletin. But CSM's class standings at graduation were calculated on 174 graduates and other official publications give 174 graduates. Even in early times, one source mentions the first MS degree being given in 1911, but the school says the first MS was awarded in 1913.

Given the difficulty in obtaining accurate figures for the granting of degrees, the alumni association's class listings were used to fill in many gaps before 1962. Since these included graduate degrees, those degrees, where known, were factored out to obtain a more accurate number of silver diplomas awarded. In short, a direct and accurate comparison between the pre-1962 numbers and those later must be made with some caution, but it is felt that the numbers are reasonably accurate.

Notes on Sources:

The Masters and Doctorates awarded prior to 1955 come from Jesse R. Morgan, *A World School The Colorado School of Mines* (Denver, CO: Sage Books, 1955).

Enrollments from 1962 to 2015 and degrees granted from 1889 to 2015 were provided courtesy of Tricia Douthit, the Office of Institutional Research, Colorado School of Mines, Golden, CO.

Enrollments prior to 1962 and all faculty numbers were gleaned from various issues of the *Mines Magazine, Quarterly of the Colorado School of Mines, The New Zealand Mines Record, CSM Bulletin,* and various reports and other publications on the internet and in the research stacks of the Arthur Lakes Library.

Professional Degrees granted from 1913 to 1988 were determined from individual historical documents at Arthur Lakes Library and the internet, as well as the Alumni Association's Network 2004/2005 (the last such publication by the Alumni Association and sorely missed by many Alumni.)

Appendix D -- Admission Requirements

Mines has always said that its admission standards were in keeping with its fame as the world's foremost mineral engineering school. In reality, until 1968, Mines depended on its instructional rigor to weed out those who couldn't meet CSM's standards. Efforts were made frequently to establish admissions standards to ensure a reasonable retention rate among each new class, but when everything was boiled down to the essentials, first and foremost was the dedication of a prospect to becoming a mineral engineer, a leader in industry and society, and a commitment to excellence in all his endeavors.

Standards were first instituted in 1879, and reformulated in 1880, 1890, 1894, 1898, 1902, 1903, 1908, 1922, 1928, 1932, 1944, 1946, 1950, 1952, 1955, 1956, 1958, 1959, 1960, 1967, 1973, 1974, and 1975. Other changes took place to the present, most notably in 1994.

1879: Applicants were to be at least 17 years old and have had a liberal education in the English branches, and to possess some knowledge of algebra and geometry. The age minimum remained in effect until 1903.

1880: Same as 1879 with the addition of having completed a satisfactory examination on the first five chapters of Peck's *Manual of Algebra* and on the first four books of *Wentworth's Geometry* or an equivalent of Davies's *Legendre*.

1890: Applicants had to pass a satisfactory examination in English composition, geography, arithmetic, and the first elements of algebra and geometry, namely the first five chapters of Wentworth's *The Complete Algebra* or an equivalent.

1894: A certificate of proficiency from an approved high school was accepted in lieu of taking an examination, but for advanced standing, an examination could be required if the faculty so deemed.

1898: Applicants had to take examinations in English, Geography, Arithmetic, Algebra, Geometry, and Zoology. English of a high school level was required. Graduation diplomas from approved high schools were accepted in lieu of examinations.

1902: Applicants from "accredited" high schools according to the State University in the candidate's state were accepted and only examinations in plane and solid geometry were required. Twenty-four high schools of high school districts were listed for Colorado. Applicants from non-accredited high schools were required to take the full range of examinations.

1903: Completion of certain course units became required for admission. A unit was defined as a course covering not less than thirty-five weeks with four or five periods of at least forty-five minutes each week. Sixteen units were required for acceptance, twelve being specified, with four being chosen from a list of electives. The specified units were Algebra (1-1/2), Plane Geometry (1), Solid Geometry (1/2), Languages other than English (2), English (3), History (2), Physics (1), Chemistry (1). The elective list included Drawing (1), Shop Work (1), Mathematics (1/2 or 1), Greek (1, 2, or 3), Spanish (1 or 2), History (1 or 2), English (1), Science (1 or 2), Psychology (1/2 or 1), Political Economy (1/2 or 1).

1908: The same as 1903 except that one-half unit of Algebra was specified to be advanced algebra and only three units were required from the elective list.

1922: The same as 1908 except that Chemistry and Physics were no longer required units.

1928: The same as 1908 (Chemistry and Physics were once more required.

1932: A rank in the upper third of an accredited high school was required to avoid examinations. The course lengths were increased to 36 weeks for a unit, with five weekly periods of at least forty-five minutes. The number of required units were lowered to fifteen with ten being specified and five coming from the list of electives.

1944: Admission requirements for students with deficiencies were lowered to make up for the catastrophic decline in enrollments. Courses were provided both in the summer and regular sessions in Advanced Algebra, Solid Geometry, Physics, and Chemistry.

1946: One half unit of Trigonometry was added to the required list of units.

1950: Non-resident applicants who were not in the upper third of their graduating classes were required to take the Pre-Engineering Inventory Test administered by the Educational Testing Service.

1952. The meeting of entrance requirements by testing in the various subjects was discontinued. In addition, the unit requirements for trigonometry and solid geometry were dropped.

1955: A formal admissions program was put into place, including orientation and registration periods during which the pre-engineering and qualifying exams for placement in Mathematics and Chemistry were introduced. Applicants that did not rank in the upper third of their high school class were required to take the Scholastic Aptitude Test administered by the College Entrance Examination Board. The specified high school units were lowered to only ten: Essentials of Algebra (1), Advanced Algebra (1/2), Plane Geometry (1), Advanced Mathematics (1/2 selected from Solid Geometry, Trigonometry, and other advanced courses), English (3), History or Social System (2), Chemistry or Physics (1), Additional Natural or physical science (1).

1956: All non-resident applicants were required to take the SATs, and all Colorado applicants not in the upper one third of their high school class also had to take the SAT.

1958: The G.E.D. Equivalency Certificate was accepted in lieu of a high school diploma, but the unit requirements remained in place.

1959: Applicants who were Colorado residents were strongly urged to take the SAT, but it was not required.

1960: All applicants were required to take the SAT.

1967: The CEEB Mathematics Achievement Test (Level 1) was required of all applicants in addition to the SAT.

1973: Either the SAT or ACT was required for admission. The CEEB Mathematics Achievement Test (Level 1) was no longer required.

1974: Trigonometry was once more made a required high school course (1/2 unit).

1975: All applicants had to be graduates of an accredited high school and should rank in the upper third of their class. The ten required units were changed somewhat: Essentials of Algebra (1), History or Social Studies (2), Advanced Algebra (1/2), Laboratory Science (2 – one unit had to be Chemistry or Physics, the second unit either Chemistry, Physics, Zoology, Botany, or Geology), Trigonometry

(1/2), English (3).

1994: The units in high school had ballooned to sixteen but were now strongly recommended instead of being required. They were: English (4), Algebra (2), Geometry (1), Advanced Mathematics, including Trigonometry (1), History of Social Studies (2), Lab Science (3), Academic electives (3 – recommended were mathematics, English, science, or foreign languages.) *Note: most of this history of admission requirements was obtained from a report presented to the Board of Trustees by Bill Young, July, 1975, and published in Mines Today, Vol 7, No. 3 (Golden, Colorado: Colorado School of Mines Publications Department, 1994).

2016: The units were now seventeen but written differently. Recommended were: four years of English, four years of college prep/ advanced mathematics (including trigonometry or pre-calculus), three years of history or social studies, three years of lab science (one year should be chemistry or physics, both are recommended if available), two years of academic electives (computer science, STEM (science, technology, engineering, mathematics), engineering), one year of a foreign language. CSM does not have a minimum requirement for a high school GPS, or the SAT or ACT scores. However, as it is currently admitting 36 out of every 100 applicants, an effective minimum high school GPA would be 3.6, the minimum SAT would be 1280 on the 1600 maximum SAT (1790 on the 2400 maximum SAT), and ACT 28 (maximum 36), with the writing portion not being required.

The startling thing about this history of admission requirements is the lack of change over the years. Mines put in the high school required courses needed for admission to Mines in 1903, and there has been very little change since then. At the current time, an applicant must have earned predominately "A" grades in high school to be accepted, unless there is some telling political consideration. On a percentage basis, having a 3.5 GPA in some high schools will not put a student in the top ten percent of his class, due to the rampant grade inflation that has swept American education. For many years Mines was required to accept applicants from Colorado who were in the top third of their class in an accredited high school, a very low standard by any analysis, but that has been eliminated. The SAT and ACT scores are still not impressive, but with the Pre-Engineering Inventory Test and all achievement tests being eliminated, it is difficult to compare Mines freshman classes in the

1950s with those currently enrolling.

President Ansell's goal of graduating students in propor-tion to their ethnic and racial percentages in the Colorado popu-lation affected the selection criteria for years, and the continued acceptance of community college graduates bypassing the first two years at Mines raises serious concern. Statistics are obscured, and interpretation of the data is sketchy. For example, one female stu-dent enrolled at CSM in 1957 but also attended three other univer-sities. She graduated four years later, but should she be considered a four-, five-, or six-year student? And what were the requirements she had to meet for admission?

The other outstanding aspect of CSM's registration require-ments is that Mines never had hard and fast rules by which to accept entering freshmen. President Chauvenet was primarily concerned with the prospective student's motivation, and this was a major factor until the school began relying on high school GPAs and test-ing services. Today, requirements are fuzzy and highly subjective, to say the least. Educational aptitude tests do not address an in-dividual's ability to innovate, his leadership potential, steadfast-ness, loyalty, and the willingness to venture into the unknown and take risks. Academicians are the worst possible individuals to teach such subjects, as they lead a safe, leisurely, and untroubled career with guaranteed lifetime employment, and they teach the same courses over and over. Yet successful Mines graduates might work eighty hours per week, take enormous physical, monetary, and so-cial risks, face the unknown with confidence, break new ground with new ideas, and be leadership models for those around them. Where is Mines measuring these qualities in the beginning fresh-men? One can't do it by following the herd of educators writing paper tests, researchers running surveys on students, or guiding students into group think while building student teams to work on glitzy projects. Mines has a long way to go, and counting numbers is not the answer.

Appendix E - Chronology of Events

1750: Indian migrations until 1850. Utes push Comanches from Mountains into Colorado and Texas plains. Cheyenne and Arapaho forced south from Black Hills by westward moving Sioux, and war continuously against Kiowa and Comanches. Colorado Indian population in 1850 estimated at 10,000.

1852: First permanent white settlement in Colorado at Conejos.

1858: Green Russell discovers placer gold near confluence of Cherry Creek and the South Platte River. Pike's Peak gold rush. Towns of Montana City, St. Charles, Denver City, and Auraria founded on site of present-day Denver. Town rivalries erupt as the area becomes Arapahoe County, Kansas Territory -- illegally, since the Denver Basin was accorded by treaty to the Arapaho Indians. Miners acquire land from Arapahos through series of barbeques.

1859: Gold discovered on Clear Creek by Jackson and Gregory. First school opened in Auraria, stimulating "School fever". Golden founded by Boston Company of thirteen men and one woman, including Edward L. Berthoud, George West, and W. A. H. Loveland. West founds Western Mountaineer, 3rd newspaper in the state. Jefferson Territory established.

1860: Census gives population as 32,654 white males, 1,577 white females, 46 Negroes. Miner's and People's courts establish law and order. Legislature of Jefferson Territory meets in Golden.

1861: Colorado Territory established with boundaries of present State. Name chosen by Governor Gilpin as source of the Colorado River. Colorado University authorized. Colorado City (western portion of Colorado Springs) named as capital. Census gives 20,798 white males (not counting absent prospectors), 4,484 white females, 89 Negroes. Edward L. Berthoud sent west from Denver assisted by mountain man Jim Bridger to survey a route to Salt Lake City. He ascended Berthoud Pass and established a route that became US 40.

1862: Golden selected as territorial capital. Meetings held in Koenig Building on Washington and 12th until 1867. Legislature passes act creating fund for schools, and first tax supported schools established.

1864: Colorado Seminary (later Denver University) established by Methodists, Loretto Academy opened by Sisters of Loretto.

1866: Bishop Randall arrives in Denver. General West founds Golden Transcript in Golden, later to become *The Colorado Transcript*.

1867: Legislature passes an act to incorporate a Colorado Mining College, January 11, 1867. Denver chosen as new territorial capital.

1868: Charles C. Welch of Golden donates 12 acres to Bishop Randall for building a university. Construction of Jarvis Hall complex begins. Nathaniel Hill builds first smelter at Blackhawk.

1869: Windstorm destroys incomplete Jarvis Hall.

1870: Legislature appropriates $3,872.45 to establish a School of Mines in the Jarvis Hall complex. Excavation for the Mines Building begins concurrent with the reconstruction of Jarvis Hall. Census gives territory population as 39,864.

1871: E. J. Mallett appointed Professor in Charge of School of Mines. Captain James T. Smith arrives in Golden.

1872: Jarvis and Matthews Hall schools open. Colorado Central Railway connects Central City, Blackhawk, Golden, and Denver through Clear Creek Canyon. Golden major smelter site.

1873: The School of Mines occupied its own building. Bishop Randall dies. Loveland and Berthoud draw up legislation to make the School of Mines a State institution.

1874: Legislature passes act establishing the Colorado School Mines as a State school at Golden and appropriates $5,000 operations. Colorado College chartered by the Legislature along with Colorado School of the Deaf and Blind at Colorado Springs. An appropriation of $15,000 was authorized for Colorado University, contingent on Boulder raising an equal sum. The first Mines catalog published, prepared by Berthoud and printed by George West. Mines faculty numbered six, including Arthur Lakes, Loveland, Berthoud, and Mallett. Colorado Territory boasts of 60 school districts, 120 schools, and a great emphasis on education.

1875: Professor Loveland assumes duties as Professor in Charge upon departure of Professor Mallett.

1876: Colorado becomes a state. Gregory Board named Professor in Charge of Mines. School receives bronze medal and diploma from Philadelphia Centennial Exposition for best geological collection. Enrollment 26.

1877: Colorado University opens at Boulder with 44 students and 2 faculty. Legislative act provides that one of Mines' five trustees must be a graduate of Mines.

1878: Milton Moss becomes Professor in Charge at Mines. Leadville strikes generate immense wealth, Central City Opera House opens.

1879: Land in Golden donated by citizens for construction of new college. Board of Trustees appropriates $7,500 for buildings, and Legislature assigns a one-fifth mill property tax statewide for the continued operation of the school. Colorado College for Agriculture and Mechanic Arts opens in Ft. Collins (becomes Colorado State University). Meeker Massacre and following battles subdue Utes -- last major Indian conflict in Colorado.

1880: Enrollment 61. Albert Hale becomes Professor in Charge. 1880 Building occupied, first building constructed by Mines on permanent campus. Colorado population 194,327.

1882: First degree granted at Mines; Honorary Engineer of Mines to Milton Moss. Additional land purchased along 14th Street west of Old Chemistry Building. Mr. Hale's title changed to President. Addition to 1880 Building completed. Enrollment; 37 students, nine faculty.

1883: First graduation with 2 graduates (some sources give 1882 for the first graduation), William Middleton of New York, and Walter Wylie of California. Regis Chauvenet becomes President. Dr. Chauvenet begins eliminating non-degree programs and miscellaneous courses. Designs an Engineering Academy, modeled on the US Naval Academy whose course of instruction was designed by William Chauvenet, Dr. Chauvenet's father. Stress on elitism and academic excellence in narrow specialties. Independent assessment of Colorado's school system prompts statement: "The creation of a system of schools on so large a scale, of such exceptional merits, and in so brief a space of time, is a phenomenon to which the history of education affords no parallel."

1888: Residence for President authorized.

1889: President's house completed.

1890: Enrollment 65. North wing to 1880 Building (Old Chemistry Building) completed. Enrollment 65 from 14 states and 2 foreign countries. Normal School (later Colorado State College at Greeley) opened. State population 413,249.

1891: Robert Womack discovers gold fields at Cripple Creek.

1893: State grants women suffrage as first state after Wyoming.

1894: Engineering Hall (Math Building) built as the Hall for Advanced Chemistry.

1899: Guggenheim brothers combine various smelters into American Smelting & Refining Company (ASARCO) based on their fortune from Leadville mines and smelters.

1900: Enrollment 236. Winfield Stratton donates $25,000 to CSM. Stratton Hall built from gift. Rocky Mountain Conference organized for athletics with initial members; Colorado University, Colorado A & M, Colorado College, Denver University, and CSM. State population 539,700.

1902: Charles Palmer elected President of CSM. Stratton Hall and Assay Laboratory built.

1903: Horace Patton Acting President during summer. Victor Alderson appointed President. Over $10,000 in gifts received for exhibits at World's Fair.

1906: Guggenheim Hall, donated by Simon Guggenheim. Largest private donation to higher education in the US at its time. Power house next to Assay Laboratory completed. Mining of tungsten begins. US mint begins operations in Denver.

1907: Gymnasium (Integral Club) completed. First major alumni contributions of $1,600 for gymnasium.

1908: "M" Built on Mt. Zion.

1909: Western State College opens at Gunnison.

1910: Enrollment 342. State population 799,024.

1911: CSM Experimental Plant acquired for Research Foundation.

1912: CSM free from debt.

1913: William Haldane elected Acting President after Dr. Alderson was terminated by Board of Trustees.

1914: World War I begins in Europe.

1915: William Phillips chosen President.

1916: Howard Parmelee chosen President. Massive trouble with students and faculty culminating in a student strike.

1917: Dr. Alderson returns as President. US. Enters World War I.

1918: World War I ends.

1919: Mines approved for an engineering detachment of the Reserve Officers Training Corps (ROTC). One of three in the US; the other two at Auburn University and the University of Alabama.

1920: Enrollment 471. State population 939,629.

1921: Edgar Mine leased for 99 years as CSM Experimental Mine in Idaho Springs.

1925: Melville Coolbaugh named President of CSM. Colorado Legislature approves oil royalties act dedicating two-thirds of the State's oil royalties to the various counties for schools, and one-third to CSM. Adams State Teachers College at Alamosa and junior colleges at Grand Junction and Trinidad established. Mines student Russell "Rut" Volk wins Rocky Mountain wrestling and boxing championships on the same day.

1926: Brooks Field completed. Rut Volk amasses a total of 14 varsity letters before graduating from Mines.

1928: Publications Building (a house on 14th Street where the current gym is) purchased. Moffat Tunnel completed, provides rail link between Denver and western Colorado.

1929: Beginning of the Great Depression.

1930: Enrollment 544. State population 1,035,791, Golden 2,426.

1931: World War II starts with Japan invading Manchuria.

1932: "M" lighting permanently added.

1936: Physics Building acquired -- was formerly Golden Elementary School built in 1873.

1937: Steinhauer Fieldhouse constructed. Mines loses accreditation from North Central Association.

1938: Berthoud Hall constructed.

1939: Mines Park constructed for faculty housing at foot of Lariat Loop. War begins in Europe.

1940: Enrollment 840. State population 1,123,296.

1941: US enters World War II.

1945: World War II ends.

1946: Ben H. Parker chosen President of Mines, only CSM graduate ever selected. Golden's Chocolate Factory becomes the Golden Nugget Saloon, and the La Ray Hotel becomes the Holland House.

1947: New President's house purchased at 17th & Illinois. Temporary structures were built at 14th Street and Maple to house the petroleum refining department and a cafeteria. Prospector Park was built of temporary wooden barracks-like buildings to house married students on 19th Street east of Mines Park. First lowering of academic standards by reducing amount of credits required for graduation. Dr. Chauvenet's design comes increasingly under attack from educators failing to understand the purpose of Mines.

1948: New Power House completed.

1949: 75th Anniversary Celebration. "M" Destroyed by vandals & reconstructed.

1950: John Vanderwilt named President. Enrollment 1,104. Building program initiated which would become the Horizon Plan in 1954. Denver-Golden Interurban railway discontinued. Korean War starts in June. State population 1,325,089.

1951: Chauvenet Hall dedicated, was formerly the old Power House. Legislature repealed the Act of Oil Royalties of 1925.

1952: Coolbaugh Hall dedicated as new Chemistry Building. Office of Dean of Students created, William Burger, first Dean. Last Senior Day.

1953: Freshman agitation reduced from 10 to 6 weeks. Course credits lowered to meet North Central Accreditation standards. Graduate School formalized, and Dean of Graduate School created. Korean War ends.

1954: Alderson Hall (Petroleum, English, Economics, and Descriptive Geometry) and Bradford Hall (dormitory) dedicated.

1955: Arthur Lakes Library built.

1957: Enrollment 1,212. Course credit again lowered without changing amount of material covered to satisfy North Central demands for less demanding student schedules. Old Chemistry Building razed. Randall Hall (dormitory) completed. October 4th, the Soviet Union sends up Sputnik.

1958: Metallurgy Building constructed. Who's Who in American Colleges & Universities started based on voting by administration and faculty and without student input. Widely seen as a reward for kowtowing to the administration. Last "milk train" to a Mines football game.

1959: "M" plastering incident. Director of Student Affairs position created, Chauncey Van Pelt first Director. Major effort by administration to take control of student activities away from students. New Gymnasium (later named Volk Gymnasium) completed.

1960: Formal bidding system inaugurated by administration for fraternity pledging. Interfraternity Council constitution created, social sanctions formalized. Mines ring designed and made available to class of 1961. Mines re-accredited by North Central Association. State population 1,753,947.

1961: Lower division courses restructured, hours for Math, Chemistry, and Geology reduced. Fraternities warned that any violation of the school's new social standards would bring social probation or revocation of a fraternity's charter. Last use of the "M" alarm and protection system provided by fraternities, also last year for *The Picker*. President Kennedy touts the study of science and engineering.

1962: Kappa Sigma House acquired through eminent domain followed by the SAE and PKA houses. Freshman gauntlet abolished.

1963: Orlo Childs named President. Fraternities begin moving to Fraternity Row on reclaimed land over the clay pits. Physics Building (Meyer Hall) completed where SAE and PKA houses once stood. President Kennedy greatly increases US involvement in Vietnam, assassinated in November.

1964: Kappa Sigma House becomes Caldwell Hall, a woman's dormitory. Freshman agitation essentially eliminated, replaced with "Freshman Orientation." College Union opens, renamed Ben H. Parker Student Center. Attempt made to rename Mines as "The Colorado Institute of Technology."

1968: New academic plan for degrees announced: beginning in 1969, Mines would grant BS degrees for a much reduced four years of study, the old Professional Degree would become a Master of Engineering. Alumni would not be grandfathered in and given the new Masters. Theta Tau put on disciplinary probation for shaving beards off freshmen. Students rebel against traditions, and wearing long hair and beards declared a "civil right."

1969: New degree programs take effect. Campus unrest surges in opposition to the Vietnam War, and ROTC comes under fire. NASA puts 1st man on the moon. Campus traditions thrown into the mix for abolition as being unnecessary and totalitarian.

1970: Guy T. McBride named President. ROTC made mandatory only for freshman (sophomore year optional). Student protests, backed by faculty, create incidents. Mines begins a struggle to find an identity and construct a plan for the future. Start of a period of disarray lasting to 1980. Enrollment 1,818. State population 2,209,596.

1971: Most Mines social traditions discontinued: i.e., beards restricted to seniors, wearing the senior Stetson, etc. The old Mines now essentially dead.

1973: Selective Service Draft eliminated in July.

1974: Major investigation of Mines made by AAUP (professor's union) to increase faculty power, salaries, and benefits, including tenure and "academic freedom."

1975: US pulls out of Vietnam. Colorado Legislature finally eliminates the offset of private gifts to Mines by reducing state appropriations. Mines launches a multi-year funding campaign.

1980: Enrollment 3,039. Brown Hall (Mining Department) built on site of former ATO house. Last fraternity to be evicted from former close-in sites. Long period of haphazard administration begins to ameliorate. Legislature gives trustees more flexibility. State population 2,889,964.

1982: Enrollments peak temporarily at 3,242.

1983: Enrollments start to decline – recovery takes until 1996. Tensions rise among faculty without tenure, administrative employee numbers increase continually.

1984: George S. Ansell named President. Mines continues to flounder.

1988: Faculty tenure recognized, faculty senate created, power of faculty rises enormously. AAUP seeks to take control of Mines through threats and intimation.

1989: Faculty no-confidence vote taken on administration leadership: Results 111-no confidence, 30-confidence, 22-abstained, 126-did not vote. Ansell continues as President.

1990: Enrollment 2,370. State population 3,294,394, Denver metropolitan area 1,622,980.

1991: Mines ROTC detachment deactivated.

1992: Mines removed from AAUP censure list.

1996: Enrollments reach level of 1982. Administration tout's vindication of growth strategies.

1998: Theodore Bickart named President.

2000: Enrollment 3,115. Parking on campus becomes major problem. Bicycles become popular on campus.

2001: John U. Trefny named President, introduces new age initiatives such as the Center for Technology and Learning Media.

2002: Banning Report still finds major problems at Mines due to being insufficiently progressive.

2006: Myles W. Scoggins becomes President.

2007: Student Recreation Center opens, largest building on campus.

2010: Enrollment 4,843. Major efforts made to attract women & minorities.

2013: West Rail Line opens providing light rail from Denver to the Jefferson County Government Complex.

2015: President Scoggins involves Mines in a ridiculous suit over an athletic locker name plate containing the word "Lord" as violating the first amendment. Paul C. Johnson named President. Enrollment 5,809. Meyer Hall razed. On-campus parking becomes massive problem. Number of student organizations exceeds 70.

2016: CoorsTek Research Center construction begins on former site of Meyer Hall.

Sigma Phi Epsilon Fraternity House (c. 1960)

Appendix F – The SSDC Reunion

As this work may be excessively serious, perhaps an offset is required. The following is the record of the reunion of the SSDC in 2011, the correspondence leading up to that august event, and the correspondence afterwards. In a large sense, this is the true Mines of old.

The SSDC managed with negligible effort to organize itself for its 50th reunion. The initial effort came from Jack, the Keeper of the Kitty. He announced that the Kitty possessed the grand sum of $5.49 and could buy the first round. Responses poured in, and most of the SSDC members promised their attendance. Oh, did I leave something out? Oh, yeah, the crafty Jack promised free beer to everyone attending.

But the SSDC possessed other crafty members, Dave knew that Jack had become really, really successful with his own hydrology company, and had made a fortune using slave labor. Having been a Mines student in Geological Engineering, Jack, of course, knew all about slave labor. Dave had heard that Jack, who was also something of a financial wizard, had used his normal nefarious contacts, invested the Kitty, and earned a vigorish of 3% per month. Quickly putting his slide rule to use, Dave calculated that the Kitty amounted to $944,635,026.21. Obviously if Jack held out, water-boarding would be necessary.

Other very, very successful SSDC members who knew their multiplication tables and how to make change, quickly pointed out that Jack would have earned 5% per week on the Kitty given his normal astuteness, and Dave recalculated. The Kitty was suddenly worth more than the Clinton Foundation, at 6.7 gazillion dollars. Even if Jack only did half that good, he could still retire the national debt.

Jack immediately pulled out the mendacity manual he had acquired from CBS News, and miss-directed the conversation. He pointed out that the members should not confuse him with the President of Stanford University, his bookstore manager, and many others in the 1990s who managed to divert millions of dollars of public money to various purposes, including their own lifestyles. Nor was he a politician like Nancy Pelosi or Dianne Feinstein, both of whom were reputed to be worth north of $300 million and had spent their entire lives as "public servants." But Jack did agree to consider starting a building program to replace the Golden Nugget.

Caving in like a Republican in Congress, Jack then sent out the following email:

"*Greetings, Serious Ex-seniors:*

The clock is ticking down to our reunion. There are a few business matters that I need to inform you of, regarding official SSDC activities. First of all, the records of this organization are in shambles (not surprisingly, since we never had a recorder, secretary, president, vice-president, sergeant at arms, social chairman, etc.). Therefore, because this meeting involves dispensing of free gratuities, it is imperative that we grant such gratuities to officially certifiable members only. Otherwise we (I) are/am subject to potential penalties under various state and federal tax and financial disclosure laws. As the only officer in this institution, it is my fiduciary responsibility to assure that any persons who plan to partake of official social activities planned in the name of the SSDC be required to verify their status as confirmed members of the original, true, and only Serious Seniors Drinking Club of the Colorado School of Mines, during the years 1960-1961. The original membership can be verified by any of the following: provide a notarized copy of the official photograph of the Club (as printed in the 1961 Prospector), signed over the face of the member; present an official certified membership card from the original club (no such cards were issued, so any such card presented will be viewed with great suspicion); provide three notarized affidavits from certified members testifying that you were, indeed, a true member.

In addition, it is necessary for me to require that some routine recertification criteria be implemented in order to maintain the standards of membership in this noble organization. This can be accomplished during one of our business meetings Thursday evening or Friday lunch, or other designated time. The agenda of the meeting(s) will include the following:

- *Minutes of the last meeting*
- *Financial report*
- *Election of officers*
- *Date of next meeting*
- *Recertification of members*

The recertification of members will involve one or more of the following tests:

- *Recognizing that many of the members have needed to greatly alter their imbibition practices in order to preserve their lives, families, careers, and/or sanity, there will no longer be any requirements for chugging a pitcher of 75-cent beer at the Golden Nugget Saloon (or replacement institution).*
- *In lieu of this, there will be a test of basic educational acuity. This test will include one or more of the following:*

1. Demonstration of disassembly and reassembly of an M1 Garand rifle

2. *Speed test on solving 5 trig problems with a slide rule*

3. *One problem involving the use of four different parts of the Great Steam Table*

4. *Correctly determining your location on this earth using a transit and north-start positioning siting*

5. *Extending and throwing a 100-ft steel chain in 30 seconds.*

6. *Provide an original copy of any Picker magazine.*

If you expect to qualify and remain as an esteemed member of this notorious and disreputable organization, come prepared to meet these requirements.

I apologize for being like Sergeant Foley, but, as the only officer of the organization, I must protect my rear against this litigious society.

Looking forward to seeing you all, Blessings,

Jack, Keep of the Kitty

The responses were predictable. Dick wrote back:

"Dear Jack,

You are to be commended for your zeal in service to the SSDC. Your attention to detail and your determination to protect the dignity of the SSDC indeed shows your devotion to maintaining the high standards of our beloved organization.

However, there are a few things that you may not have considered.

In the first place, you have deleted in your agenda any discussion of the recommendations of the Building Committee. This item was also neglected at our 40th reunion. And so, we still lack any elegant facility in which to meet.

Secondly, perhaps we should not repeal the beer chugging requirement for membership. The test can be changed to fit our member's present circumstances and conditions. Instead of "chugging a seventy-five cent pitcher of beer" the requirement would be changed to "chug seventy five cents worth of beer (and/or diet cola or warm milk)".

Thirdly, there are major problems for me with the suggested re-certification questions. Things that bother me are as follows:

A.   An M1 Garand rifle may be difficult to obtain. And in the climate of political correctness in which we live, do we want to give the impression we do not support peaceful methods of conflict resolution.

B.   It will be difficult for me to practice slide rule trig problems because my slide rule is lying in pieces on a table in the garage and can't be fixed. Besides, the Calculator function on the PC gives me better answers more quickly.

C.   My steam tables got lost when I came to California. Besides, even though I have worked on more bridges than I can remember in my professional career, I have never worked on a bridge with a boiler. *Instead, if I ever need to solve a steam table problem, I can call my youngest son who has a degree in mechanical engineering and he will give me the answer.*

D.   A transit will be hard to locate. My boss has one he keeps as a souvenir but he would never lend it out. In the late 70's and early 80's transits were universally replaced with electronic surveying equipment. The easiest way to find out where you are on earth is to use Google Earth so maybe that could be a substitute requirement. If you need to know within a few millimeters, use GPS technology.

E.   Throwing a steel chain is something I think I can still do so I won't complain about this requirement.

F.   My Picker Magazines were confiscated by either my mother or my wife as unsuitable reading material so producing one would be impossible for me.

Keep up the good work, Jack. Respectfully yours, Dick"

That epistle earned the following reply:

"Dick:

For once you had a noteworthy suggestion. I like your idea of chugging 75 cents worth of beer (or alternative beverage) as one of the recertification requirements. However, I have serious issues with some of your other hair-brained ideas:

A.   M1s are easy to get hold of. Just come to Arizona and you can buy any kind of gun you want with no questions asked and no permits. (This is where the Mexican drug and people smuggling cartels are getting their guns to wage war on one another.)

B.   Having a dysfunctional slide rule is no excuse. In fact, failing to maintain your slide rule in good working order is grounds for expulsion from the SSDC. I will have to refer this matter over to the Disciplinary Committee.

C.   Losing your steam tables constitutes another serious potentially expulsionary (is that a word?) failure to live up to the standards of SSDC membership. How could you ever design a steam-operated draw bridge without steam tables?

D.   You call yourself a civil engineer and you don't even own a transit? That's worse than a geologist without a Brunton compass.

E.   Since you are still able to throw a steel chain, I am assigning you the task of running a short workshop on that subject, so that other members can be requalified in that skill.

F.   Failure to secure your old Picker magazines — another punishable offense. You can probably find used copies on Amazon.com or EBay. I'm afraid the Disciplinary Committee is going to take a very dim view of your status.

Regarding the Building Committee, I think you were appointed chair-

man at the 40*ᵗʰ* reunion, so we will expect a report which presents your
recommendations for a suitably elegant edifice for future meetings. We
will also need a financial plan describing how the facility will be financed.
Cheers, Jack"

And more from another Dick:

"Folks,
- Lacking an M-1 to field strip we could require candidates to describe the pain of M-1 thumb and how that pain arose.
- For Miners in the Corps of Engineers during the Cuban Missile
Crisis a suitable test question could be how the ADM was armed
after installing the getaway timers.
- – then again let's not dwell on the cold war madness that thrust
an atom bomb into the hands of a 22-year-old shave-tail.
- A working real metal Brunton compass manufactured in Wyoming or a book of 9-place logarithms should sufficient to allow candidates to bypass the onerous SSDEIT (Senior Serious Drinking
Engineer in Training) exam and let the candidate move directly to
the chugging challenge (75 cents of beer at today's price is probably
50 ml or so.)
- If transits are hard to come by, Plane Tables must appear only on
such programs as the Antiques Road Show. Then again this implies
that we are rapidly getting to the point that SSDC-ers might qualify
as antiques. . .
- I think I can lend Dick a working Log-log-duplex K&E slide rule.
I lovingly protected mine to maintain my Geek status.
Dick"

And then there was Carl:

"Wait a minute. I thought we took care of all this at our last meeting in Georgetown. Certainly, the High Pu-bah of the SSDC, Dominick
Perrigo, can certify to all this from his presence at that occasion as a ba-
boon wearing (MY) senior hat. Being a former semi-civil servant, I can
understand the need for the bureaucratic trappings of any organization
(is that the correct word) but I'm too old for that crap.
As to the "recertification criteria" the following comments:
- As I recall the Nugget died before we graduated so all that is a
moot point.
- I don't know much about M-1 rifles because when I graduated I
was ushered into the U.S. Army Chemical Corps (Motto: Up your
ass with bugs and gas). Spending two fun filled years as a training
officer with that branch was, to say the least, unique, but we didn't
play with rifles. My weapon of choice is the M(whatever) Flame
Thrower. I challenge anybody at 20 meters.
- As others have related, it's sad to report that when I finally retired
and cleaned out my desk I found this crusty green leather thing in

the bottom of a drawer that turned out to be the mummified case of my K&E log, log whatever, and it was still in there! However, when attempts were made to extract it the whole works disintegrated. But I could still smell the cherry wood.

• Steam tables? Isn't that being they serve bad food in the Army?

• Believe it or not, I actually have an optical contractors' transit that somebody threw away because they didn't know how to us it. I occasionally amaze people by setting it up and leveling the beast. I use it to check my GPS.

• Item No. 5 is so easy it's not even a challenge. The challenge is to find a 100 ft steel tape. (Editor's Note: Uh, I think the length was 66 feet or 22 yards, or 100 links, or 4 rods. There are 10 chains in a furlong, and 80 chains in one statute mile. An acre is the area of 10 square chains.)

• Unfortunately, my Pickers were underneath the slide rule and are therefore history.

As a former PRE graduate who never refined any petroleum (and I'm not the only one) I look forward to all the tales and adventures of the members.

One last thought given this era of financial promiscuity, has there ever been an audit of the Kitty?

See you all soon, Carl"

The glorious reunion took place on schedule, and with all the wives attending to see just what sort of low-life their husbands caroused with, the number of bodies in the room was twice what was expected. Somehow the SSDCers' time at Mines took on new dimensions, and the good times were remembered (probably because they were so few) and the bad ones forgotten. Several celebrants offered to buy the block of Golden real estate where the luncheon was held, but one had just plunked down a couple of mil to help the college along, and the others didn't have enough cash in their billfolds. They probably weren't serious anyway, having just finished chugging their free beers.

No sooner were all the SSDC members back in their respective states that unfinished business arose:

"Jack:
It was truly great to see you and everybody else at the reunion.
However, I am hurt and disappointed that I was not allowed to give the oral report from the SSDC Building Committee that I had prepared. So I have put it in writing for consideration by all the members.
Dick"

For posterity and posteriors, Dick included the Building Committee's report:

REPORT OF THE SSDC BUILDING COMMITTEE
50TH REUNION MEETING CYCLE

June 5, 2011

INTRODUCTION

For several decades the only member of the SSDC Building Committee has dreamed of a facility that would serve as a meeting place, library and museum. This grand edifice would preserve for all times the memory of our august group and their accomplishments. Now is the proper time to bring all these dreams to fruition. Now is the time to preserve our legacy forever. Now is the time to construct a bar where we can truly enjoy the beverages of our choice.

THEME

A truly distinct architectural achievement must be centered on a significant, poignant and riveting theme. The School of Mines had an unofficial but engaging motto when we graduated. That motto was, "Don't let the dirty bastards grind you down."
Now, after more than fifty years, we can see we were not ground down. Even though, some of us must admit, we are a bit smoother than when we started. And so, the theme for our monument edifice will be: **We didn't let the dirty bastards grind us down.**

SITE LOCATION

The site of the proposed SSDC facility should be on a reclaimed mining parcel as near as possible to the Colorado School of Mines campus. This would be highest and best use of an area where argillaceous materials have been extracted in the past for the purpose of processing them for refractory and ceramic usages. Such a site would reinforce the memories of historical ties between Coors and Mines.
There are numerous places near the Mines campus where Coors extracted raw material for its refractory and ceramic products. And later some of these sites were acquired by the college for building locations as is the case in the area west of Bradford Hall. And, of course, many of us fondly remember those golden moments in the "clay pits" when someone would tap a keg of Coors for the rest of us to imbibe.

THE BUILDING STRUCTURE

The structure should make a rugged statement of our theme in simple but bold lines. It should project great inner strength and the resolve to resist the fierce elements of nature. It should reflect the influence the mineral industry has had in the lives of each of us. Obviously, it must be constructed of reinforced concrete.

Because so much tradition at our college is centered on mining, it is only fitting that much of our building be placed below ground level. And since mine shafts are cylindrical, it is only proper that the main part of our structure be cylindrical. Additional structural details will be developed as additional design work is done.

INTERIOR FEATURES

The central feature of the SSDC facility interior will be the bar. It will be large and easily accessible from the seating and table areas. Proper lighting will be important as well as adequate beverage refrigeration. Comfortable seating will be provided throughout. All other features will be detailed in later design phases.

LANDSCAPING

Landscaping shall consist entirely of native Colorado plants and shrubs. These plants are adapted to the climate and environmentally in tune with the local ambiance. We can let the area be seeded by local seeds blowing in the wind that germinate and take root. Irrigation will utilize natural precipitation. Maintenance cost for landscaping of this type will be minimal.

CONCLUSION

The next step in our planning process is for all of the SSDC members to read and consider the project that has been proposed. Your comment and input are essential before starting the initial design phase for the facility.

The long-suffering Jack took Dick's communication to heart and wrote to everyone:

"Dear Distinguished Members (not sure who, if any qualify):
We owe a vote of thanks to Dick and the Building Committee for the effort they have gone to in putting together a visionary plan for a permanent headquarters home for the SSDC, suitable for the ambiance and subtle elegance needs for our gatherings. Although I agree that the Committee captured some of the vision we collectively should have in mind, I believe the plans miss the mark in several ways.

Firstly, I agree with the general theme and motto. The fact that we are still here is strong evidence supporting the motto, 'We have not let the dirty bastards grind us down.'

Although the suggestion of placing the facility in the clay pits would be in keeping with our grubby history, unfortunately all the near-campus clay pits have been filled-in to expand available campus real estate. However, I have an alternative suggestion worthy of consideration that will capture the underground mining aspect even better, I believe. Part of the filled-in clay pit area provided the land for the CSM sorority houses. They probably used an SSDC engineering geologist for the pit filling and foundation engineering for the sorority houses because they are now sinking un-uniformly as the thick fill compacts and settles. I suggest we drive a shaft down into the pit-fill some distance away from the sorority houses, tunnel under one of the houses and excavate a sufficiently sized facility for our meeting room (bar), museum, archives, and hall of infamy directly beneath the sorority house. No one would think to look for us under a bunch of sorority girls, not even the revenuers from the federal government!

As for the actual appearance and design of the facility, I think there is only one way to go, if we are to honor our origin and tradition. We should engage a Hollywood set designer to recreate an exact partial replica of the Golden Nugget Saloon. The facade and entry can be duplicated using the photo in the 1961 Prospector. The interior need not contain the entire bar and tables etc. We used only the front large booth, so we could suffice with a re-creation of that booth (based on the SSDC photo in the 1961 Prospector). For ambiance and beer taps, we should also include perhaps a 6-ft segment of the bar with a couple of bar stools and a mirror on the wall behind. Of course, some antique Coors neon signs would need to be added.

As for landscaping, nothing will grow underground very well, so I suggest cheap plastic imitation plants like the British-owned Holiday Inns have everywhere.

Now for the real challenge: We need a Capital Campaign! The SSDC kitty could seed the campaign with $10.71. However, we will have to rely on some of our more successful members (and, as we all know, we have a few that are very successful) for the major funding of this ambitious project. Some possible supplementary funding sources also come to mind. For example, we could produce a revival Picker edition and sell it for exorbitant prices world-wide through the internet and social media.

Send your contributions in care of SSDC Building Fund Kitty, to my address (below). Also send any additional constructive suggestions you might have.

Finally, my apologies to Dick and the Building Committee for not making time for you on our agenda in Golden. The agenda was so full of

much more important business that we just couldn't find time for your report and presentation. Besides that, when I raised the question, no one was interested in hearing about it. In the meantime, between now and our next meeting in April 2016, you can begin drawing up preliminary architectural engineering plans for the facility.
Cheers to all! Jack, Keeper of the Kitty"

Pat was the first to offer his opinion:

"What a grand idea...a shrine commemorating our educational experience! I suggest that we approach Anthony Wiener as our icon and agent to sell the new "Picker" you propose as a way to fund our new headquarters. He would surely go for the underground, under coeds deal. But, Nancy Pelosi would probably steal the money and refuse to give us the requisite environmental permits. She is, I read, now involved with Al Gore in a program to cover volcanoes with cheese cloth to filter out harmful particulates and is, as always, on the warpath against plutocrats like SSDC members and rich people with indoor plumbing."

Poor us! We're stuck here in Dallas in our tiny, hot mobile home eating at the Golden Corral when the welfare check comes. But I can still have fun shooting beer cans off my collection of pink-cement birds like them what stand on one leg at Disney World.
Regards, Pat"

Jack responded:

"Great to hear from you. I'd love to come and shoot beer cans off your pink one-legged birds sometime. I recently got to shoot a diamondback off my front door entrance (although I thought about leaving him there to greet some of our Nazi Sheriff's Gestapo who take great pleasure in intruding into our private lives.) Hey, you get to eat at the Golden Corral? We're stuck with eating with our three dogs (their food costs more than Golden Corral). The local food bank is a great source for us — nothing like canned tuna and instant mac and cheese. Couldn't we have a great time with Wiener and many others on both sides with a special Picker addition? We couldn't ask for a better name than Wiener, could we?
Cheers, Jack"

A Dick (not the one who produced the report) had a better idea:

"Dick, I was pondering your specifications for the SSDC gathering spot as I drove through southern Wyoming on my way to the Chugwater Chili cook-off. There are several abandoned Titan Missile silos in that area and it struck me that many of your specifications are met in those abandoned missile silos. If I recall, there are several in Colorado. Maybe

we could pick one up and modify it. Given the tie with us graduating just in time to face the Cuban Missile Crisis it may bring back memories (editor's note: uh, the missile crisis was the following year – the Berlin Wall went up in August 1961).

On the other hand, some memories don't warrant being restored . . ."
Best, Dick

The other Dick responded to this challenge of his authority with:

"Dick, thank you for your insightful suggestion that we utilize a Titan Missile silo as a framework structure that could be remodeled into our new spectacular SSDC clubroom and international headquarters. If we can find a vacant Titan site within ten miles of Golden that can be purchased for the amount budgeted for land acquisition, we should surely investigate buying it.

My initial design ideas have centered on utilizing concepts developed when I designed and had built a major wastewater pump station for the City of Parlier, California. Because almost all the wastewater in the city passes through this pump plant before traveling the final mile and a half to the sewage plant, the structure is reasonably large. Because it is in a residential area, the structure is totally underground except for electrical panels, a stationary crane to pull pumps and a vent stack of sufficient height to prevent odors from settling in the neighbor's back yard. Because the influent lines are 22 feet below grade, the pump station wet well is thirty-five feet deep. Underground storage space for sewage is connected to the wet well so that the pumps can cycle off and on. The facility also features an attractive underground valve pit. It seems to me that the project plans from the Parlier project could be tweaked in a major way to serve our purpose.

Jack has proposed building our new facility under one of the CSM sorority houses. In my opinion, my design concepts could be utilized in such a structure as long as the main shaft (wet well) is located in the front yard of the sorority house.

Always Working in the Best Interests of the SSDC, Dick"

Somehow, all this had gotten confused with the proverbial "ten-foot shaft to Hell." The millionaires in the group (which meant probably everyone) were not impressed with meeting in an abandoned Titan silo, and also felt that digging in a sorority house's front yard was beneath their dignity (besides, their wives were opposed.) Blowing a hole in a sorority house's front yard was more appropriate, but the wives were still opposed. The project was tabled until the next reunion.

Where that will take place, with the SSDC members going the way of all Mines graduates, no matter how talented, is anyone's guess.

So Mote It Be

Appendix G - The Purpose of College & Its Cost

Many students and their parents are finding out after college that their education is worth little in the marketplace, and the repayment of five and six-digit educational loans becomes problematic. By 2016, 40% of students with outstanding loan balances did not earn enough to make a single payment during the year to lower the outstanding balance.

College educators say that is the fault of the system, not the universities, their administrations or faculties. They claim that college educations are not designed to turn out productive and skilled graduates, able to contribute to society. According to a Gallup Poll reported on March 10, 2017, college presidents saw the goal of colleges as making progressive-educated citizens out of students, teaching them to understand and accept new points of view, and making liberal education a perpetual process in their lives. In short, the goal was to make happy and well-adjusted citizens, steeped in literature, fine arts, and other "quality of life" factors. Many college presidents actually favored moving engineering out of university curricula as being excessively career-related. Preparing a person for gainful employment or a life-time career was not considered appropriate by such "educators." This was the belief of President Vanderwilt and most, if not all, of his successors at Mines.

On the other hand, college presidents have shown a marked disinclination to report graduate competence statistics and salary and employment information. 71% even want the College Scorecard reporting system eliminated because it may be harmful to low-performing colleges. Since World War II, one of the existential beliefs inherent in progressive education was that judgmental structures were to be eliminated. Students were to be supported and rewarded rather than punished. Trophies were given for participation rather than for winning, and if students and graduates were not to be judged and scored, the institutions generating those graduates were also exempt from society's judgement and criticism, even if that society was paying the lion's share of the cost in producing those graduates. Instead, "retention rates" were touted, even at Mines, and GPAs rocketed to averages of 3.0 and even 3.5 in some schools and departments.

It is the belief of the authors that colleges should be graded on the results of degree-specific proficiency examinations to the College Scorecard, a metric that can be used to determine eligibility for federal funding. After all, it is a college's role to educate and inform, not con people into supporting institutions that merely warehouse students from age 18 to 26.

The burgeoning costs of a college education attracted political attention in the 21st century as citizen debts for educational loans grew enormously. Young people demanded that the government alleviate the debts, and that it should even provide free education through four years of college, and even beyond. Blame was put on administrator and faculty salaries, astoundingly heavy costs in facilities for student housing and recreation, and instructional aids and equipment. Behind the push for new equipment lay the ever-present requirements for such equipment to perform research and help obtain government research grants.

Perhaps the most revealing defense of the educational system and its blamelessness in increasing costs was made by Terry W. Hartle, Senior Vice President of the American Council on Education (ACE) before the Committee on Ways and Means, Subcommittee on Oversight of the U.S. House of Representatives on the Rising Costs of Higher Education and Tax Policy, October 7, 2015. ACE was a Washington, DC, lobbyist organization representing over 1,700 colleges and universities.

In his testimony, Mr. Hartle claimed that the published numbers of the cost of a college education were highly inflated as only about a fourth of college students paid the full, published tuition and fees price, the remainder receiving some type of cost abatement, scholarships, federal or state grants, or other financial assistance. He chose not to discuss how that situation reflected the government's chosen ethnic, racial, and other classifications of students enjoying lower education costs than were available to non-special Americans. Obviously, the system was highly unfair and detrimental to middle-class Americans.

According to Mr. Hartle, about forty percent of students who graduated in 2012-13 had taken out student loans, borrowing an average of $27,300. Although he gave no statistics from the 20th century, by comparison, there were essentially **NO** students loans available from banks or government entities in the 1950s. Clearly, the ability of parents to foot the cost of a college education had disappeared between 1960 and 2010, even with only twenty-five percent the students in 2010 paying full price.

Showing great ingenuity in miss-directing the subcommittee, Mr. Hartle then blamed the rising costs of a college education on four factors, none of which were administration or faculty salaries.

1) A decline in state funding. To prove his point, Mr. Hartle presented data indicating that state funding sometimes declined on a per-FTE (Full Time Equivalent) basis after factoring out the rate of inflation.

(A digression: The reader is right to be skeptical of the federal government's published inflation rates, as the components change under political pressure, and even series like the cost of food and fuel have sometimes been omitted. To a large degree, the inflation rate, like the unemployment rate, is what America's political leaders want it to be. One of the authors was involved with the National Center for Statistical Analysis in 1978 and was given the mission to prove with statistics that "55 Saved Lives." The national speed limit did no such thing, but it was easy to prove it did by merely making certain invalid assumptions and adjusting the statistics accordingly.)

There is simply no way to hide the fact that at Mines tuition and fees multiplied from $840.00 per year for non-resident students in 1960 to $36,172 in 2016. That is an increase of over 43 times, reflecting the fact that college tuitions are one of the leaders in the U.S.'s rate of inflation. It is difficult to spin that away, but Mr. Hartle attempted the impossible by blaming the states because their funding has not kept up with the rate of inflation, whatever that was. (And the components of the inflation rate frequently change.)

Even more astounding was that Mines had lowered the amount of teaching during this period from around 200 semester hours to about 140, or a 30% decrease in instruction, literally all of the decrease coming in engineering and science. Therefore, on a per hour basis, the increase in tuition alone (not counting fees) went from nearly $17 per hour in 1960 to $972 in 2016, an increase of 57 times, or a 5,600% increase. One has to search long and hard to find another segment of the US economy that has risen so sharply in cost. Is the Mines education in 2016 fifty-seven times more valuable than in 1960? With the loss in engineering and technical courses, one could argue that it is actually less valuable than in 1960.

2) Increases in labor costs. Mr. Hartle danced around the enormous increases in costs in faculty and administrator salaries and benefits, saying it was unfair to quote million-dollar salaries of some head football coaches and college presidents, as they were not representative of most coaches and presidents. Maybe not, but they were there.

Faculty salaries at Mines are difficult for an outsider to obtain for some periods — especially including all sources, summer school, research, etc. —, but apparently, they went up by a factor of almost 20 from 1960 to 2016, or about half of the tuition increase. Much of the tuition increase can be explained by the supposed need for more faculty (teaching lighter loads) and other services to all of the Mines community members, students, faculty, and administration. Administrative positions have burgeoned, and salaries are set to be competitive (or better) than in private industry.

Mr. Hartle stated that faculty salaries had to be set to meet competition from industry, although in the majority of universities, there was little call for most of their faculty in private employment. And he neglected to consider the special benefits in faculty employment, such as tenure and the use of university facilities, that made faculty positions so desirable. But beyond the costs of faculty salaries, no comment was made concerning the work load on faculty which had declined dramatically and necessitated additional hiring. If faculty are reduced to teaching no more than two courses per semester in the future, which is likely, costs will take another giant leap upwards.

3) Increases in technology and equipment costs. Mr. Hartle cited extraordinary costs in equipment that, to him, were vital for undergraduate teaching. He mentioned two pieces of such equipment, an electron microscope and a DNA sequencer. He also opined that, "No college or university equipped with scientific and technological resources from 2005 can meet the needs of students in 2015, let alone 2025." All this was so much hype. The vast majority of instructional departments need students studying, not playing with the latest and greatest personal computer, tablet or cell phone.

Note the following table:

Baccalaureate Degrees issued in the U.S. in 2014-2015 by Resource Requirements

Very High Resource Demand:

Biological and biomedical sciences	109,896
Engineering	97,858 (5.2%)
Nursing & health technologies	108,114
Physical sciences	30,038
Total	345,906 (18.3%)

High Resource Demand:

Agriculture and natural resources	36,277
Family and home economics	24,584
Trade & technician technologies	17,238
Visual and performing arts	95,832
Total	173,931 (9.2%)

Medium Resource Demand:

Architecture	9,090
Communication technologies	47,893
Computer and information sciences	59,581
Homeland security, law enforcement, and firefighting	62,723
Parks, recreation, athletics, leisure, and fitness	49,006
Total	228,293 (12.0%)

Low Resource Demand:

Health service administration & services	108,114
Education	91,623
Miscellaneous	423
Total	200,160 (10.6%)

Very Low Resource Demand:

Area, ethnic, gender, and group studies	7,782
Business	368,510
Journalism	47,892
English language and literature	45,847
Foreign languages, literatures, and linguistics	19,493
Legal studies	4,420
Liberal arts, general studies, and humanities	43,647
Mathematics and statistics	21,853
Multi/interdisciplinary studies	47,556
Philosophy, theology, and religion	20,780
Psychology	117,557
Public administration and social services	34,363
Social sciences and history	166,944

Total   946,644 (50.0%)
Grand Total   1,894,934

SOURCE: U.S. Department of Education, National Center for Education Statistics, Integrated Postsecondary Education Data System (IPEDS), "Completions Survey" Fall 2000 through Fall 2015. (Prepared September 2016.)

Mines is in the "Very High Resource Demand" classification, but over 60% of the degrees granted required virtually nothing or very little in the way of equipment or even computerization in the classroom. There was no need for lectures to be podcast into classrooms, interactive whiteboards, virtual classrooms, mobile apps, and other special equipment, or even for a professor to be IT-savvy.

4) And finally, there is the excuse of excessive government regulations. According to Hartle, at one college the federal regulations represented about 7% of the college's operating budget. That sounds extraordinarily high, as such costs impact a school when a regulation's compliance is initiated, but then become relatively fixed at a low level rather than staying high or increasing every year. But does such a small component justify tuition increases that from 1961 to 2017 have increased more than 4,000%?

In 2016, CSM broke out its operating revenues and expenses as follows:

Revenues:

Tuition and Fees	53.5%
Grants and Contracts	27.8%
Services and Auxiliary Enterprises	18.7%

Expenses (omitting depreciation):

Teaching	34.2%
Academic Support	9.2%
Admin Salaries & Expenses	10.0%
Services & Auxiliary Enterprises	14.9%
Physical Plant Ops & Maintenance	10.2%
Research & Other	21.5%

As can be seen from the above table, Teaching, Academic Support, and Administrative Salaries and Expenses constitute 53.4% of the school's expenses, and it is in these areas that the greatest cost controls have to be taken. There is also a ticking time bomb here, and that is pensions and benefits. Colorado provides wonderful pensions to its retired educational employees, and by law must contribute an amount each year equal to employee contributions into the appropriate trust fund. Whether or not the trust fund generates sufficient funds to pay out retirement benefits, the State, by law, must pay out the benefit as contracted. This is truly outstanding security, paid for by the taxes of people who cannot afford to put money aside for their own retirement. That system effectively renders such people to serfdom, working for those in the governing class. It might even be appropriate if the universities as a whole produced well-educated graduates, trained to be immediately productive in the private sector, but alas, such is not the case.

Not surprisingly, Mr. Hartle had no suggestions concerning solutions other than for colleges to find creative ways to lower costs. There was not a smidgen of awareness shown that the colleges were failing to generate products that might be worth the expense, or even that colleges had the responsibility to produce graduates that could actually perform well in the private sector of the economy.

The American educational system is deeply flawed, given its failure to generate graduates, at any level, who can find fault with the sentence: "Him had done gone to Walmart, you know what I'm saying, while her sleeps." Nor can the products of the American educational system make change in a retail environment without a computer, comment on who wrote the 1st Amendment to the Constitution (it was Roger Sherman of Connecticut), read proficiently (one-third of all college graduates now complete their education without taking a single course that requires reading more than 40 pages of a textbook), state what country the United States fought in the War of 1812 (or even the Revolutionary War), and name two metals that together make brass. In short, ignorance of all things except pop culture is now standard and is deepening.

No complaint can be made of the service academies, as they produce graduates that immediately perform valiantly to keep the citizens of the United States safe from harm, both internally and externally. Mines formerly produced graduates who were immediately productive in providing engineering and other services to the citizens. Today, what amount of "bang for the buck" that universities provide the taxpayers and private benefactors is problematical in the extreme, and the best that can be said is that they produce graduates who can qualify for further training in graduate school.

Hopefully, masters and PhD degrees will produce individuals able to contribute to America's general economy, but in large measure, such individuals become employed in the educational establishment, looping back within a framework disassociated from real life in the private sector, and exacerbating the situation. There will be an end to this treadmill to oblivion, and it will not be pretty.

APPENDIX H - ENROLLMENT AT MINES

Year	UG Enroll	UG Degs	GR Enroll	MS Degs	DSc/PhD Degs
1876	26				
1877	NF				
1878	22				
1879	30				
1880	61				
1881	94				
1882	76				
1883	49	2			
1884	50				
1885	51	1			
1886	49	2			
1887	50				
1888	38	4			
1889	50	3			
1890	65	1			
1891	106	2			
1892	111	9			
1893	128	6			
1894	128	6			
1895	133	23			
1896	158	14			
1897	184	23			
1898	184	24			
1899	220	20			
1900	236	27			
1901	247	36			
1902	216	25			
1903	250	30			
1904	304	29			
1905	257	49			
1906	298	41			
1907	359	35			
1908	380	50			
1909	370	38			
1910	342	45			
1911	266	34			
1912	248	53			
1913	211	69	NF		1
1914	199	57	NF		2
1915	181	39	NF		
1916	217	28	NF		
1917	164	29	NF		

Year	UG Enroll	UG Degs	GR Enroll	MS Degs	DSc/PhD Degs
1918	275	13	NF		
1919	432	13	NF		
1920	471	41	NF		
1921	478	64	NF	1	
1922	553	78	NF	5	2
1923	493	110	NF	6	1
1924	503	72	20	1	1
1925	438	75	NF	1	
1926	420	68	NF	2	
1927	392	64	NF	1	
1928	423	53	NF	2	1
1929	463	67	16	4	
1930	544	66	NF	1	3
1931	601	68	NF	5	1
1932	529	90	29	7	3
1933	491	79	20	6	3
1934	548	75	NF	8	3
1935	603	88	16	3	
1936	631	101	NF	3	
1937	771	71	NF	4	
1938	828	101	NF	3	1
1939	813	127	NF	6	
1940	840	142	NF	4	3
1941	787	156	NF	3	2
1942	673	153	NF	6	
1943	277	173	NF	7	
1944	170	52	NF		
1945	613	25	NF	1	1
1946	1,027	15	NF	3	
1947	1,022	106	NF	10	
1948	1,285	177	NF	23	1
1949	1,200	268	NF	24	1
1950	1,075	277	NF	29	1
1951	905	225	96	42	11
1952	990	231	NF	15	10
1953	948	193	NF	16	7
1954	946	183	63	11	8
1955	1,016	122	48	11	2
1956	1,074	146	88	13	4
1957	1,043	161	84	16	1
1958	1,010	177	82	15	4
1959	980	182	100	20	1
1960	959	149	117	12	1

Year	UG Enroll	UG Degs	GR Enroll	MS Degs	DSc/PhD Degs
1961	943	176	103	15	8
1962	1,271	140	104	26	3
1963	1,309	147	124	28	7
1964	1,395	193	140	33	8
1965	1,635	174	115	37	9
1966	1,669	206	147	31	11
1967	1,718	180	142	39	9
1968	1,593	250	133	38	11
1969	1,655	266	157	35	11
1970	1,614	276	204	42	10
1971	1,552	277	217	55	12
1972	1,510	257	229	58	16
1973	1,555	256	281	62	17
1974	1,792	307	345	76	18
1975	2,101	350	333	93	22
1976	2,192	253	418	90	27
1977	2,322	288	442	113	26
1978	2,377	336	470	119	32
1979	2,460	490	511	126	31
1980	2,532	489	507	137	37
1981	2,645	465	508	136	40
1982	2,769	501	473	137	39
1983	2,602	559	512	127	35
1984	2,380	544	501	138	37
1985	2,240	535	519	135	41
1986	1,944	610	576	140	40
1987	1,800	440	537	155	39
1988	1,686	510	581	145	46
1989	1,747	293	584	110	43
1990	1,820	401	550	201	58
1991	1,980	261	594	134	31
1992	2,212	260	646	232	35
1993	2,371	317	636	174	44
1994	2,465	327	629	192	51
1995	2,535	353	653	173	35
1996	2,677	424	566	184	59
1997	2,624	454	586	181	54
1998	2,672	464	579	162	38
1999	2,690	449	587	187	57
2000	2,695	495	420	129	33
2001	2,784	451	431	136	48
2002	2,783	510	548	169	52
2003	2,929	521	516	198	50

Year	UG Enroll	UG Degs	GR Enroll	MS Degs	DSc/PhD Degs
2004	3,106	553	521	186	43
2005	3,335	505	523	210	51
2006	3,431	505	543	211	46
2007	3,523	590	614	238	53
2008	3,680	626	645	241	41
2009	3,909	652	767	280	46
2010	4,008	680	835	325	49
2011	4,185	656	873	310	50
2012	4,371	755	868	367	71
2013	4,481	871	834	358	97
2014	4,660	876	869	349	100
2015	4,771	635	1038	190	63

Bibliography

Books, Periodicals, and Reports:

Altman, Kathleen, *A Century of Women at Mines*, Golden, CO, 1999.

Ansell, George S., "The Ansell Years; Keynote Address," 1998.

Bancroft, Caroline. *Gulch of Gold*, Denver: 1958.

Baskin, O. L., and Company, *History of Clear Creek and Boulder Valleys*, Chicago: 1880.

_____, *History of the City of Denver*, Arapahoe County, and Colorado. Chicago: 1880.

Black, Robert C., *Railroad Pathfinder: The Life and Times of Edward L. Berthoud*, Evergreen, CO, 1988.

Braden, C. H. C. Ed., *Colorado School of Mines Magazine*, March 1930, Vol XX, No. 3, downloaded 6.20.2015 from Mines_Magv20.n3_1930.pdf.

Budd, Montgomery, "Colorado and Its School of Mines", *Mines Magazine*, June, 1949.

Chauvenet, Regis, *History of the Colorado School of Mines: Origin and Early Years*, unpublished manuscript, 1920.

Childs, Orlo E., *The President's Five-Year Report*, 1963-1968, Golden, CO,1968.

Clément-Grandcourt, Michel et Brigitte, *Edouard-Louis Berthoud, 1828–1908*, de Fleurier à Golden (Colorado), Attinger, Hauterive (NE), Switzerland, 2010.

Colorado School of Mines, *Quarterly of the Colorado School of Mines*, July, 1907, Vol. 2, No. 1 (CSM with Smith History.pdf), internet file downloaded 1/20/2016.

_____, *Quarterly of the Colorado School of Mines*, Vol XIII, No. 1, Golden, CO, 1918.

Eckley, Wilton, *Rocky Mountains to the World A History of the Colorado School of Mines*, Virginia Beach, VA, 2004.

Fisher, Vardis, and Opal Laurel Holmes, *Gold Rushes and Mining Camps of the Early American West*, Caldwell, Idaho, 1968.

Fossett, Frank, *Colorado, Denver*, 1876.

_____, *Colorado, Its Gold and Silver Mines*, New York, 1879.

Hoyt, Mary E., "A Short History of the Colorado School of Mines", 1949, reprinted in *The Mines Magazine*, Golden CO: February, 1988)

Langton, Jackson M., *All Trappers Don't Wear Fur Hats*, www.1stBooks.com, 2003.

Laubach v. Bradley, No. C-1131 572 P.2d 824 (1977) Internet file, down loaded 2015.

Lee, Mabel Barbee, *Cripple Creek Days*, New York: 1958.

McGrath, Maria Davies, *The Real Pioneers of Colorado*, Denver, 1934.

Melani, Debra, "Mines Building History" *Mines Magazine*, 2014, Vol. 104,

No 2, downloaded 5/30/2015 from http://minesmaga zine.com/9427/

Morgan, Jesse R., *A World School The Colorado School of Mines*, Denver, CO, 1955.

LeRossignol, James Edward, *History of Higher Education in Colorado*, Washington, DC, 1903.

Sacks, David O. & Peter A. Thiel, *The Diversity Myth, Multiculturalism and Political Intolerance on Campus*, Oakland, CA, 1998.

Shinn, Charles Howard, *Mining camps: A Study in American Frontier Government*, New York: 1884, 1948.

Sorgenfrei, Robert, "The Colorado School of Mines: Its Founding and Early Years, 1874-1902", *Quarterly Review of the Colorado School of Mines*, Vol. 100, No. 2.

Tonge, Thomas, "The Colorado School of Mines", *The New Zealand Mines Record*, Dec 16, 1905.

Vanderwilt, John W, *President's Annual Progress report, Colorado School of Mines*, 1957.

Waters, Frank, *Midas of the Rockies; the Story of Stratton and Cripple Creek*, New York: 1937.

Wessels, Gysbert, "In Memoriam: Robert Eugene Donald Woolsey (1936-2015)", Internet File, downloaded 2015.

Woolsey, Robert E. D., *The Woolsey Papers*, Marietta, GA, 2003.

Other Sources:
CSM Quarterly, various editions, 1910-1920.

Interviews with many alumni from 1954 to 1973. The SSDC members were: Dave Brightwell, Dick Collins, Jim Cox, Dave Dougherty, Dick Evans, Joe Gust, Doug Halbe, Bruce Henry, Chuck Hammerberg, Keith Jones, Miles Kara, Jim Keating, Coulter Kirkpatrick, Dick Palmer, Jim Partridge, Pat Phillips, Larry Preble, Pat Rice, Jack Robertson, John Rockaway, Chuck Schultz, Jim Simpson, Carl Sjoberg, Brad Vote, Bob Wright, and faculty advisor (silent) Dale Milich, and two juniors, Jerry Hanks, and Dave Summers.

Jarvis Annual Reports, 1870.
Mines Magazine, (CSM Alumni Magazine), Various editions from 1910 – current, many available on line.
Picker (CSM Student humor magazine, 1954-1961).
Prospector (CSM Student Yearbook, 1912-1961).
Office of Institutional Research, Guggenheim Hall, CSM, Golden, CO.
Oredigger (CMS Student Newspaper), various editions, 1921-1961.
Scientific Quarterly, 1892-1900.
Senior Day newspapers (various titles), Arthur Lakes Library, Golden, CO.
The Bulletin, 1900-1905.

Weimer, Robert J, "125 Years of Earth Science Programs At CSM – Lessons For The Future", CSM Senate Distinguished Lecture, December 1999.

Various publications and materials such as commencement programs, student transcripts and grade cards (used with permission), E-Day programs, and many other materials. Some were located in Arthur Lakes Library, many were obtained directly from graduates of Mines.

INDEX

About the Authors

Dave Dougherty served as a lieutenant and captain in Army Intelligence's 513th INTC Group, and was a Professor of Management, Business, and Computer Science, most recently at the University of Texas, El Paso. He holds advanced degrees from Colorado School of Mines and Case Western Reserve University and advanced to candidacy for a PhD at both Case Western Reserve and the University of Maryland. He is a Registered Professional Engineer, and an entrepreneur in computers, being a pioneer in the use of client-server processing, the promotion of the cloud and ARPANET all during the 1970s, and later became arguably the world's most prolific applications programmer. History was always Dave's prime avocation, and he built one of the nation's premier collections in silver and gold ancient and medieval coinage to bring history to life. In Arkansas and Missouri, Dave is a radio personality discussing political problems through the lens of history and a rigid constitutionalist. Dave has authored over twenty academic papers and a number of books, including *A Patriot's History Reader: Essential Documents for Every American, A Patriot's History of the Modern World, Volumes I and II, Starve The Beast!, The Gnosis Within, Landslide, Make Georgia Howl The 5th Ohio Volunteer Cavalry in Kilpatrick's Campaign and the Diary of Sgt. William H. Harding* and *On Hamburg Station*

Ralph Dougherty holds the professional degree of Metallurgical Engineer from Colorado School of Mines, where he was MVP on the Swimming Team, Editor of the yearbook, and served two terms as President of Alpha Tau Omega fraternity. He is a graduate of Duquesne University Law School, where he was elected to Phi Alpha Delta. In addition to being a US Army veteran, he has been a Patent Attorney for over 45 years, with U.S. Steel, Midrex Corporation, Korf Industries, and his own law firm. He currently is serving his 32nd year on the Board of Directors of the local Chapter of American Society for Metals, and is President of Parkview Community Foundation, an after-school program for at-risk children in northwest Charlotte. Ralph served two terms as International Vice President of Optimist International. He has also served 15 years as Treasurer of the US Bar / Japan Patent Office Liaison Council in Washington and Tokyo, and was on the Board of Directors of the United Methodist Foundation of Western Pennsylvania in Pittsburgh. In 2018, Ralph Dougherty was honored by the Metrolina Business Council with the presentation of the Donald Haack Community Service Award in recognition of his community involvement.

Ralph and his wife, Troyann, are enthusiastic travelers, having visited 63 countries and all seven continents. They reside in North Carolina.

Look for other books by Dave Dougherty from Pike & Powder Publishing Group, LLC